ACCOUNTING PROBLEMS
AND HOW TO SOLVE THEM

ACCOUNTING PROBLEMS

AND HOW TO SOLVE THEM

Wanda A. Wallace, Ph.D., C.P.A., C.M.A., C.I.A.
The Deborah D. Shelton Systems Professor of Accounting
Texas A&M University

James J. Wallace, M.B.A.
Texas A&M University

Originally published as
*Study Guide to Accompany Solomon/Vargo/Schroeder:
Accounting Principles*

A Barnes & Noble Book

1817

HARPER & ROW, PUBLISHERS, *New York*
Cambridge, Philadelphia, San Francisco, London
Mexico City, São Paulo, Singapore, Sydney

ACCOUNTING PROBLEMS AND HOW TO SOLVE THEM. Copyright © 1985 by Harper & Row, Publishers, Inc. All rights reserved. Printed in the United States of America. No part of this book may be used or reproduced in any manner whatsoever without written permission except in the case of brief quotations embodied in critical articles and reviews. For information address Harper & Row, Publishers, Inc., 10 East 53rd Street, New York, N.Y. 10022. Published simultaneously in Canada by Fitzhenry & Whiteside Limited, Toronto.

First BARNES & NOBLE BOOKS edition published 1985.

Library of Congress Cataloging-in-Publication Data

Wallace, Wanda A., 1953–
  Accounting principles and how to solve them.

  Reprint. Originally published: Study guide to accompany Solomon/Vargo/Schroeder Accounting principles. New York : Harper & Row, 1983.
    1. Accounting.   I. Wallace, James J.   II. Title.
HF5635.W193 1985   657   85-42598
ISBN 0-06-460207-9 (pbk.)

85 86 87 88 89 MPC 10 9 8 7 6 5 4 3 2 1

CONTENTS

PREFACE

This book was prepared to help you develop your accounting skills. It is also designed to be used as a review of accounting principles. Students in a first-year course will find it helpful in studying for examinations, whatever textbook they use. For those taking upper-level or graduate courses, it should be a valuable supplement—it facilitates self-learning of the basics, yet challenges the student through chapter demonstration problems. Business and professional people will profit from its concise but extensive coverage of the material.

Emphasized are those aspects of financial and managerial accounting that are most troublesome and most conducive to problem-solving. Each chapter begins with a summary of the topics to be covered. Key terms are highlighted in **bold type.** The summary is followed by a listing of technical points needed to work in the accounting framework.

A variety of questions—multiple-choice, true-false, classification, and matching—test the reader's grasp of the material. Rather than simply providing answers to the questions, the book offers an appropriate explanation of the erroneous responses along with a full discussion of why the preferred response is the best answer. Similarly, an analysis of the questions concerning the effects of transactions is provided with the solutions; those requiring additional help are led through the logic of the answer, step by step.

The exercises are relatively straightforward applications of key principles discussed in the chapter. In contrast, the chapter demonstration problems are intended to integrate numerous concepts from the chapter and to challenge you "to think like an accountant." The demonstration problems illustrate actual business applications of the concepts introduced in the chapter to ensure that you don't think only in terms of one-step exercises. Both the exercises and the chapter demonstration problems are accompanied by detailed explanations that "walk" you through the solution.

Appearing at intervals in the book are crossword puzzles that provide a quick review of key terms and concepts introduced in preceding chapters. For the puzzle enthusiast, they will be an especially enjoyable approach to studying the language of accounting.

**ACKNOWL-
EDGMENTS**

The authors appreciate the reviewers' comments and the able assistance provided by the publisher through the entire project.

We especially wish to thank Stephanie Perry, who typed the manuscript with great skill and painstaking care; Stephanie handled the challenge of preparing numerous crossword puzzles with her usual good nature.

We also wish to thank our parents, Mr. and Mrs. James Wallace and Mr. and Mrs. Wayne Wilson, for their encouragement and example. The enthusiastic support of our family and friends—Mary Anne and Buddy Coleman, Pat and Ken Kiernan, Babs and Marty Michael, and Alice and Bill Mitchell—is also appreciated.

Wanda A. Wallace
James J. Wallace

HOW TO USE THIS BOOK

For ease of use, each chapter contains the following sequence of elements:

Chapter summary
Technical points
Multiple-choice questions
True-false questions
Classification and matching questions
Questions concerning the effects of transactions
Exercises
Chapter demonstration problems

If you're learning accounting for the first time or reviewing the basics, it's best to work through all of the material. Should time constraints preclude such an approach, read the chapter summary and technical points and then do the exercises. At least read over the short-answer questions and their solutions. The answers, even those relating to multiple-choice and true-false questions, are accompanied by detailed explanations that should improve your understanding of critical accounting concepts. Even if you find the crossworld puzzles too time-consuming to complete, just reading over the definitions will provide a valuable review of key accounting terms.

You will probably find that the chapter demonstration problems are more challenging than the exercises and short-answer questions; these demonstration problems integrate several concepts into a single problem and require some creative thinking. When you feel that you have devoted sufficient time to trying to solve the problems, turn to the detailed solutions that are provided and check your answers; carefully study the solutions so that you have a thorough understanding of the concepts and calculations that are described.

1   *AN INTRODUCTION TO ACCOUNTING*

After completing this chapter, you should:

1 *Be able to identify the distinction between bookkeeping and accounting.*

2 *Be cognizant of the broad scope of accounting services and accounting-related careers.*

3 *Understand how indispensable accounting is to a business entity.*

4 *Comprehend the distinction between financial and managerial accounting.*

5 *Be able to define the key accounting concepts of separate entity, historical cost, and the accounting equation.*

6 *Be capable of preparing an income statement, a statement of owners' equity, and a balance sheet.*

CHAPTER SUMMARY

"At least you can balance your checkbook!" is a popular comment made by individuals when first introduced to an accountant. Such a phrase clearly misrepresents the job of an accountant. A **bookkeeper** records, summarizes, and processes data into information and assists the **accountant**, who primarily utilizes and interprets this information in such diverse fields as auditing, income tax, management advisory services, cost accounting, internal auditing, systems design, planning and forecasting, and governmental accounting. Of course, in order to be an accountant or to use reports prepared by accountants, one must first understand bookkeeping and the basic accounting equation.

Accounting records are maintained for an entity about which the users of financial reports desire information. That entity may be defined as an individual who perhaps is applying for a loan, as a sole proprietorship that wants to establish a line of credit with a supplier, as a partnership that wants some basis for dividing profits among the partners, or as a corporation that wants to attract investment capital. Once the business or individual for which records are to be maintained is identified, the **entity assumption** is invoked. This assumption clarifies, for example, that a sole proprietor's home mortgage is not recorded as a business debt (assuming the business is not located in the proprietor's home). Having determined which expenditures should be recorded in the records of the business, the next issue is at what value these expenditures should be entered in the accounting records. No matter how "good of a deal" the sole proprietor thinks an expenditure may have been, the accountant assumes that the seller is rational and would not have sold the item for less than its objectively determined value. This assumption that goods, services, and other resources acquired by the entity be recorded at cost is known as the **historical cost principle**. The assumption relies on the independence of the seller from the buyer and provides an objective and verifiable value for the accounting records whenever transactions are in fact "arms-length." The problem for the accountant which arises from requiring such objectivity is that over time, as an item appreciates in value, the recorded cost may totally misrepresent the economic worth of an item. While this problem is not typically corrected in the accounting records, disclosures as to the market value of such holdings as marketable securities (stock investments in other entities) are required to permit the users of financial statements to better assess the economic worth of an entity.

Once the entity has been defined and the historical cost value of an item has been determined, the next issue facing the accountant is how to record the item: in what *type of account* and in which *particular account* within that general class of accounts? The general types of accounts include (1) **assets**, in which resources expected to yield future benefits are recorded; (2) **liabilities**, which reflect quantities owed by an entity to creditors; (3) **owners' equity** or capital, which reports that share of the entity's assets belonging to the owners (as distinct from creditors); (4) **revenues**, which are actually a component of owners' equity and represent the amounts charged to customers for goods sold or services rendered; (5) **expenses**, which are also a component of owners' equity and record costs that are incurred in producing revenue; and (6) **withdrawals** or **dividends**, which are reductions in owners' equity that represent the removal of assets from a business for the owners' personal use. The **basic accounting equation** (Assets = Liabilities + Owners' Equity) can be rewritten as Assets = Liabilities + Beginning Owners' Equity + Revenues − Expenses − Withdrawals and adjusted for changes in Owners' Equity other than those related directly to the earnings process or to the removal of assets from a business for the owners' personal use.

Specific account titles within these general account classes typically describe the item being recorded; for example, cash, land, and equipment are all assets. Claims for cash are assets called **receivables**; cash paid by a company in advance, which is a claim for future services, is an asset referred to as a **prepaid expense**. Claims by others which will have to be paid by an entity in the future are referred to as **payables**. Examples of particular revenue sources would include sales, interest income, and fees earned, while expenses are typified by salaries expense, interest expense, and insurance expense account titles.

The basic accounting equation will always balance, as reflected in an entity's statement of financial position or **balance sheet**, which summarizes the components of assets, liabilities, and owners' equity at a particular time. Details of the transactions that generated the ending balance of owners' equity are provided in the income statement and statement of owners' equity. The **income statement** reports revenues less expenses for a period of time, resulting in a **net income** if revenues are the greater of the two amounts or a **net loss** if expenses exceed revenues. The **statement of owners' equity** reports the beginning of the period's owners' equity, owners' investments and withdrawals during the period, and the net income or loss reported on the income statement for the period. The statement of owners' equity thereby reconciles the prior period's owners' equity balance with the current period's ending balance that is reported on the balance sheet. The interrelationship of these three primary financial statements (a fourth financial statement, the statement of changes in financial position, is required, but will not be discussed until Chapter 17 of this study guide) reflects the **double-entry system** of accounting, which guarantees that the basic accounting equation will balance. If the income statement and statement of owners' equity could not reconcile the ending balances in owners' equity reported on the balance sheets of the prior and current periods, an error must exist in the accounting records for the entity. Unfortunately, it is possible for the accounting equation to balance in the presence of errors since offsetting mistakes could be made; however, the double-entry system does at least provide one check on a bookkeeper's accuracy.

TECHNICAL POINTS

√ Basic accounting equation

    Assets = Liabilities + Owners' Equity

√ If revenues > expenses

    Net Income = Revenues − Expenses

If revenues < expenses

    Net Loss = Revenues − Expenses

√   *Beginning Owners' Equity*
$$\begin{bmatrix} + \textit{Net Income} \\ or - \textit{Net Loss} \end{bmatrix}$$
        + Investments by Owners
        − Withdrawals by Owners
        Ending Owners' Equity

Note: The owners' equity account ties the balance sheet and income statement together, by reporting the extent to which changes in the assets and liabilities of a company have arisen from profitable operations (net income).

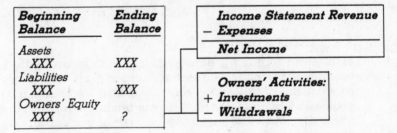

√ Allocating prepaid expenses to expense

    (Prepaid Expense ÷ Number of Periods to Which the Prepayment Relates)
    × Current Number of Periods "Used" to Generate Revenue = Expense for the
    Current Period

MULTIPLE-CHOICE QUESTIONS

Circle the letter corresponding to the best response.

1. Which of the following is primarily concerned with external reporting?
    a. managerial accounting
    b. cost accounting
    c. internal auditing
    d. financial accounting
    e. Cost Accounting Standards Board (CASB)

2. Certified public accountants (CPAs) employed in public accounting are typically involved in
   a. auditing
   b. income tax
   c. management advisory services (MAS)
   d. internal auditing
   e. all of the above
   f. a, b, and c only

3. CPAs who perform income tax services are expected
   a. to primarily prepare and file tax returns
   b. to employ techniques of tax avoidance
   c. to employ techniques of tax evasion
   d. all of the above
   e. none of the above

4. The Certificate in Management Accounting (CMA) program primarily measures the competence of
   a. public accountants
   b. internal auditors
   c. private accountants
   d. Internal Revenue Service (IRS) agents
   e. none of the above

5. The "watchdog" of Congress is the
   a. IRS
   b. General Accounting Office (GAO)
   c. Securities and Exchange Commission (SEC)
   d. CASB
   e. none of the above

MULTIPLE-CHOICE QUESTIONS (ANSWERS)

Answer   *Explanation*

1. d   Managerial accounting deals primarily with reporting the results of operations internally, and cost accounting deals with the collection, assignment, control, and evaluation of costs internally. Internal auditing emphasizes the monitoring of accounting procedures and controls internally. CASB sets standards for internal cost accounting related to contract work for the U.S. government. Only financial accounting is directed primarily to external users.

2. f   Public accountants most often work in the fields of auditing, income tax, and MAS, while private accountants perform internal auditing services.

3. b   CPAs performing income tax services do far more than prepare and file returns; they advise clients as to alternative means of minimizing their taxes and assure clients' compliance with tax laws. Tax planning for the future is more likely to be the CPA's primary task. Such planning is done within the legal boundaries of the tax statutes and is termed **tax avoidance**. In contrast, tax evasion has no regard for the law and such techniques are unacceptable when applied by any person or business, regardless of whether or not that person is a CPA.

4. c   For *(a)* the primary measure of competence is the CPA, while for *(b)* it is the certified internal auditor (CIA). The CMA covers managerial finance and economics, principles of organizational behavior, business ethics, financial and managerial accounting practices, and quantitative methods, and the CMA is directed toward the private accountant.

5. b   The IRS administers the tax laws, the SEC is commonly referred to as the "watchdog" for the *investor,* and the CASB is involved in setting cost accounting standards for companies doing contract work for the U.S. government. The GAO is known as the "watchdog" of Congress due to its responsibility for evaluating other governmental agencies and programs.

Indicate whether each of the following statements is true (T) or false (F).

_____ 1. An accountant's work can be typified by the job of maintaining a set of records for a small retail establishment to determine its profit or loss at the end of the year.

_____ 2. A CPA who performs an audit for a company is typically an employee of the company being audited.

_____ 3. Professional staff performing management advisory services (MAS) may have no accounting training whatsoever.

_____ 4. The historical cost principle states that owners' assets are not to be mixed with a company's assets for financial reporting purposes.

_____ 5. The historical cost principle relies on the transaction being at "arms-length."

_____ 6. Cash receipts is synonymous with revenues.

_____ 7. Net income is typically a very precise figure.

_____ 8. A fiscal year refers to any one-year period other than from January 1 to December 31.

_____ 9. Both an income statement and statement of owners' equity are prepared for a period of time, while a balance sheet is prepared for a particular point in time.

_____ 10. The balance sheet cannot be prepared until the net income (or loss) has been calculated.

TRUE-FALSE QUESTIONS (ANSWERS)

Answer	Explanation
1. F	The accountant's tasks cannot be characterized as a job of such narrow scope. In fact, the accountant is frequently involved in designing information systems and in performing tax services and various other activities that involve processing information far beyond the data relevant to determining profit and loss.
2. F	An audit is intended to lend credibility to the financial statements (reports) that are prepared by a business and is performed by an external independent auditor. CPAs who are employees of a company can conduct internal audits, but these focus on accounting controls and are not concerned primarily with the fairness of financial statements.
3. T	Since MAS services can be only indirectly related to traditional accounting, the use of production specialists, engineers, and computer experts on the MAS staff is not uncommon, although such nonaccounting specialists are primarily employed by larger public accounting firms.
4. F	This is the entity assumption. The historical cost principle states that acquisitions of goods, services, and other resources of a business are to be entered in the accounting records at their cost.

5. T   Unless the seller and buyer are at *arms-length* (i.e., independent of one another), the cost would not be considered objective and definite and an alternative means of valuation would be required.

6. F   Collections of prior periods' sales are cash receipts for this period; similarly, an entity can borrow $3,000 from a bank and essentially have cash receipts of $3,000, but the entity's loan is not revenue. Revenues refer to the amounts charged to customers for goods sold or services rendered.

7. F   Net income typically is not precise because it is the *residual* of recorded revenues and expenses that results from applying some subset of several generally accepted alternative accounting practices and techniques and that requires judgment in arriving at accounting *estimates*.

8. T   A year that runs from January 1 to December 31 is a calendar year, whereas all other 12-month periods are fiscal years.

9. T   The income statement and statement of owners' equity essentially explain the change in balance sheets over the period between that point in time for which the balance sheet was last prepared, and the last day of the current period. You can think of these period statements as links between balance sheets.

10. T   The net income (or loss) has to be added (or subtracted) to beginning owners' equity to arrive at the ending owners' equity. In addition, of course, owners' investments and withdrawals must be adjusted.

CLASSIFI-CATION AND MATCHING QUESTIONS

A. Classify the following items using these symbols.

A = Asset
L = Liability
R = Revenue
E = Expense
N = None of the above

_____ *1.* Accounts payable
_____ *2.* Capital
_____ *3.* Prepaid expenses
_____ *4.* Equipment
_____ *5.* Investments in bonds
_____ *6.* Notes receivable
_____ *7.* Withdrawals
_____ *8.* Sales
_____ *9.* Interest payable
_____ *10.* Rent

B. Classify the following items by indicating on which of the financial statements the item is likely to appear; some items may appear on more than one financial statement.

BS = Balance sheet
IS = Income statement
SOE = Statement of owners' equity

_____ *1.* Liabilities
_____ *2.* Net income
_____ *3.* Withdrawals
_____ *4.* Expenses
_____ *5.* Assets
_____ *6.* Revenue
_____ *7.* Owners' equity
_____ *8.* Net loss

CLASSIFICATION AND MATCHING QUESTIONS (ANSWERS)

A. *1.* L *2.* N *3.* A *4.* A *5.* A *6.* A *7.* N *8.* R *9.* L *10.* E (Prepaid rent would be an asset, and rental income would be a revenue, but rent represents a rent expense.)

B. *1.* BS *2.* IS; SOE *3.* SOE *4.* IS *5.* BS *6.* IS *7.* BS; SOE *8.* IS; SOE

QUESTIONS CONCERNING THE EFFECTS OF TRANS- ACTIONS

Indicate the effects of the following transactions on the basic accounting equation by indicating the direction and amount by which each component of the equation is affected.

$$A = L + OE$$

+\$300
−\$300 —   —   *Example:* A customer paid \$300 of her debt to the entity for goods purchased last month.

___ ___ ___ *1.* The entity ordered \$200 of materials from a supplier.

___ ___ ___ *2.* The entity sold \$700 worth of goods to customers; \$200 were cash sales and \$500 were sold on account.

___ ___ ___ *3.* The entity purchased a truck for \$6,000, paying \$1,000 in cash and signing a note for the balance.

___ ___ ___ *4.* Owners of the entity invested an additional \$12,000 in the business.

___ ___ ___ *5.* The entity paid the \$200 owed to suppliers for materials purchased in number (1) above.

___ ___ ___ *6.* Owners of the entity withdrew \$1,500 from the business.

___ ___ ___ *7.* The entity purchased a 12-month insurance policy for \$12,000 cash on November 1, 1983.

___ ___ ___ *8.* It is now December 31, 1983, and the entity wishes to reflect the fact that only 10 months of the insurance coverage [purchased in number (7) above] remains.

QUESTIONS CONCERNING THE EFFECTS OF TRANSACTIONS (ANSWERS)

Answers				Explanation
	A	= L	+ OE	In the example, cash increases by \$300, while accounts receivable decreases by \$300.
1.	+\$200	+\$200	—	Materials or inventory (an asset) increase(s) by \$200, and accounts payable increases by \$200.
2.	+\$200 +\$500	—	+\$700	Cash increases by \$200, accounts receivable increases by \$500, and revenue (a component of OE) increases by the total of \$700.
3.	+\$6,000 −\$1,000	+\$5,000	—	Trucks, an asset, increases by \$6,000, cash decreases by \$1,000, and notes payable increases by \$5,000.
4.	+\$12,000	—	+\$12,000	Cash increases by \$12,000, and capital increases by the same amount.
5.	−\$200	−\$200	—	Cash declines by \$200, and accounts payable declines by the amount paid, or \$200.
6.	−\$1,500	—	−\$1,500	Cash declines by \$1,500, and capital declines by the same amount.
7.	+\$12,000 −\$12,000	—	—	Prepaid insurance increases by \$12,000 and cash decreases by \$12,000.

8. −$2,000   —   −$2,000   Prepaid insurance declines by the amount to be allocated to expense [($12,000 ÷ 12 months) × 2 months = $2,000], and insurance expense increases by $2,000, which reduces the OE balance. (Recall that both revenues and net income increase OE, while both expenses and net loss decrease OE.)

Note: Since A = L + OE, we ought to be able to add the columns for numbers (1)–(8) and balance. Column *(A)* adds to $14,200, column *(L)* adds to $5,000, and column *(OE)* adds to $9,200, and $14,200 does equal $5,000 plus $9,200.

EXERCISE

Marty Michaels's Construction Company has provided you with the following information concerning its first year of operations, January through December, 1983.

The company purchased a truck for $4,000 cash.
The company made cash sales of $15,000.
The company made $74,000 of sales on credit, of which $52,000 have been collected.
During the past year, the company bought $200 of stock in Dakco as an investment.
Expenditures for the company include payroll of $36,000, insurance of $1,500, materials and supplies of $19,000, rent of $12,000, and miscellaneous of $1,200.
At the end of the period, the company has $2,000 of prepaid rent, $1,600 of materials and supplies on hand, and insurance coverage for three more months related to the last annual premium.
On December 31, 1983, the company borrowed $8,000.

Prepare an income statement for the company from the information provided.

EXERCISE (ANSWER)

MARTY MICHAELS'S CONSTRUCTION COMPANY
Income Statement
For the Year Ended December 31, 1983

Sales		$89,000
Less expenses		
Payroll	$36,000	
Insurance	1,125	
Materials & supplies	17,400	
Rent	10,000	
Miscellaneous	1,200	65,725
Net income		$23,275

Note that purchases of assets, including the truck and the Dakco stock are not expenses, although they do involve cash disbursements. Furthermore, the $22,000 of uncollected receivables is revenue although it does not represent cash receipts for the period. The expenditures for insurance, materials and supplies, and rents do not correspond to expenses because some of these disbursements are prepayments for future months' insurance [3 × ($1,500 ÷ 12)], rent ($2,000 of the $12,000 paid), and supplies ($1,600 of the $19,000 paid). The loan represents an exchange of a liability for an asset, with no immediate effect on the entity's income.

**CHAPTER
DEMON-
STRATION
PROBLEM**

A friend of yours, I. M. Trying started a tire-changing business four months ago. He knows that you are attending an accounting course, and he gives you a call to get some answers on how he should account for his business activities over the last few months. A summary of his remarks and questions follow.

"I've got one employee who changes the regular tires to snow tires or vice versa, depending on the season, and I pay him $5 an hour. He works 8 to 12 and 1 to 5, and I take his place over lunch time, or whenever he's ill. I've been paying him weekly from my personal checking account."

"There's a bookkeeping service down the street that has helped me by filing employer-employee tax information and deposits, including workmen's compensation, and I'm wondering whether to have that same service do my tax return."

"I need some more capital to replenish my tire inventory, so I spoke with the bank. Barbara (the banker) said she'd consider extending some credit if I prepared some financial statements for her and purchased some 'key man' life insurance. I purchased a one-year policy for cash at the end of last month for $720, but I can't figure out what kind of financial statements Barbara wants."

"The way I figure it, my total cash receipts for the period have been $60,000, my total cash disbursements have been $38,000, so my income of $22,000 ought to land me that loan."

"I know that you haven't been in that accounting course very long, but can you give me any advice?"

Required

Give I. M. Trying some advice. Then, assume that you meet with your friend, discuss his business, and identify the following transactions (in addition to those identified earlier).

October 1, 1983	$60,000 was invested in the company by I. M. Trying.
October 4, 1983	$20,000 worth of tires inventory and related supplies were purchased on account.
November 1983 through January 1984	$45,000 of revenue has been generated from selling and changing tires. $30,000 of this revenue has been collected.
January 1, 1984	Paid off $18,000 of the $20,000 bill to the supplier after borrowing $30,000 from a friend.
January 1984	Withdrew $4,000 from the business to meet personal debt commitments.

You have also ascertained that rental expense is $400 paid in cash on the first day of each month, the cost of the tires still in inventory is $5,000, and the total payments to the employee for the four months were $3,200, with an additional $500 paid for other employee-related expenses (included taxes). I. M. Trying has purchased advertising in local newspapers rather sporadically, spending a total of $550 cash. He pays interest of 20% on his friend's note on a monthly basis, with the principal due in 2 years. Prepare financial statements for your friend as of January 31, 1984.

CHAPTER DEMONSTRATION PROBLEM (ANSWER)

Several points should be discussed with I. M. Trying, to assure that his efforts pay off. One problem made clear by your friend is his lack of understanding of the entity assumption; he has told you that he uses his personal checking account to pay his one employee. You should explain the preferability of maintaining separate checking accounts: one account for his personal expenditures, and one account for the separate business entity. Otherwise, when financial statements are prepared for the tire-changing business, each separate transaction will have to be scrutinized in order to determine to which entity the transaction belongs.

A second problem involves your friend's perception of a bookkeeper's services, and his unidentified need for an accountant. A bookkeeper can file routine tax and employee-related reports, but his ability to provide tax expertise and planning advice is likely to be very limited. Explain to I. M. Trying that he should try a little harder to assure the optimal handling of his tax situation by hiring an accountant to provide tax services.

Regarding financial statements requested by the banker, you can describe the four types of financial statements typically prepared: the income statement, statement of owners' equity, balance sheet, and statement of changes in financial position (which you cannot yet elaborate upon). You should point out that the banker should specify over what period of time she wishes the first two statements to be prepared, and to what point in time the balance sheet should relate. Also, explain what an audit is and suggest that your friend verify that the banker does not require audited financial statements in order to consider extending a loan to the tire-changing business.

I. M. Trying is confusing cash disbursements with expenses and cash receipts with revenue. Explain to him that a purchase of tires represents expenditures for assets, while expenses occur in the form of cost of goods sold when these tires are sold. Similarly, the key man life insurance represents a claim for eleven additional months of coverage; only one month has expired and resulted in insurance expense, while the remainder is an asset, prepaid insurance. The $30,000 borrowed from a friend is a cash receipt, but remind I. M. Trying that the loan does not represent revenue. Besides, with personal and business expenditures being paid out of the same checking account, this estimated disbursement figure probably includes I. M. Trying's home mortgage and other personal expenditures.

After discussing these issues with I. M. Trying, you can assist him in preparing the following financial statements.

I. M. TRYING TIRE CHANGE SERVICE
Income Statement
For the Four Months Ended January 31, 1984

Revenue		$45,000
Less expenses		
Cost of goods sold (cost of tires sold)	$15,000	
Labor	3,200	
Payroll taxes	500	
Advertising	550	
Interest	500	
Insurance	60	
Rent	1,600	21,410
Net income		$23,590

I. M. TRYING TIRE CHANGE SERVICE
Statement of Owner's Equity
For the Four Months Ended January 31, 1984

Owners' equity, October 1, 1983	$60,000
Increase	
Net income for the four months ended January 31, 1984	23,590
Decrease	
Withdrawals	4,000
Owners' equity, January 31, 1984	$79,590

I. M. TRYING TIRE CHANGE SERVICE
Balance Sheet
January 31, 1984

Cash	$ 90,930
Accounts receivable	15,000
Inventory	5,000
Prepaid insurance	660
Total assets	$111,590
Accounts payable	$ 2,000
Notes payable	30,000
Total liabilities	$ 32,000
Owners' equity	79,590
Total liabilities & owners' equity	$111,590

Some helpful hints follow.

To derive the cost of tires sold, compare the $20,000 purchased, to the $5,000 still on hand at the end of the period.

To arrive at the interest charge, take the $30,000 owed to the friend, multiply by 20%, and divide by 12, since the money has only been borrowed for 1 month.

Insurance expense is one-twelfth of the $720 paid for the annual premium.

Rent is $400 a month multiplied by 4 months.

The cash balance must reflect all cash-related transactions:

+	*$60,000*	*Investment*
+	*30,000*	*Collections*
−	*18,000*	*Payments to Supplier*
+	*30,000*	*Loan*
−	*4,000*	*Withdrawal*
−	*1,600*	*Rent*
−	*3,200*	*Labor*
−	*500*	*Payroll Expenses*
−	*550*	*Advertising*
−	*500*	*Interest*
−	*720*	*Insurance*
	$90,930	*Ending Cash Balance*

2 PROCESSING ACCOUNTING INFORMATION

OBJECTIVES

After completing this chapter, you should:

1 *Have an understanding of accounts, debits and credits, journals, the chart of accounts, and their interrelationship.*

2 *Know how to journalize transactions.*

3 *Be able to summarize transactions by posting from journals to the general ledger.*

4 *Understand what a trial balance is, that inaccuracy in a trial balance is possible in spite of the equality of debits and credits, and how to proceed to locate an error in an out-of-balance trial balance.*

CHAPTER SUMMARY

As does every profession, accounting has its own language, part of which is introduced in this chapter.

When a **transaction** occurs, **source documents** (e.g., invoices, receiving reports, purchase orders, and cancelled checks) are generated that describe the exchange. Once these source documents are reviewed to verify that the transaction is substantially completed and ready to be recorded, a journal entry is prepared. For example, a purchase order is typically matched with an invoice and a receiving report as the basis for recording the purchase of inventory (goods for resale) and an obligation to suppliers (accounts payable) in a journal entry.

The **journal entry** to record any transaction has a standard form with the top line(s) representing debits to the left, and the next line(s) representing credits, slightly indented to the right. In fact, **debit** (meaning "left") and **credit** (meaning "right") are the terms used by bookkeepers to describe how a transaction is recorded. The **double-entry system** of accounting requires that the dollar amount of debits equals the dollar amount of credits in every journal entry and that the basic accounting equation is always in balance. Therefore the accounting system is structured with *assets* increasing as *debits, liabilities* increasing as *credits,* and *owners' equity* increasing as *credits.* In line with their effects on owners' equity, *revenues* increase as *credits,* and *expenses* increase as *debits.* Hence the journal entry describing the purchase of goods for resale would be a debit to inventory and a credit to accounts payable. The particular accounts used will depend on the entity's chart of accounts. Once transactions are journalized in either specialized journals, such as purchases or cash receipts journals, or the general journal, they are periodically posted, or transferred, to the general ledger accounts affected by each transaction. The journal will reference to which account each debit or credit is posted, and the general ledger will reference the journal and page number where the original entry is provided in support of the posting. These references provide an audit trail or can make easier the tracing of ledger entries back to their original entry. The general ledger presents each account of a business on a separate sheet of paper with its current dollar balance.

Periodically, the general ledger accounts are listed in a **trial balance** and the equality of debits and credits is checked to confirm that the books are in balance. Although *in balance* is not synonymous with *correct,* if debits equal credits, we assume no errors are made. Of course, this assumption is later checked directly by auditors and indirectly through related accounting procedures. Whenever the ledger is out of balance, it is possible to detect **transposition errors** (reversal of two digits) and **slides** (improper movement of the decimal point in either direction) by checking to see if the difference in the total debits and credits is divisible by 9. If not, taking one-half of the difference and comparing this amount to the trial balance may help to locate an error in which debit balances were entered in credit columns or vice versa. If these short-cuts do not locate the problem, the bookkeeper must return to the ledger and the journal, first check computations, and then, if necessary, trace from the journals to the ledger in an attempt to locate posting errors.

This chapter permits you to visualize the initial phase of the accounting process: journalizing, posting, and preparing a trial balance.

TECHNICAL POINTS

✓ Form for recording journal entries

    Account to be Debited   XX
      Account to be Credited   XX

✓ T-accounts

Account Title	
Debits ◄ (left)	*Credits* (right) ►
Footing	*Footing*
Balance if debits > credits	*Balance if credits > debits*

What Debits Do to Various Types of Accounts

Increase assets
Decrease liabilities
Decrease owners' equity
Decrease revenue
Increase expenses

What Credits Do to Various Types of Accounts

Decrease assets
Increase liabilities
Increase owners' equity
Increase revenue
Decrease expenses

√ Example of running balance form of account (assume this is the first year of operations)

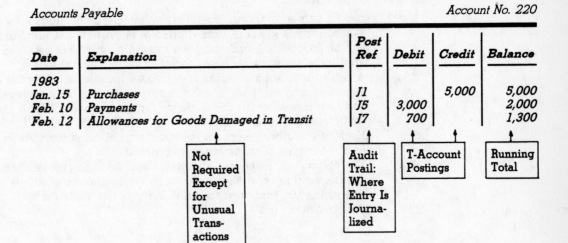

Accounts Payable   *Account No. 220*

Date	Explanation	Post Ref	Debit	Credit	Balance
1983					
Jan. 15	Purchases	J1		5,000	5,000
Feb. 10	Payments	J5	3,000		2,000
Feb. 12	Allowances for Goods Damaged in Transit	J7	700		1,300

Not Required Except for Unusual Transactions

Audit Trail: Where Entry Is Journalized

T-Account Postings

Running Total

MULTIPLE-CHOICE QUESTIONS

Circle the letter corresponding to the best response.

1. All of the accounts taken together compose a firm's
   a. financial statements
   b. T-accounts
   c. general ledger
   d. journal
   e. none of the above

2. The term debit refers to
   a. an increase in an account
   b. a decrease in an account
   c. transactions that have "bad" effects
   d. the right side of a T-account
   e. the left side of a T-account

3. A variety of transactions is recorded in
   a. the general journal
   b. the purchases journal
   c. the sales journal
   d. the cash receipts journal

4. A transposition error means
   a. the reversal of two digits, e.g., 572 as 527
   b. the decimal point of a number has been improperly moved to the left or to the right
   c. that a slide has occurred
   d. that the trial balance is in error in spite of the equality of debits and credits

Answer   *Explanation*

1. c   Only a subset of accounts appears on each type of financial statement. A T-account is a general term applied to any single account, and a journal can be specialized, including, for example, only cash receipts. The name applied to all accounts taken together is the general ledger.

2. e   A debit increases assets, but it decreases liabilities. While the debit to expenses may be "bad," a debit to assets would surely be "good"; no good or bad implication exists for debits or for credits per se. Debit means "left," while credit means "right."

3. a   Each of the other responses represents specialized journals in which only a particular type of transaction is recorded.

4. a   The *(b)* and *(c)* responses are equivalent, and the problem with *(d)* is that a transposition error should result in the inequality of debits and credits (assuming the exact transposition error is not made for both the debit and the credit entries).

TRUE-FALSE QUESTIONS

Indicate whether each of the following statements is true (T) or false (F).

____   *1.* A transaction always affects a minimum of two accounts.

____   *2.* Accounts always possess their normal balance.

____   *3.* A credit balance in the machinery account is not possible unless an error has been made.

____   *4.* The journal is a needless repetition of the information contained on the source documents.

____   *5.* In any transaction, the total dollar amount of debits must equal the total dollar amount of credits.

____   *6.* Account numbers in increments of one should be assigned to the accounts that the entity is using to record transactions, that is, the chart of accounts.

____   *7.* A trial balance is not typically issued to such parties as owners and creditors.

____   *8.* A trial balance with equal debit and credit totals does not always mean that the accounting process was free from error.

TRUE-FALSE QUESTIONS (ANSWERS)

Answer   *Explanation*

1. T   The double-entry system of bookkeeping requires that debits equal credits, which would not be possible if a transaction affected only one account.

2. F   Some accounts can carry balances that are opposite to their normal balance; for example, if an entity overpaid a supplier, a debit balance would result for accounts payable.

3. T   A company cannot have "negative" equipment.

4. F   The journal brings order to the recording process by summarizing in one place all relevant information regarding a transaction. Often a single transaction relates to a number of source documents that would require employees to scurry around to many locations whenever questions arose, if no journal existed.

5. T   This is the basis of the double-entry accounting system.

6. F   Gaps should be left in the account numbers to permit the insertion of additional accounts as the need arises. For example, increments of ten can be used.

7. T   A trial balance is not a formal financial statement but is an internally generated listing of accounts prepared to check the equality of debits and credits.

8. T   Unfortunately this is true; offsetting errors, omissions, transaction duplications, and posting errors can all occur without causing an inequality in debits and credits.

CLASSIFI-CATION AND MATCHING QUESTIONS

A. Classify the following descriptions as relating to either a debit (Dr) or a credit (Cr).

____ 1. The normal balance for assets.
____ 2. The normal balance of owners' equity.
____ 3. An increase in liabilities.
____ 4. How a collection from a customer is recorded in accounts receivable.
____ 5. The normal balance of drawing accounts.
____ 6. The normal balance of expenses.
____ 7. How a payment of accounts payable is recorded in the cash account.
____ 8. How cash sales would be recorded in the sales account.

B. Demonstrate your understanding of the sequence of the following events in the processing cycle by numbering the first event no. 1, the second event no. 2, and so on to the final event no. 6.

____ 1. Trial balance
____ 2. Posting
____ 3. Source document
____ 4. Ledger account
____ 5. Transaction
____ 6. Journal entry

CLASSIFICATION AND MATCHING QUESTIONS (ANSWERS)

A. *1.* Dr *2.* Cr *3.* Cr *4.* Cr *5.* Dr *6.* Dr *7.* Cr *8.* Cr
B. *1.* no. 6 *2.* no. 4 *3.* no. 2 *4.* no. 5 *5.* no. 1 *6.* no. 3

QUESTIONS CONCERNING THE EFFECTS OF TRANS-ACTIONS

Would the following transactions increase (+) or decrease (−) the account involved?

____ 1. A debit to equipment
____ 2. A debit to sales revenue
____ 3. A credit to Babs Michaels, capital account
____ 4. A debit to notes payable
____ 5. A credit to prepaid rent
____ 6. A debit to insurance expense

QUESTIONS CONCERNING THE EFFECTS OF TRANSACTIONS (ANSWERS)

1. +   2. −   3. +   4. −   5. −   6. +

EXERCISES

1. Describe what transaction resulted in the following journal entries. It is not sufficient to merely say that one account was debited and one account was credited; the essence of what happened should be explained. You should not repeat names of accounts or amounts in the explanation unless essential for understanding or clarification of the transaction.

a. Accounts Receivable   60
      Sales   60

_____

_____

b. Equipment   8,000
      Cash   2,000
      Notes Payable   6,000

_____

_____

c. Notes Payable   1,000
      Cash   1,000

_____

_____

d. Insurance   600
      Prepaid Insurance   600

_____

_____

e. Sales   30
      Accounts Receivable   30

_____

_____

f. Accounts Payable   700
      Cash   700

_____

_____

g. Drawing Account   200
      Cash   200

_____

_____

h. Cash   20
      Accounts Receivable   20

_____

_____

    i. Prepaid Rent 3,000
          Cash   3,000

_____

_____

2. Balance the following T-accounts and explain what happened to generate those entries that are lettered.

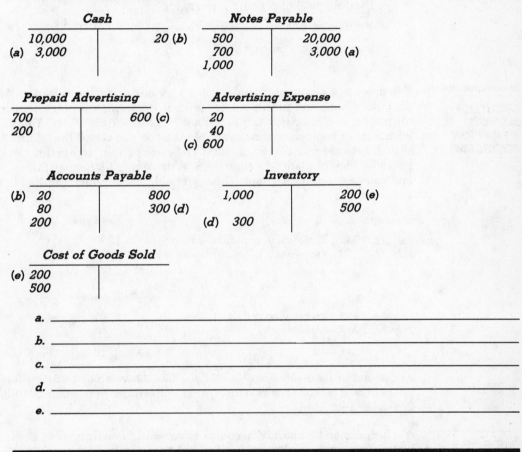

    a. _____

    b. _____

    c. _____

    d. _____

    e. _____

EXERCISES (ANSWERS)

1. a. Made a sale on account for $60.
    b. Purchased equipment, making a down payment of $2,000, and assuming a note for the balance of $6,000.
    c. Paid off $1,000 of an outstanding note payable (a liability).
    d. Used up (or had expire) $600 of prepaid insurance.
    e. Reversal of a previously recorded sale; either the goods were returned or the original entry was made in error. (Typically you do not assume a mistake was made, so the presumption would be that the customer returned merchandise purchased on credit.)
    f. Paid off a supplier ($700).
    g. The owner withdrew $200 from the business for personal use.
    h. Collected $20 from customers.
    i. Paid rent in advance for future use.

2. Balances

    Cash = $12,980 Dr
    Notes Payable = $20,800 Cr
    Prepaid Advertising = $300 Dr

Advertising Expense = $660   Dr
Accounts Payable = $800   Cr
Inventory = $600   Dr
Cost of Goods Sold = $700   Dr

a. Borrowed $3,000 in the form of a note payable.

b. Paid off $20 of an account payable.

c. Used up $600 of prepaid advertising.

d. Purchased $300 of goods on account.

e. Sold inventory costing $200.

CHAPTER DEMON-STRATION PROBLEM

You operate a plant- and house-sitting service during the summer. You attend summer school, and in this college town it is common for faculty members to leave town for a month or two and to request house-sitting services. You had been faced with a lot of competition for available jobs, so you added the "gimmick" of plant sitting, because plant lovers abound and most of your competing house sitters have no knowledge of plants. In contrast to your competition, your father owns a nursery and you've got natural talent. This approach last summer resulted in the following business:

Description		Revenue
July 31, 1983	*Three plant- and house-sitting jobs*	*$300*
July 31, 1983	*Two weekly plant checks*	*80*
		$380
		Expenses
July 31, 1983	*Transportation*	*$ 25*
July 31, 1983	*Fertilizer*	*15*
		$ 40

At the end of the summer (8/31/83) you had $3 worth of fertilizer left and still had not collected $50 of your revenue (other collections were made 8/10/83). You still owe $7 for the fertilizer.

Required

Recommend a chart of accounts to record the operations of the plant- and house-sitting service. Record the journal entries to reflect operations and diagram how these journal entries would appear in a general ledger. Also, prepare a trial balance as of the end of the summer.

General Journal

Date	Explanation	Post Ref	Debit	Credit
1983				
Aug. 10	Cash	101	330	
	Accounts Receivable	110		330
	To record collections			

General Ledger

Cash   *Account No. 101*

Date	Explanation	Post Ref	Debit	Credit	Balance
1983					
July 31		J2	33		33
July 31		J2		33	—
Aug. 10		J3	330		330

Accounts Receivable   *Account No. 110*

Date	Explanation	Post Ref	Debit	Credit	Balance
1983					
July 31		J1	380		380
Aug. 10		J3		330	50

General Journal

Date	Explanation	Post Ref	Debit	Credit
1983				
Aug. 31	Fertilizer Expense	510	12	
	Fertilizer	120		12
	To record the use of fertilizer during the summer (This is known as an adjusting journal entry.)			

General Ledger

Fertilizer Expense   Account No. 510

Date	Explanation	Post Ref	Debit	Credit	Balance
1983 Aug. 31		J4	12		12

Fertilizer   Account No. 120

Date	Explanation	Post Ref	Debit	Credit	Balance
1983 July 31 Aug. 31		J2 J4	15	12	15

Trial Balance
August 31, 1983

Cash	$330	
Accounts receivable	50	
Fertilizer	3	
Accounts payable		$ 7
Capital		33
Revenue: Plant and house sitting		300
Revenue: Plant checks		80
Transportation expense	25	
Fertilizer expense	12	
	$420	$420

3 COMPLETION OF THE ACCOUNTING CYCLE

After completing this chapter, you should:

1 *Be able to explain what an accounting period is and what its effects are on financial accounting.*

2 *Understand the difference in cash basis accounting, modified cash basis accounting, and accrual accounting.*

3 *Know how to record adjusting journal entries, why these entries are needed, and how to document these entries on a worksheet.*

4 *Be able to prepare a set of financial statements from a worksheet.*

5 *Know how to close a set of books and how to prepare a post-closing trial balance.*

CHAPTER
SUMMARY

Although accounting for an entity's operations would be greatly simplified by waiting until a business went out of business and then computing the difference in beginning and ending owners' equity to arrive at income, such an approach would obviously provide no information to investors on the entity's operations while in business. To fulfill investors' and other decision makers' need for information, an **accounting period** is defined as a discrete portion of an entity's life over which financial information is to be collected and reported. Within this period, the previously introduced terms of revenue and expense require further definition.

Revenues and expenses can be recognized on the **cash basis**, which means that cash receipts related to the earnings process of a business constitute **revenue**, while cash disbursements related to the earnings process represent **expenses**. A **modified cash basis** essentially permits cash disbursements related to assets that would provide future services beyond one accounting period to be recorded as assets instead of expenses. The **accrual basis** of revenue and expense recognition defines a matcning process by which revenues are recognized when earned, then expenses are matched to those revenues that they helped to create as such expenses are incurred. The actual timing of the exchange of cash is largely irrelevant to an accrual-based income statement.

The requirements that reports be prepared for accounting periods that are shorter than an entity's life and that accrual accounting be used as the basis for revenue recognition create the need for adjusting journal entries. Whenever multiperiod costs and revenues are split among two or more accounting periods, such as prepaid expenses, depreciation, and unearned revenues, an **adjusting process** is required that allocates to each accounting period an appropriate portion of the period's related expenses or revenues. For example, a truck with a five-year life costing $6,000 can be expected to decline in value over time. Assuming straight-line depreciation (with zero residual or salvage value), a debit to depreciation expense of $1,200 ($6,000 ÷ 5 years) and a credit to the contra-asset account (accumulated depreciation expense: truck) of $1,200 would be recorded in each of the five years until at the end of its useful life the book value [or difference between the truck (asset) and the contra-asset account of accumulated depreciation] is zero.

Similarly, any revenues and expenses that have been earned or incurred in a given period but not yet recorded in the books require adjusting entries; this is particularly applicable to accrued expenses and accrued revenues. These accruals can result from an exception to the typical equivalence of cash disbursements and expenses observed for certain items. For example, employees' wages are paid weekly with a debit to wage expense and a credit to cash. If a particular payday falls on a Friday that happens to be four days after the year-end, then disbursements will not equal expenses for this business, and the expenses must be accrued. Accruals can also result whenever the entity is not reminded (e.g., by means of a transaction with some third party) during the current period of certain revenues and expenses that arise primarily as a function of the passage of time. For example, interest receivable or payable on a long-term note receivable or payable may only be paid upon maturity, with no current notification of interest due being mailed or received, although it is actually earned or incurred as time passes.

Once adjustments are posted to a worksheet containing an entity's trial balance, the accountant can extend the original balances and prepare the foundation for the preparation of formal financial statements. After journalizing and posting the adjustments and after preparing the statements, a closing process empties nominal or temporary accounts in order that the new period's income and withdrawals can be separated from the prior years' results. After closing, the revenue, expense, and drawing accounts will have zero balances, the income summary account will be closed out to owners' equity, as will the drawing account, and a post-closing trial balance will be prepared to confirm the equality of debits and credits in the general ledger.

To facilitate routine bookkeeping in the subsequent period, reversing entries are often recorded at the beginning of that period. These entries tend to reverse accruals booked at year-end in order to avoid the double-counting that could arise if entries are routinely recorded as cash payments are made. For example, the bookkeeper routinely debits payroll expense and credits cash whenever payroll is recorded. Yet an adjusting entry may have been recorded that debited wage expense and credited wages payable. By reversing this entry—debiting wages payable and crediting wage expense—the routine journal entry recorded by the bookkeeper will result in the netting out of entries so that no wage expense is double-counted or placed in the wrong accounting period.

TECHNICAL POINTS

✓ *Supplies Expense = Prepaid Supplies − Supplies on Hand*

✓ *Straight-line Depreciation = Cost / Useful Life*

Note: This assumes no residual or salvage value.

✓ *Book Value = Original Cost − Accumulated Depreciation*

✓ *Annual Interest Expense = Note Payable × Interest Rate*

MULTIPLE-CHOICE QUESTIONS

Circle the letter corresponding to the best response.

1. Some companies do not recognize revenues until they are collected; such companies employ
   a. a cash basis of accounting
   b. a modified cash basis of accounting
   c. an accrual basis of accounting
   d. all of the above
   e. a and b only

2. On January 2, 1983, an entity pays rent for January through June, 1983; this January cash disbursement
   a. would be recorded as prepaid rent under the accrual basis of accounting
   b. would be recorded as rent expense under the cash basis of accounting
   c. is properly matched with related revenue under the cash basis of accounting
   d. all of the above
   e. a and b only

3. A building purchased for $120,000 on July 1, 1983, has an estimated useful life of 40 years and no residual or salvage value and is to be depreciated on a straight-line basis. The appropriate adjusting journal entry on December 31, 1983, is
   a. Depreciation Expense   1,500
        Accumulated Depreciation: Building   1,500

   b. Depreciation Expense   3,000
        Building   3,000

   c. Depreciation Expense   3,000
        Accumulated Depreciation: Building   3,000

   d. Depreciation Expense   1,500
        Building   1,500

   e. none of the above

4. Unearned revenue
   a. represents a liability at the time of collection
   b. represents revenue at the time of collection
   c. is recognized as revenue upon collection
   d. is the term typically associated with returned merchandise
   e. none of the above

5. Accrued expenses
   a. are expenses that have been paid but not yet incurred
   b. are expenses that have been incurred but not yet paid
   c. are expenses that have been paid and incurred
   d. are expenses that have neither been paid nor incurred

6. The statement of owners' equity can be constructed
   a. from a worksheet
   b. from a worksheet plus information on owners' investments (capital) recorded in the general ledger
   c. from a worksheet plus information on owners' investments and withdrawals recorded in the general ledger in the capital account
   d. from a worksheet plus information on owners' withdrawals recorded in the capital account of the general ledger

Answer   *Explanation*

1. e   The only distinction between cash basis and modified cash basis is with respect to disbursements: if expenditures result in assets with future value beyond a single accounting period, they are not expensed under a modified cash basis, whereas they would be under a cash basis. Both methods recognize revenue as it is collected. In contrast, accrual accounting recognizes revenue as it is earned, essentially disregarding the collection date.

2. e   Cash basis accounting would record all six months' rent as expense in the month of January and would not properly match revenues and expenses.

3. a   The cost of $120,000 divided by 40 years yields annual depreciation expense of $3,000, but the building has been used for only six months, and one-half of $3,000, or $1,500, is the appropriate adjustment. It is desirable to leave the cost of the asset intact; hence, a separate contra-asset account should be used rather than charging the building account directly.

4. a   Unearned revenue represents revenue that has been collected in advance of the earnings process (e.g., a deposit on custom-made furniture). If the entity receiving the deposit does not build the furniture to the customer's satisfaction, then the sale will not occur and the deposit will have to be returned. Hence, unearned revenue is a liability until it becomes earned and is recognized as revenue.

5. b   An accrued expense is a liability; it represents an expense incurred but unpaid. If utility bills are paid the tenth of the month and financial statements are being prepared, the two-thirds of the month for which utility expenses have been incurred but not paid would be an accrued expense requiring an adjusting journal entry.

6. b   The statement of owners' equity cannot be constructed by an accountant merely by relying on the worksheet; this is because any investments made by an owner are essentially buried in the capital account that appears in the trial balance. In contrast, the drawing account is detailed on the worksheet, so that use of the general ledger for checking withdrawals would be unnecessary. Furthermore, the drawing account would not be reflected in the capital balance until after closing.

**TRUE-FALSE
QUESTIONS**

Indicate whether each of the following statements is true (T) or false (F).

_____   *1.* A loan, which is a cash receipt, is not considered to be revenue under a cash basis of accounting.

_____   *2.* Withdrawals are expenses under a cash basis of accounting.

_____   *3.* Overall, the cash basis does not properly match revenues and expenses.

_____   *4.* Few businesses utilize a strict cash basis of accounting.

_____   *5.* An asset's book value represents the true value of the asset in the market place.

_____   *6.* On the balance sheet of a worksheet, a net loss would be listed in the debit column.

_____   *7.* Adjusting entries on a worksheet must also be journalized and posted to the general ledger.

_____   *8.* Both temporary and balance sheet accounts are closed at the end of an accounting period.

Answer	Explanation
1. T	Since the loan is not generated by an entity's earnings process, it is not considered revenue under the cash basis of accounting.
2 F	Withdrawals are not expenses; they are reductions in owners' equity.
3. T	The timing of cash receipts and disbursements is not directly related to the earnings process.
4. T	The possible mismatch of revenues and expenses under a strict cash basis of accounting encourages the use of a modified cash basis or an accrual basis of accounting.
5. F	Book value is the difference between an asset's original cost and its related accumulated depreciation and cannot be equated with the true value of the asset. Although the original cost would be expected to relate to the asset's market value, fluctuations in market value subsequent to acquisition are not typically recorded in the accounting records.
6. T	Since a net loss must reduce owners' equity, which typically has a credit balance, the loss is listed in the debit column.
7. T	The accountant wants to achieve consistency between the general ledger and the financial statement balances, as prepared from the worksheet.
8. F	Only temporary accounts are closed (reduced to a zero balance) to facilitate the recording of a single period's income. Balance sheets require carryover from period to period, as they report the financial position of an entity at a particular date (reflecting, of course, all past operations of that entity). Only revenue, expense, and drawing accounts are closed.

CLASSIFI-CATION AND MATCHING QUESTIONS

Match the following accounts with that section of the worksheet in which they would typically appear (or where amounts affecting the accounts would appear). Also indicate the normal balance of each of the accounts (Dr or Cr). Note that accounts are likely to be matched with more than one section of the worksheet.

Matching(s)	Normal Balance		
_____	_____	1. Car	a. Trial balance
_____	_____	2. Prepaid rent	b. Adjustments
_____	_____	3. John Spender, drawing	c. Income statement
_____	_____	4. Net income	d. Balance sheet
_____	_____	5. Interest expense	
_____	_____	6. Unearned commissions	

Answer		Explanation
1. a,d	Dr	Although cars will decline in book value, the car account is not adjusted directly. Instead, the contra-asset account (accumulated depreciation: cars) is created.
2. a,b,d	Dr	Typically some of the prepayment will have expired.
3. a,d	Dr	After closing, this balance disappears into the owners' equity balance, but it's carried to the balance sheet columns on the worksheet.
4. c,d	N/A	Assuming a positive income, net income is plugged into the debit column of the income statement and the credit column of the balance sheet (vice versa if negative). It does not represent an

account per se and hence has no account balance. Net income is a residual amount computed by combining revenue and expense accounts.

5. b,c   Dr   Typically, interest expense will not appear in the trial balance but will arise from adjustments made on the worksheet.

6. a,b,d   Cr   Unearned commissions represent a liability; typically, some part of such unearned revenue is earned during an accounting period and requires adjustment.

QUESTIONS CONCERNING THE EFFECTS OF TRANSACTIONS

Indicate whether the following journal entries result in either an increase (+) in net income, a decrease (−) in net income, or no effect (0) on net income.

____   *1.* Accrual of interest owed to creditors.

____   *2.* Reduction of unearned revenue.

____   *3.* Expiration of prepaid advertising.

____   *4.* Downward adjustment of supplies to the quantity of supplies on hand.

____   *5.* Increase in unearned revenue.

____   *6.* Accrual of interest on a note receivable.

____   *7.* Collection of accrued interest on a note receivable.

____   *8.* Acquisition of prepaid insurance.

QUESTIONS CONCERNING THE EFFECTS OF TRANSACTIONS (ANSWERS)

Answer	Explanation
1. −	Interest expense
2. +	Earnings process reduces liability
3. −	Advertising expense
4. −	Supplies consumed or supplies expense
5. 0	Debit cash, credit unearned revenue
6. +	Interest revenue
7. 0	Debit cash, credit interest receivable
8. 0	Debit prepaid insurance, credit cash

EXERCISE

Indicate whether the following errors would overstate (O), understate (U), or have no effect (N) on net income and on total assets.

Effect on Income	Effect on Total Assets	
____	____	*1.* The company forgot to accrue interest receivable.
____	____	*2.* The company forgot to record the use of prepaid supplies.
____	____	*3.* The company forgot to record the realization of unearned revenue.
____	____	*4.* The company forgot to record depreciation on its trucks.
____	____	*5.* The company made no adjustment for the two days' wages that were unpaid at year-end.

Effect on Income	Effect on Total Assets
1. U	U
2. O	O
3. U	N
4. O	O
5. O	N

CHAPTER DEMON- STRATION PROBLEM

American Machinery Electronics Suppliers Syndicated (AMESS) has a general ledger before adjustments as of June 30, 1984, with the following account balances.

Cash	$ 30,000
Accounts receivable	80,000
Prepaid rent	15,000
Prepaid advertising	5,000
Truck	10,000
Accumulated depreciation: truck	3,000
Building	60,000
Accumulated depreciation: building	4,000
Accounts payable	90,000
Note payable	5,000
Mortgage payable	48,000
Capital, T. Hodge	12,000
Drawing, T. Hodge	2,000
Sales revenue	400,000
Repair & maintenance expense	60,000
Sales commissions	25,000
Supplies expense	5,000
Travel expense	30,000
Wage expense	220,000
Utilities expense	10,000
Interest expense	10,000

AMESS has provided you with the following information.

(a) The truck has a useful life of five years with no expected residual value at the end of the life. Straight-line depreciation is used.

(b) The building has an estimated life of 50 years with no expected residual value; straight-line depreciation is being used.

(c) The prepaid rent was paid at the beginning of last year (July 1, 1982) in a total sum of $25,000.

(d) The prepaid advertising relates to ten radio ads, seven of which have been broadcast.

(e) The note payable bears an 18% interest rate, payable every July 1.

(f) The interest on the mortgage payable has been recorded as paid.

(g) The travel expenses include $7,000 of travel advances to the sales staff that has not yet been spent.

(h) The $5,000 of supplies purchased during the period were expensed; however, a physical count has indicated that $800 of these supplies are still on hand for future use.

(i) At year-end $400 of wages and $100 of utilities expense have been incurred, have not yet been paid, and have not yet been recorded in the books.

Required

1. When was the truck purchased?
2. When was the building purchased?
3. What is the monthly rate of rent prepaid July 1, 1982?
4. Prepare a worksheet, making all necessary adjustments.
5. Prepare financial statements for AMESS. Assume no capital contributions were made during the 1983–1984 fiscal year.
6. Prepare the closing journal entry(ies) for AMESS.
7. Prepare a post-closing balance sheet.

AMERICAN MACHINERY ELECTRONICS SUPPLIERS SYNDICATED
Worksheet
For the Year Ended June 30, 1984

Accounts	Trial Balance Debit	Trial Balance Credit	Adjustments Debit	Adjustments Credit	Income Statement Debit	Income Statement Credit	Balance Sheet Debit	Balance Sheet Credit
Cash	30,000							
Accounts receivable	80,000							
Prepaid rent	15,000							
Prepaid advertising	5,000							
Truck	10,000							
Accumulated depreciation: truck		3,000						
Building	60,000							
Accumulated depreciation: building		4,000						
Accounts payable		90,000						
Note payable		5,000						
Mortgage payable		48,000						
Capital, T. Hodge		12,000						
Drawing, T. Hodge	2,000							
Sales revenue		400,000						
Repairs & maintenance expense	60,000							
Sales commissions	25,000							
Supplies expense	5,000							
Travel expense	30,000							
Wage expense	220,000							
Utilities expense	10,000							
Interest expense	10,000							
	562,000	562,000						
Depreciation expense								
Rent expense								
Advertising expense								
Interest payable								
Prepaid travel								
Prepaid supplies								
Accrued expenses								
Net Income								

Answer	*Explanation*

1. January 1, 1982: The $10,000 Truck Cost ÷ 5-year Truck Life = $2,000 Straight-line Depreciation. Accumulated depreciation is $3,000, or 1½ years' equivalent. Since it is assumed that the trial balance is before adjustment, this 1½ years of depreciation was recorded prior to the 1983–1984 fiscal year. Hence, the truck was purchased January 1, 1982 (probably January 2, 1982).

2. March 1, 1980: The $60,000 Building Cost ÷ 50-Year Building Life = $1,200 Straight-line Depreciation. Accumulated depreciation is $4,000 or 3⅓ years. As in number (1), this depreciation was booked prior to the 1983–1984 fiscal year. Hence, the building was purchased March 1, 1980.

3. 833.3\overline{3}$ Total prepaid rent was $25,000 on July 1, 1982, and it is $15,000 on July 1, 1983 (since no adjustments to prepaid rent have been made during the 1983–1984 fiscal year). Hence, $10,000 relates to 12 months' rent, which results in a monthly rental rate of 833.3\overline{3}$.

4. See completed worksheet on pp. 35–36.

5. See income statement, statement of owners' equity, and balance sheet on pp. 36–37.

6. See closing journal entries on p. 38.

7. See post-closing trial balance on p. 38.

AMERICAN MACHINERY ELECTRONICS SUPPLIERS SYNDICATED
Worksheet
For the Year Ended June 30, 1984

Accounts	Trial Balance Debit	Trial Balance Credit	Adjustments Debit	Adjustments Credit	Income Statement Debit	Income Statement Credit	Balance Sheet Debit	Balance Sheet Credit
Cash	30,000						30,000	
Accounts receivable	80,000						80,000	
Prepaid rent	15,000			(c) 10,000			5,000	
Prepaid advertising	5,000			(d) 3,500			1,500	
Truck	10,000						10,000	
Accumulated depreciation: truck		3,000		(a) 2,000				5,000
Building	60,000						60,000	
Accumulated depreciation: building		4,000		(b) 1,200				5,200
Accounts payable		90,000						90,000
Note payable		5,000						5,000
Mortgage payable		48,000						48,000
Capital, T. Hodge		12,000						12,000
Drawing, T. Hodge	2,000						2,000	
Sales revenue		400,000				400,000		
Repairs & maintenance expense	60,000				60,000			
Sales commissions	25,000				25,000			
Supplies expense	5,000			(h) 800	4,200			
Travel expense	30,000			(g) 7,000	23,000			
Wage expense	220,000		(i) 400		220,400			
Utilities expense	10,000		(j) 100		10,100			
Interest expense	10,000		(e) 900		10,900			
	562,000	562,000						
Depreciation expense			(a) 2,000 (b) 1,200		3,200			
Rent expense			(c) 10,000		10,000			
Advertising expense			(d) 3,500		3,500			
Interest payable				(e) 900				900
Prepaid travel			(g) 7,000				7,000	
Prepaid supplies			(h) 800				800	
Accrued expenses				(j) 500				500
			25,900	25,900	370,300	400,000	196,300	166,600
Net Income					29,700			29,700
					400,000	400,000	196,300	196,300

Adjusting Journal Entries

(a)   Depreciation Expense   2,000
         Accumulated Depreciation: Truck   2,000
      To record 1983–1984 depreciation ($10,000 ÷ 5)

(b)   Depreciation Expense   1,200
         Accumulated Depreciation: Building   1,200
      To record 1983–1984 depreciation ($60,000 ÷ 50)

(c)   Rent Expense   10,000
         Prepaid Rent   10,000
      To record expiration (or use of) prepaid rent (833.3\overline{3}$ × 12 months)

(d)   Advertising Expense   3,500
         Prepaid Advertising   3,500
      To record expiration of prepaid advertising ($5,000 × ⁷⁄₁₀)

(e)   Interest Expense   900
         Interest Payable   900
      To record interest incurred during the period on the note payable ($5,000 × 18%)

(f)   No entry required

(g)   Prepaid Travel   7,000
         Travel Expense   7,000
      To reclassify travel advances

(h)   Prepaid Supplies   800
         Supplies Expense   800
      To reclassify unused supplies

(i)   Wages Expense   400
      Utilities Expense   100
         Accrued Expenses   500
      To record the liability for accrued expenses as of year-end

5.

AMERICAN MACHINERY ELECTRONICS SUPPLIERS SYNDICATED
Income Statement
For the Year Ended June 30, 1984

Sales revenue		$400,000
Less expenses		
Repair & maintenance expense	$ 60,000	
Sales commissions	25,000	
Supplies expense	4,200	
Travel expense	23,000	
Wage expense	220,400	
Utilities expense	10,100	
Interest expense	10,900	
Depreciation expense	3,200	
Rent expense	10,000	
Advertising expense	3,500	370,300
Net income		$ 29,700

AMERICAN MACHINERY ELECTRONICS SUPPLIERS SYNDICATED
Statement of Owners' Equity
For the Year Ended June 30, 1984

Beginning balance, July 1	$ 12,000
Increase:	
Net income	29,700
Decrease:	
Owner withdrawals	2,000
Ending balance, June 30	$ 39,700

AMERICAN MACHINERY ELECTRONICS SUPPLIERS SYNDICATED
Balance Sheet
June 30, 1984

ASSETS

Cash		$ 30,000	
Accounts receivable		80,000	
Prepaid rent		5,000	
Prepaid advertising		1,500	
Prepaid travel		7,000	
Prepaid supplies		800	
Truck	$10,000		
Less: Accumulated depreciation	5,000	5,000	
Building	$60,000		
Less: Accumulated depreciation	5,200	54,800	$184,100

LIABILITIES

Accounts payable		$ 90,000	
Interest payable		900	
Accrued expenses		500	
Note payable		5,000	
Mortgage payable		48,000	$144,400

OWNERS' EQUITY

T. Hodge, capital		39,700
Total liabilities & owners' equity		$184,100

Closing Journal Entries

June 30, 1984

Sales Revenue	400,000	
Income Summary		400,000
To close revenues		

June 30, 1984

Income Summary	370,300	
Repairs & Maintenance Expense		60,000
Sales Commissions		25,000
Supplies Expense		4,200
Travel Expense		23,000
Wage Expense		220,400
Utilities Expense		10,100
Interest Expense		10,900
Depreciation Expense		3,200
Rent Expense		10,000
Advertising Expense		3,500
To close expenses		

June 30, 1984

Income Summary	29,700	
T. Hodge, capital		29,700
To close income summary		

June 30, 1984

T. Hodge, capital	2,000	
T. Hodge, drawing		2,000
To close drawing		

AMERICAN MACHINERY ELECTRONICS SUPPLIERS SYNDICATED
Post-Closing Trial Balance
June 30, 1984

Cash	$ 30,000	
Accounts receivable	80,000	
Prepaid rent	5,000	
Prepaid advertising	1,500	
Prepaid travel	7,000	
Prepaid supplies	800	
Truck	10,000	
Accumulated depreciation: truck		$ 5,000
Building	60,000	
Accumulated depreciation: building		5,200
Accounts payable		90,000
Interest payable		900
Accrued expenses		500
Note payable		5,000
Mortgage payable		48,000
Capital, T. Hodge		39,700
	$194,300	$194,300

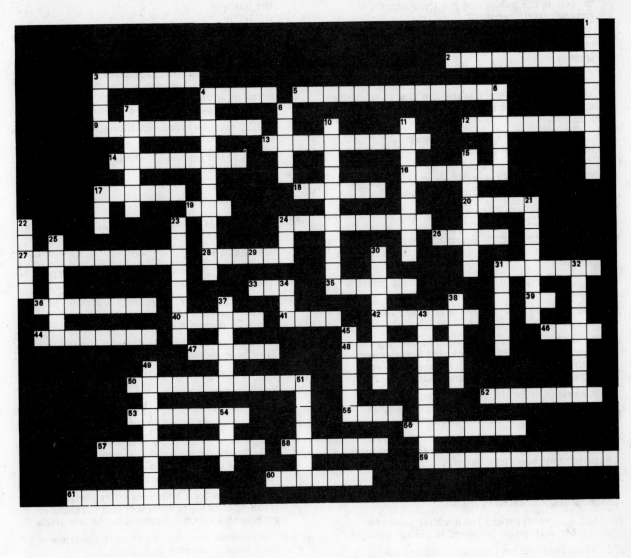

2. The _2 across_ and _52 across_ _61 across_ (abbreviated _34 down_.) was established to review the financial statements of firms that offer securities for sale to the public and has the authority to impose certain reporting standards.

3. _____ corrects the lack of agreement between the owners' equity account and the owners' equity statement.

4. The left side or column of an account.

5. The entity form which is the simplest in structure and is owned by one individual is called a _54 down_ _5 across_.

9. _____ is concerned with the recording, summarizing, and processing of data into information.

12. The _____ is a columnar form that aids in the construction of the financial statements.

13. Amounts that are owed by an enterprise are known as _____.

14. _14 across_ _39 across_ _28 across_ Equity discloses the causes of change in owners' equity during the accounting period.

16. _____ expenses are assets that provide future benefits.

17. Accumulated depreciation is an example of a _____ asset.

18. All of the accounts taken together compose a firm's _51 down_ _18 across_, a book that contains separate listings for each account that appears on an organization's financial statements.

19. Abbreviation for the agency known as the "watchdog" of Congress as it evaluates other governmental agencies and programs.

20. The accounting _____ represents the various tasks that are performed during an accounting period to process transactions.

24. _____ accounting deals primarily with reporting the results of operations for planning, control purposes, and decision making.

26. A _____ occurs when the decimal point of a number is improperly moved to the left or right.

27. When depreciation expense is debited the _____ depreciation account is credited.

28. See 14 across.

31. A _31 across_ _53 across_ year is exemplified by the professional baseball club's October 31 year-end, which is after the play-offs and world series.

33. Abbreviation for the body responsible for administering the tax laws that are passed by Congress and handed down by the courts.

35. Inventory receiving reports, bills from suppliers, customer sales slips, and customer checks are all examples of _35 across_ _49 down_.

36. _____ represents the major source of business for most public accounting firms, particularly those organized on the national or international level.

39. See 14 across.

40. See 1 down.

41. See 23 down.

42. The Income _____ account is used only in the closing process and is closed out to retained earnings, reflecting the net income or net loss of the business.

44. See 24 down.

46. A net _____ is reported for companies with expenses that exceed their revenues.

47. The _____ statement summarizes the results of operations for a business by disclosing the revenues it has earned along with the expenses incurred in producing those revenues.

48. _____ revenue represents future revenue that has been collected.

50. _____ is the process by which transactions are originally recorded.

52. See 2 across.

53. See 31 across.

55. Accounting is based on the principle of historical _____.

56. See 24 down.

57. _____ are the amounts that a business expects to collect at some future date.

58. The _____ account is a contra (opposite) owners' equity account which reduces capital and normally possesses a debit balance.

59. A _____ means that two digits of a given number have been accidentally reversed.

60. See 8 down.

61. See 2 across.

DOWN

1. The _40 across_ _1 down_ states that a business must be viewed as a unit that is separate and apart from its owners and from other firms.

3. Abbreviation for a body created by Congress as a result of millions of dollars of cost overruns on government defense contracts in the late 1960s.

4. The expense recorded to reduce the balance of a fixed asset is referred to as _____.

6. A month, quarter, or year are all examples of an accounting _____.

7. The transactions in the journal and the accounts in the ledger are linked together by a process called _____.

8. The _8 down_ _60 across_ checks the equality of debits and credits in the ledger by listing each account along with its ending balance.

10. _____ by owners decrease the equity of the owners in the assets of the business (i.e., remove assets from the business for the owners' personal use).

11. Revenue, expense, and drawing accounts are known as _____ accounts.

15. _____ refers to the practice of having expenses incurred in producing revenue deducted from the revenues they have helped to produce.

17. Arthur Andersen & Co. is one of the Big Eight _____ (abbreviation) firms.

21. The mathematical relationship, Assets = Liabilities + Owners' Equity, is known as the fundamental accounting _____.

22. The _____ of accounts is a detailed listing of a company's accounts along with their associated account numbers.

23. A _23 down_ _41 across_ basis system is adopted by most businesses that desire to use the cash basis and represents a combination of both the cash and accrual systems.

24. _43 down_ _44 across_ _56 across_ (abbreviated _24 down_.) are frequently provided by auditing firms and include projects such as inventory control, analysis and design of information-processing systems, and the implementation of production scheduling systems.

25. _____ expenses are expenses that have been incurred and not as yet paid.

29. The fifth letter of the alphabet.

30. Same as 12 across.

31. Certain account types tend to contain more debits than credits and will almost always possess a _____ balance that is a debit balance, such as assets and expenses.

32. In the _____ process, the accountant analyzes the various accounts maintained by a business to determine whether or not they are up-to-date.

34. See 2 across.

37. A _____ year is any one-year period other than from January 1 to December 31 (e.g., July 1 to June 30).

38. The right side or column of an account.

43. See 24 down.

45. Firms engaged in _____ accounting render accounting services to all types of enterprises.

49. See 35 across.

51. See 18 across.

54. See 5 across.

4 ACCOUNTING FOR MERCHANDISING OPERATIONS

OBJECTIVES

After completing this chapter, you should:

1 *Comprehend the importance of inventory to business enterprises.*

2 *Be able to diagram and explain a merchandising system, including the role of such source documents as a purchase order, invoice, customer statement, checks, credit memorandum, and debit memorandum.*

3 *Know how to record sales, sales returns and allowances, sales discounts, and freight-out expenses for a seller as well as purchases, purchase returns and allowances, purchase discounts, and freight-in expenses for a purchaser.*

4 *Be able to compute cost of goods sold, to prepare a worksheet and financial statements for a merchandising concern, and to close out accounts for an entity that uses a periodic inventory system.*

5 *Understand the distinction between a periodic and a perpetual inventory system.*

CHAPTER SUMMARY

Inventory, the good(s) that an entity is in business to sell, is perhaps the most critical asset in its operations. Too little inventory aggravates effective customer service, while excess inventory can impose such a financial burden on an entity that it is unlikely to have profitable operations. Hence, control over this asset, both its sale and purchase, is essential to efficient operations and is evident in a review of a typical merchandising operation.

Sales orders or invoices are generated for customer sales and processed by the **order processing department**, which is responsible for checking customer credit information and inventory availability, keeping track of unfilled customer orders, and informing the accounts receivable department of credit sale information via the forwarding of the invoices. The mail clerk receives customers' payments, records cash received, and forwards the cash to cash collections and the information on customer payments to accounts receivable. The **accounts receivable department** updates customers' accounts, the general ledger, and prepares customer statements. Obviously, this sales cycle relies on the inventory being available and implies a purchasing cycle to handle inventory control and the payment of suppliers. Specifically, purchase orders initiated by the **purchasing department** are sent to the **inventory control department** that monitors which purchase orders have been filled and which are unfilled, keeps a count of the goods on hand, provides information to **order processing**, analyzes the efficiency of the entity's inventory and marketing policies, and provides the accounts payable department with information on purchase invoices. The **accounts payable department**, after verifying the propriety of the bill, will issue a check and update detailed records of payables as well as the general ledger.

The actual recording of *inventory-related sales* requires a debit to cash or accounts receivable and a credit to sales, while *returns by* or *price reductions granted to customers* are recorded as a debit to sales returns and allowances and a credit to accounts receivable or cash. A **credit memo** is the source document from which such an adjustment is made; the debit is to a contra-revenue account that is listed on the income statement in arriving at net sales.

Due to the impracticality of publishing a price list for every type of customer, entities typically publish one basic **price list** representing the maximum price charged and then offer various **trade discounts** to customers who qualify for a break due to their status as a wholesaler or retailer (rather than as an individual) or due to their purchase of large quantities. Since the printed price list is never the relevant price to any party to whom a trade discount is offered, such discounts are not recorded in accounting records but are used merely to compute the actual price to a customer which, in turn, is recorded as a debit to accounts receivable and a credit to sales.

In contrast, **cash discounts** are not automatic to a given customer class but must be earned by the customer through prompt payment of bills. The common format of cash discounts is 3/10, n/60, which means that a 3% discount on the invoice (net of returns and freight costs) can be claimed if a bill is paid within 10 days of the invoice date; otherwise, the entire invoice balance must be paid within 60 days of the invoice date. These discounts are typically recorded when claimed via prompt payment and are reflected on the books of the seller by debiting sales discounts for the difference in the full invoice price credited to accounts receivable and the amount of cash received, which is debited to cash.

Freight charges are borne by the seller if the terms are *F.O.B.* (free-on-board) *destination* and by the purchaser if *F.O.B. shipping point* and are booked as either a freight-out or a freight-in expense, respectively. The result is an increase in either cost of goods sold or cost of goods purchased.

Purchases are recorded as a debit to purchases and a credit to accounts payable, net of trade discounts, and frequently net of purchase discounts (cash discounts). Although purchase discounts are equivalent to sales discounts in the way they are computed, they are perceived to be more controllable since an entity knows its intention or policy with respect to taking discounts even though it may know very little about its customers' policies. Hence, an entity that intends to take advantage of every purchase (cash) discount which is offered will frequently record purchases at their net amounts, and if a discount is lost, the difference in the gross amount paid (credited to cash) and the amount expected to be owed net of discount (debited to accounts payable) is debited to purchases discounts lost, which is an expense account. This net method permits managers to apply the concept of **management by exception** by focusing attention on only those discounts lost. The gross method of recording discounts (equivalent to that used for sales discounts) is also common. The handling of purchase returns and allowances as well as freight charges is similar to sales; a credit is made to a contra-purchase account, purchase returns & allowances (based on a debit memorandum), and a debit is made to accounts payable in the former case, while freight charges represent an additional cost of goods purchased.

A **perpetual inventory account** directly adjusts inventory every time a purchase or sale occurs, so that the general ledger account continually reports goods available. In contrast, a **periodic inventory system** leaves the beginning inventory balance in the general ledger throughout the period and sets up separate accounts to record purchases, returns and allowances, discounts, and freight costs. At year-end a physical count is made of inventory on hand and then **cost of goods sold** is computed by applying the formula: Beginning Inventory + Purchases, − Purchase Returns and Allowances, − Purchase Discounts, + Freight-in, − Ending Inventory. The entries made on the books to facilitate this computation are the closing of beginning and ending inventories to the income summary, the establishment of ending inventory as the final balance in the general ledger (i.e., providing an update to beginning inventory), and the closing of each of the purchase-related accounts to the income summary. These entries, combined with the normal closing entries discussed in Chapter 3, will result in the correct income figure that is reflected in the worksheet and the income statement. The appearance of the income statement for a merchandising firm differs from that of a service industry in its presentation of the detailed computation of cost of goods sold components and in its use of the **gross profit format** (Sales − Cost of Goods Sold = Gross Profit, and then other revenue and expense items are listed).

TECHNICAL POINTS

✓ Records are maintained net of trade discounts

List Price × (1 − Trade Discount) = Invoice Price

✓ *Cash Discounts = (Invoice Price − Returns and Allowances − Freight Costs) × (Percent Cash Discount)*

✓ Converting cash discounts to annualized interest

$$\frac{Cash\ Discount}{\substack{Number\ of\ Days\ in\ Which\ Net\ is\ to\ be\ Paid \\ -\ Number\ of\ Days\ Permitted\ to\ Qualify\ for\ Discount}} = \frac{x}{360\ Days}$$

✓ *Net Sales = Sales − Sales Returns and Allowances − Sales Discounts*

✓   *Purchases*
    + Freight-in
    − Purchase Returns and Allowances
    − Purchase Discounts
        Net Purchases

✓ *Goods Available for Sale = Beginning Inventory + Net Purchases*

✓   *Beginning Inventory*
    + Net Purchases
    − Ending Inventory
        Cost of Goods Sold

✓ *Gross Profit = Net Sales − Cost of Goods Sold*

✓ *Gross Profit Percentage =* $\dfrac{Gross\ Profit}{Sales}$

MULTIPLE-CHOICE QUESTIONS

Circle the letter corresponding to the best response.

1. Payments on customers' accounts are typically received by
  a. the mail clerk
  b. the salesperson

    c. the credit department
    d. the accounting department
    e. none of the above

2. The accounts payable department
    a. establishes records that allow for the proper payment of all purchase invoices as they come due
    b. checks the mathematical accuracy of invoices
    c. compares the initial purchase order and a report completed by warehouse personnel of the actual goods received
    d. issues checks to suppliers
    e. all of the above
    f. a, b, and c only

3. Trade discounts are intended
    a. to encourage prompt payments
    b. to adapt one price listing to all customers
    c. to cover freight costs
    d. all of the above
    e. a and b only

4. F.O.B. destination means
    a. the seller incurs transportation costs
    b. the seller pays transportation costs
    c. the buyer incurs transportation costs
    d. the buyer pays transportation costs

5. Management by exception
    a. is demonstrated by the gross method of recording sales discounts
    b. is demonstrated by the gross method of recording purchase discounts
    c. is demonstrated by the net method of recording purchase discounts
    d. none of the above

6. A 3/10, n/30 cash discount translates into an annual rate of interest of
    a. 12%
    b. 36%
    c. 108%
    d. 54%
    e. none of the above

MULTIPLE-CHOICE QUESTIONS (ANSWERS)

Answer   *Explanation*

1. a   To permit customers' payments to be handled by the sales staff or the accounting department or by personnel granting credit, would represent poor control over assets. The sales staff could promote unrecorded sales by not processing orders properly, the accounting department could adjust the books to cover up cash shortages, and the personnel granting credit could indicate a bad credit standing for a customer and remove the customer's payments. The mail clerk, by recording cash received and sending receipts to cash collections and information to the accounts receivable department, sets up a check-and-balance system over cash handling and record keeping.

2. e   The checking of math and the comparison of purchases with receipts helps to assure that goods are not paid for unless they were both ordered and delivered. Once these procedures have been performed, records are established of purchases, and checks are issued. Each of these duties is performed by the accounts payable department. (The issuance of checks is distinct from the signing of checks.)

3. b Cash discounts are intended to encourage prompt payments. Neither cash nor trade discounts are intended to cover freight costs.

4. a Sometimes a buyer may pay transportation costs that are to be incurred by the seller. F.O.B. shipping point would result in the buyer incurring transportation costs.

5. c Such an accounting treatment directs management's attention to the exception, which is the cash discount not taken in spite of the company's policy of claiming all cash discounts offered by suppliers.

6. d $3/20 = x/360$ or $3(360) = 20(x)$ or $1080 = 20x$ and $x = 54\%$

TRUE-FALSE QUESTIONS

Indicate whether each of the following statements is true (T) or false (F).

____ **1.** The mail clerk typically receives payments on account, keeps a record of all cash received, and then sends the receipts and information regarding customer checks to the accounts receivable department.

____ **2.** A merchandising firm acquires or manufactures goods for resale to others.

____ **3.** Marketing department personnel would typically desire higher levels of inventory to be on hand relative to the inventory levels desired by finance department personnel.

____ **4.** The most popular method of recording sales discounts is the gross method.

____ **5.** Under the periodic method of inventory, before year-end adjustments are made the inventory account in the general ledger will be the year's beginning inventory balance.

____ **6.** Under a perpetual inventory method, when purchases are made the inventory account is debited.

____ **7.** If a company's income statement lists cash discounts lost, that company is utilizing the gross method to record purchase discounts.

____ **8.** A debit memorandum is prepared to support a sales return and allowance.

____ **9.** F.O.B. means free-on-board.

____ **10.** The purchases account is used *strictly* to record purchases of merchandise for resale to customers.

TRUE-FALSE QUESTIONS (ANSWERS)

Answer   *Explanation*

1. F Only information is sent to the accounts receivable department, the actual checks or cash received are sent to the cash collections division of the firm. This procedure of separating cash handling from its record keeping improves control over assets.

2. F A merchandising firm acquires but does not manufacture goods for resale.

3. T Marketing personnel would tend to focus on avoiding out-of-stock situations, while the finance personnel would be concerned over the storage and investment commitment represented by inventory.

4. T Since sellers do not know customers' policies with regard to taking discounts (much less have control over such policies), companies typically choose to record sales using the gross method, recording discounts as they are actually claimed with payments.

5. T As purchases are made, temporary accounts are used to maintain records throughout the year; only when a year-end physical count is made is the inventory balance in the general ledger adjusted.

6. **T**   Instead of debiting purchases, the inventory account is adjusted directly.

7. **F**   The company would be utilizing the net method of recording purchase discounts if cash discounts lost are listed as an expense item on the income statement.

8. **F**   A credit memorandum supports a sales return and allowance, while a debit memorandum supports a purchase return and allowance.

9. **T**   In other words, the seller will place the merchandise sold on board a freight carrier at no charge.

10. **T**   Any purchases of other items are recorded in descriptive accounts such as prepaid supplies or office furniture and fixtures.

CLASSIFI-CATION AND MATCHING QUESTIONS

A. Match the following tasks to the departments that typically perform them by using these symbols.

OP = Order processing department
AR = Accounts receivable department
IC = Inventory control department
AP = Accounts payable department

____   *1.* Closely monitors the amounts owed by customers.
____   *2.* Keeps track of all unfilled customer orders.
____   *3.* Updates customer accounts.
____   *4.* Monitors which purchase orders have been filled and which are unfilled.
____   *5.* Monitors the balances owed to suppliers.
____   *6.* Is responsible for the issuance of checks to suppliers.
____   *7.* Checks customer credit from information provided by the credit department.
____   *8.* Keeps a running count of the goods on hand.

B. Classify the following accounts by using these symbols.

C = Components of the cost-of-goods-sold calculation
CR = Contra-revenue accounts
E = Expense accounts other than cost of goods sold
N = None of the above

____   *1.* Cash discounts lost
____   *2.* Sales returns and allowances
____   *3.* Freight-in
____   *4.* Freight-out
____   *5.* Trade discounts
____   *6.* Sales discounts
____   *7.* Beginning inventory
____   *8.* Purchase discounts

CLASSIFICATION AND MATCHING QUESTIONS (ANSWERS)

A. *1.* AR *2.* OP *3.* AR *4.* IC *5.* AP *6.* AP *7.* OP *8.* IC
B. *1.* E *2.* CR *3.* C *4.* E *5.* N *6.* CR *7.* C *8.* C

QUESTIONS CONCERNING THE EFFECTS OF TRANS-ACTIONS

Indicate whether the following items result in an increase (+), a decrease (−), or no effect (0) on net income. [Assume that inventory is stable, remaining unchanged over the period (i.e., the beginning inventory balance equals the ending inventory balance)].

____   *1.* Freight-in

____   *2.* Purchase discounts

___ 3. Sales returns & allowances

___ 4. Purchases

___ 5. Sales discounts

___ 6. Cash discounts lost

___ 7. Purchase returns & allowances

QUESTIONS CONCERNING THE EFFECTS OF TRANSACTIONS (ANSWERS)

1. −   2. +   3. −   4. −   5. −   6. −   7. +

EXERCISES

1. Joyce Clarks' Interior Design Shop had $102,000 of sales during the past year. Of these, $30,000 were cash sales. Joyce offers a 2/10, n/30 sales discount; 40% of the discounts offered were claimed by customers. Assume that all receivables have been collected as of year-end. Record the appropriate journal entries.

2. The general ledger for Salley's Sewing Supplies, before adjustments, includes the following balances.

Inventory	$ 72,000
Freight-in	3,000
Freight-out	1,000
Purchase discounts	900
Purchase returns & allowances	300
Purchases	330,000
Sales returns & allowances	4,000
Sales	500,000
Sales discounts	400

Salley has also told you that her total trade discounts claimed on purchases were $10,000 and that her ending inventory count was $64,000.

a. Compute cost of goods sold
b. Compute net sales
c. Compute the gross profit and the gross profit percentage

EXERCISES (ANSWERS)

1. Obviously no cash (sales) discount would be offered for cash sales. Therefore $102,000 − $30,000 = $72,000 is subject to sales discounts, and only 40% of these, or $28,800, claimed the discounts. Hence, $28,800 × 2% = $576 Sales Discounts Granted.

Accounts Receivable	72,000	
Cash	30,000	
Sales		102,000

To record cash sales and sales on credit

Cash	71,424	
Sales Discounts	576	
Accounts Receivable		72,000

To record collection of receivables net of sales discounts

Note: The net method, the most popular form for sales discounts, is used in this exercise.

2. a.

Beginning Inventory	$ 72,000
+ Purchases	330,000
+ Freight-in	3,000
− Purchase Discounts	900
− Purchase Returns & Allowances	300
− Ending Inventory	64,000
Cost of Goods Sold	**$339,800**

b.

Sales	$500,000
− Sales Returns & Allowances	4,000
− Sales Discounts	400
Net Sales	**$495,600**

Note: Trade discounts and freight-out are irrelevant. Also note that the inventory balance on the books, before adjustments, for a company with a periodic inventory system is the beginning inventory of the company for the current period.

c.

Net Sales	$495,600
− Cost of Goods Sold	339,800
Gross Profit	**$155,800**

$$\text{Gross Profit Percentage} = \frac{\text{Gross Profit}}{\text{Net Sales}} = \frac{\$155,800}{\$495,600} = 31.4\%$$

CHAPTER DEMONSTRATION PROBLEM

Cutrate Tools, Inc., has made sales totaling $600,000 in list price during one period; 30% of these sales were subject to a trade discount of 40%, 20% of these sales were subject to a trade discount of 30%, and 10% of these sales were subject to a trade discount of 20%. During the period, 5% of the goods sold were returned as defective and $4,000 of allowances were granted. All sales were made on account and all returns and allowances were granted prior to receipt of customers' payments. Although most of the company's sales are F.O.B. shipping point, $5,000 of freight expenses have been incurred.

Cutrate Tools, Inc., has purchased $250,000 of inventory during the period. The company has a policy of automatically taking 2% cash discounts that are offered on 70% of the company's purchases, although mistakes made in the timing of payments resulted in losing discounts on 10% of these purchases. The company uses the net method of recording these cash discounts. The 1% cash discounts that are offered on the other 30% of purchases are only taken if working capital permits, so the gross method of accounting is used. Over the past year, one-half of the 1% discounts offered were claimed. The total transportation expenditures on these purchases was $10,000 for F.O.B. shipping point terms and $3,000 for F.O.B. destination terms. Assume all of these purchases have been paid for as of year-end.

At the beginning of the period, inventory on hand was valued at $30,000, and a physical count at year-end indicates ending inventory is $40,000.

Required

Journalize the described transactions, compute the company's gross profit, and prepare closing entries that would be required for the accounts described.

CHAPTER DEMONSTRATION PROBLEM (ANSWER)

$ 600,000 Sales List	$ 600,000 Sales List	$ 600,000 Sales List
✕ 30%	✕ 20%	✕ 10%
$ 180,000	$ 120,000	$ 60,000
✕ (1−40% Trade Discount)	✕ (1−30% Trade Discount)	✕ (1−20% Trade Discount)
$ 108,000	$ 84,000	$ 48,000

√ *$108,000 + $84,000 + $48,000 = $240,000 Total Sales Net of Trade Discounts (Invoice Value)*

√ *1 − (30% + 20% + 10%) = 40%*

with list price equal to the invoice amount, so

√ *40% × $600,000 = $240,000 = Total Sales without Trade Discounts*

$480,000 ($240,000 Net of Discounts + $240,000 at List)
×   0.05

$ 24,000 Sales Returns
*   4,000 Sales Allowances*

$ 28,000 Sales Returns & Allowances

The following journal entries are related to sales.

Accounts Receivable   480,000
* Sales   480,000*
To record sales on account

Note: These sales are recorded net of trade discounts.

Sales Returns & Allowances   28,000
* Accounts Receivable   28,000*
To record returns and allowances granted to customers

Freight-out   5,000
* Accounts Payable (or Cash)   5,000*
To record freight expenses incurred

Purchases

$250,000	*$175,000*	*$250,000*
× 70%	*− 3,500*	*× 30%*
$175,000	*$171,500*	*$ 75,000*
× 2%		*× 50%*
$ 3,500		*$ 37,500*
× 10%		*× 1%*
$ 350		*$ 375*

The following journal entries are related to purchases.

Purchases   171,500
* Accounts Payable   171,500*
To record purchases net of cash discounts

Accounts Payable   171,500
Cash Discounts Lost   350
* Cash   171,850*
To record payment of purchases net of cash discounts, including lost discounts

Purchases   75,000
* Accounts Payable   75,000*
To record purchases gross of cash discounts

Claim against Suppliers for Freight Paid   3,000
* Cash   3,000*
To record payment of $3,000 for freight on purchases made on F.O.B. destination terms

Accounts Payable   75,000
* Purchase Discounts   375*
* Claim against Suppliers for Freight Paid   3,000*
* Cash   71,625*
To record payment of purchases, netted with those cash discounts claimed and the amount due for freight paid which was to be incurred by the supplier

Note: The freight costs do not qualify for a cash discount.

    Freight-in Expense   10,000
        Accounts Payable (or Cash)   10,000
    Record freight expense for purchases made on F.O.B. shipping point terms

Gross profit calculation

Sales	**$480,000**
— **Sales Returns & Allowances**	28,000
Net Sales	**$452,000**
Beginning Inventory	$ 30,000
+ **Purchases**	171,500
	75,000
— **Purchase Discounts**	375
+ **Freight-in**	10,000
Goods Available for Sale	**$286,125**
— **Ending Inventory**	40,000
Cost of Goods Sold	**$246,125**
Gross Profit	**$205,875**

Note: Lost purchase discounts are an expense item not included in the cost of sales calculation.

Closing entries

    Income Summary   30,000
        Inventory   30,000
    To close beginning inventory

    Inventory   40,000
        Income Summary   40,000
    To record ending inventory

    Income Summary   289,850
        Sales Returns & Allowances   28,000
        Purchases   246,500
        Freight-in   10,000
        Cash Discounts Lost   350
        Freight-out   5,000
    To close income statement debit accounts

    Sales   480,000
    Purchase Discounts   375
        Income Summary   480,375
    To close income statement credit accounts

    Income Summary   200,525
        Capital   200,525
    To close the income summary to the capital account

Note: The income summary would actually have been adjusted for all revenues and expenses before closing.

5 INFORMATION PROCESSING SYSTEMS AND INTERNAL CONTROL

OBJECTIVES

After completing this chapter, you should:

1 *Be able to recognize an audit trail.*

2 *Be familiar with what internal controls are and how they can be utilized by the smallest of business operations.*

3 *Be able to distinguish between administrative controls and accounting controls.*

4 *Know what the Foreign Corrupt Practices Act (FCPA) is.*

5 *Understand how specialized journals and subsidiary ledgers are utilized in an information-processing system.*

6 *Have some familiarity with the interaction between accounting and computers, including related advantages and problems arising from such interaction.*

CHAPTER SUMMARY

The integrity and efficiency of a company's information system rely upon *internal control*. Controls can be classified either as **administrative** in nature, relating to management's authorization of transactions for the purpose of achieving a company's objectives (such as a plan of organization to achieve the company's goals and controls directed at operational efficiency that only indirectly relate to the accounts), or as **accounting** in nature, primarily concerned with safeguarding assets and reasonably assuring the reliability of financial records (such as the authorization of specific transactions and the conformity of records with generally accepted accounting principles).

The general control features that should be incorporated into any accounting system include the following: limiting access to assets; separating duties (specifically separating the transaction authorization, the recording of the transaction, and the custody of the assets involved in the transaction); utilizing accountability procedures such as duty authorization, prenumbered documents, and verification of records; hiring qualified personnel; and subjecting controls to an independent review (particularly by internal and external auditors). Added insurance against loss can be acquired in the form of fidelity bonding of employees handling valuable assets of a company. In all cases a business must evaluate the benefits of an internal control relative to the cost of implementing the particular control as the basis for designing and installing its internal control system; expected benefits should exceed the related costs of the control. An adequate system of internal accounting control is required by law under the **Foreign Corrupt Practices Act (FCPA)**, which is primarily intended to deter the making of illegal payments to foreign firms, governments, and political officials. However, the ability of adequate controls to effectively deter such payments is questionable in light of the ability of controls to be either circumvented or "beaten" through collusion.

The audit trail is an important element of control, particularly in providing the independent auditor with a means of verifying the legitimacy of recorded transactions and the absence of unrecorded transactions. The **audit trail** takes many forms depending on the type of processing system utilized by a company; such systems range from a cardboard box holding original documents, to a computerized real-time data base that instantaneously updates inventory and permits the offering of such services as advanced seating reservations on an airline. A common information-processing system is a **general journal/general ledger system**, augmented by specialized journals and subsidiary ledgers.

Specialized journals group like transactions to save the time required to journalize and post individual entries in a general journal. For example, sales on account can all be entered in a single column of a sales journal, and the monthly total can be posted to sales (a credit) and accounts receivable (a debit). Typically, specialized journals include a sales journal, purchases journal, cash receipts journal, cash payments journal, and possibly a sales returns journal and a purchases returns journal; the type(s) of specialized journal(s) used depends on the quantity of these transactions that are typically processed. These journals take whatever form is most efficient for the particular company, including the provision of details as to types of sales or purchases being processed, if desired, and columns for recording discounts in the cash receipts and payments journals, if common. A company must have an up-to-date record from which to prepare customer statements and to validate billings received from suppliers. Such a record is prepared in **subsidiary accounts receivable** and **subsidiary accounts payable ledgers**. These books contain an alphabetic listing of customers and suppliers and show the detailed billings, collections, payments, and running balance for each one. The subsidiary ledgers are controlled via the general ledger, since the accuracy of the subsidiary ledger can be checked by adding all of the subsidiary ledger sheets and comparing it to the balance in the related general ledger (for example, customers' balances when added should equal the accounts receivable general ledger balance). In order to assure the up-to-date status of subsidiary ledgers, postings are made daily from the specialized journals to the subsidiary for each individual transaction; tick marks in the journals indicate that the posting has been completed per transaction, and a posting reference to the source journal is recorded in the subsidiary ledger to provide an audit trail. Subsidiary ledgers can be prepared as needed for inventory items, departmental salaries, and similar accounts for which detailed listings using some classification scheme are desired.

The computerization of accounting systems is becoming more common as the costs of computers decline, the availability of minicomputers and microcomputers increases, and the quantity of transactions being processed grows. The advantages of computers include the reduction of data processing costs, the availability of better information for management control, and the access to quick responses to system queries. However, such advantages come at the cost of increased exposure to computer fraud. Such exposure is particularly acute in the absence of adequate controls over computer programming and computer access and in the presence of only limited computer expertise within a business, particularly in its internal audit department.

TECHNICAL POINTS

✓ Separation of the following duties is critical.

Transaction authorization
Transaction recording
Asset custody

✓ *Examples of Specialized Journals*	*Transactions Recorded*
Sales journal	Sales of merchandise on account
Purchases journal	Purchase of merchandise on account
Cash receipts journal	All cash receipts
Cash payments journal	All cash payments
Sales returns & allowances journal	All sales returns & allowances*
Purchases returns & allowances journal	All purchase returns & allowances*

*These items refer to sales and purchases of merchandise only.

✓ *Examples of Subsidiary Ledgers*	*Typical Subdivision*
Accounts receivable subsidiary ledger	Alphabetic listing of customers
Accounts payable subsidiary ledger	Alphabetic listing of suppliers
Merchandise inventory subsidiary ledger	Listing by inventory number
Salary expense subsidiary ledger	Listing by department

MULTIPLE-CHOICE QUESTIONS

Circle the letter corresponding to the best response.

1. Administrative controls
  a. are synonymous with accounting controls
  b. are typified by employee training programs
  c. are typified by prenumbered checks
  d. all of the above
  e. none of the above

2. The use of a secret password on a computer terminal is an example of which of the following general control features?
  a. separation of duties
  b. accountability procedures
  c. hiring of qualified personnel
  d. limited access to assets
  e. independent review

3. An independent review for third parties can best be performed by
  a. a key employee not responsible for the activity being reviewed
  b. the owner/manager
  c. the internal auditor
  d. the external auditor

4. The Foreign Corrupt Practices Act (FCPA)
  a. outlaws bribes to foreign political officials
  b. makes bribes to foreign governments a criminal offense
  c. if violated can result in a fine of $1 million for companies
  d. if violated can result in directors being fined $10,000 and/or imprisoned for up to five years
  e. all of the above
  f. a and c only

5. The advantages of special journals include
  a. allowing a company to spread its work load
  b. reducing the amount of posting to the general ledger

     c. reducing the amount of posting to the subsidiary ledgers

     d. all of the above

     e. a and b only

6. The debits in the sales journal should be posted to

     a. the sales account in the general ledger

     b. the cash account in the general ledger

     c. the accounts receivable account in the general ledger

     d. the accounts receivable subsidiary ledger

     e. none of the above

     f. c and d only

7. The credits in the subsidiary accounts payable ledger originate from the

     a. purchases journal

     b. cash payments journal

     c. general journal

     d. cash receipts journal

     e. sales journal

8. Advantages of computers in data processing include

     a. the reduction of data processing costs

     b. better information for management control

     c. quick response to system queries

     d. all of the above

MULTIPLE-CHOICE QUESTIONS (ANSWERS)

Answer	*Explanation*
1. b	While administrative controls are only *indirectly* related to accounts, accounting controls are *directly* related to accounts, stressing both the safeguarding of assets and the reliability of financial statements. Hence, *(b)* relates to administrative controls, while *(c)* corresponds to accounting controls.
2. d	The password, known to a select few, is intended to limit access to a company's valuable computer time and data files.
3. d	Too often the objectivity of *(a)* and *(b)* is questionable, and some risk exists that the comments by *(c)* may not be properly recognized as being independent due to the internal auditor's employee status. Hence, the independent auditors are likely to be in the best position to independently review controls.
4. e	Each of these are provisions under the FCPA.
5. e	No reduction in postings to the subsidiary ledger results from the use of specialized journals since each individual entry must be transferred. However, specialized journals do permit one person to account for all cash receipts, another for all sales, and so on. In addition, the number of postings to the general ledger is greatly reduced by the use of specialized journals.
6. f	Since only sales of merchandise on account are recorded in the sales journal, the debits are posted to accounts receivable, both in the general ledger and in the subsidiary receivables ledgers.
7. a	The purchases journal results in debits to purchases and credits to accounts payable. The credits would be posted to both the general and the subsidiary ledgers.
8. d	All of these benefits of employing both small and large computers are commonly cited in the literature.

Indicate whether each of the following statements is true (T) or false (F).

_____ *1.* No distinction can be made between data and information.

_____ *2.* The use of posting references helps to create an audit trail.

_____ *3.* The design of a perfect system that detects and prevents all errors is an impossibility.

_____ *4.* Although it assists in error detection, the separation of duties has no effect on the ease of fraud and embezzlement.

_____ *5.* The prenumbering of documents in and of itself provides no internal control, it is the subsequent accounting for the prenumbered documents that actually constitutes a control.

_____ *6.* A fidelity bond is an example of an internal control.

_____ *7.* From a control perspective, an employee who faithfully serves the employer year after year, taking no vacations, is a valued asset of the company.

_____ *8.* Basic internal controls should be implemented by all businesses regardless of the related costs.

_____ *9.* The general ledger account of accounts payable is the control account over the accounts payable subsidiary ledger.

_____ *10.* Many companies make no attempt to assign account numbers when dealing with accounts receivable and accounts payable.

_____ *11.* Typically, each column total of the cash receipts journal is posted to the general ledger.

_____ *12.* Accountants prefer to post the sales journal before the cash receipts journal and the purchases journal before the cash payments journal.

TRUE-FALSE QUESTIONS (ANSWERS)

Answer	Explanation
1. F	Information is meaningful data useful in decision making, while data are facts and figures. The terms are not synonymous.
2. T	Posting references make it easy for the auditor to trace general ledger entries to the original journal which in turn, typically provides the information necessary to locate the underlying source documents for the transaction of interest.
3. T	Any control system can be "beaten." Since controls can be influenced by employee carelessness and fatigue, perfection, even in the absence of intentional errors, is not possible.
4. F	Fraud and embezzlement are made more difficult largely because a single individual could not easily remove assets and simultaneously adjust the books so that the assets would not be identified as "missing." Separation of duties typically requires the collusion of employees before a fraud or embezzlement can be successfully perpetrated.
5. T	If every document were prenumbered but never accounted for, no accountability control would exist.
6. F	The fidelity bond is an insurance policy that reimburses a company for losses that arise from bonded employees' dishonest practices. It's insurance for a fault in a control system, rather than an internal control.

7. F   In fact, annual employee vacations should be required to permit a regular fraudulent routine to be broken and problems to be identified. Note that it is assumed that some other person performs the activities of the vacationing employee. If the vacationer's work is simply permitted to "pile up" until he or she returns to work, the whole point of requiring annual vacations is lost.

8. F   Controls should be implemented if the benefits of their use exceed the costs of their implementation and operation.

9. T   This means that if you add up the balances due suppliers that are listed in the subsidiary ledger, the total amount would agree with the general ledger.

10. T   The subsidiary ledgers can just as easily be alphabetized, which allows for the insertion of new accounts or deletion of old accounts without having to modify an account numbering scheme.

11. F   Typically, the cash receipts journal includes a sundry column that is not posted in total. Since various accounts are affected by entries in the sundry column, each line is separately and frequently posted as the transactions occur; this posting procedure is in the interest of efficiency.

12. T   This way the sales and purchases are entered in the appropriate accounts prior to payment by customers to the firm and by the firm to its suppliers, respectively.

**CLASSIFI-
CATION AND
MATCHING
QUESTIONS**

A. Divide the following activities of a company among three employees to achieve the optimum internal control over operations. Use the following classification scheme.

    1 = First employee
    2 = Second employee
    3 = Third employee

____   *1.* Hiring of employees
____   *2.* Purchasing of inventory
____   *3.* Recording payables
____   *4.* Shipping inventory to customers
____   *5.* Receiving inventory from suppliers
____   *6.* Paying suppliers
____   *7.* Paying employees
____   *8.* Writing sales invoices
____   *9.* Collecting on customers' accounts
____   *10.* Preparing customers' statements
____   *11.* Approving credit extensions to customers
____   *12.* Maintaining the accounts payable subsidiary ledger
____   *13.* Accounting for prenumbered sales invoices
____   *14.* Reconciling the bank statement to the general ledger cash account

B. Match the following transactions with the appropriate journal that would be used to record the original journal entry. Use the following abbreviations:

    SJ = Sales journal
    PJ = Purchases journal
    CR = Cash receipts journal
    CP = Cash payments journal
    GJ = General journal

____   *1.* Collections from customers
____   *2.* Purchase of equipment
____   *3.* Cash sale of merchandise
____   *4.* Loan payment to the bank
____   *5.* Sale of merchandise on account

___   *6.* Payments to suppliers
___   *7.* Proceeds from sale of furniture
___   *8.* Contribution of $600 capital
___   *9.* Purchase of inventory
___   *10.* Traded in two cars for a truck (an even trade)
___   *11.* Adjusted prepaid advertising to reflect the use of advertising over the period
___   *12.* Closed out the income summary account

CLASSIFICATION AND MATCHING QUESTIONS (ANSWERS)

A. The three basic types of financial activities to be divided are transaction authorization (employee no. 1), transaction recording (employee no. 2), and asset custody (employee no. 3).

1. 1   *2.* 1   *3.* 2   *4.* 3   *5.* 3   *6.* 3   *7.* 3   *8.* 1   *9.* 3   *10.* 2   *11.* 1   *12.* 2   *13.* 2   *14.* 2

B.   *1.* CR   *2.* GJ   *3.* CR   *4.* CP   *5.* SJ   *6.* CP   *7.* CR   *8.* CR   *9.* PJ   *10.* GJ   *11.* GJ   *12.* GJ

QUESTIONS CONCERNING THE EFFECTS OF TRANSACTIONS

Indicate whether the following transactions are likely to increase (+), decrease (−), have no net effect (=), or have no effect whatsoever (N) on the accounts, journals, and/or ledgers listed.

A. Collection of an account receivable
___   *1.* Sales journal
___   *2.* Accounts receivable subsidiary ledger
___   *3.* Cash receipts journal

B. Purchase of furniture and fixtures on account
___   *1.* Purchases journal
___   *2.* Cash payments journal
___   *3.* General journal
___   *4.* Accounts payable

C. Paying employees
___   *1.* Accounts payable
___   *2.* Cash payments journal
___   *3.* Purchases journal
___   *4.* General journal

QUESTIONS CONCERNING THE EFFECTS OF TRANSACTIONS (ANSWERS)

Answer   *Explanation*

A.   *1.* N   Only the initial sale affects the sales journal.
    2. −   Accounts receivable decline.
    3. =   Cash is debited and accounts receivable is credited, and these together yield no net effect.

B.   *1.* N   The purchases journal only records the purchases of inventory or goods intended for resale.
    2. N   Purchase on accounts will not affect the cash payments journal until the account is paid.
    3. =   Furniture and fixtures is debited and accounts payable is credited, and these together yield no net effect.
    4. +   Accounts payable increase.

C. **1. N** Accounts payable would not typically include payroll; a separate salaries payable account would typically be available in a chart of accounts for the entity.

2. = Either salaries (wage) expense or salaries payable would be debited and cash would be credited, and these together yield no net effect.

3. N Purchases refer to the purchase of inventory not of labor.

4. N Since payroll is a frequent routine transaction, it is typical to maintain a payroll register of some sort or to record the initial expense in the cash payments journal rather than entering a journal entry in the general journal.

EXERCISES

1. Describe the audit trail for a debit entry to the general ledger account entitled sales returns & allowances.

2. It has been said that there is no such thing as a computer fraud; to refer to fraud in computerized systems as computer fraud is thought to be equivalent to referring to fraud in manual systems as pencil fraud. Provide a critical comment on this assertion.

EXERCISES (ANSWERS)

1. The general ledger will have a posting reference either to the general journal, if such entries are infrequent, or to a specialized journal for sales returns & allowances. The general ledger entry can be traced to whichever journal is referenced to identify the customer who received the allowance or who returned the merchandise. A tick mark beside the customer's name in the journal will indicate that the return or allowance was posted to the subsidiary accounts receivable ledger. The subsidiary accounts receivable ledger will typically report the recent transactions with that customer as well as the customer's outstanding balance and the customer's mailing address.

The entry in the journal should reference the sales return and allowance credit memorandum number to facilitate locating the document in the numerically filed memoranda. The memorandum should be accompanied by or make reference to other supporting documentation such as the customer's request for an allowance or a receiving department slip reflecting the return of inventory.

The assumption in the above description is that payment for the goods that were returned or on which an allowance was granted had not yet been received by the firm. If payment had already been made, the account affected could be either accounts receivable, showing credit against future sales to that customer, or cash. If cash was involved, the cash payments journal rather than the accounts subsidiary ledger and general journal would provide the described audit trail, including reference to the number of the issued check. The cancelled check could be inspected for evidence that payment was appropriately made to the customer in the amount of the return or allowance.

2. The computer, like the pencil, is merely a tool that facilitates a fraud. The actual fraud is committed by people. The same concerns exist for controls applied to manual and computer systems in the sense of the following objectives.

Proper segregation of duties
Accountability
Safeguarding of assets

However, the attributes of a computer do affect the form of these controls and typically alter the potential risk exposure of companies.

The very attribute considered to be a key advantage of a computer, the quick processing of large amounts of data, can make a company vulnerable to big losses perpetrated over a short time. The reason the term *computer fraud* has become vogue is that access to a computer can be gained from outside a business through remote terminals; computers often are not well controlled within a business. Hence, fraud has been observed on a large scale with computer systems, and in many cases the computer has been seen as the weak link. In reality the weak link is control over the computer through a control system that parallels a manual control system over a pencil adjustment to the books of original entry.

CHAPTER DEMON-STRATION PROBLEM

Joe Artistic has decided to go into business. He wishes to open an interior decorating shop, specializing in the sale of antiques, Persian rugs, and decorator items. He has asked you for advice on setting up his record-keeping system. Joe intends to have two employees, one salesperson and a part-time bookkeeper. In a manner that will be comprehensible (remember that Joe has no business training), describe to Joe the type of information system he should have and include some comment regarding internal control over operations.

CHAPTER DEMONSTRATION PROBLEM (ANSWER)

Explain to Joe that he first has to design a chart of accounts in which to record transactions. Suggest the following accounts as a basic framework.

Account No.	Account Name
100	Cash
110	Accounts receivable
120	Allowance for doubtful accounts
130	Notes receivable
140	Inventory
150	Furniture & fixtures
200	Accounts payable
210	Notes payable
220	Interest payable
230	Salaries payable
240	Taxes payable, salaries
300	Capital, Joe Artistic
310	Drawing, Joe Artistic
400	Sales
410	Interest revenue
500	Cost of goods sold
510	Advertising expense
520	Salaries expense
530	Rent expense
540	Interest expense
550	Bad debts expense

Explain the meaning of the accounts, the reason for gaps in the numbering scheme, and the flexibility that permits the insertion of new accounts for additional detail whenever desired.

Explain that there are three primary facets of operations that require control: inventory handling, sales and related cash receipts, and purchases and related cash payments. Describe the potential usefulness of each of the following ledgers and journals.

An inventory subsidiary ledger
A sales journal
An accounts receivable subsidiary ledger
A cash receipts journal
A purchases inventory journal
An accounts payable subsidiary ledger
A cash payments journal

Assuming that Joe agrees that these specialized journals and ledgers are advisable, go with him to an office supply store and purchase four ledger books and four journals. The fourth ledger is for the general ledger, and the fourth journal is for the general journal. Explain the purpose of these records.

Set up the account headings as on the seven illustrations below to facilitate the recording of future transactions. Note that following standard accounting practices, debit and credit are abbreviated as Dr and Cr, respectively.

√

Inventory Description	Invoice No.	Acquired	Cost	Date Sold

Emphasize to Joe that this record should be kept up to date and will provide information as to goods available for sale, how long goods stay in inventory, and the appropriate cost per unit of inventory.

√

Date	Customer	Invoice No.	Dr Accounts Receivable Cr Sales	Dr Cost of Goods Sold Cr Inventory

Emphasize that each entry is posted to the accounts receivable subsidiary ledger and the inventory subsidiary ledger and that monthly totals are posted to the general ledger. The reason for recording cost of sales on an ongoing basis is so that the profit of the business can be continually assessed.

√

Customer's Name Mailing Address					
Date	Post Ref	Explanation	Debit	Credit	Balance

Emphasize that the running balance provides the information for monthly billings to customers.

√

				Cr Sundry	
Date	Customer	Dr Cash	Cr Accounts Receivable	Amount	Account

Emphasize that all cash receipts are to be recorded in this specialized journal, that individual customer collections are to be posted to the accounts receivable subsidiary ledger, and that monthly totals are to be posted to the general ledger (with the exception of sundry items such as interest receivable entries which must be posted separately).

√

Date	Supplier	Purchase Order or Invoice No.	Dr Inventory Cr Accounts Payable

Emphasize that all purchases of inventory are to be recorded in this journal, with individual purchases being posted to the accounts payable subsidiary ledger and monthly totals being posted to the general ledger. Explain that the debit is to inventory rather than purchases, because it is desirable to maintain continual control over inventory and cost of sales relative to sales.

√

Supplier's Name Mailing Address					
Date	Post Ref	Explanation	Debit	Credit	Balance

Emphasize that the running balance provides the information for monthly payments to creditors.

√

Date	Supplier	Cr Cash	Dr Accounts Payable	Dr Sundry	
				Amount	Account

Emphasize that all cash payments are to be recorded in this specialized journal, that individual payments to suppliers are to be posted to the accounts payable subsidiary ledger, and that monthly totals are to be posted to the general ledger (with the exception of sundry items that must be posted separately, such as interest payable entries).

Describe the types of unusual transactions that are to be recorded in the general journal: for example, the purchase of additional furniture and fixtures on credit; additional capital contributions by Joe; and the estimation of bad debts expense.

After answering Joe's questions as to which transactions are recorded where, explain the concept of control accounts in the general ledger and how they are used to check the accuracy of the bookkeeping process. At least monthly, the accounts receivable subsidiary ledger should be footed (added) and the total sum should be compared with the balance in the accounts receivable account in the general ledger. If these two figures are unequal, an error has been made. It must be investigated and corrected. Similarly, the sum of the accounts payable subsidiary ledger sheets should tie into the accounts payable account in the general ledger, and the inventory subsidiary ledger should tie into the inventory account.

Finally, explain the primary advantage of the double-entry bookkeeping system: it self-checks itself for reasonableness via the requirement that debits equal credits. Although the books could be in error and still be in balance, the monthly preparation of a trial balance and a check that debits equal credits provide negative assurance that the records are accurate.

Describe the importance of internal controls over operations, both administrative and accounting controls. Discuss owner/manager considerations. Joe's involvement in operations permits him to oversee the operations and to monitor the performance of his employees. However, he should be encouraged to keep in mind the basic segregation of duties that is desirable in any entity: a separation of authorization, custody, and record-keeping responsibilities. The obvious lines of division would be for Joe to authorize transactions, for the salesperson to maintain custody, and for the bookkeeper to record transactions. No matter how small the operation, such a separation of duties can decrease the risk exposure of the business to errors as well as to defalcations. Explain to Joe the importance of not permitting the substitution of duties across employees, because any access to accounting records by the salesperson destroys the intended separation of duties and the potential control over operations.

To put controls into perspective, explain what is meant by an audit trail and encourage Joe to require visible evidence of who does what and, in particular, of authorizations for transactions. If the salesperson and bookkeeper have to acknowledge that they, for example, checked credit ratings or recomputed the mathematical extension on a sales invoice, and if they know that purchases and sales over a certain dollar amount are to be initialized by Joe, these duties are likely to be performed with greater care and the firm's overall operating control will be enhanced. As a final means of limiting his risk exposure, Joe should consider acquiring a fidelity bond on his employee who handles cash.

6 FINANCIAL STATEMENTS: AN IN-DEPTH VIEW

OBJECTIVES

After completing this chapter, you should:

1 *Be able to describe the form and content of a complete set of financial statements.*

2 *Understand the concept of an operating cycle.*

3 *Know how to compute the current ratio and working capital for a company as well as know how such information can be used.*

4 *Be aware of the three forms of business organization and the effect of these forms on financial statement presentation.*

5 *Be able to distinguish extraordinary items from other transactions.*

6 *Be familiar with the content of footnotes and parenthetical disclosures.*

CHAPTER SUMMARY

In order to provide users with a clear picture of financial performance that is reliable and credible, a generally accepted set of accounting principles is applied in the financial reporting process. The activities of an entity's operations are reported in four formal financial statements, one of which is the **balance sheet**. This statement lists the company's assets, liabilities, and owners' equity at a single point in time; classifies assets as *current* (convertible into cash or expected to be consumed in the normal course of business within a relatively short period of time, the longer of either one year or one operating cycle) and *noncurrent;* and provides detail on long-term investments, on property, plant, and equipment, and on intangibles. Liabilities are similarly classified as current or long-term, with current representing those liabilities that are expected to be liquidated within one year or within the operating cycle, whichever is longer. The owners' equity is classified in a single capital account for a sole proprietorship, in a capital account per partner for a partnership, and in a common stock account and a retained earnings account for a corporation.

The balance sheet can be in an account form, with assets presented to the left of (horizontal to) a listing of liabilities and owners' equity, or in a report form, with assets presented above (vertical to) the listing of liabilities and owners' equity. It provides information concerning a company's ability to meet its current debt obligations, particularly when the current ratio and working capital of the firm are computed. The balance sheet also permits financial statement users to evaluate inventory levels and similar measures of firm growth and of management's performance and to evaluate the financial dependence on the financial support of owners relative to that of creditors. Two acknowledged shortcomings of a balance sheet include the use of historical cost rather than current values and the omitting of such assets as a skilled work force from the reported assets of a firm, due to the inability to objectively value such items.

Another formal financial statement is the **income statement**, which reports **profits** (Revenues − Expenses). The income statement reports on profitability with either a **single-step approach**, in which revenues less expenses are reported in two sections, or a **multiple-step approach**, in which a distinction is made between operating and nonoperating revenues and expenses and in which a **gross profit format** (Net Sales − Cost of Goods Sold) is common. An all-inclusive approach to reporting income is generally accepted; this means that nonrecurring items are reported in addition to the recurring items. **extraordinary items**, gains or losses that arise from unusual and infrequent events, are reported on the income statement, disclosing their related tax effects. The income statement discloses sources of revenue, types of expenses, and **earnings per share** (Net Income ÷ Number of Common Shares). By comparing income statements over time, users can assess the growth rate of sales, expenses, taxes, and overall profitability. Furthermore, users of income statements frequently forecast future profitability, growth, and dividend payment from past and current income statements. The commonality of comparative data in financial statements facilitates historical comparisons.

A third formal financial statement is the **statement of owners' equity**, which provides insight into the changes in the owners' equity of a business. If the only transactions that affect the owners' equity of a corporation are the result of net income and the distribution of dividends to stockholders, then the statement is known as the **statement of retained earnings**.

The fourth financial statement required to complete the set of formal financial statements is the **statement of changes in financial position**, which presents a summary of how a business acquires and uses its capital funds. An integral part of the financial statements, beyond the four formal statements, are **footnotes** that disclose the accounting policies used by a business in keeping its accounting records as well as a firm's contingencies and commitments and the operations for each of its business segments. An alternative to footnote disclosure is parenthetical disclosure in the body of the financial statements; **parenthetical disclosures** are typically used to report estimated market values, interest rates and maturity dates for debt, and similar information that can be briefly disclosed.

TECHNICAL POINTS

✓ Balance Sheet Presentation

Account form: Asset accounts are presented on the left side of the statement, because these accounts normally have debit balances, and liability and owners' equity accounts are presented on the right side, because these accounts normally have credit balances.

Report form: Asset accounts are presented above the liability and owners' equity accounts.

✓ **Operating cycle** is the average period of time it takes a firm to buy merchandise inventory, sell it, and ultimately collect the cash.

✓   *Current Ratio* = $\dfrac{Current\ Assets}{Current\ Liabilities}$

    Note: Rule of thumb provides for a 2:1 current ratio.

✓   *Working Capital = Current Assets − Current Liabilities*

✓   *Accounting Income = Revenues − Expenses*

✓ Single-step income statement

    Revenues
    − Costs and Expenses
    _____

    Earnings before Income Taxes
    − Income Taxes
    _____

    Net Earnings

✓ Multiple-step income statement

      Sales
      − Sales Discounts
      − Sales Returns and Allowances
      _____

      Net Sales
      − Cost of Goods Sold
      _____

      Gross Profit
      − Operating Expenses
      − Selling Expenses
      − General and Administrative Expenses
      _____

      Income from Operations
      − Other Expenses
      _____

      Net Income before Income Taxes
      − Income Taxes
      _____

      Net Income before Extraordinary Items
      $\begin{bmatrix} + \textit{Extraordinary Gain} \\ or - \textit{Extraordinary Loss} \end{bmatrix}$
      $\begin{bmatrix} - \textit{Tax Liability} \\ or + \textit{Savings} \end{bmatrix}$
      _____

      Net Income

✓   *Earnings per Share* = $\dfrac{Net\ Income}{Number\ of\ Common\ Shares}$

Circle the letter corresponding to the best response.

MULTIPLE-CHOICE QUESTIONS

1. A complete set of financial statements for a business includes how many formally prepared, interrelated statements?
   a. two
   b. three
   c. four
   d. five
   e. none of the above

2. Information concerning a firm's revenue-producing activities over a period of time is furnished in
   a. a balance sheet

    b. a statement of owners' equity

    c. an income statement

    d. a and c only

    e. all of the above

3. A company purchased a piece of land five years ago for $70,000; the land is appraised today at a value of $150,000. An offer has been made to purchase the land for $120,000. On the company's balance sheet, this piece of land will be recorded at the dollar amount of

    a. $70,000

    b. $150,000

    c. $120,000

    d. none of the above

4. Which of the following items would be reported on a company's balance sheet?

    a. good management

    b. a skilled work force

    c. a prime location

    d. business contacts

    e. all of the above

    f. none of the above

5. A firm's operating cycle is the average period of time it takes a firm

    a. to buy merchandise inventory and sell it

    b. to buy merchandise inventory, sell it, and ultimately collect the cash

    c. to buy merchandise inventory

    d. to sell inventory and to collect the cash

6. Extraordinary gains and losses may arise from such events as

    a. earthquakes in Alabama

    b. the loss suffered because of a newly enacted law

    c. sale of equipment

    d. all of the above

    e. a and b only

7. Property, plant, and equipment are normally listed on the balance sheet based on

    a. the length of their service lives, from the longest life to the shortest life

    b. the length of their service lives, from the shortest life to the longest life

    c. liquidity

    d. the amount of depreciation per item

    e. none of the above

8. Which of the following forms of business organizations have the most similar presentation of owners' equity on a balance sheet?

    a. sole proprietorship and corporation

    b. sole proprietorship and partnership

    c. partnership and corporation

    d. sole proprietorship, partnership, and corporation

9. The definition of income utilized by accountants is

    a. the amount by which a business is better off at the end of a period compared to the beginning of the period

    b. a comparison of worth or value at two different times

    c. appraisers' estimates of "well-offness"

    d. revenues minus expenses

    e. an average of appraisers' opinions as to the organization's well-offness, with the high and low opinions discarded

10. Which of the following is an example of a nonoperating item in a multiple-step income statement?

    a. gross profit

    b. selling and administrative expenses

    c. income tax expense
    d. loss from hurricane (hurricanes are unusual and infrequent events in this geographical region)
    e. interest expense
    f. none of the above

MULTIPLE-CHOICE QUESTIONS (ANSWERS)

Answer   *Explanation*

1. c   The balance sheet, income statement, statement of owners' equity, and statement of changes in financial position are included in a complete set of financial statements.

2. c   A balance sheet provides information about a company's assets, liabilities, and owners' equity at a single point in time, and the statement of owners' equity provides insight into the changes in the owners' equity of a business over a period of time. Details on revenue-producing activities are reported in an income statement.

3. a   Assets are recorded on the books at their acquisition cost with only a few exceptions. Current values are not used for the valuation of land in the accounts.

4. f   Many of the assets possessed by a business, though important to its future existence and profitability, are not reported on the balance sheet because they are not measurable in dollars. The items in *(a)*, *(b)*, *(c)*, and *(d)* could not be objectively valued for accounting purposes.

5. b   For companies selling merchandise on credit, the operating cycle can be illustrated as

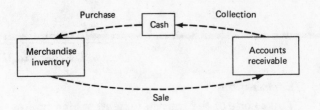

In other words, goods are acquired and sold, and related collections are made within an operating cycle of a business.

6. e   An extraordinary item must be both unusual and infrequent, as would be the case for *(a)* and *(b)* but not *(c)*.

7. a   Those assets with the greatest long-term usefulness are listed first. Liquidity, while a relevant standard for current assets, is not a particularly relevant criterion for assets that are not held for resale to customers or for direct conversion into cash.

8. b   Both sole proprietorships and partnerships report only capital balances, while a corporation reports common stock and retained earnings.

9. d   The other alternatives do not allow for the precision and the objectivity needed by accountants for the preparation and presentation of the income statement.

10. e   The rationale for this placement is that interest is related to financing and is not related to operations. Responses *(a)* and *(b)* are operating items; *(d)* is an extraordinary item. Income tax expense is typically deducted separately from the other expenses.

Indicate whether each of the following statements is true (T) or false (F).

_____   1. The statement of changes in financial position presents a summary of how a business acquires and uses its capital funds.

_____   2. Creditors generally feel that owners will work harder if they primarily rely on creditors to finance operations.

_____   3. When a balance sheet is presented in the report form, asset accounts are listed above the liability and owners' equity accounts.

_____   4. For purposes of the current asset definition, the time period is one year or the operating cycle, whichever is shorter.

_____   5. Current assets are sequenced on the balance sheet in the order of liquidity.

_____   6. The owners' equity section of a corporate balance sheet combines owner investments, net income and losses, and withdrawals in one capital account.

_____   7. At any point in time, retained earnings represents all of the profits of a corporation since it began operation.

_____   8. An all-inclusive approach to measuring and presenting net income includes all operating and normally recurring earnings of the firm and excludes only nonrecurring items.

_____   9. The practice of associating tax with the items that gave rise to the tax is known as intraperiod tax allocation.

_____   10. If the only transactions affecting owners' equity resulted from net income and the distribution of dividends to stockholders, the statement of owners' equity is properly renamed the statement of retained earnings.

TRUE-FALSE QUESTIONS (ANSWERS)

Answer	Explanation
1. T	This is one of the four statements which makes up a complete set of financial statements; due to its complex nature, it is not discussed in depth until a later chapter.
2. F	The general feeling is that owners will probably work harder if they have more of their own money to lose (i.e., if they have a sizable stake in the business).
3. T	The report form of a balance sheet is a vertical presentation, while the account form is a horizontal presentation (with asset accounts on the left side and liability and owners' equity accounts on the right side).
4. F	Whichever is longer, not whichever is shorter.
5. T	Liquidity refers to how close a current asset is to becoming cash; hence, cash is the first item listed, then short-term investments purchased with idle cash, then receivables, and so on through the accounts.
6. F	While this is true for sole proprietorships and partnerships, it is not true for corporations. Since ownership and control of operations are in the hands of different parties, different accounts are maintained for the investments made by stockholders and the net income or losses achieved by management.
7. F	Retained earnings represents all of the undistributed profits (i.e., all profits less dividends) of a corporation since it began operation.
8. F	The all-inclusive approach includes operating and nonoperating revenues and expenses, gains and losses from occasional sales of assets, and

extraordinary gains and losses. All-inclusive means that both recurring and nonrecurring items are included on the income statement, although disclosures are made concerning the unusual and extraordinary nature of some items.

9. T This is illustrated by the separate reporting of tax for normally recurring items and of tax for extraordinary items.

10. T This is due to the fact that in this situation the statement of owners' equity contains only changes in the retained earnings account.

**CLASSIFI-
CATION AND
MATCHING
QUESTIONS**

A. Indicate which financial statement is most likely to provide the information described, using the following abbreviations.

> BS = Balance sheet
> IS = Income statement
> OE = Statement of owners' equity
> CFP = Statement of changes in financial position

———— *1.* A basis upon which to judge the effectiveness of a new inventory-ordering process

———— *2.* A basis for evaluating a company's profitability

———— *3.* Dividend policy of the company

———— *4.* Assurance to creditors that sufficient cash is available to pay liabilities when due

———— *5.* How the business acquires and uses its capital funds

———— *6.* Assurance that cost of goods sold are being controlled by management

———— *7.* A basis for determining if the owners are investing their own capital in the business or relying on other creditors to finance operations

B. Classify the following items using these symbols.

> CA = Current assets
> LTI = Long-term investments
> PPE = Property, plant & equipment
> IA = Intangible assets
> OA = Other assets
> CL = Current liabilities
> LTL = Long-term liabilities
> OE = Owners' equity

———— *1.* Land purchased for speculation

———— *2.* Cash

———— *3.* Wages payable to employees

———— *4.* Retained earnings

———— *5.* Prepaid expenses

———— *6.* Louie Busman, capital

———— *7.* Investments made to acquire other firms

———— *8.* Unearned revenue

———— *9.* Franchises

———— *10.* Buildings

———— *11.* Long-term receivables

———— *12.* Common stock

———— *13.* Inventories

———— *14.* Vehicles

———— *15.* Investments set aside for the employees' pension fund

———— *16.* Short-term investments purchased with idle cash

———— *17.* Copyrights

———— *18.* Interest payable

———— *19.* Mortgages payable

———— *20.* Trademarks

CLASSIFICATION AND MATCHING QUESTIONS (ANSWERS)

A. *1.* BS *2.* IS *3.* OE *4.* BS *5.* CFP *6.* IS *7.* BS
B. *1.* LTI *2.* CA *3.* CL *4.* OE *5.* CA *6.* OE *7.* LTI *8.* CL *9.* IA *10.* PPE
  11. OA *12.* OE *13.* CA *14.* PPE *15.* LTI *16.* CA *17.* IA *18.* CL *19.* LTL
  20. IA

QUESTIONS CONCERNING THE EFFECTS OF TRANSACTIONS

Indicate whether the following transactions would increase (I), decrease (D), or have no effect upon (N) a current ratio of 2:1.

——— *1.* Purchased $300 of merchandise on account

——— *2.* Borrowed $15,000 by issuing bonds

——— *3.* Collected $50 from customers

——— *4.* Incurred wage expense

QUESTIONS CONCERNING THE EFFECTS OF TRANSACTIONS (ANSWERS)

Answer *Explanation*

Note: If a ratio is greater than 1:1 and both the numerator and the denominator increase by the same amount, the ratio will decrease.

1. D   In this problem, inventory and accounts payable both increase by $300.
2. I   Cash increases with no effect on current liabilities.
3. N   An exchange of cash for accounts receivable has no net effect on current assets.
4. D   An increase in wages payable increases the denominator of the ratio, with no influence on the numerator.

I. M. LIQUID
Balance Sheet
December 31, 1984

ASSETS

Cash		$ 6,000
Certificate of deposit		15,000
Accounts receivable		60,000
Inventory		40,000
Prepaid expenses		4,000
Buildings	$90,000	
Less: Accumulated depreciation	10,000	80,000
Copyright		30,000
Total assets		$235,000

LIABILITIES AND OWNERS' EQUITY

Accounts payable		$ 20,000
Property taxes payable		4,000
Advances from customers		11,000
Bonds payable		60,000
Total liabilities		$ 95,000
Charlie Money, capital		140,000
Total liabilities & owners' equity		$235,000

1. Using the above balance sheet, fulfill the following requirements.
   a. Compute the current ratio.
   b. Comment on the desirability of such a current ratio.
   c. Compute working capital for the firm.

2. Explain where and how the following items are likely to be disclosed and why disclosure is made in this manner.
   a. A pending lawsuit with ultimate liability ranging from $0.50 to $3 million.
   b. The percentage of a conglomerate's profits that are derived from its operations in a particular industry.
   c. A marketable security acquired for $20,000 and currently valued at $85,000.
   d. The company's accounting treatment of pension costs.
   e. The maturity date of the mortgage payable.
   f. The company's operations relative to the prior year's operations.
   g. A company's contractual obligation to purchase equipment from a particular supplier over the next three years.
   h. The loss suffered by a firm from closing a plant due to newly enacted regulation.

EXERCISES (ANSWERS)

1. a. $\text{Current Ratio} = \dfrac{\text{Current Assets}}{\text{Current Liabilities}}$

   where

   $\text{Current Assets} = \text{Cash} + \text{Certificate of Deposit} + \text{Accounts Receivable} + \text{Inventory} + \text{Prepaid Expenses}$

   $\text{Current Liabilities} = \text{Accounts Payable} + \text{Property Taxes Payable} + \text{Advances from Customers}$

thus

$$Current\ Ratio = \frac{\$6,000 + \$15,000 + \$60,000 + \$40,000 + \$4,000}{\$20,000 + \$4,000 + \$11,000}$$

$$= \frac{\$125,000}{\$35,000}$$

$$= \frac{3.57}{1}\ or\ 3.57{:}1$$

b. A 2:1 current ratio is a rule of thumb frequently preferred by creditors, and a higher current ratio is generally preferable to a lower one. However, 3.57:1 is rather high and probably is an indication that I. M. Liquid has too many current assets for the volume of business being generated. Specifically, the certificate of deposit, accounts receivable, and inventory balances appear to be excessive. Such high balances suggest that the firm is foregoing other more profitable investment opportunities, and hence the high current ratio is undesirable.

c. Working capital is calculated by taking the mathematical difference between total current assets and total current liabilities. Using the computations presented in *(a)*, total current assets are $125,000 and total current liabilities are $35,000. Hence, working capital totals $125,000 − $35,000, or $90,000.

2. **a.** Disclosure would be in a footnote, labeled "contingencies," rather than in the accounts because, while a possible liability exists, the outcome of the lawsuit is uncertain and actual liability could be zero if the case is won in court.

b. A disclosure would be in a footnote, labeled "segment data." The entity principle supports the reporting of the conglomerate's total operations on the financial statements, and the information user's desire to assess the profitability and importance of each segment of the business provides the rationale for footnote disclosure.

c. The marketable security would appear as a current asset in the amount of $20,000 on the face of the balance sheet, with a parenthetical disclosure of the estimated market value of $85,000; the historical cost principle argues for retaining the original cost basis, objectively determined through an arm's-length purchase transaction, in the accounts, while the desire to provide information on holding gains supports the parenthetical disclosure of market value.

d. Accounting policies are disclosed in footnotes and a reference to the pension footnote would typically be provided by the financial statement accounts affected by this policy; inadequate space on the face of financial statements provides a rationale for using footnotes, an integral part of the financial statements for disclosure purposes.

e. Disclosure would typically be made parenthetically beside the mortgage payable account on the balance sheet, although the maturity date could be disclosed in a separate footnote; this type of disclosure assists the user of financial statements in better understanding the presentation, and such information is not explicit in the reported account balance.

f. Except for the first period of operation, the financial statements of a firm are normally presented on a comparative basis, permitting direct comparison of the current period's operations with those of the prior year; such comparative financial presentations are generally considered to be necessary for users to assess the financial direction of a business over time.

g. Disclosure would be in a footnote, labeled "commitments"; contracts frequently represent transactions that have not yet taken place and hence cannot yet be recorded in the accounting records; however, such contracts are often substantial financial commitments that are of interest to financial statement users and warrant footnote disclosure.

h. This represents an extraordinary item and would be disclosed on the income statement with the related tax effect of the extraordinary loss; the all-inclusive approach to financial reporting supports the presentation of extraordinary items in the body of the income statement.

CHAPTER DEMON-STRATION PROBLEM

The primary stockholder of We Sell Corporation has provided you with the following information and requests that you provide him with a complete set of financial statements for the calendar year ended 12/31/83.

Property	$ 50,000	Mortgage payable	$30,000
Cash	12,000	(Current portion $5,000;	
Loss from earthquake		maturity 2005)	5,000
(tax shield $1,500)	4,000	Beginning retained earnings	37,100
Interest income	1,000	Common stock ($10 par)	60,000
Sales	110,000	Cost of goods sold	65,000
Wages expense	25,000	Land held for speculation	10,000
Trademark	3,000	Accounts payable	20,000
Inventory	35,000	Interest payable	4,500
Dividends	1,000	Sales returns	14,000
Selling expenses	2,200	Income tax expenses	900
Accounts receivable	40,000	Long-term purchase commitments	22,000
Interest expense	2,000		

Prepare the balance sheet in report form and the income statement in multiple-step form, and describe any related disclosures that should be presented.

CHAPTER DEMONSTRATION PROBLEM (ANSWER)

WE SELL CORPORATION
Income Statement
For the Year Ending December 31, 1983

Revenues		
Sales		$110,000
Less: Sales returns		14,000
Net sales		$ 96,000
Cost of goods sold		65,000
Gross profit		$ 31,000
Operating expenses		
Selling expenses		2,200
Wages expense		25,000
Income from operations		$ 3,800
Other income		
Interest income		1,000
Other expenses		
Interest expense		2,000
Net income before income taxes		$ 2,800
Income tax expenses		900
Net income before extraordinary items		$ 1,900
Less extraordinary loss*	$4,000	
Tax savings	1,500	2,500
Net income (loss)		($ 600)

*It is assumed that the earthquake loss is extraordinary.

Earnings per share disclosures

$$\text{Net Income before Extraordinary Loss} = \frac{\$1,900}{6,000 \text{ Shares}} = \$0.316$$

$$\text{Extraordinary Loss} = \frac{(\$2,500)}{6,000 \text{ Shares}} = (\$0.416)$$

$$\text{Net Income} = \frac{(\$600)}{6,000 \text{ Shares}} = (\$0.10)$$

WE SELL CORPORATION
Balance Sheet
December 31, 1983

ASSETS

Current assets		
Cash	$12,000	
Accounts receivable	40,000	
Inventory	35,000	
Total current assets		$ 87,000
Long-term investments		
Land held for speculation		10,000
Property, plant, & equipment		
Property		50,000
Intangible assets		
Trademark		3,000
Total Assets		$150,000

LIABILITIES & OWNERS' EQUITY

Current liabilities		
Accounts payable	$20,000	
Interest payable	4,500	
Current portion of mortgage payable	5,000	
Total current liabilities		$ 29,500
Long-term liabilities		
Mortgage payable (due 2005)		25,000
Total liabilities		$ 54,500
Owners' equity		
Common stock ($10 par value)	$60,000	
Retained earnings	35,500	
Total owners' equity		95,500
Total liabilities & owners' equity		$150,000

WE SELL CORPORATION
Statement of Retained Earnings
For the Year Ended December 31, 1983

Balance at beginning of year	$ 37,100
Net income (loss)	(600)
	$ 36,500
Deduct: Cash dividends	1,000
Balance at end of year	$ 35,500

There are long-term purchase commitments in the amount of $22,000. Additional footnotes would be prepared for these statements by following the list of instructions below.

Determine whether (1) any contingencies exist and (2) any segment disclosures are required.

Disclose the accounting policies used by the business.

Obtain parenthetical disclosure data as to the market value of the land held for speculation.

The full disclosure practices under generally accepted accounting principles require that the following financial statements be prepared.

Prepare a statement of changes in financial position.

Prepare comparative financial statements.

2. _____ information expands upon the body of the financial statements, assists users in the interpretation of the statements and in the making of business decisions, and frequently is flavored with specialized accounting jargon.

6. _____ disclosure is a way to add financial information in the body of the financial statements.

9. The _____ journal is used to record the purchase of merchandise on account.

11. _____ are circumstances such as lawsuits in which the outcome is uncertain.

13. A _87 across_ - _13 across_ _32 down_ _69 down_ presents revenue and expense accounts by association so that important relationships can be easily seen by readers.

14. _14 across_ _46 across_ _64 across_ _91 down_ is computed by taking the beginning inventory account and adding net purchases.

16. A _____ form balance sheet presents asset accounts above the liability and owners' equity accounts.

18. In high volume applications, the _____ is the most cost-effective method of processing data.

21. A _21 across_ _52 down_ is a convenient means of reducing list price to invoice price.

22. Sales of merchandise often give rise to _____ as customers notice defects.

24. _____ are not recorded in accounts, as that would be premature, but are disclosed in footnotes, as such disclosure is considered to be prudent.

27. A _____ system processes the transactions and events related to the sales and purchases of inventory.

28. An audit _____ is a means by which the details that underlie summarized information can be traced and accessed.

29. The _109 across_ _29 across_ _50 across_ _58 across_ _9 across_ records both purchases and accounts payable at the total invoice cost of the merchandise acquired despite the availability of discounts.

31. _53 down_ _31 across_ handle specific types of transactions and are beneficial whenever businesses have a large number of a given type of transaction to process.

33. A _____ account is a general ledger account that is composed of subsidiary ledger accounts.

36. An _36 across_ _33 across_ _59 down_ monitors which purchase orders have been filled and which are unfilled.

39. _74 down_ _50 across_ _14 across_ _39 across_ represents the total cost of the inventory that a company has sold.

42. _94 across_ . _42 across_ means the seller is responsible for goods until they arrive at the buyer's warehouse.

44. The _95 down_ _44 across_ provides insight into a firm's ability to pay its short-term obligations on time and keep its credit standing.

45. _____ information reports on the business activity of parts of a company and is typically presented in the footnotes.

46. See 14 across.

49. _____ gains and losses are the results of transactions or events that are both unusual in character and occur infrequently.

50. See 29 across and 39 across and 20 down.

51. _____ are corporate withdrawals of profits by stockholders.

54. _54 across_ _1 down_ are groups of lower-level accounts each of which composes a general ledger account.

56. A _56 across_ _48 down_ is essentially an insurance policy that reimburses a company for losses suffered from the dishonest practices of the bonded employees.

57. A _61 across_ _79 down_ _57 across_ will have a balance in the inventory account throughout the period which is equal to the balance at the beginning of the period.

58. See 29 across.

61. See 57 across.

62. A _62 across_ _70 across_ informs the seller that its account has been reduced by the purchaser.

64. See 14 across.

65. _77 down_ _65 across_ _92 across_ allocation refers to the practice of associating tax with the items that gave rise to the tax.

66. The _____ approach is the basis used by accountants to define income.

67. A _67 across_ _96 down_ is a formal document that itemizes the details of the merchandise a buyer wishes to acquire.

70. See 62 across and 72 across.

71. _____ refer to facts and figures.

72. A _72 across_ _70 across_ documents a return or allowance from a customer.

73. _107 across_ _73 across_ is the mathematical difference between total current assets and total current liabilities.

76. _84 down_ _6 down_ _76 across_ can be defined as Net Income ÷ Number of Common Shares Outstanding.

78. _94 down_ _106 across_ _78 across_ means that the seller's responsibility for freight stops when the goods are loaded for shipment.

80. _75 down_ _80 across_ or the competency of employees is an essential element of internal control.

82. Year-end _____ are typically recorded in the general journal.

86. _83 down_ _86 across_ _47 down_ is the concept reflected by management's desire for information regarding discounts that are missed rather than taken.

87. See 13 across.

89. A _89 across_ _79 down_ _12 down_ maintains a running count of inventory units on hand.

90. A _35 down_ _90 across_ is intended to encourage prompt payment by customers.

92. See 65 across.

94. See 42 across.

97. An _15 down_ _85 down_ _97 across_ records sales of merchandise on invoices.

100. The _82 down_ _100 across_ _101 across_ closely monitors the amounts owed by customers.

101. See 100 across and 78 down.

102. A _____ journal is employed to record the sale of merchandise on account.

103. To _103 across_ _105 across_ to assets is a means of safeguarding assets and is exemplified by the use of passwords for computer terminal use.

105. See 103 across.

106. See 78 across.

107. See 73 across.

108. _108 across_ _79 down_ refers to goods acquired for resale.

109. See 29 across.

DOWN

1. See 54 across.

3. _._._. must be disclosed on the face of the income statement and is frequently used to compare businesses on a common basis.

4. _4 down_ _55 down_ is computed by subtracting cost of goods sold from net sales.

5. The _37 down_ _60 down_ _40 down_ _5 down_ _9 across_ records purchases and accounts payable at the total invoice price less the anticipated cash discount.

6. See 76 across.

7. A _7 down_ _43 down_ is a detailed listing of all purchases and payments made by a customer during the billing period.

8. _11 down_ _8 down_ represents the ownership interests in corporations.

10. _._._. is the abbreviation for a past authoritative body that issued accounting pronouncements.

11. See 8 down.

12. See 89 across.

15. See 97 across.

17. The _17 down_ _41 down_ _88 down_ Act outlaws questionable payments to foreign firms, governments, and political officials.

19. Current assets are sequenced on the balance sheet in the order of _____.

20. The _20 down_ _50 across_ _51 down_ provides control by specifying that incompatible functions be performed by different employees.

23. The _23 down_ _81 down_ refers to the basic catalog price for merchandise.

25. Can be used as the impersonal subject of the verb to be.

26. A _26 down_ _57 across_ is concerned with the customer and the proper recording and processing of sales transactions.

30. An _____ expense refers to rent, advertising, or similar items incurred in the selling and administrative activities of a business.

32. See 13 across.

33. The _30 down_ _33 down_ of a business is the average period of time it takes a firm to buy merchandise inventory, sell it, and ultimately collect the cash.

34. _18 across_ _34 down_ involves the use of the computer to aid and abet in embezzlement.

35. See 90 across.

37. See 5 down.

38. An _38 down_ _33 across_ is frequently established to promote operational efficiency and to encourage adherence to management policies.

40. See 5 down.

41. See 17 down.

43. See 7 down.

47. See 86 across.

48. See 56 across.

51. See 20 down.

52. See 21 across.

53. See 31 across.

55. See 4 down.

59. See 36 across.

60. See 5 down.

61. Comparative data present the current and _____ periods' financial information.

63. Same as 37 down.

68. The _____ payments journal is used to record virtually all payments that are made by a business.

69. See 13 across.

74. See 39 across.

75. See 80 across.

77. See 65 across.

78. An _82 down_ _78 down_ _101 across_ monitors the balances owed to suppliers.

79. See 57 across, 89 across, and 108 across.

81. See 23 down and 93 down.

82. See 78 down and 100 across.

83. See 86 across.

84. See 76 across.

85. See 97 across.

88. See 17 down.

91. See 14 across.

93. _93 down_ _81 down_ is defined as list price less applicable trade discounts.

94. See 78 across.

95. See 44 across.

96. See 67 across.

98. Same as 62 across.

99. Same as 16 across.

104. _._._._. is an authoritative body that currently issues pronouncements that have a significant impact on financial statement presentation and preparation.

7 CASH AND SHORT-TERM INVESTMENTS

OBJECTIVES

After completing this chapter, you should:

1 *Understand the meaning of all key terms presented in the text material.*

2 *Be able to evaluate an internal control system over cash receipts and disbursements.*

3 *Know how to reconcile a bank account.*

4 *Be acquainted with the journal entries necessary to establish, to replenish, and to record errors in a petty cash fund.*

5 *Know the proper accounting treatment of short-term investments, particularly the recording of changes in market value.*

6 *Be able to describe how a voucher system operates.*

CHAPTER SUMMARY

While you might think the term *cash* does not require a definition, how would you classify IOUs, money orders, certificates of deposit (CDs), and similar items if no directions were provided? The key consideration is *negotiability*.

Cash includes all currency, checks, money orders, travelers' checks, and checking and savings account funds not penalized for day-to-day withdrawal or restricted from being used for operations due to a **compensating balance agreement** (i.e., a commitment by the borrower to maintain a portion of the loan balance on deposit). Postdated checks, IOUs, and travel advances are receivables, while CDs are investments. Compensating balances are stated separately in the current assets section of the balance sheet as *restricted deposits held against short-term borrowing* or, if not legally restricted from use in operations, footnote disclosure is sufficient.

Sinking funds or similar funds restricted for future use for plant expansion or some similar long-term project are classified as noncurrent assets.

The "more cash the better" notion is totally inefficient, because cash earns little return relative to other investment forms. **Cash management** involves cash planning systems, including the preparation of a cash budget, the investment of excess cash (e.g., in common and preferred stock, corporate and municipal bonds, treasury bills, CDs, and commercial paper), and the maximizing of return on cash used in operations through such devices as NOW accounts (interest-bearing checking accounts). Cash management also involves **cash control systems** that establish adequate internal control over cash; typical controls include separation of incompatible duties; the use of a cash register; the use of accountability procedures such as prenumbered checks, daily deposit of cash receipts, the use of a voucher system; and monthly preparation of bank reconciliations. **Reconciliations** compare the cash balance on the company's records with the bank's balance per the monthly bank statement, timing differences such as deposits in transit or outstanding checks frequently explain any differences. However, transactions originating with the bank such as service charges, collections of notes, or discovery of checks drawn on nonsufficient funds (NSF) are not mere timing differences and must be recorded on the company records. In addition, if a reconciliation indicates any company errors in recording either checks or deposits, the company's books must be corrected. Two rather recently implemented techniques, *truncation* and *electronic funds transfer systems,* are expected to reduce the paperwork involved in cash handling and in the preparation of reconciliations.

Petty cash funds allow a company to make small cash payments more economically than via a 100% check disbursement system. A fund custodian maintains petty cash on a **imprest basis**, meaning that the sum of petty cash vouchers (documenting disbursements) and cash in the petty cash box at any time will add up to the amount originally established in the fund (with the exception of slight errors charged to cash short and over). When the fund is replenished (whenever it gets low and at year-end), a check is cashed for the total of the petty cash vouchers netted with the cash short and over balance, and the petty cash vouchers are recorded in the appropriate accounts.

Cash management typically involves investing in securities with values that change frequently. A company expects that some of its marketable securities will increase in value and that some will decrease in value, but on average, the company expects a net profit from its aggregate investment. The accountant understands this **portfolio approach** to investments and focuses upon the portfolio or group of marketable securities, rather than upon individual securities, when determining the reported value of such investments. Specifically, the **net change in market value** for the entire portfolio, in the aggregate, is calculated and any net losses are recorded in a **valuation account** (contra to short-term investments recorded at cost) to arrive at what appears to be the **net realizable value** of marketable securities, if below cost, for the portfolio. Subsequent net increases in the portfolio's market value decrease or eliminate the valuation account; however, no net increases beyond the balance of the valuation account are recorded. While conservative, the potential understatement effect of only recording the downside of initial market changes is offset, in part, by decreasing the valuation account (contra to short-term investments) for subsequent recovery, on a portfolio basis, of prior periods' losses; also, the portfolio basis of valuation which records only net declines is much less conservative than recording all declines in value for each individual marketable security.

TECHNICAL POINTS

√ *Effective Rate of Interest* $= \dfrac{Interest\ Expense}{Principal - Compensating\ Balance}$

√   **Balance per Bank**
+ **Deposits in Transit**
− **Outstanding Checks**
──────────────────────
Adjusted Bank Balance

┌─────────────────────┐
│ These adjusted balances │
│ should be equal │
└─────────────────────┘

Cash Balance per Books
+ **Collections by Banks or Other Credit Memos**
− **NSF Checks or Other Debit Memos**
− **Service Charges**
± **Record-Keeping Errors Discovered during**
Reconciliation
──
Adjusted Cash Balance per Books

√   **Cash Remaining in Petty Cash Fund**
+ **Petty Cash Vouchers**
± **Cash Short and Over**
──────────────────────────
Original Amount of Petty Cash Fund

√   **Purchase Price of Stock**
+ **Costs Incurred Incidental to Transaction**
    (e.g., Brokerage Fees and Taxes)
──────────────────────────────────────
Short-Term Investment in Stock

√ **Portfolio's Original Cost − Allowance for Decline in Market Value of Short-Term**
Investments − Portfolio's Market Value = x

If x is negative, *then* record the lesser of |*x*| and the balance in the valuation
account as a recovery in value of short-term investments.
If x is positive, *then* record the entire amount as a loss on short-term investments.

Circle the letter corresponding to the best response.

**MULTIPLE-
CHOICE
QUESTIONS**

1. A customer has agreed to pay $10,000 of interest for a $100,000 one-year loan. In addition, the customer is obligated to keep a $20,000 compensating balance at the lending bank. What is the effective rate of interest being paid by the customer?
   a. 10%
   b. 12.5%
   c. 8%
   d. 30%

2. Which of the following are properly classified as current assets?
   a. special fund established for plant expansion
   b. compensating balances
   c. cash in foreign banks (with restrictions on transfer of funds out of the foreign country)
   d. sinking funds

3. The term NOW account refers to
   a. securities sold by banks to allow companies and individuals to invest cash for short periods of time
   b. requirements that a portion of any amount loaned to customers remain on deposit in the bank for the duration of the loan period
   c. day-to-day withdrawal account
   d. interest-bearing savings account on which customers are permitted to write checks

4. The cash account of a depositor on the books of the bank is carried as an
   a. asset
   b. liability
   c. stockholders' equity account
   d. revenue
   e. expense

5. Mary Anne Wallace shows a cash balance in her checkbook of $120, but the bank statement, just received, reports a balance of $90. Which of the following possibilities could account for this $30 difference?
   a. $30 of outstanding checks
   b. $30 notes receivable were collected by the bank
   c. $30 of deposits in transit
   d. a $30 credit memo
   e. the bank made an error, cashing a $50 check for $20

6. A check written by Wilson Contractors, Inc., for $53.90 was incorrectly recorded in the accounting records as $35.90.
   a. This error results in an $18 understatement of the accounting records.
   b. This error should be corrected by the bank's issuance of a debit memo.
   c. This error should be corrected by the bank's issuance of a credit memo.
   d. This error requires an upward adjustment of the ending cash balance per the company records.
   e. This error requires a downward adjustment of the ending cash balance per the company records.

7. Mitchell Company's bank statement reports that a note receivable of $30,000 and interest of $2,000 was collected by the bank. The general journal entry required on the company records is
   a. *Interest Expense*   2,000
      Note Receivable   30,000
         Cash   32,000

   b. *Cash*   32,000
         Note Receivable   32,000

   c. *Cash*   32,000
         Note Receivable   30,000
         Interest Revenue   2,000

   d. *Cash*   30,000
      Interest Receivable   2,000
         Note Receivable   32,000

   e. No entry is required.

8. The term truncation refers to
   a. the practice of shortening petty cash vouchers by only requiring initials rather than signatures
   b. cut-off bank statements
   c. the practice of having the bank perform the reconciliation of customers' accounts as a banking service
   d. the nonreturn of canceled checks to customers after payment has been made

9. At all times, for a petty cash system, the following relationship should be true.
   a. Petty Cash = Cash in the Petty Cash Box
   b. Petty Cash = Cash in the Petty Cash Box + Petty Cash Vouchers
   c. Petty Cash = Petty Cash Vouchers
   d. Petty Cash = Cash in the Petty Cash Box − Petty Cash Vouchers

10. Which of the following journal entries could be utilized to record the replenishment of the petty cash fund?
   a. *Postage Expense*   60.00
      Miscellaneous Expense 90.00
         Cash   150.00

   b. *Postage Expense*   60.00
      Miscellaneous Expense 90.00
         Petty Cash   150.00

   c. *Petty Cash*   150.00
         Cash   150.00

   d. *Petty Cash*   150.00
      Accounts Receivable: Employees   150.00

11. If cash short and over possesses a credit balance
    a. it would be shown as a miscellaneous revenue
    b. it would be shown as a miscellaneous expense on the income statement
    c. it is reported as a liability account
    d. it is reported as an asset account

12. A means of reducing both the time lag in banking transactions and the need for physical documents associated with cash handling systems is
    a. the use of NOW accounts
    b. the use of a voucher system
    c. the use of computerized electronic funds transfer systems
    d. the implementation of a good system of internal control over cash

13. Anderson, Inc., acquired $60,000 of stock, incurring a $600 brokerage fee and $180 tax. How is this transaction recorded?

    a. *Short-Term Investment in Stock 60,780*
          Cash   60,780

    b. *Short-Term Investment in Stock 60,600*
       Taxes (Expense)   180
          Cash   60,780

    c. *Short-Term Investment in Stock 60,180*
       Brokerage Fees   600
          Cash   60,780

    d. *Short-Term Investment in Stock 60,000*
       Brokerage Fees   600
       Taxes (Expense)   180
          Cash   60,780

14. Securities purchased for management control are classified as
    a. short-term current assets (provided a secondary market exists which makes the securities readily salable)
    b. short-term current assets (provided no documentation exists in the company records that management does not intend to convert the securities into cash within the operating cycle or one year, whichever is longer)
    c. long-term investments
    d. short-term current assets (provided the securities are readily salable *and* no documentation exists in the company records that management does not intend to convert the securities into cash within the operating cycle or one year, whichever is longer)

15. During 1984, Kiernan, Inc., received $3,200 of dividends. The entry to record these dividends would be

    a. *Short-Term Investment in Stock 3,200*
          Dividend Revenue   3,200

    b. *Cash   3,200*
          Dividend Revenue   3,200

    c. *Cash   3,200*
          Short-Term Investment in Stock   3,200

    d. *Cash   3,200*
          Recovery in Value of Short-Term Investments   3,200

    e. *Short-Term Investment in Stock   3,200*
          Recovery in Value of Short-Term Investments   3,200

16. On January 1, 1983, Big Jim Contractors acquired $4,000 of stock in Johanna Company for $50 per share, and $2,000 of stock in Pat's Pride, Inc., for $20 per share. At December 31, 1983, Johanna Company's stock sold for $40 a share and Pat's Pride, Inc., stock sold for $25 per share. The journal entry that should be recorded on the books of Big Jim Contractors is

    a. *Loss on Short-Term Investments 800*
          Short-Term Investments   800

    b. *Loss on Short-Term Investments   800*
          Allowance for Decline in Market Value
            of Short-Term Investments   800

   c.   Loss on Short-Term Investments   300
         Short-Term Investments   300

   d.   Loss on Short-Term Investments   300
         Allowance for Decline in Market Value
            of Short-Term Investments   300

   e.   Loss on Short-Term Investments   800
         Increase in Value of Short-Term Investments   500
         Allowance for Decline in Market Value
            of Short-Term Investments   300

MULTIPLE-CHOICE QUESTIONS (ANSWERS)

Answer   **Explanation**

1. b

$$\frac{Interest}{Principal - Compensating\ Balance} = \frac{\$10,000}{\$100,000 - \$20,000} = \frac{\$10,000}{\$80,000}$$

= *12.5% Effective Interest Rate*

2. b   Compensating balances would be reported as cash, if such balances are not legally restricted and are available to companies for operating purposes, or as a separate line item (restricted deposits held against short-term borrowings) if legally restricted. In either case, the compensating balances are current assets.

3. d   Response *(a)* defines CDs, and *(b)* defines compensating balances. The acronym *NOW* stands for negotiated orders of withdrawal.

4. b   While cash is an asset on the books of the depositor, it represents a liability to the bank.

5. c   The rest of the transactions would increase the bank balance relative to the checkbook balance.

6. e   Since the error involves the books of Wilson Contractors, Inc., while the bank can be expected to deduct the correct amount of the check ($53.90) when it is received for payment, only a downward adjustment of the book's cash balance is required.

7. c   Both the note and interest were collected by the bank. Only the principal of the note is chargeable against the note receivable account; interest revenue must be recorded in a separate account.

8. c   Reconciliations of bank accounts would still be performed by the customer, but the paperwork involved would be reduced by having the bank retain the canceled checks.

9. b   The sum of the cash on hand and the petty cash vouchers, which represent disbursements from the petty cash fund, should at all times equal the original amount of the fund.

10. a   The petty cash fund is only charged when establishing, increasing, decreasing, or eliminating the fund balance. However, once established, at a given balance, the petty cash fund is replenished by cashing a check drawn on the company's regular checking account.

11. a   A credit balance reports that underpayments were made out of the petty cash fund; such underpayments are typically classified as miscellaneous revenue.

12. c   Electronic funds transfer systems (EFTS) permit the transfer of huge sums of money among banks without checks and with an instantaneous updating of account balances.

13. a   Brokerage fees and taxes are considered part of the acquisition price of the securities and are not charged to expense.

14. c   Management control is a long-term goal and requires that securities, despite their negotiability and the absence of *written* documentation of management's intentions, be classified as long-term investments.

15. b   Dividend revenue is distinct from the carrying value of securities.

16. d   The lower-of-cost-or-market rule is applied on a portfolio basis; therefore gains are offset against losses before recording any adjustment of the carrying value. Furthermore, no direct write-off of investments is appropriate; instead a valuation or contra-account is utilized. Increases in individual market values are not recorded; only recoveries are separately reported—to the extent that they offset prior losses (beyond current period losses).

TRUE-FALSE QUESTIONS

Indicate whether each of the following statements is true (T) or false (F).

____   1. All cash items are normally combined and listed as a single figure on the balance sheet.

____   2. Sinking funds are classified as current assets.

____   3. All compensating balances, even if available for operating purposes, must be reported as a separate line item in the current asset section of the balance sheet.

____   4. The effective interest rate for a borrower is decreased through the use of compensating balances.

____   5. Returns earned on NOW accounts are comparable to those earned on short-term securities.

____   6. A firm's cash balance should represent 10% of total current assets, if the business is properly managing its cash balances.

____   7. Cash planning systems are primarily concerned with adequate internal control over cash.

____   8. It is usual for a bank statement cash balance and a company's cash records not to be in agreement.

____   9. No general journal entries are required on a company's books for adjustments made to the ending bank statement on a bank reconciliation.

____   10. The general journal entry typically recorded to reflect an NSF check involves a debit to bad debt expense and a credit to cash.

____   11. NSF checks are frequently reported on the bank statement via a credit memo notation.

____   12. Every time that a disbursement is made from the petty cash fund, a journal entry is recorded.

____   13. In an entry to replenish the petty cash fund, the credit is to the cash account and not petty cash.

____   14. The petty cash fund should be replenished at the end of each period.

____   15. The amount of cash short and over is usually shown as a miscellaneous expense on the income statement.

____   16. Frequently, the sum of petty cash vouchers and cash in the petty cash fund will not equal the original fund balance.

____   17. Electronic funds transfer systems (EFTS) have little influence on the way in which accountants traditionally ascertain that all cash receipts and disbursements have been properly handled and recorded.

____   18. Investments that are readily salable should be reported as current assets on the balance sheet.

____   19. The carrying value of securities is never increased above cost.

_____ **20.** Once the carrying value of securities is decreased to the lower of cost or market, it cannot be increased until the ultimate sale of those securities.

_____ **21.** Brokerage fees incurred in the acquisition of securities are charged to expense.

_____ **22.** The lower-of-cost-or-market method is the generally accepted method for recording the carrying value of all short-term investments.

_____ **23.** Revenue from temporary investments such as dividends and interest is recorded as it is earned by the investor, regardless of whether the historical-cost method or the lower-of-cost-or-market method is used to record the value of the investments.

_____ **24.** It is possible for a single period's income statement to report both a loss on short-term investments and a recovery in value of short-term investments.

_____ **25.** The lower-of-cost-or-market method is consistent with the accounting concept of conservatism.

_____ **26.** The column totals of the voucher register are all posted to the general ledger.

_____ **27.** A voucher register is somewhat similar to an all-encompassing purchases journal.

_____ **28.** The check register typically has a debit column for vouchers payable and for purchases discounts and a credit column for cash.

_____ **29.** While a voucher system establishes control over cash disbursements in the sense that all payments must be approved, it does not eliminate the possibility of paying the same approved invoice twice.

_____ **30.** The unpaid voucher file comprises a subsidiary ledger for the vouchers payable control account.

_____ **31.** In order to find out whether a particular voucher has been paid, it is necessary to refer to the check register.

TRUE-FALSE QUESTIONS (ANSWERS)

Answer   *Explanation*

1. T   Details by cash item are not provided.

2. F   Since sinking funds are restricted and not available to settle current obligations, they should not be classified as current assets.

3. F   If compensating balances are not restricted in the sense that they are available for operating purposes, footnote disclosure is appropriate. Only legally restricted compensating balances are required to be reported as a separate line item.

4. F   The effective rate of interest is increased through the use of compensating balances.

5. F   NOW accounts are low-interest-bearing savings accounts on which checks can be written; the return on such accounts is not comparable to that earned on short-term securities.

6. F   The amount of cash necessary to meet current obligations varies between businesses. Hence, there is not one optimal percentage (let alone 10%) applicable to all businesses.

7. F   Cash planning is directed at ensuring that adequate cash is available to meet current obligations and that any excess cash is invested. The question refers to the objective of cash control systems.

8. T These normally are not in agreement due to timing differences associated with the use of a checking account (i.e., a transaction frequently is recorded on the depositor's books or the bank's books but not on both books at the same time).

9. T These items are already on the books and need no further updating; they simply are not yet on the bank statement.

10. F The debit should be charged to accounts receivable, because a claim still exists against that party who wrote the NSF check.

11. F Since the bank reduces the company's account for NSF checks, a debit memo is issued.

12. F To make a formal journal entry for each disbursement would necessitate considerable bookkeeping work and posting and would eliminate the time-saving and economical benefits associated with using a petty cash system. A journal entry is not recorded until the fund is replenished; typically, replenishment occurs when the amount of cash in the fund becomes low.

13. T The balance in the petty cash account remains intact at the original amount and payment is actually made from the cash account.

14. T End-of-period replenishment is necessary because no formal journal entries have been recorded for individual disbursements from the fund; replenishment ensures that all expenses are charged to the period in which they occurred.

15. T This is because overpayments are more likely than underpayments.

16. T This is due to errors made by the fund custodian, some in the company's favor and some against.

17. F EFTS eliminates much of the traditional written evidence supporting cash transactions (e.g., deposit tickets and checks), requiring accountants to employ other than visual examination of documents to verify the proper handling and recording of all cash receipts and disbursements.

18. F Two requirements must be met in order for investments to be reported as a current asset: they must be readily salable *and* intended to be converted into cash within the operating cycle or one year, whichever is longer.

19. T Cost is the effective ceiling since loss recoveries are only recognized to the extent of previously recorded losses.

20. F Loss recoveries are recognized to the extent of previously recorded losses by decreasing the allowance for decline in value of short-term investments.

21. F Brokerage fees and similar costs of acquisition, such as taxes, are capitalized in the short-term investment in stock account. They represent part of the acquisition price of the securities.

22. F While the lower-of-cost-or-market method is used for short-term investments in stock, the historical-cost method has been used for all other short-term investments.

23. T The historical-cost and lower-of-cost-or-market methods differ only in their reporting of the carrying value of securities not in the reporting of revenue from those securities in the form of dividends or interest.

24. F Since the carrying value of short-term securities is determined on a portfolio basis, either a loss or a recovery, but not both, can be reported.

25. T Conservatism basically states that all losses should be anticipated but no gains should be anticipated. Since the lower-of-cost-or-market method recognizes losses in market value while holding securities but does not recognize increases in market value above the original cost, it is entirely consistent with the concept of conservatism.

26. F The sundry total is not posted since different accounts are affected by its detailed entries. Each item in the sundry column must be individually posted to the general ledger.

27. T A voucher system establishes control over all cash disbursements by check.

28. F The purchases discounts would be a credit column, indicating less cash was disbursed because the invoice was paid within the discount period.

29. F   Since all vouchers are marked *paid* and are filed in a paid voucher file, no single invoice should be paid twice.

30. T   The total amount of unpaid vouchers should equal (and provide a detailed record of) the difference in vouchers recorded and checks written.

31. F   The payment of a voucher, including the date of payment and the check number, is cross-referenced in the voucher register.

CLASSIFI-CATION AND MATCHING QUESTIONS

A. Classify the following items using these symbols.

C = Cash
R = Receivable
I = Investment
S = Supplies

_____ 1. IOUs
_____ 2. Savings accounts
_____ 3. Money orders
_____ 4. Travel advances
_____ 5. Checks
_____ 6. Postdated checks
_____ 7. Currency
_____ 8. Postage stamps
_____ 9. Certificates of deposit
_____ 10. Checking accounts

B. Classify the following control descriptions as primarily one of the following items.

G = General internal control features
CR = Procedures utilized for cash receipts
CD = Procedures utilized for cash disbursements

_____ 1. Use of a cash register
_____ 2. Use of a petty cash system
_____ 3. Access to cash limited to only a few authorized personnel
_____ 4. Daily bank deposits
_____ 5. Separate incompatible duties
_____ 6. Examination of receiving reports
_____ 7. Follow accountability procedures

C. Match the following terms with their definitions; each definition cannot be used as a response for more than one term.

_____ 1. Corporate bonds
_____ 2. Commercial paper
_____ 3. Preferred stock
_____ 4. Municipal bonds
_____ 5. Common stock
_____ 6. Treasury bills

a. Securities sold by banks to allow companies and individuals to invest cash for short periods of time
b. An investment on which the investor is entitled to dividend payments prior to any dividend payments on other classes of investments
c. Ownership rights of a corporation
d. Obligations of the U.S. Government
e. Short-term notes sold by large businesses to investors and other corporations
f. Obligations of cities or counties
g. A promise to repay a certain amount in the future on which interest is typically payable semiannually

CLASSIFICATION AND MATCHING QUESTIONS (ANSWERS)

A. *1.* R *2.* C *3.* C *4.* R *5.* C *6.* R *7.* C *8.* S *9.* I *10.* C

B. *1.* CR *2.* CD *3.* G *4.* CR *5.* G *6.* CD *7.* G

C. *1.* g *2.* e *3.* b *4.* f *5.* c *6.* d

QUESTIONS CONCERNING THE EFFECTS OF TRANS- ACTIONS

A. Johanna Doyle has a checking account at First National Trust Bank, and this account is affected by numerous types of transactions. Indicate whether the following items would increase (+) or decrease (−) Johanna's account.

_____ *1.* Checks

_____ *2.* Other credits by the bank

_____ *3.* Note collection

_____ *4.* Other debits by the bank

_____ *5.* Deposits

_____ *6.* Service charge

QUESTIONS CONCERNING THE EFFECTS OF TRANSACTIONS (ANSWERS)

A. *1.* − *2.* + *3.* + *4.* − *5.* + *6.* −

EXERCISES

1. You commonly shop at Bargain Center Retailers and observe the following procedures of the store's personnel.

a. When you select your purchase, a sales clerk writes up a sales ticket and asks you to take the ticket and merchandise to the cash register.

b. The cashier rings up the sale on the register.

c. Although at times you've only purchased a pack of gum, the cashier always insists on putting the purchase in a paper bag.

d. Whenever you offer currency in a denomination greater than a $20 bill in payment, the cashier rings a bell that summons a floor clerk. This floor clerk takes the bill and returns with change.

e. When you have returned merchandise, you have been required to sign a receipt for the cash provided you by the cashier.

Describe how each of these observed procedures relates to the store's internal control system.

2. Forsythe Furniture Company received a bank statement on June 20, 1983, which reported a bank balance of $46,000. With the statement were included checks numbered 101 through 205 and 208, deposits made weekly through June 24, 1983, a debit memo reporting an NSF check from Mr. Taylor (deposited on June 17, 1983), a credit memo for $1,700 collection of a note and interest (the interest portion was $200), and a service charge of $40.00.

According to the company's records, checks numbered 101 through 210 have been written, deposits were made weekly, including one on June 30, 1983, for $7,600, and the check received from Mr. Taylor was in the amount of $430.00. Detailed information follows:

Check nos. 101 through 205	$185,000
Check no. 206	3,000
207	1,000
208	860
209	2,400
210	300

The cash account in the general ledger on June 30, 1983, has a balance of $45,670.

a. Prepare a bank reconciliation.

b. Record all necessary journal entries.

c. Assume that instead of a balance of $45,670, the books had a balance of $45,490, and that after careful scrutiny of the bank statement, it was discovered that check no. 208 to a supplier cleared the bank at the amount of $680 and that due to a transposition error, the check register had reflected an $860 payment. What must be done by the bank and/or the company to correct the company's records of cash transactions?

3. Efficiency Electro, Inc., established a petty cash fund for $200 on January 1, 1983. On February 15, 1983, the fund was reimbursed for $80 of petty cash vouchers that represented disbursements for $20 of postage, $40 of transportation in freight costs, and $20 of coffee. On March 1, 1983, the firm determines that a petty cash fund of $150 would be adequate and reduces the balance of the fund to reflect this decision. On March 15, 1983, the petty cash box has $90 of cash and $58 of vouchers that represent $20 of coffee, $30 of supplies, and $8 of refunds for vending machines which are expected to be paid back to the fund by the vending company. Record the necessary journal entries on the following dates.

a. January 1, 1983

b. February 15, 1983

c. March 1, 1983

d. March 15, 1983

4. Meddaugh Movers, Inc., owns the following short-term securities as of January 31, 1983.

Hoff's Housing Co.
  20 shares @ $40 $ 800
Sorce Seed Co.
  50 shares @ $15   750
Barbado Boating Co.
  10 shares @ $70   700
                    $2,250

The market values for the stocks as of December 31, 1983, are

Hoff's $50 a share
Sorce   5 a share
Barbado   50 a share

On June 15, 1984, Meddaugh Movers, Inc., sold 40 shares of Sorce Seed Co. for $8 a share.

As of December 31, 1984, the market values for the stocks are

Hoff's $70 a share
Sorce   10 a share
Barbado   50 a share

Record all of the necessary journal entries for Meddaugh Movers, Inc., on the following dates.

a. As of December 31, 1983

b. As of June 15, 1984

c. As of December 31, 1984

5. Briefly explain why a voucher system provides improved control over cash disbursements.

1. The discussion of how these procedures relate to the internal control system of the store will be outlined to correspond to the lettered procedures.

a. The store's use of sales clerks and cashiers reflects a key separation of incompatible duties. The sales ticket will report the amount of cash that the cashier will receive from you. The cashier has no opportunity to ring up a smaller amount on the register and remove the cash difference in what you pay and what is entered in the register without this practice being detected, unless the cashier and sales clerk collude with one another.

It is assumed that the sales tickets are prenumbered and checked for completeness as an accountability control to prevent the cashier's removal of a ticket to cover up a shortage in the register.

b. The use of a cash register represents a control over cash sales. The cashier is in full view of the customer and provides the customer with receipts, if an attempt is made to not ring up a sale or to ring up the sale at a lesser amount than the cash actually paid by the customer, it is likely to be detected and possibly reported by the customer.

Presumably, the store manager will compare the cash collected in the register against the total sales per the cash register tape.

c. The insistence that sold merchandise be bagged is a means of exercising control over inventory. Shoplifting can be more easily detected because a bag and receipt must be in the possession of the customer when leaving the store with merchandise; a person who is observed with something in his or her pocket cannot reasonably claim that the item was purchased.

d. The use of a floor clerk for making change of a $50 bill and greater denominations reflects the store's desire to keep a relatively minimal amount of cash in the register drawers. Larger currency is probably out of public view, in a safe in a well-guarded section of the store. This practice better safeguards the cash on hand and reduces the company's risk of large losses from theft from the registers.

Lower amounts of cash in the registers also reduces the temptation to employees to steal from the firm and reduces the likelihood of a large honest error being made by a cashier when giving change.

e. The authorization of payments is important as a control over disbursements, and the customer's signature exercises some control over customer refunds. However, since it is preferred in a control system to separate the authorization and custody functions, there should be a separate desk to which customers report to have a credit memo authorized and issued as the source document for a refund by the cashier. If such memos are prenumbered and accounted for and there is a review of the customer's signature (to check that one customer is not receiving excessive refunds), the control over such disbursements is substantially improved.

2. *a.*

Ending balance per bank statement	*$46,000*
Add: Deposits in transit (June 30, 1983)	*7,600*
Deduct: Outstanding checks (nos. 206, 207, 209, 210)	*6,700*
Adjusted cash balance, Bank	*$46,900*
Ending balance per company records	*$45,670*
Add: Collection by bank	*1,700*
Deduct: NSF check (Mr. Taylor)	*430*
Service charge	*40*
Adjusted cash balance, Company records	*$46,900*

b.

Cash	*1,700*	
Notes Receivable		*1,500*
Interest Revenue		*200*
To record note and interest collected by bank		

Miscellaneous Expense (Service Charge)   40
Accounts Receivable, Taylor   430
    Cash   470
To record bank service charge and NSF check

   c. Essentially a $180 ($860 − $680) error has been made in recording check no. 208. The bank cashed the check for the appropriate amount, so no entry needs to be booked by the bank. However, the following entry is required on the company records.

Cash   180
   Accounts Payable   180
To correct the error in recording the check

(Since the check register presumably balanced, it is assumed accounts payable was inappropriately debited for the $180 transposition error amount.)
    After this entry, the $45,490 will be raised to $45,670 and will reconcile to the bank statement balance as demonstrated in (*a*).

3.   **a.** *Petty Cash*   200
      Cash   200
      To establish the petty cash fund

   b. *Postage*   20
      Transportation-in   40
        Miscellaneous (Coffee)   20
        Cash   80
      To replenish the petty cash fund

   c. *Cash*   50
      Petty Cash   50
      To reduce the petty cash fund from its original balance of $200 to a $150 level

   d. *Supplies*   30
      Accounts Receivable: Vending Co.   8
      Miscellaneous (Coffee)   20
      Cash Short and Over   2
        Cash   60
      To replenish the petty cash fund and record an error in disbursements (an overpayment) of $2.00

4.   **a.**

	December 31, 1983	
	Cost Basis	**Market Value**
Hoff's	$ 800	20 @ $50 = $1,000
Sorce	750	50 @ 5 = 250
Barbado	700	10 @ 50 = 500
	$2,250	$1,750

The lower-of-cost-or-market rule requires an adjustment based on the portfolio of $2,250 − $1,750 = $500.

Loss on Short-Term Investments   500
   Allowance for Decline in Market Value
      of Short-Term Investments   500
To record the decline in market value

   b. On June 15, 1984, Meddaugh Movers, Inc., sells 40 shares of Sorce Seed Co. for $8 a share, or $500. The use of a valuation account in (*a*) means that the basis of Sorce stock on the books of Meddaugh Movers, Inc., is still the original cost, or $15 a share, all of which must be removed for those shares of stock which are sold.

Cash	500	
Loss on Sale of Short-Term Investment	100	
Short-Term Investments (40 @ $15)		600
To record sale of stock		

c.

December 31, 1984

	Cost Basis	Market Value
Hoff's	$ 800	20 @ $70 = $1,400
Sorce ($750 − $600)	150	10 @ 10 = 100
Barbado	700	10 @ 50 = 500
	$1,650	$2,000

Currently the books are reporting the following amounts.

Short-term investments	$1,650
Less: allowance for decline in market value of short-term investments	500
	$1,150

However, the $500 valuation account has been recovered, and should be eliminated so that the lower-of-cost-or-market amount ($1,650) appears on the books as the value of short-term investments. Note that ($1,650 − $1,150) leads to the $500 adjustment; the amount by which market value has increased beyond mere recovery ($2,000 − $1,150 − $500, or $350) is not recorded in the books.

Allowance for Decline in Market Value of Short-term Investments	500	
Recovery in Value of Short-Term Investments		500
To record recovery in market value		

5. The following points summarize why a voucher system improves control over cash disbursements.

Since invoices are controlled upon receipt, through the assignment of a voucher number, it is unlikely that an invoice will be lost.

The formalized approval process, the reporting of account distribution on the face of the voucher, and the attachment of supporting documents to each voucher make it extremely unlikely that unauthorized payments will occur.

The maintenance of the voucher register, which reports invoices chronologically, facilitates the payment of the oldest invoices first and also makes it easy to identify payments that offer discounts and should be paid within the discount period.

The cross-referencing of check numbers to the face of the voucher and from the check register to the voucher register, as well as the marking of vouchers as *paid,* make it extremely unlikely that a single invoice will be paid twice.

CHAPTER DEMONSTRATION PROBLEM

Fuson Electronics reported the following information in its 1983 financial statements.

Balance Sheet: **12/31/83**

Current assets
  Coins & currency $ 4,000
  Checking account*   30,000
  Savings accounts & certificates of deposit   15,000
  IOUs   100
  Sinking fund for plant expansion   5,000
  Petty cash: Cash remaining in the fund   200
  Petty cash vouchers   300
  Short-term investments   4,000
  Allowance for decline in
    market value of short-term
    investments   (500)   3,500
Current liabilities
  NSF check   180
  Travel advances   (300)
  Unpaid voucher file   6,500

Income Statement: **1983**

Revenue from NOW accounts $ 1,500
Cash short and over   100
Brokerage fees   110
Loss on short-term investments   700
Sundry expenses   600

*$3,000 of this balance is a legally restricted deposit held against short-term borrowings according to a compensating balance agreement with the lender.

Instructions   Critique the form and content of these financial disclosures. Make suggestions regarding future financial statement presentation and management action.

CHAPTER DEMONSTRATION PROBLEM (ANSWER)

Cash is typically presented as a single figure; therefore the separation of coins & currency from the checking account is inappropriate.

Footnote disclosure of the compensating balance is inadequate. Restricted deposits held against short-term borrowings should be stated separately in the current assets section of the balance sheet.

Certificates of deposit are investments, while savings accounts are cash; these should not be combined.

IOUs are typically reported as receivables.

The sinking fund should appear as a noncurrent asset, because it is unavailable to meet current debt obligations.

Petty cash should always be reported at its original fund balance, as a part of the cash account. The disclosures indicate that the petty cash fund was not replenished at year-end; this means that $300 of expenses (the petty cash vouchers listed on the balance sheet) have not been properly recorded. Furthermore, the $500 implied balance of petty cash is rather large; management should reevaluate the need to maintain this large of a fund.

The NSF check is not a liability; it is a receivable.

Similarly, travel advances with a debit balance should be reclassified as receivables.

The unpaid voucher file is the subsidiary ledger for the vouchers payable control account; however, the typical balance sheet presentation is termed accounts payable.

The revenue from the NOW accounts and the relatively small balance of short-term investments suggests management may not be maximizing its return on excess cash. The interest rate on savings accounts is fairly low when compared with other alternatives available. Large cash balances held in regular checking or NOW accounts represent a loss of earnings potential. Cash that is not currently needed should be invested in short-term securities to earn higher rates of return.

The cash short and over amount is extremely large relative to the balance of petty cash. The procedures followed by the fund custodian and general controls over petty cash should be reviewed by management to ascertain the reason for this large "error" balance.

Brokerage fees should not appear on the income statement but should be added to the short-term investment account as part of the cost of acquisition.

If the loss on short-term investments is $700, the allowance for decline in market value of short-term investments must have a balance of at least $700. The accounting for short-term investments must be corrected.

Sundry expenses is a column title in the voucher register or similar journals of original entry for all entries that are not charged to the specialized columns. The items in the column should be individually posted to the general ledger and reported by expense type on the income statement (e.g., as advertising expense).

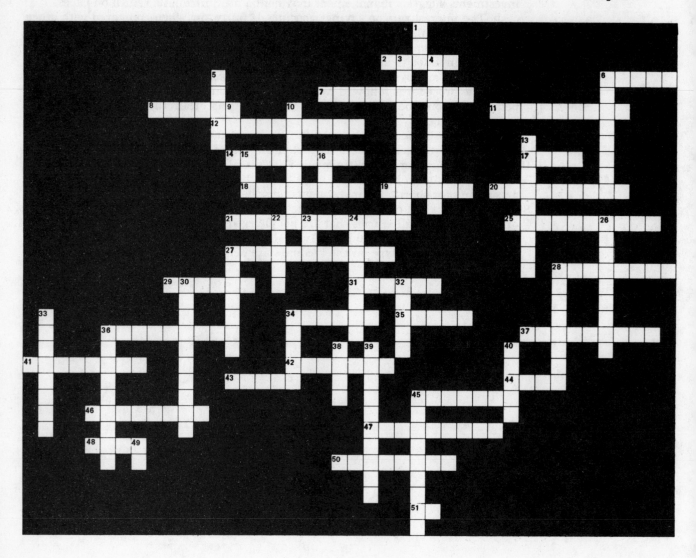

ACROSS

2. <u>2 across</u> <u>49 down</u> <u>38 down</u> <u>51 across</u> <u>8 across</u> recognizes changes in the value of short-term securities and enters those changes in the accounting record.

6. <u>12 across</u> <u>6 across</u> refers to short-term notes sold by large businesses to investors and other corporations.

7. A <u>27 across</u> <u>49 down</u> <u>42 across</u> is a security that pays a guaranteed interest rate and is sold by banks to companies and individuals; it should be classified on the balance sheet as a(n) <u>7 across</u>.

8. See 2 across.

11. The person who controls the petty cash box is known as the fund _____.

12. See 6 across.

14. To _____ a bank account means to periodically prove that accuracy of the balance that is shown in the cash account in the general ledger.

17. A decline in the market value of short-term securities is recorded as a _____.

18. <u>18 across</u> <u>35 across</u> are obligations of the U. S. Government that pay a fixed amount after a specified number of days.

19. Deposits in transit is an example of a _____ difference that frequently causes recorded cash balances to differ from bank statements.

20. _____ fees are costs frequently incurred when acquiring stock and are recorded in the short-term investment account.

21. _____ balances refer to that portion of the amount loaned to a customer which must remain on deposit in the lending bank for the duration of the loan period.

25. Effective cash _____ dictates the investment of idle funds from the time of peak inflows until a need for the funds arises by the firm.

27. See 7 across.

28. In a voucher system, disbursements are recorded in a <u>5 down</u> <u>28 across</u>.

29. Short-term investments acquired by an organization are reported as current assets on the balance sheet if they are readily salable and if it is management's _____ to convert them into cash within the operating cycle or one year, whichever is longer.

31. Since there is no special column in the voucher register to record advertising expense, such expenditures are recorded in the _____ accounts column.

34. A cash _____ is an overall plan of activity that depicts cash inflows and outflows for a stated period of time.

35. See 18 across.

36. The lower-of-cost-or-market rule is applied to the entire short-term stock investment _____, not to individual securities.

37. Checks that become payable on a date subsequent to the issue date are called _____ checks.

41. _____ in value of short-term investments is the account in which the excess of market over carrying value is recognized to the extent of previously recorded losses.

42. A _____ in transit is a receipt recorded on the company records but not yet recorded at the bank.

43. Automated tellers are an example of <u>4 down</u> <u>43 across</u> <u>24 down</u> systems.

44. When errors are made in the handling of petty cash, these errors are accumulated in an account called cash <u>40 down</u> and <u>44 across</u>.

45. A _____ system establishes control over all cash disbursements made by check.

46. Bank service charges are _____ to cash on the company's records upon receipt of the bank statement.

47. To _____ the petty cash fund, debit office supplies expense and credit cash.

48. Customer checks returned for a lack of funds are frequently reported on the bank statement via a <u>32 down</u> <u>48 across</u>.

50. Credits by the bank _____ a company's bank account.

51. See 2 across.

DOWN

1. _____ accounts allow customers to write checks on their interest-bearing savings accounts.

3. Checks written but not yet recorded at the bank for processing are called _____ checks.

4. See 43 across.

5. See 28 across.

6. Cash _____ systems consist of those procedures adopted to ensure that adequate cash is available to meet current obligations and that any excess cash is invested.

9. The fourth and fifth letters of 11 across.

10. Banks that _____ retain canceled checks instead of returning them to the customers with the monthly bank statement.

13. To record the decline in market value of common stock held for short-term investment, a company debits _____ for the decline in market value.

15. Computerized _._._. systems greatly reduce the time lag and the need for physical documents associated with cash handling systems.

16. An acknowledgement of a debt that is not negotiable and is therefore classified as a receivable until collected is called an _____.

22. A _____ cash system allows a company to make small cash payments that are impractical or uneconomical to make by check.

23. Customer checks returned for a lack of funds are called _____ checks.

24. See 43 across.

26. Securities that are similar to corporate bonds except that they are offered for sale by cities or counties are called _____ bonds.

27. Cash _____ systems are the procedures adopted to ensure the safeguarding of an organization's funds.

28. A voucher, once it has been examined for accuracy and has been approved, is recorded in a voucher _____.

30. The N in NOW account stands for _____.

32. See 48 across.

33. The separation of incompatible duties such as the authorization of cash transactions, the entry of cash transactions in the accounting records, and the custody of cash is an example of _____ control over cash.

34. Securities offered for sale by corporations that promise to repay a certain amount (usually $1,000 per security) in the future are called corporate _____.

36. A special class of stock in which the investor is entitled to dividend payments prior to any common stock dividends is known as _____ stock.

38. Under the _39 down_ _38 down_ method, short-term investments are reported on the balance sheet at their acquisition cost until they are sold.

39. See 38 down.

40. See 44 across.

45. The difference between total cost and total market value is disclosed by using a "_____" account which is offset against the original cost of the short-term investment.

49. See 2 across.

8   *RECEIVABLES*

After completing this chapter, you should:

1 *Be able to describe factors that influence the credit-granting decisions of companies.*

2 *Understand the distinction between trade and nontrade receivables.*

3 *Know how to account for uncollectible accounts under the direct write-off method and the allowance method by utilizing both the income statement and the balance sheet approaches.*

4 *Be able to compute net realizable receivables, to age accounts receivable, to write-off an uncollectible account, and to reinstate an account.*

5 *Be cognizant of the variety of receivables that involve interest and be able to record transactions involving these receivables, including installment sales and receipts and credit card sales and collections.*

6 *Know the pledging, factoring, and assignment options available to a firm to secure immediate cash from outstanding accounts receivable.*

7 *Understand the attributes of a note receivable and how to account for a note, for interest on a note, for a discounted note receivable, and, when appropriate, for a dishonored note.*

CHAPTER SUMMARY

Most business transactions involve the extension or use of *credit*. The amount of credit extended will depend on the seller's ability to increase sales by extending credit and the extent to which such increased revenue is offset by the increased expenses of operating a credit department, securing operating funds, and incurring bad debts expense. Credit is extended to customers in the form of **trade receivables** and to such parties as employees and utility companies in the form of **nontrade receivables**.

Current trade receivables, termed **accounts receivable**, can be substantial for many businesses and should be reported at their net realizable value, which is the amount the company has a reasonable expectation of collecting. One means of reflecting bad debts is the direct write-off method which debits bad debts expense and credits accounts receivable as actual losses become known. Such an approach is deficient in the matching of revenues and expenses, as well as in its compliance with the guidelines of the Financial Accounting Standards Board (FASB). Rather than permitting companies to wait for information on actual losses, the FASB requires that losses be charged against income when it is probable that a loss has occurred and its amount can be reasonably estimated. Such is typically the case for a company's uncollectible accounts; as soon as a firm extends credit it expects to incur bad debts expense and can estimate the expense related to a period's sales by analyzing historical experience or the experience of competitors.

The allowance method utilizes a valuation account entitled **allowance for bad debts** (or **allowance for doubtful accounts**), to record estimated bad debts expense. Two primary approaches to estimating the amount of bad debts exist, one of which is the **income statement approach**. Sales, or more specifically credit sales, essentially are the focus of this approach. Since bad debts are incurred at the point of sale, the historical experience of bad debts for this quantity of sales (adjusted, of course, for known changes in conditions) is used to compute the percentage of sales to be recorded as bad debts. While credit sales is the preferred base for computation, sales can be used, provided that a stable relationship exists between cash and credit sales from one period to the next. When using this percentage-of-sales approach to estimate bad debts, the journal entry is recorded as a debit to bad debts expense and a credit to the allowance for doubtful accounts; the balance of the valuation account is simply the result of matching revenues and expenses on the income statement. In contrast, the **balance sheet approach** considers the objective of recording bad debts expense to be the appropriate reporting of net realizable receivables. Either an historical percentage of accounts receivable experienced to be uncollectible is computed or a set of such percentages is applied to aged accounts receivable (e.g., 30 days old, 30 to 60 days old, 60 to 90 days old, 90 to 120 days old, and over 120 days old; receivables outstanding for over 120 days are expected to result in a higher percentage of uncollectibles than those accounts outstanding for only 30 days), and the sum of the amount of uncollectibles per age classification is computed. These two computations, since they are based on outstanding receivables, are estimates of the valuation account balance at year-end, rather than estimates of bad debts expense. For this reason, the estimate of the ending balance that is desired in the allowance for doubtful accounts will be compared to the existing balance in the valuation account; the amount of the adjustment will be whatever is required to reach the desired ending balance in the valuation account, typically with a debit charge to bad debts expense (if the existing balance in the valuation account is larger than the desired ending balance, a credit to bad debts expense would be recorded).

The valuation account allowance for bad debts is used in the **allowance method** of estimating uncollectibles because the particular accounts that are uncollectible cannot be identified at the time of the sale. When these particular accounts are identified, they are written off by debiting the allowance for bad debts account and crediting each of the individuals' accounts receivable; these write-offs are entries that are intended to clean up the account, and they affect neither net realizable receivables nor bad debts expense. If an error is made and an account receivable that is collected was previously written off, the account is reinstated by reversing the write-off entry, and collection is then recorded in the usual manner.

While accounts receivable are not typically interest bearing, installment sales accounts receivable will have a related interest charge for the customer's use of funds. Generally accepted accounting principles require that installment revenues be recorded at the time of sale, unless collection is not reasonably assured. The related interest is recorded as it is earned; the interest is based on the amount of the

10. a   Notes receivable are typically negotiable and can be transferred among parties by endorsement.

11. c   An adjusting entry would have been recorded on 12/31/83 as follows.

> Dr Interest Receivable   75
>   Cr Interest Revenue   75
>   *($4,000 × 0.15 × 45/360 = $75)*

Hence, upon receipt of the full amount of cash, $4,150 [$4,000 + ($4,000 × 0.15 × 90/360)], only $75 of the interest had not previously been recognized. The prior year's interest revenue of $75 for the period from November 15 to December 31, 1983, has been collected during 1984 and is appropriately credited to interest receivable.

12. f   The original payee will reclassify the note receivable to an account receivable in hopes of future collection. Only if collection attempts fail will the receivable be written off as a bad debt. An original payee is contingently liable for a discounted note, should it be dishonored. Hence, (*b*) and (*c*) are true, and (*f*) is the best answer.

TRUE-FALSE QUESTIONS

Indicate whether each of the following statements is true (T) or false (F).

_____ *1.* Receivables are reported on the balance sheet as either a current or noncurrent asset.

_____ *2.* When utilizing the allowance method, the current estimate of uncollectible accounts is usually in the form of a percentage and is applied to current sales or to the year-end accounts receivable balance.

_____ *3.* Most accountants favor the estimation of bad debts on the basis of total sales when applying the income statement approach.

_____ *4.* When using the balance sheet method it is necessary to consider the previous balance in the allowance for bad debts account.

_____ *5.* The allowance for bad debts may possess a debit balance.

_____ *6.* The write-off of an uncollectible account lowers the carrying value of the accounts receivable balance on the balance sheet.

_____ *7.* An entry to reinstate an account receivable is simply a reversal of the write-off journal entry.

_____ *8.* If a customer does not pay the amount owed within a certain amount of time, the seller is permitted to add a finance charge to the balance due.

_____ *9.* The Accounting Principles Board studied the issue of installment sales and concluded that installment revenues generally should be recognized at the time of collection.

_____ *10.* The credit card sale made on a bank card is really a cash sale.

_____ *11.* When pledging its accounts receivable, the borrower generally does not retain account collection responsibilities.

_____ *12.* When accounts receivable are assigned, the lending institution suffers any losses from uncollectible accounts.

Answer	Explanation
1. T	The classification depends on the timing of collection. Those receivables expected to be collected within one year or the operating cycle, whichever is longer, are classified as current assets; all other receivables are classified as noncurrent.
2. T	The allowance method is applied to current sales when using the income statement approach and to the year-end accounts receivable balance when using the balance sheet approach.
3. F	Most accountants favor the use of credit sales because it is more rational, that is, in the sense that bad debts are not incurred on cash sales. In addition, the use of total sales can yield inappropriate estimates from one period to the next if an unstable relationship exists between cash and credit sales.
4. T	Since the balance sheet method yields an estimate that is based on gross accounts receivable, the estimate will include bad debts that have already been estimated from prior periods, as reflected in the current balance of the allowance for doubtful accounts. The bookkeeper avoids double-counting such expense by netting the current balance of the allowance for bad debts account with the estimate of bad debt expense.
5. T	If bad debts have been underestimated in prior periods relative to the number of accounts receivable that are written off, a debit balance will result in the allowance account.
6. F	A write-off does not affect the carrying value of the accounts receivable balance on the balance sheet, because the carrying value is the net accounts receivable balance. Recall that net accounts receivable refers to the difference in accounts receivable and the allowance for bad debts. Since a write-off lowers both receivables and the allowance account by the same amount, the net value of the two accounts is not affected.
7. T	Accounts receivable is debited and the allowance for doubtful accounts is credited. Essentially, the bookkeeper is reversing an entry because better information has become available. Note, however, that reinstatement does not affect the recorded bad debt expense, as the company still believes that the estimate of bad debts is accurate, it simply does not know yet who is not going to pay.
8. F	Only if agreed to in the original sales agreement can the seller add a finance charge to the balance due from a customer.
9. F	In Opinion of the Accounting Principles Board (APB) No. 10, the APB concluded that installment revenues should be recognized at the time of sale since the collection of installment sales is reasonably assured.
10. T	This is due to the bank's instantaneous increasing of sellers' bank accounts upon receipt of credit card sales drafts.
11. F	Generally, the borrower collects the receivables, using the proceeds to repay the loan and related interest expense.
12. F	The borrower suffers losses from uncollectible accounts in addition to paying interest charges and a service fee to the lending institution.

CLASSIFI-CATION AND MATCHING QUESTIONS

A. Classify the following phrases as being either a description of the income statement approach (I) to estimating uncollectibles or a description of the balance sheet approach (B) to estimating uncollectibles.

___ *1.* The prior period's balance in the allowance for bad debts is ignored when estimating bad debts expense.

___ *2.* The method achieves a good matching of revenues and expenses.

_____   **3.** The method focuses on obtaining an estimate of net realizable receivables.
_____   **4.** The method often involves an aging of accounts receivable.

B. Match each of the following terms with either accounts receivable (A) or notes receivable (N).

_____   **1.** Write-off   _____   **7.** Protest fee
_____   **2.** Discounting   _____   **8.** Maturity date
_____   **3.** Dishonoring   _____   **9.** Factoring
_____   **4.** Principal   _____   **10.** Maker
_____   **5.** Pledging   _____   **11.** Installment sales
_____   **6.** Assignment   _____   **12.** Credit card sales

---

CLASSIFICATION AND MATCHING QUESTIONS (ANSWERS)

A. *1.* I *2.* I *3.* B *4.* B
B. *1.* A *2.* N *3.* N *4.* N *5.* A *6.* A *7.* N *8.* N *9.* A *10.* N *11.* A *12.* A

QUESTIONS CONCERNING THE EFFECTS OF TRANS-ACTIONS

Indicate whether the following transactions increase (+), decrease (−), or have no effect on (0) gross accounts receivable, the allowance for bad debts, net realizable receivables, and bad debts expense. Quantify the amount of each increase or decrease; assume that the current balance (before each transaction) in the allowance for bad debts is a credit of $800. Consider each transaction independently.

Gross Accounts Receivable	Allowance for Bad Debts	Net Realizable Receivables	Bad Debts Expense	
_____	_____	_____	_____	**1.** Reinstatement of a $400 customer account.
_____	_____	_____	_____	**2.** One percent of the $500,000 of credit sales are estimated to be uncollectible.
_____	_____	_____	_____	**3.** Six percent of the $60,000 accounts receivable are estimated to be uncollectible.
_____	_____	_____	_____	**4.** A $200 account receivable is written off.

QUESTIONS CONCERNING THE EFFECTS OF TRANSACTIONS (ANSWERS)

Answer				Explanation
1. + $400	+ $ 400	0	0	Debit accounts receivable, Credit allowance
2. 0	+ $5,000	− $5,000	+ $5,000	Debit bad debts, Credit allowance
3. 0	+ $2,800	− $2,800	+ $2,800	*Note:* $60,000 × 0.06 = $3,600 − $800 = $2,800. Debit bad debts, credit allowance.
4. − $200	− $ 200	0	0	Debit allowance, Credit accounts receivable

1.

Accounts Receivable		
1/1/84 120,000		?
200,000		190,000
12/31/84 ?		

Allowance for Bad Debts		
3,500	23,000	1/1/84
	?	
	?	12/31/84

Bad Debts Expense

7,300

a. What were total write-offs during 1984?
b. What were total collections from customers during 1984?
c. Provide the following balances.

Accounts receivable 12/31/84 $_____

Allowance for doubtful accounts 12/31/84 $_____

2. Collier's Collectibles Corporation's accounts receivable subsidiary ledger follows.

A. Anderson Co.

Date	Debit	Credit	Balance
12/01/82	2,000		2,000
2/30/83		1,500	500
4/15/83	700		1,200

B. Bowers, Inc.

Date	Debit	Credit	Balance
1/01/83	1,000		1,000
2/15/83	7,000		8,000
3/15/83	1,500		9,500
4/15/83		5,000	4,500
5/15/83		2,000	2,500

C. Christies Corp.

Date	Debit	Credit	Balance
3/10/83	3,200		3,200
4/15/83	5,000		8,200
5/10/83		3,200	5,000
6/10/83	1,000		6,000
6/20/83		4,000	2,000

2 Discounting makes cash available at an earlier date than the maturity date and has increased return possibilities.

$ 732,639 Net Revenue Alternative VIII
+   1,500
_____

$ 734,139 Net Revenue

Based on the information provided, Alternative III is substantially better than the other eight alternatives and Alternative I is the worst. The company may wish to combine the financing options into different alternatives (e.g., sales on others' credit cards and cash sales, as well as sales on the company's credit card to encourage store loyalty).

While the ranking of the alternatives in this problem will not universally hold, the effects of the alternatives on credit department and bad debts expense can generally be expected, as can the effect of extending credit on the total sales volume relative to a "cash sales only" policy.

9 *INVENTORY*

After completing this chapter, you should:

1 Be able to define goods in transit and goods on consignment and to determine who owns which inventory units.

2 Be aware of the problems that are commonly confronted in the taking of a physical inventory, and know the importance of the counting process.

3 Understand the effects of inventory errors on the financial statements.

4 Know how to compute the specific identification method; the first-in, first-out (FIFO) method; the last-in, first-out (LIFO) method; and the weighted-average method of inventory.

5 Be aware of the factors that are typically considered when selecting an inventory cost flow assumption and the effects of such a selection on the financial statements.

6 Understand the concept of inventory profits.

7 Know how to apply the lower-of-cost-or-market rule and how to formulate inventory estimates utilizing the gross profit method and the retail method.

8 Be able to distinguish between a periodic and perpetual inventory system and to understand both their relative advantages and their operation from a record-keeping perspective.

CHAPTER SUMMARY

Inventory refers to goods acquired or manufactured for resale to customers; it is divisible into raw materials, work in process, and finished goods for a manufacturer. Inventory encompasses all goods for which the company has legal title, including goods sent F.O.B. shipping point at the purchase date and goods sent to customers

F.O.B. destination at the sales date (until arrival at the customer's warehouse), as well as goods on consignment. Inventory records can be maintained on either a *periodic* or a *perpetual basis;* the key distinction is that no record of goods available for sale exists under a periodic system. Regardless of the system employed, a *physical inventory* is taken annually to obtain a correct ending inventory and to verify the accounting records if a perpetual system is in use. When errors are made in an inventory count, they permeate both the balance sheet and the income statement and affect statements over two years, because each year's ending inventory becomes the following year's beginning inventory.

In addition to determining the particular units to include in ending inventory, the company must select a **cost assignment process** to value the ending inventory and to calculate cost of goods sold. The **specific identification method** identifies each individual unit of merchandise with its cost and utilizes that value for cost assignment. For example, serial numbers of used cars would frequently facilitate a specific identification accounting system for a used car dealership. Obviously, such a technique can increase in complexity and cost as the quantity and variety of inventory grows; hence, rather than tracing costs per specific unit, the accountant typically makes an assumption regarding the flow of costs through the accounting system. This assumption has no necessary relationship to the physical flow of goods. The **first-in, first-out (FIFO)** method assumes that the oldest units in inventory are sold first, while the **last-in, first-out (LIFO)** method assumes that the newest units in inventory are sold first. The **weighted-average method,** a compromise between LIFO and FIFO, ignores old-versus-new units and simply computes the weighted-average unit cost and applies that average cost to each unit of inventory.

The selection of an inventory technique will consider income tax, cash flow, financial statement presentation, and investor reaction effects of each method relative to the alternative approaches to inventory valuation. During *inflationary periods,* LIFO will result in lower income, lower taxes, and lower valued inventory than FIFO; during *deflationary periods,* the relationship of the two methods reverses. The weighted-average method will usually result in an income figure that is between the FIFO and LIFO calculations. In general, LIFO results in better matching than FIFO, while FIFO values inventory closer to current market values than LIFO. However, neither method actually charges replacement cost to cost of goods sold; therefore, inventory profits are commonly reported which in actuality must be used to replenish inventory and cannot be distributed as dividends. The Financial Accounting Standards Board Statement No. 33 is an attempt to reflect the effects of inflation on both inventory and cost of sales.

Whichever method of inventory valuation is selected, the *lower-of-cost-or-market rule* is applied to assure that inventory is not stated in excess of its market value. This method is an example of the conservative approach of accounting to inventory valuation, because write-ups of inventory are not recorded but write-downs are.

Frequently, an entity wishes to estimate inventory on hand at interim dates for reporting purposes: at the date of a disaster involving physical damage to inventory (for the filing of insurance claims) and at year-end (for comparison to physical counts made for periodic inventory systems). An estimate of inventory on hand might also be made as a means of estimating losses from pilferage as distinct from cost of goods sold. The two widely used estimation procedures are the **gross profit method**, which applies an historical gross profit rate to sales to impute cost of goods sold and ending inventory, and the **retail method**, which applies the ratio of cost to retail prices (frequently by product line) to ending inventory at retail to estimate inventory at cost.

✓   *Financial Statement Account*   *Ending Inventory Overstatement Effects*

Income statement	
Cost of goods sold	Understated
Gross profit	Overstated
Net income	Overstated
Statement of owners' equity	
Ending owners' equity	Overstated
Balance sheet	
Ending owners' equity	Overstated
Total current assets	Overstated

Note: The results of an understatement of inventory would be just the opposite.

✓   *Beginning Inventory*
+ Net Purchases
_____

    Goods Available for Sale

✓   *Goods Available for Sale*
− Cost of Goods Sold
_____

    Ending Inventory

✓   *Weighted-Average Cost per Unit* $= \dfrac{\text{Cost of Goods Available for Sale}}{\text{Units Available for Sale}}$

✓ Assuming inflation, the following relationship holds true for net income computed by these three methods.

    FIFO > Weighted Average > LIFO

✓   *Inventory Profit = Current Cost to Replace − Historical Cost Charged to Cost of Goods Sold*

✓ Lower-of-cost-or-market (LCM) method

Market is defined as replacement cost provided that

    Replacement Cost ≥ (Net Realizable Value − Normal Profit Margin)

and

    Replacement Cost ≤ Net Realizable Value

where

    Net Realizable Value = Selling Price − Costs to Complete and Dispose of the Item

and the amount that can be obtained from disposal is substituted for replacement cost in the case of damaged goods.

✓   *Sales*
× Gross Profit Rate
_____

    Estimated Gross Profit
− Sales
_____

    Estimated Cost of Goods Sold
− Goods Available for Sale at Cost
_____

    Ending Inventory Estimate per the Gross Profit Method

Note: The first four lines of the computation could be replaced by Sales × (1 − Gross Profit Rate).

√   *Goods Available for Sale at Retail*
     — Sales
     _____

     Ending Inventory at Retail
     × *The Cost to Retail Ratio*
     _____

     Ending Inventory at Cost under the Retail Method

where

$$\text{Cost to Retail Ratio} = \frac{\text{Beginning Inventory at Cost} + \text{Net Purchases at Cost}}{\text{Beginning Inventory at Retail} + \text{Net Purchases at Retail}}$$

√ Journal entries recorded at point of sale by two methods

By the periodic method

   Accounts Receivable
      Sales

By the perpetual method

   Accounts Receivable
   Cost of Goods Sold
      Sales
      Inventory

MULTIPLE-CHOICE QUESTIONS

Circle the letter corresponding to the best response.

1. Incorrect accounting for sales and purchases will influence
   a. inventory
   b. cost of goods sold
   c. net income
   d. accounts receivable
   e. accounts payable
   f. all of the above

2. Goods on consignment
   a. should be included in the consignee's ending inventory
   b. should be included in the consignor's ending inventory
   c. should be included in the consignee's inventory when in the possession of the sales agent
   d. are goods for which ownership is transferred to sales agents until the point of sale
   e. none of the above

3. If purchase discounts and transportation costs for acquiring inventory are not significant
   a. it is common to charge them in entirety to ending inventory
   b. it is common to charge them in entirety to cost of goods sold
   c. it is still conceptually preferred to prorate them between cost of goods sold and the total ending inventory balance
   d. a and c only
   e. b and c only

4. The specific identification method
   a. deters management's manipulation of net income
   b. is used frequently in business
   c. matches actual costs of the units sold against their sales revenues
   d. a and c only
   e. b and c only
   f. all of the above

5. Replacement cost
   a. is currently required to be disclosed under Accounting Series Release (ASR) No. 190

b. is the cost of acquiring the same merchandise at year-end prices

c. of both ending inventories and the cost of goods sold was required to be disclosed under ASR No. 190

d. all of the above

e. a and b only

f. b and c only

6. The lower-of-cost-or-market (LCM) method

   a. is utilized with specific identification, FIFO, LIFO, or weighted average

   b. defines market value as the greater of replacement cost or net realizable value

   c. defines market value as the lesser of replacement cost or net realizable value less a normal profit margin

   d. permits inventory write-ups

   e. all of the above

   f. a, b, and c only

7. The retail method of inventory requires accumulation of the following information.

   a. the beginning inventory valued at both cost and retail amounts

   b. net purchases priced at both cost and retail

   c. net sales for the period

   d. net sales at cost for the period

   e. all of the above

   f. a, b, and c only

8. Which of the following are not generally considered to be problems with a periodic inventory system?

   a. It entails considerable record keeping.

   b. It provides no basis of accountability for theft of merchandise or errors made in the physical inventory count.

   c. It provides no record regarding the number of units in stock at any given time.

   d. It can lead to stockouts and poor customer service.

   e. None of the above.

MULTIPLE-CHOICE QUESTIONS (ANSWERS)

Answer	Explanation
1. f	All of the accounts are influenced: sales are related to accounts receivable and net income, while purchases are related to inventory, cost of goods sold, accounts payable, and net income.
2. b	While possession is transferred to the sales agent, title is not transferred. Goods on consignment should not appear in the inventory account of the agent at any point in time.
3. e	For expediency, option (b) is acceptable, but conceptually, (c) is preferable.
4. c	Specific identification allows management to manipulate net income by selectively selling those goods with either higher or lower costs. The method is used infrequently, largely due to the costs and impracticality of maintaining the required records for the method's use. Response (c) appropriately defines the specific identification method of costing inventory.
5. f	The SEC's requirements were withdrawn when the FASB issued Statement No. 33.
6. a	Response (b) should be the "lesser of" and response (c) should be the "greater of." The LCM method is an example of conservatism which does not permit inventory write-ups. The LCM method is utilized with all cost flow assumptions as a final test of the reasonableness of the reported inventory value.

7. f   Sales at cost is what will be computed through applying the retail method of estimating inventory; *ending* inventory at cost will also be computed (but it is not given as a choice for this question).

8. a   In fact, the primary advantage of a periodic system is the minimal record keeping involved relative to a perpetual inventory system.

TRUE-FALSE QUESTIONS

Indicate whether each of the following statements is true (T) or false (F).

____   1. Inventory is usually listed immediately following accounts receivable as a current asset on the balance sheet.

____   2. Ownership is determined by the transfer of legal title to the goods and the physical possession of the merchandise.

____   3. It is mandatory that a firm hand-count the goods that are in its possession at the end of the accounting period when a firm utilizes a periodic inventory system; however, the taking of a physical inventory is optional for firms that utilize a perpetual inventory system.

____   4. The observance of a client's physical count of inventory by an outside independent auditor has always been a required auditing rule.

____   5. There is no direct connection between the physical flow of goods and the cost flow assumption used in their accounting.

____   6. The FIFO method of inventory, when prices are rising, results in higher income taxes for the user.

____   7. The specific identification method of inventory will report a higher net income than the weighted-average method during an inflationary period.

____   8. Income tax regulations require that if LIFO is used for tax purposes it must also be used for financial reporting.

____   9. From an income measurement viewpoint, LIFO is superior to FIFO.

____   10. Net income is more appropriately defined as profits available for distribution when a company utilizes the FIFO method of inventory during an inflationary period than when a company utilizes the LIFO method.

TRUE-FALSE QUESTIONS (ANSWERS)

Answer   Explanation

1. T   Because inventory is one step further removed from cash via the operating cycle, it typically is reported after accounts receivable. Recall that all current assets are listed in the order of liquidity and that the term *current* reflects the company's intention that most inventory will be used or sold and converted into cash within one year.

2. F   Physical possession of merchandise is irrelevant; the sole determinant of ownership is title.

3. F   The taking of a physical inventory is mandatory for companies utilizing either a periodic or a perpetual inventory system. Such a count serves to verify the accounting records maintained in a perpetual inventory system.

4. F   The observation of physical inventory counts was not required until after the McKesson & Robbins fraud discovery in which there were reported fictitious inventories and receivables that totaled $19 million for the year 1937. Presumably the twelve-year fraud would have been precluded had the auditor observed inventory and confirmed accounts receivable (as currently required by auditing rules).

5. T   No necessary relationship exists between the flow of cost and the flow of goods; for example, a laborer is likely to shovel from the top of a pile of coal, even though the accounting for raw materials may assume that the oldest coal (that on the bottom of the pile) is being used in production.

6. T   FIFO will charge older, lower costs to cost of goods sold, increasing the net income on which taxes are incurred (during such inflationary periods).

7. F   The income effects of specific identification are dependent upon which batch of goods management selects for sale and cannot be generalized relative to the weighted-average method.

8. T   However, the regulation has been contested by subsidiaries of consolidated entities. Precedent exists for a subsidiary to use LIFO for taxes and for consolidated financial statements to use FIFO, but the court case is on appeal at this writing.

9. T   LIFO allows net income to be measured by charging the most recent costs against current sales, whereas FIFO charges older costs.

10. F   Inventory profits are greater during an inflationary period when FIFO is utilized because a larger part of reported net income is required to replenish inventory. If net income was distributed, the operations of the entity would have to contract, as sufficient resources to maintain the size of inventory required to sustain the past level of sales would be unavailable. Although inventory profits can also be a problem when utilizing LIFO, the definition of income as profits available for distribution would be more appropriate for a company applying LIFO during an inflationary period than for a company applying FIFO, because LIFO charges income with higher cost of goods sold.

CLASSIFI-CATION AND MATCHING QUESTIONS

Classify the following items as describing the FIFO method (F), the LIFO method (L), the weighted-average method (W) of inventory, or none (N) of these methods. More than one response may be appropriate per item.

_____ 1. Results in a higher net income.

_____ 2. Does not focus on when costs are incurred in terms of old-versus-new units.

_____ 3. Achieves a better matching of current costs with current revenues.

_____ 4. Results in an inventory valuation that frequently is close to the current value of inventory.

_____ 5. Results in higher taxes being paid during an inflationary period.

_____ 6. Results in understated inventory values on the balance sheet.

_____ 7. Results in a higher gross profit during a deflationary period.

_____ 8. Is based on the notion that all goods available for sale in a period should reflect the same cost.

_____ 9. Results in a higher inventory value during a period of deflation.

_____ 10. Consistently results in a higher cost of goods sold than that computed using FIFO during an inflationary period.

CLASSIFICATION AND MATCHING QUESTIONS (ANSWERS)

Answer	Explanation
1. N	This cannot be resolved unless an economic trend description is provided (i.e., is inflation or deflation occurring?).
2. W	The method averages old and new costs, whereas FIFO costs out old units first and LIFO costs out new units first.
3. L	In all cases LIFO matches the most current costs with current revenues.
4. F	In all cases the most recent purchase prices are reflected in the ending inventory derived from the FIFO method of inventory.

5. F   Since inflation results in lower (the older) costs being charged to cost of goods sold, FIFO results in higher net income, implying higher taxes.

6. N   As in number (1), an economic trend description is required.

7. L   LIFO will charge the most recent and lowest costs against sales, resulting in a higher gross profit during a period of deflation.

8. W   Essentially, the weighted-average method charges each unit sold and each unit retained in inventory at the same cost.

9. L   Since the oldest, most expensive items are assumed to be in the inventory when LIFO is utilized, during a period of deflation LIFO will report a higher inventory value.

10. W & L   Both the weighted-average method and LIFO will result in higher cost of goods sold than will FIFO during a period of inflation; in addition, LIFO will be consistently higher than the weighted-average cost of sales.

QUESTIONS CONCERNING THE EFFECTS OF TRANS-ACTIONS

Indicate whether the following errors result in overstated (O), understated (U), or correct (C) account balances. Consider each error independently and assume no other errors were made.

Net Income 1983	Retained Earnings 12/31/83	Net Income 1984	Retained Earnings 12/31/84	
____	____	____	____	1. Four thousand dollars of inventory was counted twice during the physical inventory count at 12/31/83.
____	____	____	____	2. Two thousand dollars of inventory stored in a closet was overlooked as of 12/31/84.
____	____	____	____	3. Goods on consignment valued at $30,000 were omitted from the 12/31/83 inventory.

QUESTIONS CONCERNING THE EFFECTS OF TRANSACTIONS (ANSWERS)

1. O   O   U   C
2. C   C   U   U
3. U   U   O   C

EXERCISES

1.

	Units	Cost per Unit	Cost
Beginning inventory	1,000	5.00	$ 5,000
Purchase (Jan. 31)	2,000	4.00	8,000
Purchase (Apr. 30)	3,000	3.00	9,000
Purchase (Aug. 31)	1,500	2.00	3,000
Purchase (Nov. 30)	2,500	2.00	5,000
Purchase (Dec. 15)	3,500	1.00	3,500
Goods available for sale	13,500		$33,500

During the year the following sales were made for $7 per unit.

Month of Sale	Units Sold	Alternative I	Alternative II
Feb.	1,000 units	From beginning inventory	From Jan. purchases
May	500 units	From Jan. purchases	From Jan. purchases
Sept.	3,000 units	500 From Jan. purchases	1,500 From Apr. purchases
		2,500 From Apr. purchases	1,500 From Aug. purchases
Dec.	2,000 units	1,000 From Jan. purchases	From Dec. purchases
		500 From Apr. purchases	

Utilizing the specific identification method, compute both the gross profit and the ending inventory under each of the following assumptions.

a. Assume Alternative I describes the specific units that were sold

b. Assume Alternative II describes the specific units that were sold

2.

	Historical Cost	Market	Net Realizable Value	Net Realizable Value Less a Normal Profit Margin
a.	$6	$6.20	$5.90	$5.60
b.	6	5.90	6.30	5.95
c.	6	5.90	6.30	6.10
d.	6	5.95	6.00	5.90

What would be the appropriate per-unit inventory value, utilizing the lower-of-cost-or-market method, which should appear on the balance sheet for *(a)*, *(b)*, *(c)*, and *(d)*?

EXERCISES (ANSWERS)

1. *a.* Cost of goods sold calculation

1,000:	1,000 @ $5 =	$ 5,000
500:	500 @ $4 =	2,000
3,000:	500 @ $4 =	2,000
	2,500 @ $3 =	7,500
2,000:	1,000 @ $4 =	4,000
	500 @ $3 =	1,500
		$22,000

Gross Profit = Sales − Cost of Goods Sold

Sales = 6,500 Units × $7 Selling Price = $45,500

$45,500 − $22,000 = $23,500 Gross Profit

Goods Available for Sale	$33,500
− Cost of Goods Sold	22,000
Ending Inventory	$11,500

Ending inventory can be calculated directly.

Aug. 1,500 @ $2 = $ 3,000
Nov. 2,500 @ $2 =   5,000
Dec. 3,500 @ $1 =   3,500
                   $11,500

b. Cost of goods sold calculation

1,000 @ $4 = $ 4,000
  500 @ $4 =   2,000
1,500 @ $3 =   4,500
1,500 @ $2 =   3,000
2,000 @ $1 =   2,000
              $15,500

$45,500 − $15,500 = $30,000 Gross Profit

Goods Available for Sale $33,500
− Cost of Goods Sold   15,500

Ending Inventory $18,000

Ending inventory can be calculated directly.

Beginning Inventory 1,000 @ $5 = $ 5,000
        Jan.   500 @ $4 =   2,000
        Apr. 1,500 @ $3 =   4,500
        Nov. 2,500 @ $2 =   5,000
        Dec. 1,500 @ $1 =   1,500
                           $18,000

2. a. $5.90 b. $5.95 c. $6.00 d. $5.95

CHAPTER DEMONSTRATION PROBLEM

We've Got the Selection Retailers has provided you with the following information on one of its product lines.

7/01/83   Beginning inventory 500 @ $8
7/31/83   Purchases 1,000 @ $10
10/31/83 Purchases 500 @ $15
3/31/84   Purchases 200 @ $20
5/31/84   Purchases 300 @ $25

Month	Sales in Units
July 1983	200
Aug. 1983	700
Sept. 1983	100
Oct. 1983	50
Nov. 1983	300
Dec. 1983	150
Jan. 1984	50
Feb. 1984	100
Mar. 1984	50
Apr. 1984	100
May 1984	100
June 1984	150

Selling price is $30 from July 1, 1983, through December 31, 1983, and $50 from January 1, 1984, through June 30, 1984.

Cost to complete and dispose of each item is $3.

Replacement cost at June 30, 1984, was $22.

Normal profit margin is 50%.

Estimated gross profit margin is 70%.

a. Assuming a periodic inventory system, compute cost of goods sold for the fiscal year ended 6/30/84 utilizing the FIFO, LIFO, and weighted-average estimation techniques. Compute the reported inventory profit for each method.

b. Assuming a perpetual method of inventory, compute cost of goods sold as of October 31, 1983, utilizing the FIFO and LIFO techniques.

c. Compute the ending inventory balance that should be reported on the 6/30/84 balance sheet utilizing FIFO, LIFO, and weighted-average inventory cost flow assumptions.

d. Utilizing the gross profit method, estimate inventory as of 12/31/83.

e. Utilizing the retail method of inventory, estimate inventory as of 12/31/83.

f. Assume that the company has a periodic inventory system and suspects that it has a problem with pilferage. What could you recommend as an approach to estimating such theft losses (as distinct from the cost of goods sold)?

CHAPTER DEMONSTRATION PROBLEM (ANSWER)

a. Total of units sold is 2,050.

2,050 Units × Replacement Cost of $22 per Unit = $45,100

$$
\begin{aligned}
500 \ @ \ \$8 &= \$ \ 4,000 \\
1,000 \ @ \ \$10 &= \ 10,000 \\
500 \ @ \ \$15 &= \ 7,500 \\
50 \ @ \ \$20 &= \ 1,000
\end{aligned}
$$

Cost of Goods Sold with FIFO $22,500

Inventory Profit with FIFO = $45,100 − $22,500 = $22,600

$$
\begin{aligned}
300 \ @ \ \$25 &= \$ \ 7,500 \\
200 \ @ \ \$20 &= \ 4,000 \\
500 \ @ \ \$15 &= \ 7,500 \\
1,000 \ @ \ \$10 &= \ 10,000 \\
50 \ @ \ \$8 &= \ 400
\end{aligned}
$$

Cost of Goods Sold with LIFO $29,400

Inventory Profit with LIFO = $45,100 − $29,400 = $15,700

Weighted average

Total of units available for sale is 2,500.
Total of cost of goods available for sale is $33,000.

$$Average\ Cost = \frac{\$33,000}{2,500} = \$13.20$$

$$2,050 \times \$13.20 = \$27,060$$

Inventory Profit = $45,100 − $27,060 = $18,040

b. FIFO

July Sales 200 @	$ 8 =	$1,600	
Aug. Sales 700: 300 @	$ 8 =	2,400	
400 @	$10 =	4,000	
Sept. Sales 100 @	$10 =	1,000	
Oct. Sales 50 @	$10 =	500	
		$9,500	

LIFO

July Sales 200 @ $10 =	$ 2,000	
Aug. Sales 700 @ $10 =	7,000	
Sept. Sales 100 @ $10 =	1,000	
Oct. Sales 50 @ $15 =	750	
	$10,750	

Note: It is assumed that the cost of sales is adjusted at month-end, at which time the month's latest purchases are known. Also, it is acknowledged that this is a simplified calculation, which does not portray LIFO reserve estimates that are commonly used in practice and will be studied in advanced accounting coursework.

c. Ending inventory value

2,500 − 2,050 = 450 Units

FIFO

300 @ $25 =	$ 7,500	
150 @ $20 =	3,000	
Cost	$10,500	

Market

450 @ $22 = $9,900 Market

Ceiling = Net Realizable Value = Selling Price − Costs to Complete and Dispose of the Item = $50 − $3 = $47

Floor= Net Realizable Value − Normal Profit Margin = $47 − 50% ($50) = $47 − $25 = $22

Therefore, market rate meets the floor and ceiling tests.

> LCM = $9,900 Market Value

LIFO: 450 @ \$8 = \$3,600 Cost
Market: 450 @ \$22 = \$9,900 Market
Ceiling: \$47
Floor: \$22

Therefore, market rate still meets the floor and ceiling tests.

> **LCM = \$3,600 Cost**

Weighted average: 450 @ \$13.20 = \$5,940 Cost
Market = 450 @ \$22 = \$9,900 Market
Ceiling: \$47
Floor: \$22
Therefore, market rate still meets the floor and ceiling tests.

> **LCM = \$5,940 Cost**

d. Net Sales = 200 + 700 + 100 + 50 + 300 + 150 = 1,500 Units @ \$30 = \$45,000

Beginning Inventory, July 1	*500 @ \$ 8*	*\$ 4,000*
Net Purchases: 1,000 @ \$10		*10,000*
	500 @ \$15	*7,500*
Goods Available for Sale		*\$21,500*

Current gross profit is 40%

Gross Profit = \$45,000 × 70% = \$31,500

Cost of Goods Sold = \$45,000 − \$31,500 = \$13,500

Ending Inventory = \$21,500 − \$13,500 = \$8,000

e.

	Cost	Retail
Beginning inventory, 7/1/83	\$ 4,000	\$15,000
Net purchases, July through Dec.	17,500	45,000
Goods available for sale	\$21,500	\$60,000

$$\text{Ratio of Cost to Retail Prices} = \frac{\$21,500}{\$60,000} = 35.83\%$$

\$ 60,000	*Goods Available for Sale at Retail*
− 45,000	*Sales*
\$ 15,000	*Ending Inventory at Retail*

Ending Inventory at Cost = \$15,000 × 35.83% = \$5,375

f. The company could employ the retail method to judge the extent of theft and shoplifting by comparing the physical inventory count to that ending inventory balance computed by applying the retail method. To improve the accuracy of such estimation procedures, ratios of cost to retail can be developed for each major product line.

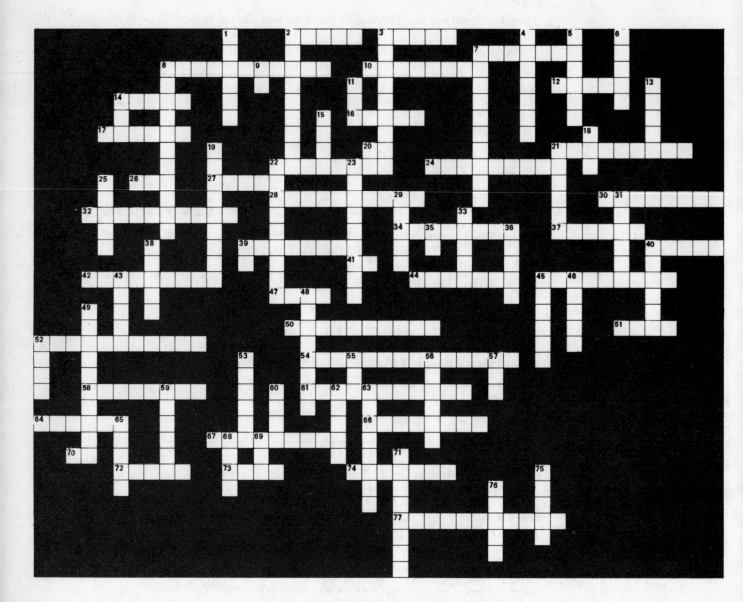

ACROSS

2. The _____ is the party to whom a note is to be repaid.

3. The _3 across_ - _20 across_, _14 across_ - _26 across_ inventory cost flow assumption will result in higher costs for ending inventory in inflationary periods.

7. The _34 across_ _7 across_ method is, in effect, a compromise between FIFO and LIFO.

8. Mr. Smith is _8 across_ his _75 down_ if he is in default of his debt obligations.

10. See 7 down.

12. The _74 across_ _12 across_ _30 across_ to estimating bad debts focuses on reporting accounts receivable at its net realizable value.

14. See 3 across.

16. The _47 across_ - _35 down_, _16 across_ - _57 down_ inventory cost flow assumption charges the most recent costs to cost of goods sold.

17. See 1 down (also, same as 37 across).

20. See 3 across.

21. The _45 down_ _21 across_ _63 down_ to estimating bad debts emphasizes the proper matching of expenses with revenues.

22. _____ of accounts receivables essentially involves using the accounts as collateral for a loan.

24. _____ can be defined as goods acquired for resale to customers (same as 19 down, 23 down, and 45 across).

26. See 3 across.

27. _40 down_ _27 across_ is defined to be replacement cost or the cost that must be paid to reproduce or repurchase the item.

28. See 8 down.

30. See 12 across.

32. A note between the discount date and the maturity date represents a _32 across_ _42 across_ to the payee.

34. See 7 across.

37. See 6 down and 48 down (also, same as 17 across).

39. Finance charges made for the use of borrowed funds are termed _____.

40. The person or firm that promises to pay a stipulated amount is the _____ of the promissory note.

41. See 5 down and 29 down.

42. See 32 across.

44. See 14 down.

45. See 21 down (same as 19 down, 23 down, and 24 across).

47. See 16 across.

49. See 23 down.

50. See 46 down.

51. The _71 down_ _51 across_ is when a note becomes due.

52. Companies transfer possession of merchandise to sales agents without transferring ownership through a process known as _____.

54. See 48 down.

58. When a firm has a _____ inventory system, purchases are recorded in the purchases account throughout the year and the inventory account balance is constant throughout the year.

61. The sales of many retail products such as automobiles and large appliances are on an _61 across_ _62 down_ basis.

64. See 23 down.

66. See 23 down.

67. See 5 down.

70. Same as 20 across and 20 down.

72. Same as 36 down.

73. _____ (an abbreviation) method of inventory during inflationary periods will result in lower (older) costs for cost of goods sold.

74. See 12 across and 33 down.

77. See 76 down.

DOWN

1. The _25 down_ _1 down_ _17 across_ is an inventory estimation procedure developed from recent past experience.

2. _____ represents the amount on which the interest is computed.

3. The sale or _____ of accounts receivable involves transferring the ownership of individual customer accounts to a finance company.

4. _65 down_ _20 down_ _4 down_ between the buyer and seller should be included in the inventory of the party that possesses legal ownership of the goods based on freight terms.

5. The _67 across_ _5 down_ _41 across_ _18 down_ _36 down_ associates the revenue and expense related to uncollectibles in the same accounting period.

6. The _59 down_ _6 down_ - _11 down_ _37 across_ of accounting for uncollectible accounts enters bad debts in the accounting records when the actual loss is incurred.

7. The _7 down_ _9 down_ _10 across_ _28 across_ refers to the result of an agreement of a lending institution with a company in which cash is advanced by the lender as sales on account occur, in exchange for rights to the collections of accounts receivable.

8. _8 down_ _75 down_ _28 across_ allows the payee to sell a note to the bank with a guarantee of payment at maturity should the maker default.

9. See 7 down.

11. See 6 down.

13. The amount due on the maturity date (principal plus interest) is commonly referred to as the _71 down_ _13 down_.

14. The party that discounts a note, if the note is dishonored, must pay the maturity value of the note plus a service charge (termed a _44 across_ _14 down_).

15. In _56 down_ _15 down_ _62 down_ the seller does not have to wait for the purchaser to pay the bill; reimbursement takes place shortly after the sale is made.

18. See 5 down and 36 down.

19. Fictitious _19 down_ _31 down_ arises due to inflation because the cost of goods sold is computed by using old (and fairly low) cost.

20. See 4 down.

21. A _22 down_ _45 across_ _21 down_ maintains a continuous record of the inflows and outflows of merchandise and results in a running count of the goods on hand.

22. See 21 down.

23. Regardless of whether a company has a periodic or a perpetual system, it is mandatory that the company make a hand-count of the goods in its possession; this process is known as _64 across_ _49 across_ _66 across_ _23 down_.

25. See 1 down.

29. Accountants can justify the use of the _29 down_ _41 across_ _52 down_ or _40 down_ _37 across_ when the market potential for a particular product has been significantly reduced.

31. See 19 down (same as 1 down).

33. When using the _74 across_ _33 down_ _37 across_ to estimate bad debts, it is necessary to consider the previous balance in the allowance for bad debts account.

35. See 16 across.

36. When estimating uncollectible accounts, _18 down_ _36 down_ expense is debited.

38. A _38 down_ - _69 down_ of an individual account, when using the allowance method, is recorded by debiting the allowance for bad debts accounts and crediting accounts receivable.

39. Same as 20 down and 20 across.

40. See 29 down.

43. _____ accounts receivable involves categorizing individual accounts based upon the length of time they have been outstanding.

45. See 21 across.

46. Offsetting the allowance for bad debts account against accounts receivable informs financial statement users of the expected _55 down_ _50 across_ _46 down_ or the amount of cash expected to be collected from the current accounts receivable.

48. The _48 down_ _54 across_ _37 across_ matches the actual cost of the units sold against their sales revenues.

49. FIFO is an example of a _52 down_ _60 down_ _49 down_.

52. See 49 down.

53. The _53 down_ _37 across_ is widely used by department stores and discount stores to estimate inventory for interim financial statements.

55. See 46 down.

56. See 15 down.

57. See 16 across.

59. See 6 down.

60. See 49 down.

62. See 15 down.

63. See 21 across.

65. See 4 down.

68. _____ (an abbreviation) method of inventory during inflationary periods will result in lower reported net income.

69. See 38 down.

71. See 13 down.

75. See 8 across and 8 down.

76. _76 down_ _77 across_ arise from the sale of a company's products or services to customers.

10 PROPERTY, PLANT, AND EQUIPMENT: ACQUISITION AND DEPRECIATION

After completing this chapter, you should:

1 *Be able to identify expenditures that are to be capitalized as the cost of acquiring (or constructing) property, plant, and equipment, including lump-sum purchases.*

2 *Know how to account for leasehold improvements.*

3 *Understand how to determine the service life of a depreciable asset and its residual value and how to compute depreciation using the straight-line, units-of-output, double-declining balance, sum-of-the-years'-digits, composite, and inventory methods for both complete- and partial-operating periods.*

4 *Be able to describe the differential financial reporting and income tax effects of the alternative depreciation methods.*

5 *Be aware of common fallacies about depreciation.*

6 *Know how to calculate depreciation when the estimates of service life and/or residual value are revised.*

7 *Be cognizant of the efforts by the Securities and Exchange Commission (SEC) and the Financial Accounting Standards Board (FASB) to require disclosure on the effects of inflation on reported property, plant, and equipment.*

Assets used to manufacture products or to provide services to a business are generally classified as **property, plant, and equipment**. Other than land, these assets are depreciated over their service lives, selected by considering the expected effects of physical deterioration, obsolescence, and growth (which can make existing equipment inadequate).

The historical cost of physical assets is adjusted for the negotiated purchase price, cash discounts offered (even if not claimed by the buyer), and all related costs of acquisition that are required for subsequent asset use. Examples of **capitalizable costs** for land include attorney's fees, real estate (escrow) fees, commissions to realtors, the assumption of past taxes, and the costs associated with clearing land. Examples of capitalizable costs for equipment include freight, electrical wiring, and installation costs. Any expenditure that fails to provide future benefits, such as restoring an automobile involved in an accident to its original condition, are called **revenue expenditures** and are expensed. Similarly, purchases of wastepaper baskets and other items with long lives but low prices are frequently handled as revenue expenditures. In addition, the interest incurred under a deferred payment plan is not capitalizable into the related asset account; it is an operating expense of the accounting period.

Material, labor, and indirect costs that are spent to build self-constructed assets are capitalized. Such costs include the allocation of salaries for supervisory personnel and of utilities expenses associated with the construction. Assets acquired in lump-sum purchases are recorded at an allocated cost that is based on each asset's relative appraised value. **Leasehold improvements**, which are assets invested in leased property by the lessee, normally become the property of the lessor at the termination of the lease. Such assets are valued at cost but are written off to expense over the shorter of the service life of the asset or the remaining term of the lease, whereas all other physical assets of a business are written off over their service lives.

Depreciation, which is an allocation of cost over an estimated service life, neither generates funds nor provides for asset replacement. It can be computed in a **straight-line** fashion, resulting in a stable expense charge per year (or a proportionate charge for a partial period) until the total depreciable basis (Cost − Residual Value) of the asset is depreciated. The balance sheet reflects the expiration of useful life by reporting property, plant, & equipment; its contra-asset account entitled **accumulated depreciation**; and the net amount or book value of property, plant, & equipment for the business. The **units-of-output method**, also termed the units-of-production or units-of-activity method, is an expense that is stable per unit of output thereby fluctuating per period as activity fluctuates for the business operation.

When compared to straight-line depreciation methods, **accelerated depreciation** methods result in higher depreciation charges in the earlier years of service life and lower charges in later years. **Double-declining balance** results in the most rapid depreciation by applying twice the straight-line rate to the book value of the depreciable properties. **Sum-of-the-years'-digits** applies a successively lower rate to the depreciable basis of properties, for a full twelve months, allocated appropriately to partial periods. Some of the factors considered in the selection of depreciation methods are simplicity, the stability of the depreciation charge, the tax effects, the maintenance costs required over time for the equipment being depreciated, and the matching of revenues and expenses.

An alternative to individual asset depreciation is the **composite method**, which groups assets and applies an average depreciation rate. For low-cost, short-lived items like hand tools, the inventory method whereby depreciation expense is calculated in the same manner as cost of goods sold is commonly applied. Whenever service lives or residual value estimates are revised, the remaining depreciable base of the asset is appropriately allocated over the remaining life, but no corrections are made to prior years' recorded depreciation since those numbers were based on the best available estimates.

Businesses commonly use straight-line depreciation for financial reporting and accelerated depreciation or cost recovery for income taxes; such use of these methods permits higher reported earnings and lower cash outflows in early years (i.e., an interest-free loan is implicitly obtained from the government). Supplemental information on the current cost of property, plant, and equipment and related depreciation expense is required under Statement of Financial Accounting Standards No. 33; the intention is to reflect inflationary effects upon operations.

TECHNICAL POINTS

✓   **Negotiated Purchase Price**
    + Capitalizable Costs of Acquisition
    − Cash Discount Offered

    Historical Cost (Accounting Cost of Long-Lived Asset)

where   Acquisition costs include freight, installation, broker's fees, and expenditures that are necessary to place the asset in a position to serve the firm (e.g., clearing of land and wiring of equipment).

and   The cash discount is deducted regardless of whether or not the firm takes advantage of the discount.

Note: List price is irrelevant when determining accounting historical cost.

✓   **Apportionment of Lump-Sum Purchases to an Individual Asset**

$$= \text{Historical Cost} \times \frac{\text{Individual Asset's Appraised Value}}{\text{Appraised Value of the Total Purchase}}$$

✓   **Factors Affecting Service Life**

Physical deterioration
Maintenance policies
Obsolescence
Inadequacy

✓   **Straight-Line Method of Depreciation** $= \dfrac{\text{Historical Cost} - \text{Residual Value}}{\text{Service Value}}$

✓   **Depreciable Base = Historical Cost − Residual Value**

✓   **Book Value = Historical Cost − Accumulated Depreciation**

✓   **Units-of-Output Method of Depreciation = [(Historical Cost − Residual Value) ÷ Total Estimated Units-of-Output during the Service Life] × Yearly Output**

✓   **Double-Declining Balance Method of Depreciation = 2 × Straight-Line Rate of Depreciation × Book Value**

Note: In the last year of depreciation, do not reduce the book value below the estimated salvage value.

✓   **Sum-of-the-Years'-Digits Method of Depreciation = (Historical Cost**

    − Residual Value) $\times \dfrac{\textbf{Remaining Number of Years of Service Life}}{\Sigma\textbf{(Total Service Years of Asset)}}$

For example, the first year of depreciation for a 6-year service life would be computed as

   Depreciable Basis $\times \dfrac{6}{1 + 2 + 3 + 4 + 5 + 6}$

✓   **Composite Method of Depreciation* = (Σ Annual Depreciation per Asset or Group of Assets Using the Straight-Line Method ÷ Total Cost) × Total Historical Cost**

    *Calculated for the Weighted-Average Service Life $= \dfrac{\textit{Depreciable Base}}{\textit{Annual Depreciation}}$

✓   **Beginning Inventory of Tools**
    + All Purchases of Tools during the Year
    − Ending Inventory of Tools

    Inventory Method of Depreciation

√ Change of estimates

Salvage value:

> *Historical Cost*
> *— Accumulated Depreciation*
> *— New Salvage Value*
> _____
> *Remaining Depreciable Base*

Service life:

> *Historical Cost*
> *— Accumulated Depreciation*
> _____
> *Amount to Treat as If It Were*
>   *Historical Cost over the Remaining*
>   *Life of the Asset, as Reestimated*

After these computations, depreciation is calculated for future periods in the usual manner, depending on which depreciation method is selected.

Circle the letter corresponding to the best response.

1. A piece of equipment is being purchased by We Construct Anything, Incorporated. The equipment has a list price of $60,000 and a negotiated purchase price of $50,000, with a 3% cash discount offered if payment is made within 10 days. The company is unable to qualify for the cash discount because of its limited working capital, but it does arrange to make payment within 30 days. The equipment will be recorded on the books of We Construct Anything, Incorporated, at
   a. $60,000
   b. $50,000
   c. $48,500
   d. $58,500
   e. $51,500
   f. $61,500

2. A company purchases a plot of land, a building, and a parking lot for a total price of $140,000. An appraiser estimates that the land is worth $80,000, the building is worth $60,000, and the parking lot is worth $10,000. The parking lot
   a. would be recorded on the books at $10,000
   b. would be recorded on the books at $9,333.33
   c. would be recorded in the land account, which would then total $90,000
   d. would be recorded in the land account, which would then total $65,333

3. Leasehold improvements
   a. normally become the property of the lessor at the end of the lease period
   b. are written off over the shorter of the remaining life of the lease or the life of the improvement
   c. normally become the property of the lessee at the end of the lease period
   d. are written off over the life of the lease to which the improvements are made
   e. a and b only
   f. b and c only
   g. a and d only

4. Items such as wastepaper baskets and office clocks
   a. are typically handled as revenue expenditures
   b. are typically classified as elements of property, plant, and equipment
   c. are written off as expense over rather long lives
   d. are generally capitalized no matter what the purchase price is

5. In accounting, depreciation
   a. is a process of allocation and valuation
   b. is a process of allocation, not valuation
   c. measures the decrease in value that the owners have experienced
   d. is a process of valuation, not allocation
   e. a and c only
   f. b and c only

6. In determining an asset's service life, which of the following must be considered?
   a. physical deterioration
   b. obsolescence
   c. inadequacy
   d. all of the above

7. Residual value
   a. is synonymous with salvage value
   b. is the amount a business expects to receive if the asset were disposed of today
   c. is allocated equally over the estimated service life
   d. a and b only

MULTIPLE-CHOICE QUESTIONS (ANSWERS)

Answer   **Explanation**

1. c   The list price is irrelevant. The discount lost is a financing expense and is not capitalized. Hence, $50,000 − (3% × $50,000), or $48,500 would be the recorded value of the equipment.

2. b   Lump-sum purchases are apportioned among the assets acquired based on the assets' relative sales value. Hence,

$$\frac{\$10,000}{\$80,000 + \$60,000 + \$10,000} \times \$140,000$$

is the amount to be recorded in the land improvements account.

3. e   Leasehold improvements are typically permanently attached to the leased property and therefore will typically become the property of the lessor at the end of the lease period. For this reason, the lessee's books cannot use an asset life that extends beyond the asset's usefulness to the lessee, defined both in physical terms and in legal terms via rights to use the property as defined by a lease.

4. a   In order to reduce paperwork costs, most businesses establish a companywide minimum dollar level below which expenditures are written off at the time of purchase as a revenue expenditure.

5. b   Depreciation allocates historical cost as expense to the years receiving service or benefits; it ignores fluctuations in market value.

6. d   Each of these factors warrants consideration.

7. a   Response *(b)* is incorrect because residual value represents the amount a business expects to receive from disposal of an asset at the end of the asset's life. Response *(c)* is incorrect because the residual value is not depreciable (i.e., it is not allocated over the estimated service life but is intended to be the book value of the asset at the end of its service life).

**TRUE-FALSE
QUESTIONS**

Indicate whether each of the following statements is true (T) or false (F).

_____   *1.* Idle buildings and machinery are properly classified as property, plant, and equipment.

___ **2.** When a company purchases property, plant, and equipment on a deferred payment plan, it is important to recognize that any interest incurred under the plan is included in the asset account.

___ **3.** It is proper to capitalize utilities expense when valuing a self-constructed asset on the books.

___ **4.** Typically, land and land improvements are recorded in one account.

___ **5.** Physical deterioration normally establishes the maximum limit for the estimate of service life.

___ **6.** Businesses purchasing identical items of property, plant, and equipment routinely estimate different service lives for these assets and are correct in doing so.

___ **7.** When an asset is fully depreciated it will have a book value of zero.

___ **8.** The same amount is ultimately depreciated by all depreciation methods.

___ **9.** Depreciation generates funds.

___ **10.** The accumulated depreciation account contains cash that will be used to replace existing depreciable assets at the end of their service lives.

___ **11.** Corrections of previous years' depreciation amounts are not made because of new estimates of service life and residual value.

___ **12.** The SEC currently requires the disclosure of the replacement cost of property, plant, and equipment in the accounting records, and the FASB requires the disclosure of the current cost of property, plant, and equipment.

TRUE-FALSE QUESTIONS (ANSWERS)

Answer   *Explanation*

1. F   Only long-lived assets currently used in a business are considered to be part of property, plant, and equipment.

2. F   Such interest is *not* included in the asset account but is treated as an operating expense of the accounting period.

3. T   The acquisition cost of a self-constructed asset includes material, labor, and indirect costs. Utilities expense represents an indirect cost that frequently needs to be allocated to numerous activities, but it is properly capitalized in self-constructed asset accounts.

4. F   Since land improvements have a limited life and must be depreciated, they are segregated from land, which has an indefinite life and is not subject to depreciation.

5. T   A company cannot utilize physical assets beyond the point at which they wear out; however, rarely is this point reached by a company due to the effects of obsolescence and business growth on the usefulness of property, plant, and equipment.

6. T   Each service life decision uniquely reflects the way assets are being used and management's view of the effects of obsolescence and inadequacy on the asset's useful life to a particular business.

7. F   A fully depreciated asset has a book value equal to the asset's residual value, which will frequently differ from zero.

8. T   The depreciable basis, or cost less residual value, is the total amount depreciated over the service life of an asset regardless of the depreciation method in use.

9. F   The cash account is not increased nor are liabilities decreased by depreciation charges; depreciation generates no funds, it merely allocates historical cost over an estimated service life.

10. F   This is a common fallacy of depreciation; there is no cash in the accumulated depreciation because all cash is in the cash account. Just as depreciation is a bookkeeping allocation with no effect on funds, accumulated depreciation merely represents the total of these allocations per asset group with no effect on available funds.

11. T   This is not considered to be an accounting error, because the estimates used in previous years were used in good faith.

12. F   The SEC withdrew its disclosure requirements when the FASB issued Statement No. 33.

**CLASSIFI-
CATION AND
MATCHING
QUESTIONS**

A. Classify the following items using these symbols.

> B = Capitalized to the buildings account
> L = Capitalized to the land account
> E = Capitalized to the equipment account
> X = Expensed

____   1. Payment of delinquent property taxes by the buyer of land
____   2. Freight charges incurred by the buyer of equipment
____   3. Expenditure to repair damage to equipment caused during installation
____   4. Cost of clearing land for construction of shopping center
____   5. Broker's fee for building purchased
____   6. Surveying costs
____   7. Cost of special electrical wire used for installing equipment
____   8. Interest on purchase of old building
____   9. Proceeds received from selling materials salvaged from the demolition of buildings to prepare for future construction
____ 10. Salary of supervisory personnel overseeing the company's construction of a new building

B. Classify the following items as descriptions of these four methods of depreciation. More than one response may be appropriate.

> SL = Straight-line
> SYD = Sum-of-the-years'-digits
> DDB = Double-declining balance
> UP = Units-of-production

____   1. The most widely used depreciation method.
____   2. Produces more depreciation expense in earlier years of the service life.
____   3. This method can only be used when a direct relationship exists between an asset's use and its decline in service potential.
____   4. Preferred by some investors because it does not cause net income to fluctuate.
____   5. The method's popularity is largely due to its simplicity.
____   6. This method was proposed by the federal government in the 1950s to increase employment.
____   7. Produces the highest first-year depreciation expense, generally speaking.
____   8. Permits a better allocation of cost when the amount of output from an asset varies considerably from period to period.
____   9. Depreciates over the life of the asset an amount equal to the depreciable basis.
____ 10. Ignores residual value in the computation of annual depreciation expense.
____ 11. Provides a constant depreciation expense per year.
____ 12. Frequently used for tax purposes.

CLASSIFICATION AND MATCHING QUESTIONS (ANSWERS)

A. *1.* L   *2.* E   *3.* X   *4.* L   *5.* B   *6.* L   *7.* E   *8.* X   *9.* L   *10.* B
B. *1.* SL   *2.* SYD, DDB   *3.* UP   *4.* SL   *5.* SL   *6.* DDB   *7.* DDB   *8.* UP   *9.* SL, UP,
SYD, DDB   *10.* DDB   *11.* SL   *12.* DDB, SYD

QUESTIONS CONCERNING THE EFFECTS OF TRANS-ACTIONS

Will each of the following items increase (I), decrease (D), or have no effect upon (N) the current period's net income?

——   *1.* Increase in estimated salvage value.

——   *2.* Decrease in estimated service life.

——   *3.* Use of double-declining balance in year of acquisition rather than sum-of-the-years'-digits.

——   *4.* Use of sum-of-the-years'-digits depreciation instead of straight-line in the final year of useful life.

——   *5.* The use of accelerated depreciation methods for tax purposes instead of straight-line.

QUESTIONS CONCERNING THE EFFECTS OF TRANSACTIONS (ANSWERS)

Answer   *Explanation*

1. I   Increase in salvage value decreases depreciation expense, thereby increasing net income.

2. D   Decrease in estimated service life increases depreciation expense, thereby decreasing net income.

3. D   Double-declining balance results in higher depreciation expense in year one and therefore lower income.

4. I   Sum-of-the-years'-digits results in lower depreciation in later years and higher reported income.

5. I   Accelerated methods increase the tax shield and lower taxes paid thereby enhancing cash flow and obviating the need for borrowing with related interest costs. Hence, the use of accelerated methods for taxes implies that the business will be better off with higher income. Obviously this idea is distinct from the depreciation method being applied for financial reporting purposes.

EXERCISES

1. On January 1, 1984, a company acquired a $33,000 piece of equipment for which it estimated a $3,000 salvage value and a 10-year useful life. It is now December 29, 1987, and new information becomes available that the residual value is actually $2,000 and that the remaining useful life is actually 2 years. Record depreciation expense for 1987 as of December 31 and report how the equipment would appear on the 12/31/85 balance sheet as well as on the 12/31/87 balance sheet.

2. We Service Everywhere, Inc., leases property on which it has made leasehold improvements. Specifically, on January 2, 1984, the construction of sidewalks costing $8,000 with a useful life of 50 years and a storage shed costing $20,000 with a useful life of 20 years was completed. The lease will be terminated in 40 years. What is the related write-off to expense in 1984?

Indicate whether each of the following statements is true (T) or false (F).

_____ 1. Assessments are generally added to the land account.

_____ 2. Gains and losses on the disposal of depreciable assets are common because book value does not represent the true worth of an asset in the marketplace.

_____ 3. The accounting for the exchange of similar assets for financial reporting purposes is the same as for federal income tax purposes.

_____ 4. The accounting treatment of the exchange of similar assets, for which the fair market value exceeds the book value of the asset being relinquished, results in higher depreciation expense over the service life of the new equipment than the depreciation which would result from the accounting treatment for dissimilar assets.

_____ 5. Periodically, the subsidiary ledger of property, plant, and equipment should be verified by taking a physical inventory.

_____ 6. The costs incurred in purchasing a patent or in internally developing a patent are carried as an asset.

_____ 7. To properly match revenues and expenses, periodic amortization of intangible assets is recorded, typically with a debit to amortization expense and a credit to accumulated amortization.

_____ 8. It is now accepted practice not to amortize intangible assets with unlimited service lives.

_____ 9. The depletion computation is similar to the units-of-output depreciation method.

_____ 10. The procedure for revision of depletion rates is identical to that followed for depreciation and amortization.

TRUE-FALSE QUESTIONS (ANSWERS)

Answer   Explanation

1. T   Since assessments are relatively permanent and make the land more valuable, they are generally added to the land account.

2. T   Since depreciation is a process of allocation, not valuation, since service life and residual value are only estimates, and since assets are often sold before the end of their useful lives, gains and losses are common.

3. F   For financial reporting purposes, gains on the exchange of similar assets are ignored while losses are recognized. In contrast, for tax purposes no gains or losses are recognized on the exchange of similar assets.

4. F   The depreciation expense over the service life is reduced since the gains that would otherwise be recorded are not recognized whenever similar assets are exchanged. The new equipment is recorded below the invoice price, resulting in less depreciation than would have resulted from the accounting treatment for dissimilar assets.

5. T   A physical inventory verifies that the property, plant, and equipment is still on hand and is serving the firm.

6. F   While the purchase cost of an intangible is carried as an asset, research and development costs that are incurred in developing a patent are expensed in accordance with FASB Statement No. 2.

7. F   An accumulated amortization account is rarely used; the credit would be charged directly to the intangible asset account that is being amortized.

8. F   Such intangibles are to be amortized, as are all intangibles, over a period not to exceed 40 years. (However, a grandfather clause does exist under generally accepted accounting principles.)

9. T   The cost of the natural resource less any residual value is first divided by the total units of resources estimated to be available and then is multiplied by the number of units extracted during the period.

10. T   In all cases, revisions of estimates are allocated over the remaining life rather than recorded as corrections of write-offs made in past years.

CLASSIFICATION AND MATCHING QUESTIONS

A. Classify the following items using these symbols.

    B = A betterment
    C = A capitalizable addition
    X = An expensed item

___   *1.* Painting
___   *2.* New engine in a vehicle
___   *3.* Construction of a new wing on a building
___   *4.* Inspection costs
___   *5.* Placement of air conditioning in a truck

B. Match each of the following descriptions with the intangible asset to which it relates; some assets may have more than one response.

___   *1.* Copyright   *a.* Provides owner with 17-year exclusive rights
___   *2.* Trademark   *b.* Prior to 1978 was granted for 28 years, renewable for a
___   *3.* Patent   second 28 years
___   *4.* Franchise   *c.* May have a definite or an indefinite life
                            d. Has a legal life equal to the life of its creator plus 50 years
                            e. Is registered for 20 years with unlimited renewals possible for the same term

CLASSIFICATION AND MATCHING QUESTIONS (ANSWERS)

A. *1.* X   *2.* B   *3.* C   *4.* X   *5.* C
B. *1.* b, d   *2.* e   *3.* a   *4.* c

QUESTIONS CONCERNING THE EFFECTS OF TRANSACTIONS

Would the following items increase (I), decrease (D), or have no effect upon (N) depreciation, amortization, or depletion expense?

___   *1.* The trade-in of an old asset in which the book value of the old asset is greater than its fair market value relative to a purchase with no trade-in.

___   *2.* For tax purposes, the trade-in of an old asset in which the book value of the old asset is greater than the fair market value, relative to a purchase with no trade-in.

___   *3.* Compliance with generally accepted accounting principles relative to the use of the expected service life of 50 years for goodwill.

___   *4.* The use of successful efforts rather than full cost for recording oil resources.

QUESTIONS CONCERNING THE EFFECTS OF TRANSACTIONS (ANSWERS)

Answers *Explanation*

1. N Dissimilar and similar assets both record the new equipment at its invoice price for financial reporting purposes; hence, depreciation expense would be the same for both transactions.

2. I Higher depreciation would be recorded for tax purposes since the denied loss is capitalized in the new asset account.

3. I Generally accepted accounting principles would require the use of a 40-year life for amortization.

4. D Since fewer costs would be capitalized, subsequent depletion, depreciation, and amortization costs would be lower.

EXERCISES

1. A piece of equipment was acquired on January 2, 1978, at a cost of $45,000. The machine had a residual value of $3,000 and an estimated useful life of 7 years at the date of acquisition. On July 1, 1983, the equipment was sold for $6,200. Record the July 1st transaction, assuming straight-line depreciation.

2. A truck costing $8,000 on December 31, 1981, is estimated to have a 5-year useful life with a $2,000 salvage value, and is depreciated using the sum-of-the-years'-digits method. This truck was traded for a new truck on December 31, 1984. The new truck had an invoice price of $15,000, and a trade-in allowance of $4,200 was granted for the old truck. Record the transaction on December 31, 1984.

EXERCISES (ANSWERS)

1. $$\frac{\$45,000 - \$3,000}{7 \ Years} = \$6,000 \ per \ Year$$

$6,000 per Year $\times$ 5 = $30,000 for 1978–1982

$$\$6,000 \times \frac{6}{12} = \$3,000 \ for \ 1983$$

July 1, 1983

Dr Depreciation Expense	3,000	
Cr Accumulated Depreciation: Equipment		3,000

July 1, 1983

Dr Cash	6,200	
Dr Accumulated Depreciation: Equipment	33,000	
Dr Loss on Sale	5,800	
Cr Equipment		45,000

Note: $45,000 − $30,000 − $3,000 = $12,000 Book Value. $12,000 Book Value − $6,200 Cash = $5,800 Loss. Whenever an asset is sold mid-year, its depreciation since the end of the last accounting period must be updated before recording the disposal.

2. $$\$8,000 - \$2,000 = \$6,000 \times \frac{5}{1 + 2 + 3 + 4 + 5} = \$2,000 \ Depreciation \ in \ 1982$$

$$\$6,000 \times \frac{4}{15} = \$1,600 \ Depreciation \ in \ 1983$$

$$\$6,000 \times \frac{3}{15} = \$1,200 \ Depreciation \ in \ 1984$$

$2,000 + $1,600 + $1,200 = $4,800

$ 8,000 Cost
— 4,800 Accumulated Depreciation

$ 3,200 Book Value at Trade-in

$15,000 Invoice Price of New Truck
— 4,200 Fair Market Value of Old Equipment

$10,800 Cash Paid for New Truck

December 31, 1984

Truck (New)	14,000	
Accumulated Depreciation, Truck	4,800	
Truck (Old)		8,000
Cash		10,800

CHAPTER DEMON-STRATION PROBLEM

A growing entity named We R Researching, Inc., with a 12/31 year-end, has asked that you assist them in setting up their newly acquired equipment, intangibles, and natural resources on their books. The entity has provided you with the following details concerning acquisition.

a. A silver mine was acquired on June 30, 1983, for $800,000 and is estimated to contain 15 ounces of silver per ton of ore, with 2 million tons of ore in the mine. During 1983, $75,000 of equipment with no residual value and an estimated service life of 80 years was constructed to remove the ore. This equipment will not be able to be moved when the mine is closed. In 1983, 500,000 ounces of silver were removed from the mine; in 1984, 1 million ounces were removed. Assume that only 1.3 million ounces were sold as of 12/31/84.

b. The government permits 15% percentage depletion. Silver is currently selling for $15 an ounce.

c. On June 30, 1985, a discovery of an improved grade of silver resulted in a reestimate that the silver resources in the mine were 18 ounces of silver per ton of ore. Assume that 1.5 million ounces of silver were extracted in 1985.

d. During 1983 (June 30th) $50,000 was paid and a $150,000 mortgage at 15% was assumed to acquire an administrative office building. Its useful life was estimated to be 40 years, and straight-line depreciation is to be used. Ten percent of the price was for the lot.

e. In April of 1984 a central air conditioner was installed in the building for $20,000; the unit was guaranteed for 50 years with an estimated scrap value of $2,000. In May, 1984, the office building was painted throughout at an expense of $30,000; this paint job is expected to last for 4 years.

f. The hot water heater in the administrative building in January 1985 had a major part replaced at a cost of $1,400; the replacement part has a 60-year service life and no salvage value.

g. The municipality assessed the business $10,000 for new sidewalks in 1984.

h. Office machinery with a book value as of January 2, 1984, of $3,100 (cost $10,000) was sold for $2,800. Office furniture with a cost of $8,000 and accumulated depreciation of $7,800 was sold for $1,000 on that same date.

i. Sales staff automobiles, with a fair market value of $20,000, had an original cost of $35,000 and accumulated depreciation of $8,000 as of December 31, 1984. The automobiles were traded in for new automobiles with a list price of $50,000.

j. The firm has purchased a patent for $100,000 (on June 30, 1983) and has invested an additional $15,000 during 1984 to adapt the mining process to the company's operations. The service life of the process is estimated to be 25 years.

k. The firm acquired a small mining company for $700,000 on December 1, 1984; the acquired company's financial condition is reflected by the following summarized balance sheet accounts.

	Historical Cost	Market Value
Assets	$ 940,000	$1,500,000
Liabilities	1,000,000	1,000,000

l. The firm has developed a trademark; its related expenditures include $3,000 for market research, $10,000 for design fees, $15,000 for attorney fees, and $500 for registration fees. The company estimates an indefinite life for the trademark as of 12/31/84.

m. The firm has expanded its operations into the oil industry during 1983. Over the past years it has drilled two wells: one (a dry hole) cost $150,000, and the other, close by the first, cost $200,000 and resulted in a producing well with an estimated 1 million barrels of oil, 100,000 barrels of which were removed in 1984. The firm is undecided as to the appropriate accounting treatment for its oil property.

Outline the accounting effects of all of the information provided by We R Researching, Inc., for 1983, 1984, and 1985, tying your analysis by letter to the information being utilized. Also, to the extent possible, provide guidance as to how the firm should monitor its property in the future.

CHAPTER DEMONSTRATION PROBLEM (ANSWER)

a. Silver mine, 6/30/83, $800,000 cost

$$2,000,000 \text{ Tons of Ore}$$
$$\times \quad 15 \text{ Ounces of Silver per Ton of Ore}$$
$$\overline{30,000,000 \text{ Ounces of Silver}}$$

$$\frac{\$800,000}{30,000,000 \text{ Ounces}} = \$0.027 \text{ per Ounce Cost}$$

$$\$75,000 \text{ Equipment Installed 1983}$$
$$- \quad 0 \text{ Residual Value}$$
$$\overline{\$75,000 \text{ Depreciable Basis}}$$

Journal entries for 1983

Silver Mine	800,000	
Equipment	75,000	
Cash		875,000

| Depletion Expense | 13,500 | |
| Accumulated Depletion: Silver Mine | | 13,500 |

$$\$0.027 \times 500,000 = \$13,500$$

| Depreciation Expense | 1,250 | |
| Accumulated Depreciation: Equipment | | 1,250 |

$$\frac{500,000}{30,000,000} \times \$75,000 = \$1,250$$

Journal entries for 1984

Inventory: Silver	5,400	
Depletion Expense (0.8)	21,600	
Accumulated Depletion: Silver Mine		27,000

$$\$0.027 \times 1,000,000 = \$27,000$$

Depreciation Expense ... 2,500
　Accumulated Depreciation: Equipment ... 2,500

$$\frac{1,000,000}{30,000,000} \times \$75,000 = \$2,500$$

Note: Since the equipment cannot be removed from the silver mine, and it appears that at the present rate of extraction silver will be removed from the mine in less than 80 years, the units-of-production method of depreciation, based on the rate of cost depletion, is appropriate for the equipment.

Since 200,000 ounces of silver were not yet sold as of 12/31/84, 20% of the 1984 depletion expense is deferred into inventory. In 1985 both the silver mine and the equipment would continue to be depreciated using the units-of-output approach.

b. The government's 15% depletion is applied to revenues and would result in the following tax shields.

$$\begin{array}{r} 500,000 \text{ Ounces} \\ \times \quad \$15 \\ \hline \$7,500,000 \text{ Revenue} \\ \times \quad 0.15 \\ \hline \$1,125,000 \text{ Percentage Depletion 1983} \end{array}$$

$$\begin{array}{r} 800,000 \text{ Ounces} \\ \times \quad \$15 \\ \hline \$12,000,000 \text{ Revenue} \\ \times \quad 0.15 \\ \hline \$ \ 1,800,000 \text{ Percentage Depletion 1984} \end{array}$$

c. June 30, 1985, revision of estimate

$$\begin{array}{r} 2,000,000 \text{ Tons} \\ - \quad 33,333 \text{ Tons in 1983} \\ - \quad 66,667 \text{ Tons in 1984} \\ \hline 1,900,000 \text{ Tons Left} \\ \times \quad 18 \text{ Ounces per Ton} \\ \hline 34,200,000 \text{ Ounces Left} \end{array}$$

$$\begin{array}{r} \$ 800,000 \text{ Original Cost} \\ - \quad 13,500 \text{ Depletion 1983} \\ - \quad 21,600 \text{ Depletion 1984} \\ - \quad 5,400 \text{ Adjustment in 1985 for 1984 Depletion} \\ \hline \$ 759,500 \text{ Available for Depletion} \end{array}$$

$$\frac{\$759,500}{34,200,000} = \$0.022 \text{ per Ounce Cost}$$

$$\$0.022 \text{ per Ounce Cost} \times 1,500,000 \text{ Ounces} = \$33,000 \text{ Depletion}$$

$$\frac{1,500,000}{34,200,000} \times \$75,000 = \$3,289 \text{ Depreciation}$$

Journal entries for 1985

Depletion Expense ... 5,400
　Inventory ... 5,400

Depletion Expense ... 33,000
　Accumulated Depletion: Silver Mine ... 33,000

Depreciation Expense ... 3,289
　Accumulated Depreciation: Equipment ... 3,289

Percentage depletion tax effects

$$
\begin{array}{r}
1{,}500{,}000 \ \textbf{Ounces} \\
\times \qquad \$15 \\
\hline
\$22{,}500{,}000 \ \textbf{Revenue} \\
\times \qquad 0.15 \\
\hline
\$ \ 3{,}375{,}000 \ \textbf{Percentage Depletion}
\end{array}
$$

Note: Depletion revisions affect only subsequent years' depletion and related depreciation, not prior years' charges.

d.
$$
\begin{array}{r}
\$200{,}000 \ \textbf{Cost} \\
\times \quad 0.10 \\
\hline
\$ \ 20{,}000 \ \textbf{Land Value}
\end{array}
$$

Journal entries for 1983

Land	20,000	
Cash		20,000
Building	180,000	
Cash		30,000
Mortgage Payable		150,000

40 years depreciation; no salvage value; ½-year use

$$
\frac{\$180{,}000}{40} \times \frac{6}{12} = \$2{,}250
$$

Depreciation Expense	2,250	
Accumulated Depreciation: Building		2,250

1984 and 1985 [given no other information than provided in (*d*)]

Depreciation Expense	4,500	
Accumulated Depreciation: Building		4,500

Note: Land is not depreciated, and interest is not capitalized.

e.   April 1984 addition of $20,000

Air Conditioner	20,000	
Cash		20,000

Since building has a remaining useful life of 39¼ years, which is less than the 50-year estimated life of the addition, the 39¼-year life is used for depreciation.

$$
\frac{\$20{,}000 - \$2{,}000}{39.25} = \$459 \times \frac{9}{12} = \$344.25
$$

1984

Depreciation Expense	344.25	
Accumulated Depreciation: Air Conditioner		344.25

1985

Depreciation Expense	459.00	
Accumulated Depreciation: Air Conditioner		459.00

1984

Repairs Expense	30,000	
Cash		30,000

Note: Painting is not considered to be other than a cost of maintaining existing property.

f. Betterment

1/85

> Accumulated Depreciation: Building   1,400
>   Cash   1,400

Affect on subsequent depreciation: $4,500 depreciation expense for 1985 per part *(d)* of problem. As of the beginning of 1985, the book value is $180,000 − $2,250 − $4,500 + $1,400 = $174,650 ÷ 38.5-Years Useful Life Remaining = $4,536 Depreciation.

1985

> Depreciation Expense   4,536
>   Accumulated Depreciation: Building   4,536

g. 1984

> Land   10,000
>   Cash   10,000

Note: Land and its related assessments are not depreciated.

h.   **$ 10,000   1/2/84 Cost**
        − 3,100   Book Value

        $ 6,900   Accumulated Depreciation

        $ 2,800   Proceeds
        − 3,100   Book Value

        ($ 300) Loss

        $ 8,000   1/2/84 Cost
        − 7,800   Accumulated Depreciation

        $ 200   Book Value
        1,000   Proceeds

        $ 800   Gain

        Cash   2,800
        Accumulated Depreciation   6,900
        Loss on Sale   300
            Office Machinery   10,000

        Cash   1,000
        Accumulated Depreciation   7,800
            Office Furniture   8,000
            Gain on Sale   800

i.   **$ 35,000 Cash**
        − 8,000 Accumulated Depreciation

        $ 27,000 Book Value

        $ 20,000   Fair Market Value (FMV)
        27,000   Book Value

        ($ 7,000) Loss

        $ 50,000 List − $20,000 FMV = $30,000 Cash

12/31/84

Automobiles (New)	50,000	
Accumulated Depreciation: Automobiles	8,000	
Loss on exchange	7,000	
Equipment (Old)		35,000
Cash		30,000

Note: For tax purposes, the new asset would be recorded at a value of $50,000 + $7,000 = $57,000; rather than recognizing the loss immediately, the loss is reflected in higher depreciation expense in subsequent years.

j.

Patents	100,000	
Cash		100,000

Research and Development Expenses	15,000	
Cash		15,000

Note: While purchased patents are capitalized, internal developments are not. Furthermore, since 17 years is the legal life of patents, the 25-year life estimate is inappropriate. The shorter of legal or useful life is the relevant life for amortization.

$$\$100,000 \div 17 \text{ years} = \$5,882 \times \frac{6}{12} = \$2,941$$

1983

Amortization Expense	2,941	
Patent		2,941

1984 and 1985

Amortization Expense	5,882	
Patent		5,882

Note: No valuation account is typically used for recording amortization.

k. Market value of firm acquired is $1,500,000 − $1,000,000 = $500,000 and the purchase price is $700,000. Goodwill is defined as the excess of purchase price over current value, or $200,000. When no other life is provided, the 40-year maximum life that is required under generally accepted accounting principles is assumed to apply.

$$\frac{\$200,000}{40 \text{ Years}} = \$5,000 \times \frac{1}{12} = \$416.67$$

1984

Amortization Expense	416.67	
Goodwill		416.67

1985

Amortization Expense	5,000	
Goodwill		5,000

l. All of the costs are capitalizable.

Trademark	28,500	
Cash		28,500

1985

Amortization Expense	712.50	
Trademark		712.50

$$\$28,500 \div 40 \text{ Years} = \$712.50$$

Note: It is assumed that the trademark is renewed legally, as permitted.

m. Under the successful-efforts approach

1983

    Oil Properties   200,000
        Cash   200,000

    Exploration Expenses   150,000
        Cash   150.000

1984

$$\frac{100,000}{1,000,000} \times \$200,000 = \$20,000$$

    Depletion Expense   20,000
        Accumulated Depletion: Oil Property   20,000

Under the full-cost approach

1983

    Oil Properties   350,000
        Cash   350,000

1984

$$\frac{100,000}{1,000,000} \times \$350,000 = \$35,000$$

    Depletion Expense   35,000
        Accumulated Depletion: Oil Property   35,000

Note: Either accounting method is acceptable, although the FASB has expressed its preference for successful efforts in a recently withdrawn accounting pronouncement. Essentially, the difference in the methods is one of timing; the successful-efforts approach expenses dry holes immediately, while the full-cost approach permits such expenses to be matched with revenue from productive wells through depletion charges.

Overall Recommendations

The firm should set up subsidiary property ledgers to facilitate asset management. The wide variety of assets requires detailed records for financial reporting and for tax purposes, as well as to facilitate a periodic comparison of physical assets and documentary evidence of intangibles with the accounting records. Since the recorded book value of intangible assets is substantially affected by estimates, these estimates should be subjected to periodic review and revision whenever deemed to be appropriate.

Management should be cognizant of the tax advantages to exchanging similar assets whenever a gain is expected to result from the disposal of old assets. Moreover, managers should be aware that a full-cost approach to valuing oil property may well overstate the asset base, since dry holes are permitted to be capitalized when such a technique is used for accounting purposes. Finally, in selecting the life over which an intangible is to be amortized, management should recognize that a maximum period of 40 years is permitted for amortization and that goodwill amortization is not a tax-deductible expense, although it does, of course, lower reported net income. These facts should be considered in accounting for assets and in monitoring their usefulness in operations.

12 CURRENT LIABILITIES AND PAYROLL

After completing this chapter, you should:

1 Be able to describe the typical current liabilities for a business and the circumstances in which they are likely to arise.

2 Know how to estimate and record accrued expenses, including property taxes.

3 Understand how the accounting treatment of notes payable differs when interest is included in the face value of a note relative to when interest is recorded separately.

4 Be able to recognize contingent liabilities that are to be recorded in the accounts and those for which footnote disclosure is deemed to be adequate.

5 Be aware of how warranty costs are estimated.

6 Understand the accounting for payroll, including the role of internal control, the information requirements for employers, and the treatment of taxes (such as FICA and withholding for federal, state, and local taxes) and other deductions in the accounting records.

CHAPTER SUMMARY

In the course of doing business, **debts** arise which are obligations to be paid within one year or within the operating cycle, if longer than a year. **Accounts payable** correspond to purchases of goods or services and are typically repaid within 30 to 60 days; this short time frame makes year-end cut-off critical, because unrecorded liabilities can arise simply from delays in processing or in shipping. Some operations receive substantial deposits and prepayments from customers for future services; until earned, such payments are **current liabilities**.

The tax system requires businesses to act as collectors of revenue for the state, and such withholdings and collections are current liabilities while in the possession of the business. At times businesses voluntarily act as collectors for such charities as United Fund; the charitable payroll deductions authorized by employees also represent current liabilities until they are disbursed to the appropriate party.

Accrual accounting regularly results in accrued liabilities for salaries, taxes, interest, and similar items. Essentially, **accrued expenses** refer to expenses incurred but not yet paid. Property taxes are, for example, typically accrued on a monthly basis over the taxing authority's fiscal period, although payments are usually made on an annual basis. Whenever tax rates are changed, differences between estimated and actual expenses are adjusted in the subsequent accrual (assuming such a difference is not significant).

Often, accounts payable that are past-due are replaced by **notes payable** as a means of improving the security of the liability by obtaining a signed note and of generating interest revenue over the collection period. Notes payable are also commonly obtained as short-term credit, frequently with the interest included in the face value of the note (in which case a contra-liability termed **discount on notes payable** quantifies the future interest not yet incurred). Discounts are amortized over time, and the total interest recorded will be comparable across notes of differing form.

Contingent liabilities are potential obligations; if such uncertainties both are probable and can be reasonably estimated (as is likely for items like warranty claims) they are recorded in the accounts. If only one of these conditions is met, footnote disclosure is appropriate.

Payroll, due to its liquidity and typical magnitude, requires strong internal controls to guard against defalcations. **Employee payroll** is typically maintained in a specialized payroll register, with individual earnings records that facilitate the preparation of information and tax forms for both employees and governmental agencies. The typical gap between gross pay and take-home pay is due to the combination of deductions for the Federal Insurance Contributions Act, or FICA (6.7% of up to $33,900 of gross pay as of 1983), for federal, state, and city income tax withholdings (to comply with the pay-as-you-go requirements), and for other items like insurance, savings bonds, and charitable contributions.

An employer's cost of payroll includes matching the FICA contributions of each employee, a Federal Unemployment Tax Act payment of 0.7% and a state unemployment payment of 2.7% of each employee's first $6,000 of gross earnings (although states typically give merit reductions to employers with stable work forces), and payments for numerous fringe benefits. In addition, substantial costs are associated with record keeping as well as with acting as a collector for the government and charitable organizations.

TECHNICAL POINTS

✓ Balance sheet disclosure of long-term debt with a short-term portion that will be liquidated by the use of current assets or by the creation of other current liabilities

Current Liabilities = Current Portion of Long-Term Debt

Long-Term Liabilities = Loan Payable − Balance Due Currently

✓ Accrue property taxes monthly over the fiscal period of the taxing authority

✓ *Interest Expense = Principal × Rate × Time*

✓ *Discount on Notes Payable = Interest That Is Included in the Face Value of a Note and Is Termed a Contra-Liability*

Balance sheet disclosure

Current Liabilities = Notes Payable − Discount on Notes Payable

✓ $\text{Discount Amortization} = \text{Discount} \times \dfrac{\text{Number of Days for Which Note Has Been Outstanding}}{\text{Total Number of Days for Which Note Will Be Outstanding}}$

✓ Criteria for contingent liability to be recorded in a journal entry

It is probable that the future event will occur.
The amount of the liability can be reasonably estimated.

Otherwise footnote disclosure is appropriate.

✓   **Warranty Expense = Number of Items Sold × Percentage for Which Warranty Work Is Likely to Be Required × Average Repair Expense per Item**

✓ Two methods of balance sheet presentation of current liabilities

Liabilities ordered according to due date (from earliest to latest)
Liabilities ordered according to maturity value (from largest to smallest)

✓   **Take-Home Pay = Gross Pay − Deductions**

Typical Deductions Include

FICA at 6.7% of earnings on a base of $33,900 (as of 1983)
Withholding for federal, state, and local income taxes
Voluntary payments for U.S. Savings Bonds, insurance programs, pension plans, and charity

✓   **Payroll Taxes of Employer**

FICA at 6.7% of earnings on a base of $33,900 (as of 1983)
Federal Unemployment Tax Act payments of 0.7% of each employee's first $6,000 of gross earnings
State Unemployment Tax of 2.7% of each employee's first $6,000 of gross earnings (netted with merit reductions)

MULTIPLE-CHOICE QUESTIONS

Circle the letter corresponding to the best response.

1. A $10,000 note payable, of which $2,000 is a discount, has been outstanding for 90 days. Four hundred dollars of the discount has been amortized. How will this current liability be reflected on the balance sheet?

   a. Current liabilities
   Notes payable $10,000
   Less: Discount on notes payable   2,000 $8,000

   b. Current liabilities
   Notes payable $ 8,000
   Interest payable $ 2,000

   c. Current liabilities
   Notes payable $10,000
   Less: Discount on notes payable   1,600 $8,400

   d. Current liabilities
   Notes payable $ 9,600
   Less: Discount on notes payable   1,600 $8,000
   Interest payable   400

   e. none of the above

2. Contingent liabilities should be recorded in the accounts when
   a. it is probable that the future event will occur
   b. the amount of the liability can be reasonably estimated
   c. either a or b occurs
   d. both a and b occur
   e. none of the above

3. Social Security taxes are
   a. only paid by the employer

    b. paid by both the employee's and the employer's contributions

    c. progressive taxes with no specified maximum

    d. a uniform tax of approximately $2,000 per person

    e. a and c only

    f. b and c only

    g. b and d only

    h. a and d only

4. The amount withheld from an employee's earnings for federal income taxes depends on

    a. employee earnings

    b. the frequency of pay

    c. the employee's marital status

    d. the number of withholding allowances claimed

    e. all of the above

    f. a and d only

    g. a, b, and d only

5. A company sells 100 appliances, 10% of which are likely to require repair costing $35 within the warranty period. During this year only two units have been repaired under warranty. What would be the appropriate journal entry to record the warranty liability at the end of this period?

a.	*Warranty Expense*	*350*	
	Estimated Liability for Warranties		*280*
	Parts Inventory		*70*
b.	*Warranty Expense*	*350*	
	Estimated Liability for Warranties		*350*
c.	*Warranty Expense*	*70*	
	Parts Inventory	*70*	
d.	*Warranty Expense*	*3,500*	
	Estimated Liability for Warranties		*3,500*
e.	*Warranty Expense*	*3,500*	
	Estimated Liability for Warranties		*3,430*
	Parts Inventory		*70*
f.	*Warranty Expense*	*420*	
	Estimated Liability for Warranties		*350*
	Parts Inventory		*70*

MULTIPLE-CHOICE QUESTIONS (ANSWERS)

Answer   *Explanation*

1. c   The face value of the note includes the entire discount and must be reported in the notes payable account. No separate account is required for interest payable, because it is in fact part of the note's face value. The $1,600 discount reflects the original $2,000 discount net of amortization.

2. d   Both criteria must be met to warrant a journal entry.

3. b   While the taxes are progressive they are limited by a ceiling on the tax per person once income exceeds the FICA base. The tax is not uniform; if a person earns less than the FICA base, less tax is paid.

4. e   Each of these factors affects the amount of withholding.

5. a   Assuming the $70 repair was not yet recorded for the two returned items and related only to parts inventory, *(a)* is the best response. Estimated Expenses = 100 × 10% × $35 = $350, of which $70 has already resulted in the use of parts inventory.

Indicate whether each of the following statements is true (T) or false (F).

_____   *1.* The short-term portion of long-term debt should be reported as a current liability.

_____   *2.* The account entitled discount on notes payable is a contra-liability that is deducted from notes payable on the balance sheet.

_____   *3.* Footnote disclosure of contingent liabilities is deemed appropriate when either the future event is considered probable or the amount of the liability can be reasonably estimated.

_____   *4.* Independent contractors are typically employees of the company for which the service is being provided.

_____   *5.* Businesses determine their own pay rates, including overtime pay.

_____   *6.* A form W-2 informs an employer, at the time of an employee's employment, of the number of allowances claimed by the employee for withholding purposes.

_____   *7.* Withholdings become smaller as the number of allowances claimed increases.

_____   *8.* Taxes collected under the Federal Unemployment Tax Act (FUTA) are distributed to people who are out of work.

TRUE-FALSE QUESTIONS (ANSWERS)

Answer   *Explanation*

1. F   Only if the short-term portion can be presumed to be liquidated by the use of current assets or by the creation of other current liabilities should it be reclassified. If not, such amounts should remain in the long-term liability section of the balance sheet.

2. T   The discount essentially represents the prepayment of future interest expense.

3. T   Only if both criteria are met is a journal entry appropriate.

4. F   Independent contractors do not have an employer-employee relationship with clients; they perform services for several businesses concurrently on a fee basis.

5. F   Federal regulations exist which require businesses engaged in interstate commerce to pay overtime of at least one and one-half times the regular rate for hours worked in excess of 40 per week. Businesses must comply with this Federal Fair Labor Standards Act and are not free to set company policy below a 150% overtime rate.

6. F   A form W-4 is the appropriate form and is entitled the withholding allowance certificate; a W-2 form is utilized by a business to report to employees as to their gross wages and the taxes withheld from their pay.

7. T   The federal income tax deduction tables are constructed in this manner, presumably because the total tax liability for the year will be lower the greater the number of exemptions.

8. F   The funds are used to support the administrative costs of state unemployment programs and are not distributed directly to those out of work.

**CLASSIFI-
CATION AND
MATCHING
QUESTIONS**

Match the following items using these symbols. Both symbols may be appropriate for some items.

> B = Expense incurred by the business
> E = Expense incurred by the employee or a deduction voluntarily authorized by the employee

--- 1. Withholding allowance
--- 2. FUTA payments
--- 3. FICA
--- 4. U.S. Savings Bond purchase
--- 5. Christmas bonus

CLASSIFICATION AND MATCHING QUESTIONS (ANSWERS)

1. E   *2.* B   *3.* E and B   *4.* E   *5.* B

**QUESTIONS
CONCERNING
THE EFFECTS
OF TRANS-
ACTIONS**

Indicate whether each of the following transactions increases (+), decreases (−), or has no effect on (0) the account balances listed below. Quantify each effect.

Net Income	Total Liabilities	Total Current Liabilities	
----	----	----	*1.* Received $5,000 on January 2, 1983, for 1983 magazine subscriptions.
----	----	----	*2.* Passengers of We Fly Airlines used $60,000 of previously purchased tickets.
----	----	----	*3.* Current assets will be used to pay off $20,000 of a long-term debt that is due within one year.
----	----	----	*4.* Issued a $40,000 note with a $5,000 discount included.

QUESTIONS CONCERNING THE EFFECTS OF TRANSACTIONS (ANSWERS)

	Net Income	Total Liabilities	Total Current Liabilities
1.	0	+$ 5,000	+$ 5,000
2.	+$60,000	−$60,000	−$60,000
3.	0	0	+$20,000
4.	0	+$35,000	+$35,000

EXERCISES

1. Real Estate, Inc., has a fiscal year from July 1, 1983, through June 30, 1984. The taxing authority's fiscal year is on a calendar year basis. The tax statement is received May 1, 1984, with taxes due by June 30, 1984.

During January 1984, Real Estate, Inc., estimated its property taxes for January through December 1984 to be $42,000. On May 1, 1984, Real Estate, Inc., received a tax statement for $39,000. On June 20, 1984, Real Estate, Inc., paid its tax bill.

Record the necessary journal entries as of January 31, 1984, May 31, 1984, and June 20, 1984.

2. We Give U A Break, Inc., has issued 10,000 coupons for a $5.00 rebate on appliances sold during 1983. These coupons must be redeemed by December 31, 1984. The corporation expects 70% of the coupons to be redeemed in total; as of December 31, 1983, 30% have been redeemed. Assuming that no entries have been made to date to record any transactions related to these coupons, what adjustments would be required as of December 31, 1983?

1. Estimated tax bill

$42,000 ÷ 12 Months = $3,500

January 31, 1984

Property Tax Expense   3,500
  Property Taxes Payable   3,500
To record the monthly property tax accrual

Actual tax bill

$39,000 ÷ 12 Months = $3,250

Past accruals: Jan., Feb., Mar., Apr.

4 Months × ($3,500 − $3,250) = $1,000 Over-Accrual

May 31, 1984

Property Tax Expense   2,250
  Property Taxes Payable   2,250
To record the monthly property tax accrual, net of corrections for prior months' over-accrual ($3,250 − $1,000 = $2,250)

As of June 20th, accruals were made from January 31st through May 31st, totaling $3,500 + $3,500 + $3,500 + $3,500 + $2,250 = $16,250.

June 20, 1984

Property Taxes Payable   16,250
Prepaid Property Taxes   22,750
  Cash   39,000
To record payment of property taxes

2. The coupons represent a contingent liability that should be recorded in the accounts because redemption is both probable and estimable.

To record the coupons already redeemed

```
  10,000 Coupons Issued
×   30%
  _____
   3,000 Coupons Redeemed
×    $5
  _____
 $15,000
```

Rebate Expense   15,000
  Cash   15,000

To record the liability as of December 31, 1983

10,000
$\times$ *40% (70% − 30%)*

4,000 Coupons
$\times$ *$5*

$20,000

Rebate Expense	20,000	
Estimated Liability for Rebates		20,000

CHAPTER DEMON-STRATION PROBLEM

A company named Overextended, Incorporated, which is involved in interstate commerce, has three employees for whom it has collected the following information.

Joyce Clarke

Employee in the office
Hours worked, 90
Earnings, $15 an hour
Authorized voluntary deductions: insurance, $40.00; parking, $10.00; payment on an account receivable for employee purchase, $60.00
Year-to-date earnings, $2,000 prior to this pay period
Number of exemptions claimed, 5
Withholding, $285.20

Buddy Hiller

Employee in sales
Hours worked, 80
Earnings, $16 an hour
Authorized voluntary deductions: United Way, $5.00; insurance, $50.00
Year-to-date earnings, $33,850 prior to this pay period
Number of exemptions claimed, 4
Withholding, $234.10

Rod Davis

Employee in sales
Hours worked, 100
Earnings, $13 an hour
Authorized voluntary deductions: insurance, $55.00; parking, $10.00; U.S. Savings Bond, $100.00
Year-to-date earnings, $15,000 prior to this pay period
Number of exemptions claimed, 3
Withholding, $313.60

Assume that

1. New York State, the state of employment, has a 10% income tax.
2. FICA taxes are 6.7% on a base of $33,900.
3. Federal Unemployment Tax Payments are 0.7% and state unemployment tax rates are 2.7% of the employees' first $6,000 of gross earnings.
4. Overextended has positive working capital and has an open line of credit that will provide a note with interest included in the face value, at a rate of 22%, to cover the cash flow requirements for payroll.

Calculate each employee's net pay and record the payroll journal entry on Overextended's books, including the financing transaction.

Joyce Clarke

90 Hours × $15 = $1,350.

With no other information, assume one and one-half pay rate for overtime in excess of 40 hours per week: Biweekly 80 Hours − 90 Hours = 10 Hours × (½ × $15 per Hour) = $75.

Gross Pay = $1,350 + $75 = $1,425.

Year-to-date earnings of $2,000 is less than $33,900 FICA base; FICA taxes: $1,425 × 0.067 = $95.475.

New York State income taxes: $1,425 × 0.10 = $142.50.

$1,425 Gross Pay − $95.48 FICA − $142.50 NY − $285.20 Federal − $40 Insurance − $10 Parking − $60 Payment = $791.82 Net Pay

Buddy Hiller

80 Hours × $16 = $1,280 Gross Pay.

Year-to-date earnings of $33,850 is less than $33,900 FICA base by $50.

Therefore, $50 × 0.067 = $3.35 FICA taxes for this pay period. The remaining $1,230 of gross pay is not subject to FICA.

New York State income taxes: $1,280 × 0.10 = $128.00.

$1,280 Gross Pay − $3.35 FICA − $128 NY − $234.10 Federal − $50 Insurance − $5 United Way = $859.55 Net Pay

Rod Davis

100 Hours × $13 = $1,300.

Assume one and one-half overtime pay: Biweekly 80 Hours − 100 Hours = 20 Hours × (½ × $13 per Hour) = $130.

Gross Pay = $1,300 + $130 = $1,430.

Year-to-date earnings of $15,000 is less than $33,900 FICA base; FICA taxes: $1,430 × 0.067 = $95.81.

New York State income taxes: $1,430 × 0.10 = $143.00.

$1,430 Gross Pay − $95.81 FICA − $143.00 NY − $313.60 Federal − $55 Insurance − $10 Parking − $100 U.S. Savings Bond = $712.59 Net Pay

Payroll: Employer's considerations FICA contributions

> $ 95.48 Clarke
>   3.35 Hiller
> 95.81 Davis
>
> $194.64

Unemployment tax payments on Clarke

> $ 1425 $ 1425
> 0.007   0.027
>
> $ 9.98 Federal $38.48 State

Subtotal

> $194.64
>   9.98
> 38.48
>
> $243.10

Salaries

$1,425	
1,280	$1,280
1,430	1,430
$4,135 *Gross Pay*	$2,710 *Sales Salaries*

Federal income taxes payable

$285.20
234.10
313.60
$832.90

State income taxes payable

$142.50
128.00
143.00
$413.50

FICA

$ 95.48
3.35
95.81
$194.64

Employees' insurance program payable

$ 40.00
50.00
55.00
$145.00

Subtotal

$ 832.90	$ 4,135.00
413.50	− 1,751.04
194.64	
145.00	$ 2,383.96 *Net Pay to Employees*
$1,586.04	× 0.22 *Interest Rate*
+ 100.00 *Bonds*	524.47 *Interest*
+ 5.00 *United Way*	+ 2,383.96 *Principal*
+ 60.00 *Accounts Receivable*	$ 2,908.43 *Note Payable*
$1,751.04	− 524.47 *Discount*

Note: The assumption is made that a loan is assumed only for the cash requirements of payroll; although the payables will have to be paid in the near future, they are not intended to be liquidated by this loan.

Journal entries

Cash	*2,383.96*	
Discount on Note Payable	*524.47*	
Note Payable		*2,908.43*
Office Salaries Expense	*1,425.00*	
Sales Salaries Expense	*2,710.00*	
Payroll Tax Expense	*243.10*	
FICA Taxes Payable		*389.28*
Federal Unemployment Taxes Payable		*9.98*
State Unemployment Taxes Payable		*38.48*
Employees' Federal Income Taxes Payable		*832.90*
Employees' State Income Taxes Payable		*413.50*
Employees' Insurance Program Payable		*145.00*
Savings Bond Payable		*100.00*
United Way Contributions Payable		*5.00*
Accounts Receivable: Clarke		*60.00*
Cash		*2,383.96*

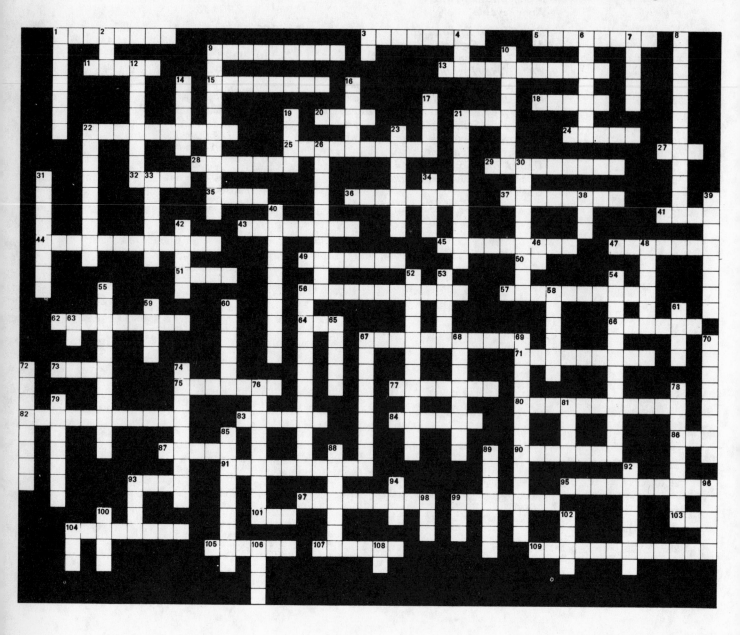

1. A _1 across_ _95 across_ is an advance that is typified by magazine subscriptions and gift certificates and is an unearned revenue.

3. A _____ is a promise made by a seller or manufacturer to remedy defects in product quality and performance.

5. _7 down_ _5 across_ are the total wages of an employee from which deductions are made for taxes and other items to arrive at _51 across_ - _100 down_ _104 down_.

9. The _105 across_ - _9 across_ _88 down_ _107 across_ (_98 down_._._.) was proposed by the federal government in the 1950s to increase employment and the rate of investment in plant and equipment.

11. _99 down_ _108 down_ _2 down_ _11 across_ _84 across_ (_27 across_._._.) depreciation applies a successively lower depreciation rate to a constant depreciable base.

13. _____ are expenditures that improve or increase the future service potential of an asset.

15. A _35 across_ - _99 down_ _15 across_ is one in which a number of assets are acquired together for a single amount.

18. The _40 down_ _94 down_ - _18 across_ _77 across_ could well include temporary holding of sales taxes by retailers.

20. The _20 across_ _19 down_ _36 across_ charges the costs of successful and unsuccessful exploration ventures to asset accounts.

21. The _21 across_ market _14 down_ of an asset is its current market price.

22. _____ is an economic determinant of service life and refers to the likely effects of business growth upon property, plant, and equipment.

24. _104 across_, _24 across_, and _71 across_ are assets with long lives that are acquired for use in the operations of a business.

25. The _25 across_ _23 down_ _37 across_ expenses the exploration costs that are associated with nonproductive drilling efforts of an oil company as soon as a drilling location is deemed a failure.

27. See 11 across.

28. Property, plant, and equipment is frequently acquired by using a _10 down_ _28 across_ plan; under such a plan a predetermined payment is sent to the seller each period until the purchase price is paid off.

29. _____ are items that provide future benefits and will be affixed to existing assets.

32. _99 across_ _32 across_ is the time period that depreciable assets are useful to a business.

35. A _35 across_ _101 across_ purchase is an acquisition of a number of assets, all for a single amount (i.e., a single purchase price).

36. See 20 across.

37. See 25 across.

41. Rather than account for the individual _____, composite depreciation accounts for a group of assets.

43. _____ represents the amount paid by a purchaser of a business in excess of the current value of the assets and liabilities acquired.

44. _97 across_ _44 across_ would include buildings that are constructed on leased property by the lessee.

45. _____ is the allocation of the cost of natural resources to the resources extracted during the current period.

47. A _47 across_ _55 down_ benefits future periods and are typified by purchases of assets such as equipment.

49. _10 down_ _49 across_ are essentially long-term prepaid expenses and include plant rearrangement costs.

50. A _65 down_ - _50 across_ _67 down_ is that fair market value which is granted for an old asset given in exchange for a new asset.

51. _51 across_ - _100 down_ (net) _104 down_ is typically less than gross earnings.

56. _____ are improvements that are made for the benefit of property owners by the municipality and are exemplified by street lights and sidewalks.

57. _57 across_ _83 across_ are long-lived assets that lack physical existence and contribute to the earnings capability of a firm.

62. _____ depreciation uses an average rate to depreciate groups of assets.

64. The life of a patent runs _____ after 17 years.

66. _42 down_ - _108 down_ - _66 across_ depreciation is frequently used for depreciable assets where the service life can be expressed in terms of miles, hours, and so on.

67. _67 across_ _52 down_ methods generate relatively large amounts of depreciation in the early years of asset use and smaller amounts in later years.

71. See 24 across.

73. _73 across_ _44 across_ are exemplified by parking lots and lawn sprinkler systems and are recorded in a separate account from the property on which they're constructed or installed.

75. _____ are amounts spent to maintain the normal operating condition of an asset and include painting and cleaning.

77. See 18 across.

80. _80 across_ _19 down_ is the cost of acquiring the same asset new at this time.

82. _82 across_ _52 down_ is the contra-asset account that reflects the total depreciation to date on the assets used in operations.

83. See 57 across.

84. See 11 across.

86. The number of that chapter which discusses successful-efforts and full-cost accounting methods.

87. Full-cost accounting may give the _____ of assets where none exist.

90. A _90 across_ _55 down_ is a disbursement that provides no future benefit, such as the repair cost of a piece of equipment that was accidentally dropped.

91. _91 across_ _30 down_ has been allowed by the Internal Revenue Service to stimulate discovery of new resource deposits and the development of existing deposits.

93. Employees _____ the cost of personal taxes through payroll deductions.

95. See 1 across.

97. See 44 across.

99. See 32 across.

101. See 35 across.

103. A _34 down_ _38 down_ _103 across_ _78 down_ (_3 down_) reports yearly totals of the employee's earnings record.

104. See 24 across.

105. See 9 across.

107. The _22 down_ depreciation _107 across_ is often used for hand tools and resembles the handling of prepaid office supplies on the books.

109. _33 down_ _103 across_ _109 across_ are required to facilitate a pay-as-you-go tax system.

DOWN

1. _1 down_ _19 down_ is defined as the number of dollars required to purchase or manufacture assets having the same service potential as the assets already owned.

2. See 11 across.

3. See 103 across.

4. Same as 2 down.

6. _6 down_ _76 down_ are often called wasting assets and are typified by oil wells and standing timber.

7. _____ earnings are the total amounts paid to an employee for the employee's services.

8. _53 down_ _8 down_ _96 down_ are typically charged as 2.7% of an employee's first $6,000 of gross pay.

9. The _9 down_ _93 down_ represents the total amount that will be written off to depreciation expense over the assets' useful lives.

10. See 28 across and 49 across.

12. The _12 down_ _14 down_ is the amount a business expects to receive from disposal of an asset at the end of the asset's life.

14. See 12 down.

16. _106 down_ _16 down_ is the cost of an asset less the accumulated depreciation of the asset.

17. Same as 20 across.

19. See 1 down, 20 across, and 80 across.

21. _____ give their owner the right to manufacture or sell certain products or perform certain services in a specific area.

22. See 107 across.

23. See 25 across.

26. _____ provide owners, or heirs, the exclusive right to produce and sell an artistic, musical, or published work.

30. See 91 across.

31. _31 down_ _69 down_ is caused by use in the normal course of business and is termed wear and tear; this is one factor that influences the selection of a service life.

33. See 109 across.

34. See 103 across.

38. See 103 across.

39. An _____ is a person who works for a specific business and is directed and closely supervised by that business.

40. See 18 across.

42. See 66 across.

46. Same as 50 across.

48. A _____ provides its owner the exclusive right to use, manufacture, and sell a product or process for a period of 17 years.

52. See 67 across and 82 across.

53. See 8 down.

54. _____ is a technological factor related to being out-of-date, which is a consideration when selecting a service life.

55. See 47 across and 90 across.

56. _____ is the process of allocating an intangible's cost over its service life.

58. To _____ a liability means to recognize unpaid expenses, such as salaries and interest, at the period's end.

59. _._._._., commonly called Social Security, is paid through both employer and employee contributions.

60. A _____ liability is the term applied to a discount on notes payable, deducted from the notes payable account on the balance sheet.

61. _._._._. is a joint program between the federal government and the various states to financially assist the unemployed.

63. _70 down_ _63 down_ _102 down_ _92 down_ is an account that is required to appropriately record a note in which interest is included in the face value.

65. See 50 across.

67. See 50 across.

68. The _89 down_ _68 down_ summarizes a firm's entire labor costs for employees.

69. See 31 down.

70. See 63 down.

72. The _72 down_ - _81 down_ depreciation method is the most widely used due to its simplicity as a means of accounting for fixed assets.

74. A _____ is an intangible asset that brings to mind a product or service, often by means of a symbol.

76. See 6 down.

78. See 103 across.

79. An _79 down_ _92 down_ represents an amount owed to suppliers for the purchase of goods or services.

81. See 72 down.

85. Same as 30 down and 45 across.

88. See 9 across.

89. See 68 down.

92. See 79 down.

93. See 9 down.
94. See 18 across.
96. See 8 down.
98. See 9 across.
99. See 11 across.

100. See 51 across.
102. See 63 down.
104. See 51 across.
106. See 16 down.
108. See 11 across and 66 across.

13 PARTNERSHIPS AND CORPORATIONS

OBJECTIVES

After completing this chapter, you should:

1 *Know the distinctive features of a partnership and a corporation, as well as their relative advantages.*

2 *Be able to account for partnership formation, income distribution, admission of a new partner, exchange of partnership interests, investment in a partnership, withdrawal of a partner, and liquidation of a partnership.*

3 *Understand the accounting treatment of organization costs, stock subscriptions and issuance, and preferred stock dividends of a corporation.*

4 *Be able to describe the rights of common stockholders and to compare these rights to those of preferred stockholders.*

CHAPTER SUMMARY

Two principal forms of business organization are the partnership and the corporation. **Partnerships,** common in accounting, law, and other professions, offer the advantages of ease of formation, operating flexibility, a means of increasing capital and specialized skills beyond the sole proprietor's abilities, and, frequently, a preferred tax treatment. Articles of partnership detail the rights, duties, and responsibilities of each of the partners and can help to assure smooth operations with a minimal number of disputes among the partners. The disadvantages of partnerships include unlimited liability because the partnership form of business is not a legal entity, high risk due to the mutual agency among partners (each partner acts as an agent of the other partners), the costs associated with a limited life, and, for individuals in a high-personal-tax bracket, taxes related to partnership operations.

Partnership accounting of assets and liabilities is identical to both sole proprietorships and corporations; however, the owners' equity section takes the form of multiple capital accounts and temporary drawing accounts—one per partner. In forming a partnership, the fair market value of noncash assets is entered on the books. When a new partner is admitted by means of purchasing an existing partnership interest, the capital on the books is merely transferred from the old partner(s) to the new partner with no reflection of the individuals' gain or loss on such an exchange. If, instead, the new partner is admitted by contributing additional capital, the share of the partnership purchased is compared to the reported book values of the other partners' capital balances. Often, a **bonus** to existing owners is implied, in which case it is shared according to the profit and loss ratio. Of course, the setting could be reversed, with the existing partners implicitly giving a new partner a bonus by permitting the purchase of a share of the partnership below its book value; the cost of such a bonus is shared by the old partners according to the profit and loss ratio. A parallel accounting treatment applies to withdrawals of partners.

When a partnership distributes its income, it is customary to initially pay partners a salary allowance and an interest allowance to compensate them for disproportionate time and capital commitments to operations. Unlike employees' salaries, the salaries to partners are not tax-deductible expenses; instead, salaries to partners are, in substance, a distribution of profits. Once salary and interest allowances are paid, any remaining profit, loss, or earnings deficiency thereby created are distributed in accordance with the partnership agreement (in equal shares if not specified in the agreement). If a partnership has to be liquidated, noncash assets are sold and the related profits or losses are allocated among the partners in accordance with the profit and loss ratio. Creditors are paid, and any partners' capital deficiencies are settled by the remaining partners according to their relative profit and loss sharing ratios. If any excess of assets over liabilities exists, it is distributed to the partners in the amount of their capital balances.

A **corporation** offers the advantages of having easily transferable ownership shares known as stock, of being perpetually in existence (unaffected by transactions among individual stockholders), of being able to limit stockholders' liability to their original investments (or to the par value of their stock if greater than the total investment), and of having more ease than a partnership in raising capital. On the other hand, disadvantages include double taxation, whereby income is first taxed to the corporation and then is taxed a second time when distributed to the stockholders in the form of dividends, and heavy regulation of operations.

A corporation is created by obtaining a charter; its organization costs, including state incorporation fees, are typically capitalized as either an intangible or other asset and written off over 5 years (in no case is the write-off period in excess of 40 years). Ownership of the corporation is represented by **common stock** (with dividend, preemptive, liquidation, and voting rights) and by **preferred stock** (with no voting rights, dividend preference, and asset preference at liquidation and sometimes with participative rights, call features, and provisions for conversion into common stock). Other classes of stock may be created with a hybrid of the typical rights for these major classes of stock. Rights of stockholders involve new accounting terms: a **preemptive right** means that existing common stockholders are given an opportunity to maintain their percentage of stock holdings by purchasing shares of each new stock issue; **cumulative preferred stock** means that any year for which dividends are not declared is accumulated with prior years until dividends are declared, at which time all dividends in arrears are paid prior to the payment of common stock dividends; and **participative preferred stock** shares in dividend distributions and their otherwise stated (fixed) return.

Par value represents legal capital per share of stock and is recorded separately from either paid-in capital in excess of par or a discount on capital stock (which arises for shares issued below par). **No-par stock** often has a stated value to provide a means of quantifying legal capital. Although stock can be sold by an underwriter, one means of selling stock directly to investors is on a subscription basis; this technique is particularly popular with smaller corporations. The means of stock payment may be either cash or noncash assets. If noncash assets are used, the fair market value that is more identifiable, either the stock's value or the noncash asset's value, is used for accounting purposes to record the transaction.

✓ Noncash assets are entered in the records of a partnership at their fair market value—the actual acquisition cost to the partnership—rather than at the book value of the asset to the contributing partner.

✓ If no provisions for the division of net income are described in the partnership agreement, profits and losses are divided equally.

✓ *Interest Allowance = Rate × Beginning, Ending, or Average Capital Balance*

✓ *(Σ Existing Capital Balances and Investment) × Percentage Interest of Partnership Being Purchased = Value of Share of Partnership*

Value of Share of Partnership − Price Paid by New Partner = Implied Bonus

Implied bonus goes either to existing partners (if price paid is greater than value of share) or to new partner (if value of share is greater than price paid).

✓ Order of liquidation process

Noncash assets are sold.
Creditors are paid.
Deficiencies of any of the partners are covered by solvent partners.
Remaining cash is distributed to the partners based on their capital balances.

✓ *Total Dividends Distributed*
 − *Dividends in Arrears to Cumulative Preferred Stockholders*
 − *Dividends to Preferred Stockholders*
 _____

Dividends to Common Stockholders

✓ *Legal Capital = Par Value × Number of Shares of Stock Outstanding*

✓ *Paid-in Capital in Excess of Par Value = Total Proceeds from Stock Issuance − Legal Capital*

✓ Issuance of stock for noncash assets or services is recorded at the fair market value of the stock or the noncash items, whichever is more clearly discernible.

Circle the letter corresponding to the best response.

1. In which of the following areas do transactions arise that are recorded in partnership accounting in a manner different from that used in sole proprietorships and corporations?
   a. income distribution
   b. owners' equity accounting
   c. asset accounting
   d. liquidation
   e. liability accounting
   f. all of the above
   g. a, b, c, and d only
   h. a, b, and d only

2. John James, a sole proprietor, invested $2,000 cash and $4,000 worth of furniture with a book value of $4,300 ($20,000 Cost − $15,700 Accumulated Depreciation), in a new partnership; this transaction would be recorded on the books of the partnership as follows:

	a.	Cash	2,000	
		Furniture	20,000	
		Accumulated Depreciation		15,700
		John James, Capital		6,300

	b.	Cash	2,000	
		Furniture	4,000	
		John James, Capital		6,000

	c.	Cash	2,000	
		Furniture	4,300	
		John James, Capital		6,300

	d.	Cash	2,000	
		Furniture	19,700	
		Accumulated Depreciation		15,700
		John James, Capital		6,000

3. When an earnings deficiency arises for a partnership, typically
   a. Salary and interest allowances are met to the extent possible.
   b. All salary and interest allowances are first met, then the total deficiency is shared by all partners.
   c. No salary and interest allowances are met; the deficiency is shared by the partners.
   d. Salary allowances are met, but interest allowances are not; the residual deficiency is then shared by all partners.

4. Tim Tendy, who has a capital balance of $180,000, agrees to sell 30% of his interest to Joe Tendy for $40,000. How is this transaction recorded on the partnership's books?

	a.	Cash	40,000	
		Loss on Transfer of Partnership Interest	14,000	
		Joe Tendy, Capital		54,000

	b.	Tim Tendy, Capital	40,000	
		Loss on Transfer of Partnership Interest	14,000	
		Joe Tendy, Capital		54,000

	c.	Tim Tendy, Capital	40,000	
		Joe Tendy, Capital		40,000

	d.	Tim Tendy, Capital	54,000	
		Joe Tendy, Capital		54,000

5. A corporation's organization costs are disclosed
   a. as an expense
   b. as an intangible asset
   c. as an "other asset"
   d. all of the above
   e. b or c only

MULTIPLE-CHOICE QUESTIONS (ANSWERS)

Answer	Explanation
1. h	Asset and liability accounting is identical; however, (a), (b), and (d) all represent areas in which transactions that are unique to partnerships arise.
2. b	Fair market value represents the actual acquisition cost to the partnership; the $300 implied loss is incurred by John James, not by the partnership.

3. b   The idea is to proportionately compensate for services and capital before sharing the effects of the partnership's operations.

4. d   The price paid for the partnership share is a personal matter between Tim Tendy and Joe Tendy; only the recorded capital balance need be transferred on the partnership's books.

5. e   Organization costs are disclosed on the balance sheet as either an intangible or an "other asset."

TRUE-FALSE QUESTIONS

Indicate whether each of the following statements is true (T) or false (F).

____ *1.* If a partnership becomes insolvent, the partners are required to furnish proportionate shares of their personal assets to settle the firm's obligations.

____ *2.* In a partnership, each partner acts as an agent of the partnership in business transactions.

____ *3.* A business operating as a partnership does not pay income taxes.

____ *4.* If no provisions for income distribution are stated in a partnership agreement, distribution is based on the proportionate capital balances of the partners.

____ *5.* Salary allowances for partners are considered to be business expenses of the partnership.

____ *6.* Interest paid on a partner's invested capital is a business expense of the partnership.

____ *7.* Most firms amortize organization costs over a minimum period of five years in accordance with existing income tax regulations.

____ *8.* Daily purchases and sales of shares by stockholders do not result in any journal entries for the corporation.

____ *9.* Paid-in capital in excess of par value is revenue for a corporation.

____ *10.* Common stock subscribed is a current asset on the balance sheet.

TRUE-FALSE QUESTIONS (ANSWERS)

Answer   *Explanation*

1. F   A partner must furnish as many personal assets as required to settle the partnership's obligations regardless of how much his other partners contribute. Wealthier partners are entitled to reimbursement by fellow partners in such a case; nonetheless, if partners have insufficient personal assets to proportionately bear responsibility, the wealthy partner must settle the entire partnership's debts.

2. T   The entire partnership is bound by any single partner's commitments and obligations that involve the partnership.

3. T   The partners pay income taxes, not the partnership, and such taxes are computed using each partner's personal tax rate.

4. F   If no provisions are stated, both net profits and losses are divided equally among the partners regardless of their relative capital balances.

5. F   Partners are not employees; they are owners. Hence, salary allowances represent income distributions, not expenses.

6. F   The interest paid on a partner's invested capital is merely another means of distributing net income to owners, it is not a business expense.

7. T　Organization costs tend to be relatively small, so this expedient amortization is typically deemed to be desirable.

8. T　The number of shares outstanding is unaffected and no cash is received by the corporation. Other than updating its list of stockholders, a corporation makes no record of such transactions.

9. F　Paid-in capital in excess of par value is simply additional invested capital; a corporation cannot earn revenues directly by dealing in its own stock.

10. F　It is a temporary paid-in capital account; subscriptions receivable is the related current asset account.

**CLASSIFI-
CATION AND
MATCHING
QUESTIONS**

A. Classify the following items using these symbols.

　　P = A distinctive feature typical of partnerships
　　C = A distinctive feature typical of corporations

____　　*1.* Limited liability
____　　*2.* Not a separate legal entity
____　　*3.* Mutual agency
____　　*4.* Ownership is easily transferable
____　　*5.* Perpetual existence
____　　*6.* Ease of formation
____　　*7.* Heavy regulation
____　　*8.* Is not a taxable entity
____　　*9.* Greatest ease of raising capital
____　　*10.* Double taxation
____　　*11.* Unlimited liability
____　　*12.* Limited life
____　　*13.* Co-ownership of property and income
____　　*14.* Greater operating flexibility

B. Match the following terms as being typically associated with common stock (C) or with preferred stock (P).

____　　*1.* Voting rights
____　　*2.* Cumulative
____　　*3.* Participative
____　　*4.* Preemptive right
____　　*5.* Dividends in arrears
____　　*6.* Proxy
____　　*7.* Callable
____　　*8.* Convertible

CLASSIFICATION AND MATCHING QUESTIONS (ANSWERS)

A.　*1.* C　*2.* P　*3.* P　*4.* C　*5.* C　*6.* P　*7.* C　*8.* P　*9.* C　*10.* C　*11.* P　*12.* P　*13.* P　*14.* P

B.　*1.* C　*2.* P　*3.* P　*4.* C　*5.* P　*6.* C　*7.* P　*8.* P

**QUESTIONS
CONCERNING
THE EFFECTS
OF TRANS-
ACTIONS**

Quantify the effect of each of the following transactions on the balance in stockholders' equity; provide both the direction of the change and the amount.

_____　　*1.* Issued 200 shares of common stock with par value $10, market value $40.

_____　　*2.* Investors subscribe 100 shares of stock at $10 par value, market value $40, by paying down $15 a share, agreeing to pay the remainder at a future date.

_____ **3.** Issued 30 shares of a closely held corporate stock with par value of $10 per share and estimated market value of $50 per share in exchange for a plot of land valued at $900.

_____ **4.** There are 1,000 shares of preferred stock outstanding; these shares are cumulative with a 15% rate and a $100 par value. At the date of dividend declaration, $12,000 of dividends were declared.

_____ **5.** Investors pay the $25 a share they owe on the 100 shares of stock previously subscribed [as explained in number (2) above].

QUESTIONS CONCERNING THE EFFECTS OF TRANSACTIONS (ANSWERS)

Answer

Explanation

1. + $8,000   Two Hundred Shares × $10, or $2,000, is recorded in the common stock account, with 200 × $30, or $6,000, recorded in paid-in capital in excess of par. The total credits are $8,000 in the stockholders' equity section.

2. + $4,000   One Hundred Shares × $40, or $4,000, is recorded as 100 × $10, or $1,000, common stock subscribed (a temporary paid-in capital account) and 100 × ($40 − $10), or $3,000, paid-in capital in excess of par value. Cash would be debited for $1,500 and subscriptions receivable (i.e., subscriptions receivable: common stock) would be debited for the balance of $2,500.

3. + $900   The rule is to use the fair market value that is most clearly discernible. Since closely held corporate stock is unlikely to have a verifiable market value, the $900 estimate of the land's value, rather than the $1,500 estimated market value of the stock, would be used. Common stock would be credited for par value of $300, and $600 would be recorded in the paid-in capital account in excess of par value.

4. − $12,000   Dividends are only liabilities and reductions of stockholders' equity upon declaration. The difference in the $15,000 expected dividend and the $12,000 declared, or $3,000, is dividends in arrears. While these $3,000 of dividends in arrears are disclosed in a footnote, they do not affect the account balances.

5. 0   Upon receipt, cash will be debited and subscriptions receivable will be credited. In addition, common stock subscribed will be debited, and common stock will be credited. Within the stockholders' equity section this amounts to a reclassification; there is no change in the total balance.

EXERCISES

1.

Capital, Jones		Drawing, Jones	
	14,000 1/1/84	3/31/84 2,000	
		4/30/84 5,000	
		8/31/84 3,000	

Salary allowance $3,000 per month
Interest allowance 10% on average capital balance
Profit sharing ratio 20%
Total 1984 profits of the partnership $90,000

Make the necessary journal entries at 12/31/84.

2. A partnership's books prior to liquidation appear as follows.

ASSETS

Cash	$ 90,000
Property, plant, & equipment	130,000
	$220,000

LIABILITIES AND OWNERS' EQUITY

Accounts payable	$ 20,000
Notes payable	140,000
Bowie, capital	29,000
Christopher, capital	32,000
Dally, capital	(1,000)
	$220,000

The property, plant, and equipment were sold for $85,000. The profit and loss sharing ratio is Bowie 25%, Christopher 60%, and Dally 15%. Make all the necessary journal entries to record the liquidation process.

EXERCISES (ANSWERS)

1. $3,000 × 12 = **$36,000 Salary Allowance**

Average capital balance

$$\$14,000 \times 3 \text{ months} = \$42,000$$
$$12,000 \times 1 \text{ month} = 12,000$$
$$7,000 \times 4 \text{ months} = 28,000$$
$$4,000 \times 4 \text{ months} = 16,000$$
$$12 \qquad\qquad \$98,000$$

$98,000 ÷ 12 = $8,167 × 0.10 = **$816.77 Interest Allowance**

Profit sharing: Assuming no other partners have either a salary allowance or an interest allowance.

$90,000 − $36,000 − $816.77 = $53,183.23 × 20% = **$10,636.65 Share of Profit**

12/31/84
    Income Summary   47,453.42
        Capital, Jones   47,453.42
        To record the division of income

$36,000 + $816.77 + **$10,636.65**

12/31/84
    Capital, Jones   10,000
        Drawing, Jones   10,000
        To close the Jones drawing account

2. Cash   85,000
    Bowie, Capital   11,250
    Christopher, Capital   27,000
    Dally, Capital   6,750
        Property, Plant, & Equipment   130,000
    To record the sale of noncash assets at a $45,000 ($130,000 − $85,000) loss, shared according to the profit and loss sharing ratio

Accounts Payable   20,000
Notes Payable   140,000
    Cash   160,000
To record payment of liabilities

Cash

90,000	
85,000	160,000
15,000	

Capital, Bowie		Capital, Christopher		Capital, Dally	
	29,000		32,000	1,000	
11,250		27,000		6,750	
	17,750		5,000	7,750	

Since cash available is less than the capital balances and one of the capital accounts has a deficiency, the liquidation process is recorded as follows.

Assuming Dally cannot pay the deficiency, charge Bowie and Christopher according to their profit and loss ratio, or 29% (25/25 + 60) for Bowie and 71% (60/25 + 60) for Christopher.

Capital, Bowie   2,247.50
Capital, Christopher   5,502.50
    Capital, Dally   7,750.00
To distribute Dally's capital deficiency and close Dally's capital account

At this point, Bowie's capital balance is $15,502.50 and Christopher's balance is a debit balance of $502.50. Assuming Christopher cannot pay the deficiency, it is charged to the only solvent partner who remains, and that is Bowie.

Capital, Bowie   502.50
    Capital, Christopher   502.50
To distribute Christopher's deficiency and close Christopher's balance

Finally, the $15,000 cash balance is distributed to Bowie.

Capital, Bowie   15,000
    Cash   15,000
To record cash distribution to partner

CHAPTER DEMON-STRATION PROBLEM

I. M. Frugal is considering an investment in something other than a savings account. He has gathered information concerning the return on an investment in a local partnership and an alternative investment in a small corporation. He has asked your assistance in evaluating what he would have earned in 1982 and in 1983, if he had invested in one of these enterprises.

Partnership

Number of Partners, 3
Simmonds: salary allowance, $15,000
Snow: interest allowance, 15%
Smith: salary allowance, $6,000; interest allowance, 15%

Total Distributions 1982

Simmonds: $69,000
Snow: $69,000
Smith: $72,000

Total Distributions 1983

Simmonds: $80,000
Snow: $83,000
Smith: $90,500

Capital balances are assumed to be stable.

Capital Balances 12/31/82

Simmonds: $10,000
Snow: $100,000
Smith: $80,000

Capital Balances 12/31/83

Simmonds: $9,000
Snow: $120,000
Smith: $130,000

Proposed Investment

1982: Purchase 25% at $60,000 for interest allowance and equal distribution of
    profits and losses
1983: Purchase 25% at $90,000 for interest allowance and equal distribution of
    profits and losses

Corporation

Capital Structure at 12/31/82 Includes the Following

Common stock ($10 par): $100,000
Preferred stock (12%, cumulative, $100 par, convertible into common stock on a 2 to 1
    basis): $200,000

1982

Preferred stock includes 1,500 shares newly issued during 1982.
Dividends declared: $7,000.
No dividends in arrears exist for prior years.
Stock prices: common $54; preferred $120.

1983

Issued 500 additional shares of common stock.
Converted 1,300 shares of preferred stock.
Dividends declared: $298,895.
Stock prices: common $95; preferred $130.

Proposed Investment

1982: Purchase 1,000 shares of newly issued preferred stock
1983: Purchase 200 shares of newly issued common stock

Assist I. M. Frugal in evaluating these proposed investments; also, provide the necessary journal entries on the books of the partnership and the corporation which would be required in the year of investment, had I. M. Frugal made each of the investments.

CHAPTER DEMONSTRATION PROBLEM (ANSWER)

Partnership 1982

$ 69,000
– 15,000 Simmonds Salary Allowance

$ 54,000 Simmonds Profit

$ 69,000
– 54,000 Equal Share of Profit

$ 15,000 Smith Interest Allowance ($100,000 × 15%)

$ 72,000
– 6,000 Smith Salary Allowance

$ 66,000
– 54,000 Equal Share of Profit

$ 12,000 Smith Interest Allowance ($80,000 × 15%)

$ 10,000 Simmonds
 100,000 Snow
  80,000 Smith
  60,000 Investment

$250,000

$250,000 × $\dfrac{1}{4}$ = $62,500 – $60,000 = $2,500 Bonus to New Partner

$54,000 × 3 = $162,000 Profit for General Distribution

$60,000 × 15% = $9,000 Interest Allowance
$162,000
– 9,000

$153,000
$153,000 ÷ 4 = 38,250 Equal Shares

I. M. Frugal would have received

$ 9,000 Interest Allowance
+ 38,250 Profit Share

$ 47,250

On an investment of $60,000, the return is

$\dfrac{\$47,250}{\$60,000}$ = 78.75%

Required journal entry for purchase of partnership interest

Cash	60,000.00	
Simmonds, Capital	833.33	
Snow, Capital	833.33	
Smith, Capital	833.34	
Frugal, Capital		62,500.00

Required journal entry for distribution of income

Income Summary	210,000	
Simmonds, Capital		53,250
Snow, Capital		53,250
Smith, Capital		56,250
Frugal, Capital		47,250

Partnership 1983

$ 80,000
− 15,000 Simmonds Salary Allowance

$ 65,000 Simmonds Profit

$ 83,000
− 65,000 Snow Equal Share of Profit

$ 18,000 Snow Interest Allowance ($120,000 × 15%)

$ 90,500
− 6,000 Smith Salary Allowance

$ 84,500
− 65,000 Equal Share of Profit

$ 19,500 Smith Interest Allowance ($130,000 × 15%)

$ 9,000 Simmonds
120,000 Snow
130,000 Smith
90,000 Investment

$349,000

$349,000 × $\frac{1}{4}$ = $87,250 − $90,000 = $2,750 Bonus to Existing Partners

$65,000 × 3 = $195,000 Profit for General Distribution

$90,000 × 15% = $13,500 Interest Allowance

$195,000
− 13,500

$181,500

$181,500 ÷ 4 = 45,375 Equal Shares

I. M. Frugal would have received

$ 13,500 Interest Allowance
+ 45,375 Profit Share

$ 58,875

On an investment of $90,000, the return is

$$\frac{\$58,875}{\$90,000} = 65.42\%$$

Required journal entry for purchase of partnership interest

Cash	90,000.00	
Simmonds, Capital		916.66
Snow, Capital		916.67
Smith, Capital		916.67
Frugal, Capital		87,250.00

Required journal entry for distribution of income

Income Summary	253,500	
Simmonds, Capital		60,375
Snow, Capital		63,375
Smith, Capital		70,875
Frugal, Capital		58,875

Corporation 1982

$200,000 **Preferred Stock**
$\times$ 0.12 **Dividends Stated Rate**

$ 24,000
− 7,000 **Total Dividends Declared**

$ 17,000 **Dividends in Arrears**

$$\frac{\$7,000}{\$200,000 \div \$100\ Par} \times 1,000\ Shares = \$3,500\ \textbf{Frugal's Dividends}$$

Purchase Price = $120 $\times$ 1,000 Shares = $120,000

Appreciation = $130 − $120 = $10 $\times$ 1,000 Shares = $10,000

Conversion Feature = 1,000 Shares $\times$ 2 = 2,000 Shares

2,000 **Shares**
$\times$ $41 ($95 − $54 Appreciation)

$82,000

Frugal would receive:

$ 3,500 **Dividends**
10,000 **Appreciation on Preferred Stock upon Sale**

$13,500

On an investment of $120,000, the return is

$$\frac{\$13,500}{\$120,000} = \underline{11.3\%}$$

However, if Frugal converted the preferred stock during 1983, no dividends would be received as a common stockholder, but appreciation of $82,000 would be realized. On an investment of $120,000, the return is

$$\frac{\$82,000}{\$120,000} = \underline{68.3\%}\ \textit{upon Sale}$$

Required journal entries

Cash	120,000	
Preferred Stock		100,000
Paid-in Capital in Excess of Par Value: Preferred Stock		20,000

Note: This represents a portion of the 1,500 shares issued.

Dividends	7,000	
Cash		7,000

Conversion of the stock would also be recorded, but the journal entry is beyond the scope of this chapter.

Corporation 1983

200 **Shares**
$\times$ $95

$19,000 **Investment**

$ 200,000 *Preferred Stock*
− 130,000
_____

70,000
×   0.12 *Dividends Stated Rate*
_____

8,400
+   17,000 *Dividends in Arrears*
−   11,050 *Dividends in Arrears on Converted Stock*
_____

14,350 *Preferred Stock Dividends*
− 298,895 *Total Dividends*
_____

$ 284,545 *Dividends Available for Common Stockholders*

Number of Stockholders = 10,000 + 500 *Additional Issue* + 2,600 *Conversions*
= 13,100

$284,545
÷ 13,100 *Stockholders*
_____

21.72
×   200 *Shares*
_____

$ 4,344 *Frugal's Dividends*

Note: No information is provided concerning the stock's 1983 to 1984 appreciation.

On an investment of $19,000 the return is

$$\frac{\$4,344}{\$19,000} = \underline{\underline{22.9\%}}$$

Required journal entries

Cash	19,000	
Common Stock		2,000
Paid-in Capital in Excess of Par Value: Common Stock		17,000

Note: This represents a portion of the 500 shares issued.

Dividends	298,895	
Cash		298,895

Conversion of the stock would have been recorded to yield the preferred stock dividend calculation in which only $70,000 of preferred stock was subject to current dividends and in which dividends in arrears were decreased by $11,050, which is the amount related to the converted shares of preferred stock.

After reviewing these calculations with Mr. Frugal, emphasize to him why he might have expected higher returns on the partnership investment: it carries higher risk in the form of unlimited liability. Also, explain the differential tax treatment of corporations and of partnerships and how it might affect the relative merits of the investments. For example, the 1982 corporate investment is likely to qualify for reduced capital gains tax treatment for the return from the appreciation of the converted stock, upon sale; whereas dividend income is taxed at the stockholder's personal tax rate. Of course, all of the income is subject to double taxation in the sense that corporations will have already incurred taxes of approximately 50% of their income, before distributing the remainder as taxable dividends. In contrast, the partnership pays no taxes and all income is taxed to the partners at their personal tax rates whether or not they withdraw the funds from their capital accounts.

14 CORPORATIONS: ADDITIONAL EQUITY ISSUES AND INCOME REPORTING

OBJECTIVES

After completing this chapter, you should:

1 *Be able to define treasury stock and record its acquisition and reissuance.*

2 *Understand how to account for donated capital.*

3 *Know how to prepare an income statement and statement of retained earnings in proper form, including the accounting treatment of discontinued operations, extraordinary items, intraperiod tax allocation, prior period adjustments, and appropriations.*

4 *Be able to compute the appropriate earnings per share (EPS) statistics for income statement presentation, including both primary and fully diluted EPS.*

5 *Understand the distinction between cash dividends, property dividends, stock dividends, and stock splits and how to account for each of these items.*

6 *Be able to explain the significance of the date of declaration, date of record, and date of payment.*

7 *Know how to compute book value per share for a corporation with more than one class of outstanding stock and how to interpret the statistic, once it is derived.*

A company has incentives to purchase its own stock for use in company retirement programs, for acquisitions of other companies, for investment purposes, and in order to lower costs related to dividend payments and annual report distribution to investors who own a small number of shares. Such shares are reported at cost in a treasury stock account, which is a contra-account to stockholders' equity, reducing temporarily the number of shares of stock outstanding. When reissued above cost, the excess of proceeds over original cost is placed in a paid-in capital from treasury stock account; when reissued below cost, the deficiency in proceeds is first charged against this paid-in capital from treasury stock balance and then, if necessary, is charged against retained earnings.

Donations from stockholders represent additional paid-in capital to the firm and are recorded in a separate donated capital account.

Whenever a company disposes of a segment of the business, the results of the discontinued operations are separately reported to permit the user to distinguish such revenue and related gains and losses from those earned from continuing operations. Similarly, extraordinary items, or events that are both unusual and infrequent, are separately reported on the income statement, following discontinued operations. In all cases, intraperiod tax allocation is applied and items that are listed below income from continuing operations on the income statement are presented net-of-tax.

Earnings per share (EPS) must be presented for the major categories of income that are reported on the face of the income statement; typically, this will include EPS from continuing operations, discontinued operations, extraordinary items, and net income. Both primary EPS and fully diluted EPS are presented for each category. **Primary EPS** computes earnings available to common stockholders per weighted-average common share outstanding, while **fully diluted EPS** stresses the effect of satisfying all existing dilutive commitments at the beginning of the accounting period by assuming that all convertible securities were converted, thereby increasing the number of common shares outstanding.

On the date of declaration, dividends become legal liabilities of a corporation; the date of record establishes to whom the dividends will be distributed on the date of payment. Stock is said to be selling **ex-dividend** after the date of record. Dividends when paid may be in the form of cash or noncash assets; in the latter case they are termed **property dividends**.

A **stock dividend** distributes additional shares of stock to existing stockholders in direct proportion to their existing ownership interest; the result is that each shareholder has more pieces of paper representing the same percentage of ownership interest in a company with the same net assets as reported prior to the stock dividend. On the books of the corporation, such a dividend simply reclassifies an amount of retained earnings that is equal to the market value of the shares being distributed as a stock dividend into the common stock and paid-in capital accounts. Hence, the amount of retained earnings that is available for future dividends is reduced, although total stockholders' equity remains the same. Stock dividends are said to be issued in order to provide a good news signal while conserving cash and to expand the ownership base by reducing the shares' market price. If the latter reason is primary, the stock dividend is likely to exceed 20 to 25% because a significant decline in the per-share market price is desired to attract more investors; accounting treatment for such large dividends is unique, requiring a debit to retained earnings at par or stated value and a credit to stock dividend distributable. A more direct means of achieving a reduced market price is the **stock split**. Essentially, a 2-for-1 stock split doubles the number of shares outstanding and halves both the par value and market value of the stock. Similarly, a 4-for-1 split quadruples the shares, cutting par value and market value to one-fourth. Stock splits require no formal journal entry; only a memorandum is recorded in the journal to document the new number of outstanding shares.

Prior period adjustments are made for accounting errors that were recorded in previous years; the beginning balance in retained earnings is charged, since the revenue or expense account involved in a prior period has already been closed out to the retained earnings account. Such adjustments do not appear on the income statement, but are reported on the statement of retained earnings.

As a means of informing financial statement users of that portion of retained earnings actually available for distribution, companies will set up appropriations or restrictions on retained earnings for planned expansion and replacement of property, plant, and equipment. These appropriations merely subclassify retained earnings as either unappropriated or appropriated.

Book value per share is commonly utilized by investors as a means of determining the stockholders' equity per share of stock. It can be computed for preferred stock: [(Call Value of Preferred Stock + Dividends in Arrears) ÷ Number of Outstanding Preferred Shares]; and for common stockholders: [(Stockholders' Equity − Sum of the Preferred Stockholders' Call Value and Dividends in Arrears) ÷ Number of Common Shares Outstanding]. Book value is frequently used in contracting among stockholders and with lenders; however, since it is based on historical costs, it is only coincidentally related to the market value of stock.

TECHNICAL POINTS

√ Treasury stock is recorded at cost.

√ Journal entry form for reissuing treasury stock

Cash	*XX*	
Paid-in Capital from Treasury Stock	*XX*	
or *Retained Earnings*	*XX*	
Paid-in Capital from Treasury Stock		*XX*
Treasury Stock		*XX*

Note: Paid-in capital is debited until the account reaches zero before retained earnings is debited for the amount that reissue price is below the cost of the treasury stock. The credit to paid-in capital results from reissue at a price above the cost of treasury stock.

√ Income statement format

> **Earnings from continuing operations**
> **Discontinued operations net-of-tax**
> ± **Earnings from operations**
> ± **Gain or loss from disposal**
> _____
> **Net earnings**
> ± **Extraordinary items net-of-tax**
> _____
> **Net income**

Earnings per share required disclosures

Primary

Income from continuing operations
Income from discontinued operations
Extraordinary items
Net income

Fully diluted

Income from continuing operations
Income from discontinued operations
Extraordinary items
Net income

√   *Price-Earnings (P/E) Ratio* $= \dfrac{\textit{Market Price of a Share of Common Stock}}{\textit{Annual Earnings per Share}}$

✓ *Weighted-Average Number of Shares Outstanding = Number of Common Shares Outstanding × Fraction of the Year the Shares Were in the Hands of Stockholders*

✓ *Primary Earnings per Share =* $\dfrac{Earnings\ Available\ to\ Common\ Stockholders}{Weighted\text{-}Average\ Common\ Shares\ Outstanding}$

where

Net Income − Dividends on Preferred Stock = Earnings Available to Common Stockholders

✓ *Fully Diluted Earnings per Share = (Earnings Available to Common Stockholders + Dividends on Converted Preferred Stock) ÷ [Weighted-Average Common Shares Outstanding + Number of Converted Shares, Assuming Conversion at the Beginning of the Period or on Date of Original Issue if Later]*

✓ *Pay-out Ratio =* $\dfrac{Dividends\ per\ Share}{Earnings\ per\ Share}$

✓ Stock dividends

If less than 20 to 25%

Dr Retained Earnings (Market Value × Number of Shares to Be Distributed)   XX
  Cr Common Stock (Par Value × Number of Shares to Be Distributed)   XX
  Cr Paid-in Capital in Excess of Par [(Market Value − Par Value) × Number of Shares to Be Distributed]   XX

If greater than 20 to 25%

Dr Retained Earnings (Par or Stated Value × Number of Shares to Be Distributed)   XX
  Cr Stock Dividend Distributable (Par or Stated Value × Number of Shares to Be Distributed)   XX

where

Number of Shares to Be Distributed = Dividend Percentage × Number of Shares of Stock Outstanding

✓ Stock splits

Increase number of shares outstanding
Reduce the par or stated value of the stock
Reduce the market value of the stock in direct proportion to the split

Note: Memorandum is required to note the stock split and the related number of shares that are issued and outstanding.

✓ *Prior Period Adjustment = Net-of-Tax Adjustment to the Retained Earnings Balance at the Beginning of the Year in Which the Correction of Prior Years' Accounting Errors Is Made*

✓ Retained earnings statement format

Retained earnings (prior year, as reported)
± Prior period adjustments

Retained earnings (restated)
+ Net income
− Cash dividends
− Stock dividends

Retained earnings (ending balance)

However, appropriated and unappropriated sections are common, and a combined income and retained earnings statement is acceptable.

$\checkmark$ **Book Value per Share** $= \dfrac{Total\ Assets\ -\ Total\ Liabilities}{Number\ of\ Shares\ of\ Stock\ Outstanding}$

where the following adjustments are made if there are more classes of stock outstanding than common stock:

Book Value per Share of Preferred Stock = (Redemption Value of Preferred Stock + Dividends in Arrears) ÷ Number of Shares of Preferred Stock Outstanding

Book Value per Share of Common Stock = (Stockholders' Equity − Redemption Value of Preferred Stock − Dividends in Arrears) ÷ Number of Shares of Common Stock Outstanding

MULTIPLE-CHOICE QUESTIONS

Circle the letter corresponding to the best response.

1. If We Buy Us, Incorporated, purchases 3,000 shares of its $1 par-value common stock with a $90 market value for $300,000, this transaction would commonly be recorded as follows:

    a.   Treasury Stock   270,000
           Cash   270,000

    b.   Treasury Stock   300,000
           Cash   300,000

    c.   Treasury Stock   270,000
           Loss on Overpayment of Stock   30,000
           Cash   300,000

    d.   Common Stock   3,000
           Paid-in Capital in Excess of Par Value   267,000
           Cash   270,000

    e.   Common Stock   3,000
           Paid-in Capital in Excess of Par Value   297,000
           Cash   300,000

    f.   none of the above

2. Fully diluted EPS
    a. adjusts primary EPS for converted stock
    b. adjusts primary EPS assuming that all dilutive securities were converted into common shares at the end of the accounting period
    c. adjusts primary EPS assuming that all dilutive securities were converted into common shares at the beginning of the accounting period
    d. adjusts primary EPS assuming securities were converted into common shares at the beginning of the accounting period (except for securities which were actually converted, in which case the date of actual conversion is used)

3. A stock dividend
    a. is merely a shifting or recapitalization of the stockholders' equity section
    b. increases stockholders' equity
    c. decreases stockholders' equity
    d. reduces the amount of retained earnings available for distributions
    e. a and d only
    f. c and d only

4. A 3-for-1 stock split
    a. triples the number of outstanding shares
    b. triples the market price of the stock
    c. reduces the number of outstanding shares by two-thirds
    d. reduces the market price of the stock to one-third of its pre-split value
    e. reduces the par value to one-third of the pre-split value
    f. a and b only

g. a, d, and e only

h. a and d only

5. Prior period adjustments

   a. are adjustments to the retained earnings balance at the beginning of the year

   b. are shown net-of-tax on the income statement

   c. are utilized to correct errors made in the current fiscal year

   d. none of the above

6. To record an appropriation for the replacement of equipment

   a. Dr Retained Earnings   XX

       Cr Retained Earnings Appropriated for Equipment Replacement   XX

   b. Dr Retained Earnings Appropriated for Equipment Replacement   XX

       Cr Retained Earnings   XX

   c. Dr Equipment   XX

       Cr Retained Earnings   XX

   d. Dr Equipment   XX

       Cr Retained Earnings Appropriated for Equipment Replacement   XX

   e. Dr Cash   XX

       Cr Retained Earnings Appropriated for Equipment Replacement   XX

MULTIPLE-CHOICE QUESTIONS (ANSWERS)

Answer   *Explanation*

1. b   The purchase of the 3,000 shares is recorded at cost. Companies may pay more than the market value of stock because they want to buy a particular stockholder's shares (perhaps to have more control over a future stockholder vote); however, no gain or loss is ever realized by buying one's own stock. Par value is irrelevant, and no adjustment is made to either common stock or paid-in capital in excess of par value when treasury stock is acquired.

2. c   The idea is to present the maximum possible dilution; hence, the first day of the period is assumed to be the day of conversion, regardless of the actual date on which conversion occurred or whether conversion has occurred.

3. e   Total stockholders' equity is the same before and after a stock dividend; however, the amount of retained earnings is reduced by the market value of the stock dividend and is transferred to the common stock and paid-in capital accounts.

4. g   A split multiplies the number of shares by the size of the split and divides both the market price and the par value of stock by the size of the split.

5. a   Prior period adjustments are shown net-of-tax on the statement of retained earnings, not on the income statement. They are required to correct errors made in prior periods, not the current periods.

6. a   Simply restrict a portion of retained earnings as unavailable for dividends due to plans to replace equipment. Appropriations do not involve cash; they simply reclassify previously unappropriated retained earnings.

TRUE-FALSE QUESTIONS

Indicate whether each of the following statements is true (T) or false (F).

_____   1. The purchase of treasury stock reduces the number of shares issued.

_____   2. Cash dividends declared by the board of directors on treasury shares are paid to the company and recorded in the treasury stock account.

_____ *3.* Treasury stock is an asset if the shares are purchased for investment purposes.

_____ *4.* Donated stock can be sold at any price, even below par or stated value, with no worry of creating a contingent liability.

_____ *5.* The results of discontinued operations must be disclosed net-of-tax in a separate category on the income statement immediately after income from continuing operations.

_____ *6.* The reason that certain dividends are called special or extra dividends is to inform stockholders that management has made no commitment to an increased dividend rate in the future.

_____ *7.* Stock dividend distributable is a liability.

_____ *8.* Large stock dividends (those in excess of 25%) are recorded by debiting retained earnings for the par or stated value of the dividend with a corresponding credit to stock dividend distributable.

_____ *9.* A stock split requires no formal journal entry.

_____ *10.* An appropriation reduces total retained earnings.

TRUE-FALSE QUESTIONS (ANSWERS)

Answer	Explanation
1. F	It reduces the number of shares outstanding but the number of shares issued is unaffected. Only if shares are retired are the number of shares issued reduced.
2. F	No cash dividends are paid on the treasury shares; since the stock is not outstanding, it is not entitled to dividends.
3. F	A corporation cannot own part of itself; it can only reduce others' holdings by debiting stockholders' equity. Treasury stock is never regarded as an asset.
4. T	This is the reason that contributed shares are considered to be more easily marketed than unissued shares.
5. T	Intraperiod tax allocation requires net-of-tax presentation, and the desire to distinguish operating activities from those that are being discontinued explains the requirement for separate presentation.
6. T	It typically reflects a good year of operations, and it is labeled to assist managers in maintaining an image of a stable dividend policy without having to retain a large percentage of earnings in an unusually good year.
7. F	Since neither cash nor other assets are used to settle this obligation, it is considered an addition to the common stock account and upon distribution is closed out to common stock.
8. T	This accounting treatment reflects the fact that large stock dividends are very similar to stock splits, but do not affect the par value or stated value of stock. Hence, this simple entry is required to increase the legal capital on the books.
9. T	Since no account balances are affected, only a memorandum is required in the journal; this memorandum should note that the stock split has been declared, as well as the new number of shares that are consequently issued and outstanding.
10. F	It restricts those earnings that are available for dividends but does not reduce total retained earnings. Essentially, an appropriation reclassifies part of the unrestricted retained earnings to inform the financial statements' readers of the purpose for which such earnings are retained.

**CLASSIFI-
CATION AND
MATCHING
QUESTIONS**

A. Classify the following items as being likely to be either an extraordinary item (E)
or something other than an extraordinary item (O).

——   *1.* Earthquake
——   *2.* Gain on disposal of a business segment
——   *3.* Financial effects of new regulation
——   *4.* Effects of a strike, including those against competitors and major suppliers
——   *5.* Flood
——   *6.* Write-down of an intangible asset
——   *7.* Hurricane
——   *8.* Write-off of receivables
——   *9.* Loss on abandonment of property, plant, and equipment
——   *10.* Seizure of assets by a foreign government

B. Match the following terms with their definitions. Each definition cannot be used
as a response for more than one term; however, some terms may be defined by
more than one response.

————   *1.* Date of record
————   *2.* Date of payment
————   *3.* Date of declaration

a. The date the dividend is distributed.
b. The date that the corporation becomes
legally liable for payment.
c. No journal entry is required on this date.
d. Date on which it's determined who will receive
the dividend.
e. The typical journal entry on this date is a debit
to retained earnings and a credit to dividends
payable.
f. Date when dividend is formally approved.
g. After this date, stocks are sold ex-dividend.
h. The typical journal entry on this date is a debit
to dividends payable and a credit to cash.

CLASSIFICATION AND MATCHING QUESTIONS (ANSWERS)

A.   *1.* E   *2.* O   *3.* E   *4.* O   *5.* E   *6.* O   *7.* E   *8.* O   *9.* O   *10.* E
B.   *1.* c, d, g   *2.* a, h   *3.* b, e, f

**QUESTIONS
CONCERNING
THE EFFECTS
OF TRANS-
ACTIONS**

Which of the following transactions increases (I), decreases (D), or has no effect (N)
on the following balances?

Retained Earnings	*Stockholders' Equity*	*Common Stock*	
——	——	——	*1.* A 10% stock dividend is declared.
——	——	——	*2.* Five thousand dollars of stock has been donated to the corporation.
——	——	——	*3.* Six thousand dollars of retained earnings has been appropriated.
——	——	——	*4.* Twenty shares of treasury stock are reissued above their original cost.
——	——	——	*5.* A 4-for-1 stock split has been declared.

QUESTIONS CONCERNING THE EFFECTS OF TRANSACTIONS (ANSWERS)

1. D N I
2. N I N
3. N N N
4. N I N
5. N N N

EXERCISES

1. We're Worth It, Inc., has 5,000 shares of $10 par-value common stock outstanding. The stock's market value is $20. On January 2, 1983, the corporation, for the first time in its existence, purchases 500 shares of its own stock for $9,500. On June 30, 1983, the corporation reissues 100 shares for $16 a share. On August 31, 1983, the corporation reissues 200 shares at $23 a share. On October 31, 1983, the corporation reissues 80 shares at $8 a share. Make all of the necessary journal entries in 1983 to record these transactions.

2. A company had 200,000 shares outstanding on January 2, 1984. On March 31, 1984, an additional 50,000 shares were issued, and on June 30, 1984, an additional 20,000 shares were issued. Compute the weighted-average shares outstanding.

EXERCISES (ANSWERS)

1. January 2, 1983

```
Treasury Stock    9,500
    Cash                    9,500
    To record cost of treasury stock
```

June 30, 1983

```
Cash              1,600
Retained Earnings   300
    Treasury Stock          1,900
    To record reissue of 100 shares costing $19 ($9,500 ÷ 500 Shares) for $16 per share
    (Since this is the first treasury stock transaction of the firm, no paid-in capital account
    from treasury stock exists; therefore, retained earnings is charged directly.)
```

August 31, 1983

```
Cash                              4,600
    Treasury Stock                       3,800
    Paid-in Capital from Treasury Stock    800
    To record reissue of 200 shares costing $19 at $23 a share
```

October 31, 1983

```
Cash                                640
Paid-in Capital from Treasury Stock  800
Retained Earnings                     80
    Treasury Stock                        1,520
    To record reissue of 80 shares costing $19 at $8 a share
```

2.

Outstanding Shares	Fraction of Outstanding	Weighted-Average
200,000	12/12	200,000
50,000	9/12	37,500
20,000	6/12	10,000
		247,500

We Help U Profit, Inc., has made the following information available.

WE HELP U PROFIT, INC.
Stockholders' Equity Section
12/31/83

Common stock ($10 par)	$ 900,000
Paid-in capital in excess of par value	2,500,000
Preferred stock ($100 par value, 10% cumulative, callable at $120, 1,000 shares authorized, 800 issued and outstanding, convertible 2 to 1 into common stock)	80,000
Paid-in capital in excess of par value	140,000
Retained earnings	1,000,000
Total stockholders' equity	$4,620,000

Transactions during 1984

Revenue totals $24 million.

Operating expenses total $18 million.

One segment of the business was disposed of at a gain of $12,000, taxed at a 40% tax rate, and had earnings from operations for the pre-disposal period of ($200,000), with an applicable tax rate of 40%.

Unusual hurricane damage of $400,000 has been incurred.

A $140,000 correction in the prior year's accounting records, increasing the accumulated depletion account, has been located and requires adjustment.

A 2-for-1 stock split is declared. Market price before the split was $80.

An investor donated $600 of land to the corporation.

Subsequent to the split, a 10% stock dividend was declared, at which time the stock price was $60 on June 30, 1984.

The company purchased 100 shares of its common stock for $4,200 on August 31, 1984.

Retained earnings of $300,000 has been earmarked for future plant expansion.

A $2 per share cash dividend has been declared on common; with full payment to preferred stockholders, including $5,000 of dividends in arrears.

Assuming a 40% tax rate applies to all transactions, prepare the required journal entries for the itemized transactions. Upon completion, prepare an income statement for 1984, the stockholders' equity section of a 12/31/84 balance sheet, and a statement of retained earnings for 1984. Also, compute the book value of We Help U Profit, Inc., shares as of 12/31/84.

Required journal entries

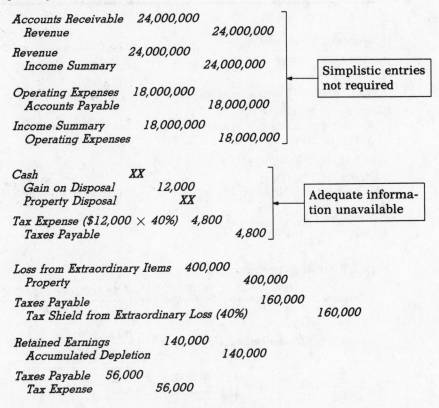

Accounts Receivable	24,000,000	
Revenue		24,000,000
Revenue	24,000,000	
Income Summary		24,000,000
Operating Expenses	18,000,000	
Accounts Payable		18,000,000
Income Summary	18,000,000	
Operating Expenses		18,000,000

Simplistic entries not required

Cash	XX	
Gain on Disposal		12,000
Property Disposal		XX
Tax Expense ($12,000 × 40%)	4,800	
Taxes Payable		4,800

Adequate information unavailable

Loss from Extraordinary Items	400,000	
Property		400,000
Taxes Payable	160,000	
Tax Shield from Extraordinary Loss (40%)		160,000
Retained Earnings	140,000	
Accumulated Depletion		140,000
Taxes Payable	56,000	
Tax Expense		56,000

Note: There is a 40% tax shield from increased expenses attributable to prior year.

Memorandum entry

$$2 \times \frac{\$900,000}{\$10 \ Par} = 180,000 \ Shares \ Outstanding$$

$$Par \ Value = \frac{\$10}{2} = \$5 \ Par$$

Note: Market value is expected to be $80/2 = $40.

Land	600	
Donated Capital		600
Retained Earnings	1,080,000	
Common Stock ($5 Par × 18,000 Shares)		90,000
Paid-in Capital in Excess of Par Value		990,000
Treasury Stock	4,200	
Cash		4,200
Retained Earnings, Unappropriated	300,000	
Reserve for Future Plant Expansion		300,000
Dividends	372,800	
Dividends Payable: Preferred Stock		13,000
Dividends Payable: Common Stock		359,800
(180,000 − 100 Treasury Shares × $2)		

WE HELP U PROFIT, INC.
Income Statement
For the Year Ended 12/31/84

Revenues	$24,000,000
Less operating expenses	18,000,000
Earnings before taxes	$ 6,000,000
Taxes @ 40%	2,400,000
Earnings from continuing operations	$ 3,600,000
Discontinued operations	
Earnings from operations net-of-tax ($200,000 loss shielding $80,000 of taxes)	($ 120,000)
Gain from disposal, net-of-taxes of $4,800	7,200
Loss from discontinued operations	($ 112,800)
Net earnings	$ 3,487,200
Loss from extraordinary item less tax savings of $400,000 × 40%, or $160,000	(240,000)
Net income	$ 3,247,200

Primary earnings per share

$$\text{Income from Continuing Operations} = \left(\frac{\$3,600,000 - \$13,000}{\$188,967} \right) = \$18.98$$

$$\text{Loss from Discontinued Operations} = \left[\frac{(\$112,800)}{\$188,967} \right] = (\$0.60)$$

$$\text{Extraordinary Loss} = \left[\frac{(\$240,000)}{\$188,967} \right] = \underline{(\$1.27)}$$

$$\text{Net Income} = \$18.98 + (\$0.60) + (\$1.27) = \underline{\$17.11}$$

Fully diluted earnings per share

$$\text{Income from Continuing Operations} = \left(\frac{\$3,600,00}{\$188,967 + (\$4 \times 800)} \right) = \$18.73$$

$$\text{Loss from Discontinued Operations} = \left[\frac{(\$112,800)}{\$192,167} \right] = (\$0.59)^*$$

$$\text{Extraordinary Loss} = \left[\frac{(\$240,000)}{\$192,167} \right] = \underline{(\$1.25)}^*$$

$$\text{Net Income} = \$18.73 + (\$0.59) + (\$1.25) = \underline{\$16.91}$$

*As you will learn in advanced accounting courses, these calculations have an antidilutive effect upon EPS and would not be reported in this manner; however, such details are beyond the scope of this chapter.

where

Numerator for primary EPS is adjusted for 13,000 preferred stock dividends: $5,000 Dividends in Arrears + ($80,000 × 10%).

Denominator for primary EPS is adjusted for weighted-average number of shares: ($180,000 Stock Split × 12/12) + ($18,000 Stock Dividend × 6/12) − ($100 Treasury Stock × 4/12).

Numerator for fully diluted EPS ignores preferred stock dividends since conversion is assumed.

Denominator for fully diluted EPS adds the converted preferred stock, adjusted for the 2-for-1 stock split.

WE HELP U PROFIT, INC.
Stockholders' Equity Section
12/31/84

Preferred stock ($100 par value, 10% cumulative, callable at $120, 1,000 shares authorized, 800 issued and outstanding, convertible 4 to 1 into common)	$ 80,000
Common stock ($5 par value, 198,000 shares authorized* and issued, 197,900 shares outstanding)	990,000
Paid-in capital in excess of par value: Preferred	140,000
Paid-in capital in excess of par value: Common	3,490,000
Donated capital	600
Retained earnings	
Appropriated: Reserve for future plant expansion	300,000
Unappropriated	2,410,400
Less treasury stock	(4,200)
Total stockholders' equity	$7,406,800

*It is assumed that 198,000 is the total number of authorized shares of common stock.

WE HELP U PROFIT, INC.
Statement of Retained Earnings
For the Year Ended 12/31/84

Retained earnings, 12/31/83	$1,000,000
Less: Correction of prior year ($140,000 − $56,000)	84,000
Retained earnings (restated), 12/31/83	$ 916,000
Add: Net income	3,247,200
	$4,163,200
Less: Cash dividends on preferred stock	13,000
Less: Cash dividends on common stock	359,800
Less: Stock dividends on common stock	1,080,000
Retained earnings, 12/31/84	
Appropriated for future plant expansion	300,000
Unappropriated	2,410,400
Total retained earnings, 12/31/84	$2,710,400

Book value as of 12/31/84

Common stock

$$\frac{\$7,406,800 \;\textbf{Stockholders' Equity} - \;96,000}{}$$

$$\frac{7,310,800}{\div \;188,967}$$

$ **38.69** **Book Value per Share of Common Stock**

Preferred stock

Call Value = 800 Shares × $120 = $96,000

Dividends in arrears (none as of 12/31/84)

$$\frac{\$96,000 + \$0}{800 \;\textbf{Shares}} = \$120 \;\textbf{Book Value per Share of Preferred Stock}$$

ACROSS

1. _1 across_ _105 across_ are frequently provided in partnership agreements as a basis for income distribution and recognize differences among partners in terms of time devoted to the enterprise.

2. When stock is issued at a price above par, the difference between the issue price and par value is often called a _2 across_ _18 across_ _88 down_ _64 across_.

4. The _4 across_ _42 down_ is computed by dividing dividends per share by earnings per share.

6. Most distributions of income to stockholders are in the form of _6 across_ _106 across_.

10. The _45 across_ _48 down_ _28 across_ _10 across_ _13 across_ is recorded based on the partners' capital balances, because the price paid by one partner to another is a personal matter among the parties involved.

11. Some preferred stock is _____ into common stock at the option of the stockholder.

13. See 10 across.

15. The process of terminating a partnership and discontinuing operations is termed _____.

17. _17 across_ _64 across_ represents an ownership interest that controls corporate management by its voting rights.

18. See 2 across.

19. The _19 across_ _48 down_ _70 down_ is when the dividend is formally approved and the corporation becomes legally liable for payment.

23. A partnership agreement is commonly referred to as the _23 across_ _65 across_ _55 across_ and details the rights, responsibilities, and duties of the partners.

25. If a partnership incurs a net loss, an _25 across_ _32 across_ arises.

28. See 10 across.

29. Same as 4 across.

31. A _47 across_ _85 across_ _31 across_ is required to correct an error that affects the net income of a previous period.

32. See 25 across.

33. _53 across_ _33 across_ is the term used to describe the taxing of income to the corporation and the subsequent taxing of dividends to the stockholder.

34. A _12 down_ _101 across_ _59 down_ _71 across_ _49 across_ _34 across_ _26 down_ will be paid either to attract a partner who possesses unique skills or significant capital or to compensate present partners for the value of past earnings records.

35. The owners of a corporation are termed its _____.

37. The _37 across_ - _25 across_ _36 down_ is a popular measure of the relationship between market price and earnings per share.

39. _____ preferred stock entitles preferred stockholders to extra dividends beyond the usual fixed return—typically an equal distribution to preferred and common stockholders.

43. Stock _____ are a means of selling stock directly to investors rather than using the services of an underwriter.

45. See 10 across.

46. _46 across_ _105 across_ are often provided to the "silent" partner as a basis for income distribution.

47. See 31 across.

49. See 34 across.

50. Market _____ quantify the cost of buying and selling shares of stock.

53. See 33 across.

55. See 23 across and 61 across.

59. _106 across_ _104 down_ _59 across_ are rights to preferred dividends which are omitted in a given year on _11 down_ preferred stock.

60. _90 across_ _60 across_ exists because of the partnership not being a legal entity and is considered to be a strong disadvantage of the partnership form of organization.

61. An _61 across_ _103 down_ _105 down_ _55 across_ will increase the assets of the partnership by the negotiated percentage of total capital in the new entity.

62. The _95 down_ _65 across_ _62 across_ is when the dividend will be distributed to the stockholders.

64. See 2 across and 17 across.

65. See 23 across and 62 across.

66. _66 across_ _78 down_ _76 across_ means that the issuer retains the rights to recall the stock at a preset price.

69. Partnerships have _69 across_ _5 down_; that is, each partner acts as an agent of the partnership in business transactions.

71. See 34 across.

72. _72 across_ _79 down_ _25 across_ _62 down_ _1 down_ (_3 down_ .) is based on the assumption that all dilutive securities were converted into common shares at the beginning of the accounting period.

74. _102 across_ _74 across_ are one-time state incorporation fees and legal expenses which are disclosed on a balance sheet as either an intangible asset or an "other asset."

75. _____ items must be unusual in nature and occur infrequently.

76. A _76 across_ _19 down_ is a distribution of additional shares of a corporation's own stock in proportion to each stockholder's present ownership in the firm.

81. The _81 across_ - _103 down_ _88 down_ account records the difference in issue price and par value.

84. A _9 down_ _84 across_ is often considered to be a disadvantage of a partnership, as the partnership is dissolved upon a partner's death.

85. See 31 across.

86. A _44 down_ - _96 across_ _86 across_ is a business in which stock is owned by only a few persons.

89. If allowance for salary and interest do not _____ within the net income (i.e., are not, in combination, less than net income), an earnings deficiency results.

90. See 60 across.

91. A corporation is created by obtaining a _____ from one of the states.

92. The ___39 down___ ___92 across___ gives existing stockholders the opportunity to maintain their respective interests in a corporation by acquiring additional shares on a pro rata basis.

93. ___93 across___ ___21 down___ stock has a fixed amount per share printed on the face of the stock certificate, representing the legal capital per share of stock.

94. A stock sold between the record date and the date of distribution is sold ___94 across___ - ___19 down___.

96. See 86 across and 37 down.

97. A _____ is defined as a component of a company whose activities represent a major line of business or class of customer.

99. ___57 down___ ___63 down___ ___99 across___ recognizes that various factors contribute to a corporation's tax bill.

101. See 34 across.

102. See 74 across.

105. See 1 across and 46 across.

106. See 6 across and 59 across.

DOWN

1. ___40 down___ ___27 down___ ___62 down___ ___1 down___ ignores the dilutive effect of convertible securities, providing a summary statistic of financial performance.

3. See 72 across.

5. See 69 across.

7. A debit balance in a partner's capital account is commonly referred to as a ___88 down___ ___7 down___.

8. The ___95 down___ ___48 down___ ___8 down___ determines who will receive the dividend payment.

9. See 84 across.

11. See 59 across.

12. See 34 across.

14. A debit (negative) balance can arise in retained earnings and is referred to as a _____.

16. ___100 down___ - ___87 down___ ___16 down___ stated value stock do not have a fixed amount per share printed on the face of the stock certificate.

19. See 76 across and 94 across.

20. A _____ is an association of two or more persons to carry on, as co-owners, a business for profit.

21. See 93 across.

22. A ___76 across___ ___22 down___ is a way of reducing the market price of common stock outstanding.

23. An _____ is the transfer of some of the retained earnings balance into a separate account for such items as plant expansion.

24. Shares held by stockholders are known as _____ shares.

26. See 34 across.

27. See 1 down.

30. Same as 18 across.

36. See 37 across.

37. A ___37 down___ - ___96 across___ ___86 across___ must follow the financial reporting regulations of the Securities and Exchange Commission.

38. ___38 down___ ___77 down___ are those segments of a business sold, abandoned, or otherwise disposed of.

39. See 92 across.

40. See 1 down.

41. ___41 down___ ___76 across___ appeals to investors who want a safe investment with a steady dividend.

42. See 4 across.

44. See 86 across.

47. The sale of stock is typically made on the basis of a _____, a document required by the SEC which contains information on the corporation's products, management, and financial affairs.

48. See 10 across, 19 across, and 8 down.

51. Same as 92 across.

52. Same as 37 across.

54. The significance of par value is that it represents ___54 down___ ___74 down___ per share of stock.

56. ___56 down___ ___76 across___ refers to shares of a corporation that are reacquired by the corporation for reissuance at a later date.

57. See 99 across.

58. Same as 99 across.

59. See 34 across.

62. See 72 across and 1 down.

63. See 99 across.

67. The number of shares allowed by the charter is termed the ___67 down___ ___76 across___.

68. Same as 60 across.

70. See 19 across.

73. The investment banker, often referred to as an _____, has the responsibility of selling the stock at a set price to the public.

74. See 54 down.

77. See 38 down.

78. See 66 across.

79. See 72 across.

80. Same as 47 across.

82. Stockholders that ___82 down___ ___88 down___ essentially contribute shares or other assets to the corporation, thereby increasing stockholders' equity by the value received for the shares or assets.

83. ___83 down___ ___25 across___ represent the portion of owners' equity that has been generated by profitable operations.

87. See 16 down.

88. See 2 across, 81 across, 7 down, and 82 down.

95. See 8 down and 62 across.

98. __.__.__. represents a summarization of all items affecting profitability; such data are widely disseminated in the financial press and must be disclosed on the face of the income statement.

100. See 16 down.

101. Same as 101 across.

103. See 61 across and 81 across.

104. See 59 across.

105. See 61 across.

15 *LONG-TERM LIABILITIES*

After completing this chapter, you should:

1 *Be able to describe how a bond issue is typically handled and what the role of the trustee is; you should also be able to describe the bond indenture agreement, a sinking fund, and serial bonds and how debt financing can be compared to stock financing.*

2 *Understand the difference between secured, debenture (unsecured), and subordinated debt.*

3 *Be able to explain how interest on bonds is typically disbursed by corporations.*

4 *Know the rationale for issuing convertible and callable bonds as well as the accounting treatment for the conversion and for the refunding or the retirement of bonds.*

5 *Understand how to account for bonds that are issued between interest dates at a premium, a discount, or at face value, as well as the reason for differences in the issue price and the face value of bonds.*

6 *Be able to amortize bond discounts and premiums utilizing both straight-line and the effective-interest methods of amortization.*

7 *Be aware of how mortgages are typically paid.*

8 *Know the basic differences between operating and capital leases and their accounting treatment.*

9 *Understand the concept of present value and how to calculate the issue price of a bond (assuming, you have read the Appendix to Chapter 15 of Accounting Principles).*

Issuing **debt** is an alternative to stock financing which avoids diluting the ownership of a company and results in tax-deductible interest expense. Bonds facilitate the spreading of a large dollar amount of debt with various maturity dates (serial bonds) over a number of individuals and are commonly issued through underwriters. A trustee is appointed to protect the bondholders' interests by assuring compliance with the terms of the bond indenture agreement, which often includes the maintenance of a sinking fund for repayment of the debt. Types of bonds include secured debt such as mortgage bonds secured by property, debenture bonds with no pledged security, and subordinated debentures which rank behind unsecured debt; these bonds will frequently have convertible and call provisions. Bonds represent more risk to a company during hard times, as the fixed interest obligations must be met regardless of how well the business performs financially; such interest is paid either directly by the company (for registered bonds) or indirectly by big banks on behalf of the company upon presentation of coupons.

Since a bond issuance to the public typically requires approval by the Securities and Exchange Commission, an interest rate that is printed on the debt instrument will often differ from the going market rate for similar bonds on the date of issuance. As a consequence, either no one will buy the new issue because its stated rate is too low or the company would be acting irrationally and paying more than it had to for debt, given the stated rate is higher than the market rate. The solution is not to reprint the bonds (possibly "missing" the market rate again and incurring higher costs of issuance); the solution is to adjust the *issue price* of the bond in order to reflect the interest differential in the market rate and the rate that will be paid (which is always the rate that is printed on the bond) while the issue is outstanding. The bond is issued at a **discount** if the coupon rate (also known as the contract interest or stated rate) is *lower* than the market rate (also known as the yield or effective rate); it is issued at a **premium** if the coupon rate is *higher* than the market rate. The recorded discount (a contra-liability) or premium (liability) is separated from the bond payable account, which records the face value of the bond (its principal), and is amortized until it reaches a balance of zero on the maturity date. Amortization is either by the straight-line method, dividing the total discount or premium by the term of the bond, and annually charging that amount to interest expense or by the effective interest method, multiplying the market rate of interest by the carrying value of the bond (either bond payable minus the discount or bond payable plus the premium) and amortizing the difference between this amount and the interest paid each period. A bond is said to be issued at par if it is issued at face value.

If bonds are issued between interest dates, the purchaser buys the accumulated interest, as the full period's interest will be received on the next interest payment date. If an issuer believes that lower cost debt is available or that more flexibility in operations would be obtained by retiring debt, the call feature can be exercised and the bond can be refunded or retired. The difference in the bond's carrying value and call price is an extraordinary gain or loss on the income statement.

Other types of long-term obligations include mortgage notes, for which collateral is pledged and repayment is typically made in installments which include principal and interest, and capital leases. While an operating lease is a short-term rental of an asset, a capital lease is in substance an installment purchase plan which is to be recorded as an asset and a long-term liability on the books of the lessee.

The concepts of present value are important in the determination of the issue price for bonds. Essentially, the **present value** of money recognizes that the earlier money is received, the earlier it can be reinvested and the shorter the period of uncertainty over which there exists a risk of nonpayment. Hence, money received earlier in time is worth more than the same sum of money received at a later date. The present value concept is reflected in the computation of a bond's issue price. A bond promises the repayment at maturity of the principal and the periodic payment of interest over the life of the obligation. The present value of these two amounts are computed by multiplying the future dollar amounts to be received by a present value factor that discounts each amount according to how much time will pass before the payment is received and according to the desired return on the obligation by investors. The sum of the present value of the principal and the interest payments is the issue price of the bond.

TECHNICAL POINTS

✓ *Interest Paid = Face Value × Coupon Rate*[*]

[*]*The coupon rate is the contract interest rate.*

✓ *Purchase Price for Bond Issued between Interest Dates = Issue Price + Accumulated Interest from Last Interest Payment Date*

✓   *Bonds Payable*
$\left[\text{or} \begin{array}{l} + \textit{Premium on Bonds Payable} \\ - \textit{Discount on Bonds Payable} \end{array} \right]$
Carrying Value of Bond

✓ *Straight-line Amortization =* $\dfrac{\textit{Discount or Premium}}{\textit{Term of Bond}}$

✓ *Effective-Interest Amortization = Effective Interest Rate × Carrying Value of Bond*

✓ *Extraordinary Gain or Loss on Refunding or Retirement = Carrying Value of Bond − Call Price*

✓ *Paid-in Capital in Excess of Par Value for Converted Bonds Payable = Carrying Value of Bond − Par Value of Shares into Which Bond is Converted*

✓ *Mortgage Payment = Interest Charge + Principal Payment*

Technical Points from the Appendix

✓ *Compound Interest = Principal × (1 + r)^n*

where r = interest rate
     n = number of periods

✓ *Present Value = Future Amount ×* $\dfrac{1}{(1 + r)^n}$

where r = interest rate
     n = number of periods

✓ *Issue Price of Bond = Present Value of Principal + Present Value of Interest*

where the present value of the principal is calculated by multiplying the principal dollar amount by the present value factor for the term of the bond at the effective rate of interest

and   the present value of interest is calculated by discounting each interest payment by the present value factor at the effective rate of interest for the period of time that will elapse between the bond issuance and the particular interest payment date and then adding these discounted values.

When the interest payment period is less than one year, treat the subperiod as equivalent to one period of time and divide the interest rate by the number of subperiods in a year as a means of adapting a present value table to the interest-payment basis of the bond issue. For example, if payment is made 4 times a year for 5 years at an effective interest rate of 20%, the number of periods before maturity is 20 (4 × 5) and the applicable rate is 5% (20% ÷ 4).

MULTIPLE-CHOICE QUESTIONS

Circle the letter corresponding to the best response.

1. A trustee
   a. is usually appointed by the issuing firm
   b. plays the role of a third party to monitor the issuer's adherence to stipulated terms of the bonds

      c. can initiate foreclosure of any property that is pledged as collateral on the bond issue

      d. all of the above

      e. b and c only

2. Bondholders

      a. are paid interest only if earnings are sufficient to do so

      b. have a residual claim on business assets

      c. are repaid in periodic installments over a number of years when they purchase serial bonds

      d. all of the above

      e. a and b only

      f. a and c only

      g. b and c only

3. Which of the following would not be considered to be a secured debt?

      a. mortgage bond

      b. debenture bond

      c. collateral-trust bond

      d. none of the above

4. Coupon bonds

      a. are handled the same as registered bonds

      b. eliminate the need for the issuing company to maintain an up-to-date list of bond owners

      c. have small detachable coupons that can be deposited at a bank for collection

      d. have small detachable coupons that are typically mailed to the issuing corporation for collection

      e. b and c only

      f. b and d only

5. The amount an investor is willing to pay for a bond is determined by

      a. the cash flows connected with the bond issue

      b. the timing of the cash inflows

      c. the rate of return acceptable to the investor

      d. all of the above

      e. a and b only

      f. a and c only

6. The advantages of leasing include

      a. Leasing is usually less expensive than purchasing.

      b. Lease payments are 100% tax deductible in the year they are paid.

      c. Usually no down payment is necessary.

      d. The risk of obsolescence rests with the lessor.

      e. All of the above.

      f. a, b, and d only.

      g. b, c, and d only.

MULTIPLE-CHOICE QUESTIONS (ANSWERS)

Answer   *Explanation*

1. d   The issuer does typically appoint the trustee, and that trustee is empowered to take whatever action deemed necessary to protect the bondholders' interests.

2. c   Bondholders are to receive interest regardless of the company's level of income (i.e., prior years' income may have to be used for payment). Bondholders have a prior claim on assets in the event of bankruptcy, whereas stockholders have a residual claim.

3. b   Responses *(a)* and *(c)* are examples of secured debt, whereas debenture bonds are defined as bonds with no assets pledged as security; their marketability is based on the issuing company's general credit.

4. e   The coupon bonds are intended to shift the responsibility for collection to the bondholder and the bank; hence, the coupons are not typically mailed to the issuing corporation for collection. The role of the bank eliminates the need for notifying an issuing company that a bond has been sold; as required for registered bonds.

5. d   These are the three determinants of the issue price for a bond.

6. g   Leasing is usually more expensive than purchasing.

TRUE-FALSE QUESTIONS

Indicate whether each of the following statements is true (T) or false (F).

_____ *1.* Bonds payable should be reclassified as a current liability one year prior to the maturity date.

_____ *2.* No gain or loss can result from converting a bond payable to common stock.

_____ *3.* If a sinking fund earns more income than required to pay the bondholders the amount that is due, the excess is shared by the bondholders, according to their relative debt holdings.

_____ *4.* The issuance of debt instead of stock decreases earnings per share.

_____ *5.* When registered bonds are sold, the issuing company must be notified so that interest can be paid to the proper owner.

_____ *6.* The periodic interest payments made on a bond that is issued at a discount will be greater than the periodic interest payments made on that same bond if it is issued at a premium.

_____ *7.* Capital leases provide off-the-balance-sheet financing.

_____ *8.* Under an operating lease, the lessee signs a short-term lease agreement and treats the amounts paid under the agreement as expense.

TRUE-FALSE QUESTIONS (ANSWERS)

Answer   *Explanation*

1. F   This is true only if the bonds are to be retired with current assets. A common exception to such a reclassification is the retirement of bonds through the use of a sinking fund, which is a noncurrent asset.

2. T   This is not an earnings activity; it is merely an exchange of debt for stock, altering the company's capital structure.

3. F   Any excess cash is returned by the trustee to the contributing company, not to the bondholders.

4. F   It can increase earnings per share if the interest costs net-of-tax are less than the dilutive effect of issuing more shares of common stock.

5. T   This is necessary because the disbursing company mails interest checks to the bond's registered owner.

6. F   Periodic interest payments remain constant, at the contract interest rate, regardless of whether a bond is issued at a premium, a discount, or at face value.

7. F   The Financial Accounting Standards Board requires that both the assets leased under a capital lease agreement and the liability to the lessor be disclosed on the balance sheet.

8. T   This is the proper accounting treatment for an operating lease agreement.

CLASSIFI-CATION AND MATCHING QUESTIONS

Classify the following items using these symbols. More than one symbol may be appropriate for some of the items.

P = Premium bond
D = Discount bond
F = Bond issued at face value (par)

____ *1.* Is issued whenever the market rate exceeds the contract interest rate.
____ *2.* Its carrying value increases over the term of the bond.
____ *3.* Its interest expense is constant over the term of the bond.
____ *4.* Its interest payments are constant over the term of the bond.
____ *5.* Amortization charges to interest increase over the term of the bond.

CLASSIFICATION AND MATCHING QUESTIONS (ANSWERS)

1. D   *2.* D   *3.* F   *4.* P, D, F   *5.* P

QUESTIONS CONCERNING THE EFFECTS OF TRANS-ACTIONS

Indicate whether the following transactions will result, over time, in an increase in net income (I), a decrease in net income (D), or in no effect upon net income (N).

____ *1.* Financing by debt instead of stock.

____ *2.* Issuing debt with a call provision rather than debt with no such provision.

____ *3.* Issuing debt with conversion rights rather than debt with no such rights.

____ *4.* Issuing collateral-trust bonds instead of subordinated debentures.

____ *5.* Issuing a bond at a discount rather than at par value.

____ *6.* Issuing a bond between interest dates rather than on an interest payment date.

____ *7.* Using straight-line amortization instead of the effective-interest method for a bond issued at a discount: give the effect on income in the first year the debt is outstanding.

____ *8.* The effect of a newly issued mortgage note on the first year's net income relative to its effect on the second year's net income (i.e., the second year in which the mortgage note is outstanding).

QUESTIONS CONCERNING THE EFFECTS OF TRANSACTIONS (ANSWERS)

Answer	Explanation
1. D	Total dollars of income will decline due to interest expense; for stock financing, dividends do not reduce, they distribute net income. Note, however, that earnings per share may go in either direction as a result of selecting debt financing.
2. D	The corporation must compensate creditors for the right of the corporation to call the bond; therefore, interest expense will be greater and income will be lower.
3. I	The creditors will give up some interest income for the right to convert the bond into stock, and this results in higher income for the corporation.
4. I	The creditors will assume less risk when purchasing secured debt than assumed when purchasing subordinated debt and can be expected to demand lower interest income, thereby increasing the net income of the issuer.

5. D   Issuing a bond at a discount implies that interest expense will be greater than stated on the certificate.

6. N   Total interest expense will be the same. Bonds issued between interest dates only differ in issue price due to the concurrent purchase of accrued interest which is returned to the purchaser on the next interest payment date; this is done for administrative convenience and does not affect the income of the issuer.

7. D   In the first year, the effective-interest method reflects the lower carrying value of the bond relative to later years, whereas the straight-line method spreads the discount evenly across time.

8. D   The first year will have a larger proportion of the mortgage allocated to interest due to the higher unpaid note balance in the first year relative to the second year.

EXERCISES

1. A company wishes to compare the financing alternatives of debt and stock. Currently, its earnings before interest and taxes are $500,000, its financing needs are $1,200,000, and its options are to
 a. Issue 60,000 additional shares of common stock with a par value of $1 and a market value of $20 per share
 b. Issue 15%, 10-year bonds
Currently the company is in a 35% tax bracket and has 100,000 shares of common stock outstanding. Compare the financing alternatives in the first year and advise the company as to the preferable means of financing.

2. A $60,000, 10%, 5-year bond is issued on January 1, 1983, at 103. Its interest is paid annually on January 1. The company utilizes straight-line amortization. Record all related journal entries for 1983 and 1984, assuming the company has a 12/31 year-end.

EXERCISES (ANSWERS)

1.

	Issue 60,000 Shares of Common Stock	*Issue 15%, 10-Year Bonds*
Total financing needed	$1,200,000	$1,200,000
Earnings before interest and taxes	$ 500,000	$ 500,000
Less: Bond interest ($1,200,000 × 0.15)	—	180,000
Earnings before income taxes	$ 500,000	$ 320,000
Less: Income taxes at 35%	175,000	112,000
Net income	$ 325,000	$ 208,000
Common shares outstanding	160,000	100,000
Earnings per share of common stock	$2.03	$2.08

Assuming earnings are expected to remain stable or to increase over time, stockholders will benefit from the issuance of debt. However, the company should acknowledge that the obligation to pay fixed interest charges increases the company's risk relative to the issuance of stock.

2. *$60,000 × 103 = $61,800 Issue Price of Bond*

January 1, 1983

Cash	61,800	
Bonds Payable		60,000
Premium on Bonds Payable		1,800
To record issuance of bond		

December 31, 1983

Interest Expense	6,000	
Interest Payable ($60,000 × 10% = $6,000)		6,000
To record annual interest related to payment to be made 1/1/84		

Straight-line amortization

$$\frac{\$1,800\ Premium}{5\text{-}Year\ Life\ with\ Annual\ Interest\ Payments} = \$360\ Annual\ Amortization$$

December 31, 1983

Premium on Bonds Payable	360	
Interest Expense		360
To record amortization of premium		

January 1, 1984

Interest Payable	6,000	
Cash		6,000
To record payment of interest		

December 31, 1984

Interest Expense	6,000	
Interest Payable		6,000
To record annual interest related to payment to be made 1/1/85		

December 31, 1984

Premium Bonds Payable	360	
Interest Expense		360
To record amortization of premium		

CHAPTER DEMONSTRATION PROBLEM

We're Expanding, Inc., issues $30,000 of 5-year bonds payable, with a contract interest rate of 14%, interest payable twice a year, on June 30 and December 31. Consider (a) and (b) independently. Excerpts from a present value table are provided at the end of the problem for your reference.

a. Assume the bonds are issued December 31, 1983, when the market rate for similar bonds is 20%. Record the issue, the related journal entries to be recorded during 1983 and 1984, and the early retirement of the bonds on December 31, 1985, assuming they were called at 105. Utilize the effective-interest method of amortization and assume annual amortization.

b. Assume the bonds are issued August 31, 1983, when the market rate for similar bonds is 10%. Record the issue, the related journal entries to be recorded during 1983 and 1984, and the conversion of the bonds on October 31, 1985, assuming each $1,000 bond may be converted into 20 shares of $10 par-value common stock. Utilize the effective-interest method of amortization and assume annual amortization.

The present value of $1 is summarized in the following table.

			Rate		
Periods	5%	7%	10%	14%	20%
1	0.95	0.94	0.91	0.88	0.83
2	0.91	0.87	0.83	0.77	0.69
3	0.86	0.82	0.75	0.68	0.58
4	0.82	0.76	0.68	0.59	0.48
5	0.78	0.71	0.62	0.52	0.40
6	0.75	0.67	0.56	0.46	0.34
7	0.71	0.62	0.51	0.40	0.28
8	0.68	0.58	0.47	0.35	0.23
9	0.65	0.54	0.42	0.31	0.19
10	0.61	0.51	0.39	0.27	0.16
11	0.59	0.48	0.35	0.24	0.14
12	0.56	0.44	0.32	0.21	0.11

CHAPTER DEMONSTRATION PROBLEM (ANSWER)

a. Issue price calculation

> **$30,000 5 Years at 20% Effective Rate**
> **× 0.40**
> _____
>
> **$12,000 Present Value of Principal**

Interest paid

> **$30,000 × 14% = $4,200 per Year or $2,100 Semiannually**
>
> **$2,100 At 1 Period at One-Half Rate (20% Effective Rate)**
> **× 0.91**
> _____
>
> **$1,911**

Twice the number of periods at one-half the interest rate, due to semiannual payment of interest

> **$2,100 × 0.83 = $1,743**
> **$2,100 × 0.75 = $1,575**
> **$2,100 × 0.68 = $1,428**
> **$2,100 × 0.62 = $1,302**
> **$2,100 × 0.56 = $1,176**
> **$2,100 × 0.51 = $1,071**
> **$2,100 × 0.47 = $ 987**
> **$2,100 × 0.42 = $ 882**
> **$2,100 × 0.39 = $ 819**
>
> **Sum of 10 Interest Rates = $12,894 Present Value of Interest**
>
> **$12,000 + $12,894 = $24,894 Issue Price of Bond**

December 31, 1983

Cash	24,894	
Discount on Bonds Payable	5,106	
Bonds Payable		30,000

June 30, 1984

Interest Expense	2,100	
Cash		2,100

To record one-half year of interest payment

December 31, 1984

> *Interest Expense   2,100*
>   *Cash   2,100*
> *To record one-half year of interest payment*

> *$ 24,894 Carrying Value of Bond*
> *×   20% Effective Rate*
> _____
> *$ 4,978.80 Interest Expense*
> *− 4,200.00 Interest Paid*
> _____
> *$ 778.80 Amortization*

December 31, 1984

> *Interest Expense   778.80*
>   *Discount on Bonds Payable   778.80*

December 31, 1985, early retirement entry requires adjustment of carrying value.

> *$ 24,894.00 Issue Price*
> *+   778.80 Amortization of Discount in First Year*
> _____
> *$ 25,672.80 Carrying Value*
> *×   20% Effective Rate*
> _____
> *$ 5,134.56 Interest Expense*
> *− 4,200.00 Interest Paid*
> _____
> *$ 934.56 Amortization*

December 31, 1985

> *Interest Expense   934.56*
>   *Discount on Bonds Payable   934.56*

Note: It is assumed that interest payments have been appropriately recorded in 1985.

Bond principal is $30,000: At a call price of 105, the cash required for retirement is $31,500. The carrying value of the bond is $25,672.80 + $934.56 = $26,607.36.

> *$ 26,607.36 Carrying Value*
> *− 31,500.00 Cash for Retirement*
> _____
> *$ 4,892.64 Loss on Bond Retirement*

December 31, 1985

> *Bonds Payable   30,000.00*
> *Loss on Bond Retirement   4,892.64*
>   *Discount on Bonds Payable   3,392.64*
>   *Cash   31,500.00*

b. Issue price calculation

> *$30,000 5 Years at 10% Effective Rate*
> *×   0.62*
> _____
> *$18,600 Present Value of Principal*

Interest paid

> *$30,000 × 14% = $4,200 per Year or $2,100 Semiannually*

Discount interest payments using twice the number of periods at one-half the interest rate, due to semiannual payment of interest.

$2,100 \times 0.95 = \$1,995$
$2,100 \times 0.91 = 1,911$
$2,100 \times 0.86 = 1,806$
$2,100 \times 0.82 = 1,722$
$2,100 \times 0.78 = 1,638$
$2,100 \times 0.75 = 1,575$
$2,100 \times 0.71 = 1,491$
$2,100 \times 0.68 = 1,428$
$2,100 \times 0.65 = 1,365$
$2,100 \times 0.61 = 1,281$

Sum of 10 Interest Rates = $16,212 *Present Value of Interest*

$18,600 + $16,212 = **$34,812** *Issue Price of Bond without Interest for Between Date Issuance*

Issue at August 31, 1983, implies that interest is not earned in July or August, and therefore 2 months of the 6-month payment of $2,100 on December 31, 1983, needs to be purchased.

$$\$2,100 \times \frac{2}{6} = \$700 \text{ Accrued Interest}$$

August 31, 1983

Cash	35,512	
Bonds Payable		30,000
Premium on Bonds Payable		4,812
Bond Interest Payable		700

December 31, 1983

Bond Interest Payable	700	
Interest Expense	1,400	
Cash		2,100

To record one-half year payment of interest, including repayment of accrued interest as of the issue date

$34,812.00 *Carrying Value of Bond*
$\times$ 10% *Effective Rate*

$ 3,481.20
$\times$ 4/12 *September–December*

$ 1,160.40 *Interest Expense*
− 1,400.00 *Interest Paid*

$ 239.60 *Amortization*

December 31, 1983

Premium on Bonds Payable	239.60	
Interest Expense		239.60

June 30, 1984

Interest Expense	2,100	
Cash		2,100

To record one-half year of interest payment

December 31, 1984

Interest Expense	2,100	
Cash		2,100

To record one-half year of interest payment

$34,812.00 *Carrying Value of Bond*
−   239.60
─────────────
$34,572.40
×   *10% Effective Rate*
─────────────
$ 3,457.24 *Interest Expense*
− 4,200.00 *Interest Paid*
─────────────
$ 742.76 *Amortization*

December 31, 1984

Premium on Bonds Payable   742.76
   Interest Expense   742.76

October 31, 1985, conversion requires the following adjustment of carrying value.

$34,572.40
−   742.76
─────────────
$33,829.64
$33,829.64 *Adjusted Carrying Value*
×   *10% Effective Rate*
─────────────
$ 3,382.96 *Interest Expense*
− 4,200.00 *Interest Paid*
─────────────
$ 817.04 *Amortization for Year*

Only 10 months of year require adjustment, therefore

$$\$817.04 \times \frac{10}{12} = \$680.87 \textit{ Partial Year Adjustment}$$

October 31, 1985

Premium on Bonds Payable   680.87
   Interest Expense   680.87

Note: It is assumed that interest payments have been appropriately recorded in 1985.

There are 30 $1,000 bonds, each convertible into 20 shares of $10 par-value stock (or 30 × 20 × $10 = $6,000 Par).

$33,829.64 *Carrying Value of Bond*
−   680.87 *Amortization of Premium on Bonds Payable*
─────────────
$33,148.77

October 31, 1985

Bonds Payable	30,000.00	
Premium on Bonds Payable	3,148.77	
Common Stock		6,000.00
Paid-in Capital in Excess of Par Value		27,148.77

16   *LONG-TERM INVESTMENTS*

OBJECTIVES

After completing this chapter, you should:

1 *Understand how to account for investments in bonds; understand the initial investment, bond interest revenue, amortization using the straight-line and the effective-interest rate method, and the sale of bonds before maturity.*

2 *Know how to record investments in stock.*

3 *Be able to explain when the lower-of-cost-or-market method, equity method, or equity method with consolidated statements is the appropriate method of reporting for stock investments.*

4 *Know how to prepare 100% consolidated financial statements, as well as those with minority interests.*

5 *Be able to describe the difference in purchase and pooling-of-interests accounting and the effects of each method on the financial statements.*

CHAPTER SUMMARY

Companies that invest funds in other companies' securities, which either are not readily salable or are not intended to be converted into cash within the longer of one year or the operating cycle of the investor, have acquired **long-term investments**. If the securities that are acquired are bonds, they are recorded at cost, including brokerage fees, with no separate recording of the bond's face value, discount, or premium balance on the date of purchase. However, such details are noted in the journal for subsequent calculation of bond interest revenue and amortization of the applicable premium or discount by either the *straight-line method* or the *effective-interest method*. The amortization calculation is identical to that utilized by bond issuers, except that the relevant bond life is the remaining life as of the purchase date, and the amortization affects interest revenue rather than interest expense. Due to their investment nature, bonds are frequently sold before maturity; to record such a transaction, the books must first be updated to reflect interest revenue through the date of sale and then, by comparing the bonds' carrying value to their selling price, the related gain or loss to be recorded for the sale can be computed.

If the securities that are acquired are shares of stock, they are initially recorded at cost, including brokers' fees and transfer taxes. If less than 20% of the stock of an *investee* is acquired, the *lower-of-cost-or-market* method of accounting is appropriate. This accounting treatment reflects the absence of any significant influence on the investee's operations by recognizing dividends as revenue and recognizing any net declines in the aggregate market value of the investment portfolio. In contrast, if between 20% and 50% of the stock of an investee is acquired, the investor is thought to be capable of significantly influencing dividend policy and thereby controlling its revenue. Therefore, the **equity method** of accounting is appropriate; this method reflects the investor's share of the investee's net income or loss in the investment account, reducing this balance by declared dividends.

If the investor owns more than 50% of an investee's stock, a controlling interest is held, and the equity method is required with reporting of consolidated statements. Each legal entity, the parent and its subsidiary, maintains separate accounting records; however, for the economic union of the two entities, **consolidated financial statements** are prepared. Such statements merely combine revenues and expenses on the income statement and reported assets and liabilities on the balance sheet, eliminating any intercompany transactions (transactions not involving third parties) and substituting an investment account and a *minority interest account* (when less than 100% of a subsidiary has been acquired) for the subsidiary's stockholders' equity.

If a **purchase** has occurred, the combined financial statements will reflect the investee's fair market value of assets and any excess of the company's purchase price over its fair market value will be recorded as **goodwill**. Similarly, any excess of the company's reported value over its cost is often termed negative goodwill and reported as the *excess of book value of investment in subsidiary over cost.* Such intangibles must be amortized over a period not to exceed 40 years.

If a **pooling of interest** has occurred, the book values of the combining firms are added, with no reflection of market values. A pooling implies that no sale has occurred, only a joining of interests and is restricted in its application. Since a pooling will combine total earnings for the entire period in which it occurs (whereas a purchase only combines earnings subsequent to the date of purchase), will continue to depreciate book values (rather than market values), and will not have any goodwill that requires amortization, it will typically result in higher earnings than a purchase.

TECHNICAL POINTS

√   *Purchase Price*
    + *Brokerage Fees*
    + *Any Other Costs Related to Acquisition*

    Bond Investment

√ Discounts and premiums on bonds that are purchased by investors are recorded in the investment in bonds account, not in separate valuation accounts.

√ *Effective Interest Amortization = (Face Value × Coupon Interest Rate)*
    − (Carrying Value × Effective Interest Rate)

Note: The **coupon interest rate,** also known as the nominal rate, is the rate printed on the face of the bond, while the **effective interest rate** is the market rate, also known as the yield, at the time the bond is issued.

√ *Straight-line Amortization =* $\dfrac{\text{Face Value − Carrying Value}}{\substack{\text{Number of Years of Bond} \\ \text{Life Remaining at Purchase}}}$

√ *Gain (Loss) on Sale of Bond = Bond Selling Price − Investment's Carrying Value*

✓ *Stock Investment = Purchase Price + Any Related Acquisition Costs Such as Brokers' Fees and Transfer Taxes*

✓ If less than 20% of an investee is owned, stock investments are initially recorded at cost, dividends received are recorded as revenue, and the lower-of-cost-or-market for the investment portfolio is recorded to reflect net downward changes in market value.

✓ If between 20% and 50% of an investee is owned, stock investments are initially recorded at cost, earnings (losses) increase (decrease) the investment account balance, and dividends decrease the investment account balance.

✓ If greater than 50% of an investee is owned, consolidated statements are prepared, utilizing either the purchase or the pooling-of-interests method.

Consolidated Statements

Purchase method: At purchase date, combine assets and liabilities at fair market value, record difference in purchase price and fair market value in a goodwill account (or an account entitled excess of book value of investment in subsidiary over cost), eliminate intercompany accounts, eliminate the subsidiary's stockholders' equity against the investment account and minority interest account (if less than 100% of the subsidiary is purchased).

Pooling method: At beginning of fiscal year in which pooling occurs, combine assets and liabilities at book value, eliminate intercompany accounts, and eliminate the subsidiary's stockholders' equity against the investment account.

MULTIPLE-CHOICE QUESTIONS

Circle the letter corresponding to the best response.

1. The investment in bonds account includes
   a. the face value of long-term investments
   b. the face value of long-term investments net of any premium or any discounts
   c. the face value of long-term investments net of any premium or any discount plus brokerage fees and any other costs related to acquisition
   d. the face value of long-term investments net of any premium or any discount plus brokerage fees and any other costs related to acquisition plus accrued interest which has accumulated since the last interest date

2. A 15%, 5-year, $20,000 bond that pays interest annually on December 31 is purchased for 105, at the end of the second year it is outstanding, when the effective interest rate is 13%. Assuming the effective-interest method of amortization is used, interest revenue during the first year of acquisition would be
   a. $3,000
   b. $2,800
   c. $2,667
   d. $2,730

3. Dividends received from an investment are recorded as revenue under
   a. the equity method
   b. the lower-of-cost-or-market method
   c. the equity method and the lower-of-cost-or-market method
   d. the equity method with consolidated statements

4. Alamand, Inc., invested in 1,000 shares of Axond, Inc., at a price of $50 a share and 2,000 shares of Berrick Corporation at a price of $20 a share. At year-end the price of Axond stock was $40 a share and the price of Berrick stock was $22 a share. Alamand, Inc.,
   a. will make no adjustment to long-term stock investments
   b. will record the downward stock price movement of Axond, Inc., with an adjustment of $10,000
   c. will record the downward stock price movement of Axond, Inc., with an adjustment of $6,000

    d. will record the upward stock price movement of Berrick Corporation with an adjustment of $4,000

5. Consolidation reflects
    a. the legal entities in operation
    b. the economic entity in operation
    c. both the legal and economic entities in operation
    d. neither the legal nor economic entities in operation

6. Reasons for operating separate subsidiaries, rather than merging all activities into one entity, do not include
    a. a reduction of risk
    b. conformity with governmental regulation
    c. a savings in income tax
    d. the enhancement of decentralized operations

7. Intercompany transactions
    a. are handled like all other transactions on the consolidated financial statements
    b. present no special accounting problems for the individual entities involved
    c. such as a sale of merchandise should be separately reported on the consolidated balance sheet as related party receivables and payables
    d. must be eliminated from the accounts of both the parent and its subsidiaries

8. Minority interests
    a. appear in the stockholders' equity section of the balance sheet
    b. appear between the liability and stockholders' equity sections on the balance sheet
    c. both a and b, as practice varies
    d. neither a nor b

MULTIPLE-CHOICE QUESTIONS (ANSWERS)

Answer   *Explanation*

1. c   The accrued interest is recorded separately in the bond interest receivable account.

2. d $20,000 × 105 = $21,000 Investment in Bonds; $21,000 × 13% Effective Rate = $2,730 Interest Revenue

3. b   Only the lower-of-cost-or-market method records dividends as revenue; under the equity methods the dividends reduce the recorded investment, as they represent distributions of income previously recorded.

4. c   Adjustments for decreases in the market value of long-term investments are calculated for the aggregate portfolio; hence, the $10,000 drop in Axond stock value is netted with the $4,000 appreciation in Berrick stock and results in a $6,000 adjusting entry.

5. b   Each unconsolidated subsidiary is the legal entity; however, the single economic entity formed by the subsidiaries is reflected in consolidated financial statements.

6. d   Operations can be decentralized without forming separate subsidiaries; in fact, separate subsidiaries can make control over decentralized operations more difficult. In contrast, responses (*a*), (*b*), and (*c*) are common rationales for maintaining separate subsidiaries.

7. b   Problems do not arise concerning the books, but on the worksheet eliminations must be made to generate consolidated financial statements. For example, the intercompany receivables and payables cancel each other out and the net result is reported. Such eliminations are *never* entered in the accounts.

8. c   In practice either presentation is common; however, it is recommended that disclosure be made in the stockholders' equity section.

Indicate whether each of the following statements is true (T) or false (F).

____ 1. When bonds are purchased at an amount different from their face value, a separate account is used to record the bonds' discount or premium.

____ 2. Investments for which an active secondary market is available for resale, yet are not intended to be converted into cash within one year (or the current operating cycle, if longer), are classified as noncurrent (long-term) assets on the balance sheet.

____ 3. Bond discounts and premiums respectively increase and decrease the interest revenue earned by the investing corporations.

____ 4. The equity method of accounting focuses on changes in the market value of the investee's stock.

____ 5. Elimination entries are made on the worksheet only; they are *never* entered in the accounts of either a parent or its subsidiaries.

TRUE-FALSE QUESTIONS (ANSWERS)

Answer *Explanation*

1. F No separate valuation account is used; the discount or premium is comingled with the investment and is amortized over the bonds' life.

2. T Short-term investments must be both readily salable and intended to be converted into cash within the longer of one year or the current operating cycle.

3. T The investor pays less than face value for the bond, resulting in higher interest revenue for discounted bonds than for bonds issued at par value. The investor pays more than face value, resulting in lower interest revenue for premium bonds than for bonds issued at par value.

4. F Market value of the investee's stock is considered only in the lower-of-cost-or-market method; the equity method focuses on changes in the investee's retained earnings.

5. T Each legal entity's books are maintained separately.

Identify the appropriate accounting method for reporting the following investments by using these symbols.

L = Lower of cost or market
E = Equity
C = Equity with consolidated statements

____ 1. Investments in which no significant influence is exercised over the investee
____ 2. Investments in which greater than 50% of the investee is owned
____ 3. Investments in which less than 20% of the investee is owned
____ 4. Investments in which a significant influence is exercised over the investee
____ 5. Investments in which a controlling interest is exercised over the investee
____ 6. Investments in which between 20% and 50% of the investee is owned

CLASSIFICATION AND MATCHING QUESTIONS (ANSWERS)

1. L   2. C   3. L   4. E   5. C   6. E

QUESTIONS CONCERNING THE EFFECTS OF TRANSACTIONS

Indicate whether each of the following transactions will increase (+), decrease (−), or have no effect (0) on the account or balance described.

_____ 1. The effect on consolidated net income of a pooling in December, 1982, (before a December 31 year-end) of two firms with positive earnings, relative to a purchase in December 1982.

_____ 2. Assuming the companies combining have no intangible assets prior to merger, the effect on amortization of a pooling in which the purchase price exceeds book value.

_____ 3. The effect on recorded value of total assets for a purchase when negative goodwill is present relative to a pooling.

_____ 4. The effect on the parent's investment account of a subsidiary's dividends, assuming an equity method of accounting.

_____ 5. The effect on net income of an investee's dividends, assuming the lower-of-cost-or-market method of accounting.

QUESTIONS CONCERNING THE EFFECTS OF TRANSACTIONS (ANSWERS)

Answer   Explanations

1. +   The pooling will permit the entire 1982 earnings to be recorded, whereas the purchase method would only combine December's revenue.

2. 0   Pooling results in no goodwill; hence, no amortization is required.

3. −   Pooling will combine book values, whereas purchasing will involve a write-down of recorded assets as well as the establishment of the contra-asset account, excess of book value of investment over cost.

4. −   Since earnings are increases, distributions of earnings in the form of dividends are decreases.

5. +   Dividend revenue is recorded upon receipt.

EXERCISES

1. On June 30, 1983, Benstonsen, Inc., issued $1 million of 16%, 5-year bonds with interest paid annually on December 31. Roan Corporation purchased $400,000 of these bonds for $370,000 on May 1, 1984.
a. Record the bond purchase.
   b. Record the adjusting journal entry on December 31, 1984, assuming straight-line amortization.
   c. Record the adjusting journal entry on December 31, 1984, assuming effective-interest amortization at an 18% effective rate.
   d. Assuming the effective-interest amortization method is in use, record the sale of the Benstonsen, Inc., bonds by Roan for $390,000 plus accrued interest on September 1, 1985.

EXERCISES (ANSWERS)

1. a. May 1, 1984

Investment in Bonds	370,000	
Bond Interest Receivable	21,333	
Cash		391,333

$$\$400,000 \times 16\% = \$64,000 \times \frac{4}{12} = \$21,333 \text{ Accrued Interest}$$

b. December 31, 1984

Cash	64,000	
Investment in Bonds	600	
Bond Interest Receivable		21,333
Bond Interest Revenue		43,267

$$\$64,000 \times \frac{8}{12} = \$42,667 \text{ Interest Paid and Earned}$$

$$\$400,000 - \$370,000 = \frac{\$30,000}{50 \text{ Months}} = \$600 \text{ Amortization}$$

$$\$42,667 + \$600 = \$43,267 \text{ Interest Revenue}$$

c. December 31, 1984

Cash	64,000	
Investment in Bonds	1,733	
Bond Interest Receivable		21,333
Bond Interest Revenue		44,400

$$\$370,000 \times 18\% = \$66,600 - 64,000 = \$2,600 \times \frac{8}{12}$$

$$= \$1,733 \text{ Amortization}$$

$$\$66,600 \times \frac{8}{12} = \$44,400 \text{ Interest Revenue}$$

d. First, record the amortization of the discount for January through August, 1985

$$
\begin{array}{r}
\$370,000 \\
+\ \ \ \ 1,733 \\
\hline
\$371,733 \\
\times\ \ \ \ \ 18\% \\
\hline
\$\ \ 66,912 \\
-\ \ 64,000 \\
\hline
\$\ \ \ \ 2,912 \\
\times\ \ \ \ 8/12 \\
\hline
\$\ \ \ \ 1,941 \\
\end{array}
$$

Investment in Bonds	1,941	
Bond Interest Revenue		1,941

$$\$390,000 \text{ Sales Price}$$
$$+\ 42,667 \text{ Accrued Interest } (\$400,000 \times 16\% \times 8/12)$$

$$\$432,667 \text{ Proceeds from the Sale}$$

Cash	432,667	
Investment in Bonds		373,674
Bond Interest Revenue		42,667
Gain on Sale of Bonds		16,326
To record the sale of the bond investment		

Note: The $390,000 selling price exceeded the investment's carrying value $373,674 ($371,733 + $1,941) by $16,326, resulting in a gain.

For the year ended December 31, 1983

	Carusac, Incorporated	Frickle, Incorporated
Revenue	$ 500,000	$ 200,000
− Cost of Goods Sold	− 300,000	− 100,000
Gross Profit	$ 200,000	$ 100,000
− Other Expenses	− 75,000	− 50,000
Net Income	$ 125,000	$ 50,000
− Dividends	− 75,000	− 25,000
Earnings Retained	$ 50,000	$ 25,000

December 31, 1983

	Carusac, Incorporated	Frickle, Incorporated
Cash	$1,000,000	$ 400,000
Accounts receivable (net)	1,000,000	1,500,000
Inventories	1,500,000	1,500,000
Long-term investments (net) and property, plant, & equipment (net)	3,500,000	600,000
Total assets	$7,000,000	$4,000,000
Accounts payable	$1,700,000	$1,300,000
Bonds payable	300,000	100,000
Common stock ($10 par)	4,000,000	2,000,000
Retained earnings	1,000,000	600,000
Total liabilities & stockholders' equity	$7,000,000	$4,000,000

1. Carusac, Incorporated, purchased 1,000 shares of Frickle, Incorporated, on January 2, 1983, for $60 a share plus brokers' fees of $700. Record this long-term investment. On December 31, 1983, the market price was $50 a share and Carusac held no other long-term investments. Record the adjusting entry on December 31, 1983.

2. Carusac, Incorporated, purchased 80,000 shares of Frickle, Incorporated, on January 2, 1983, for $70 a share plus transfer taxes of $2,000. Record the journal entries on January 2, 1983, and on December 31, 1983, that are related to this investment.

3. Carusac, Incorporated, purchased 100% of Frickle, Incorporated, on December 31, 1983. Appraisals of property resulted in a $100,000 write-up. The purchase price was $3 million. How would this purchase be reported?

4. Carusac, Incorporated, purchased 80% of Frickle, Incorporated, at its book value on December 31, 1983. Two hundred thousand dollars of the receivables of Frickle were payables of Carusac. How would this purchase be reported?

5. Carusac, Incorporated, pooled its interests with Frickle, Incorporated, on December 31, 1983. Frickle had been offered a $2,800,000 price for its operations by a third party but rejected the offer. Record the pooling.

1. 1,000 Shares × $60 = $60,000 + $700 = $60,700 Cost

January 2, 1983

    Investment in Frickle, Incorporated   60,700
      Cash   60,700

December 31, 1983

    Cash   125
      Dividend Revenue   125

$$\frac{\$25,000 \times 1,000\ Shares}{200,000\ Shares} = 125$$

December 31, 1983

    Unrealized Loss on Long-Term Investments   10,000
      Allowance for Decline in Market Value of
        Long-Term Investments   10,000

    $60 − 50 = $10 × 1,000 Shares = $10,000

2. 80,000 Shares × $70 = $5,600,000 + $2,000 = $5,602,000 Cost

The 80,000 shares purchased represent 40% of the 200,000 shares outstanding, which is a significant influence. The investment is recorded at cost.

January 2, 1983

    Investment in Frickle, Incorporated   5,602,000
      Cash   5,602,000
    To record the acquisition of 80,000 shares of Frickle at $70 per share

December 31, 1983

    Investment in Frickle, Incorporated 20,000
      Investment Revenue   20,000
    To record appropriate share of Frickle, Incorporated, earnings

    ($50,000 × 0.40 = $20,000)

    Cash   10,000
      Investment in Frickle, Incorporated   10,000
    To record receipt of cash dividends

    $25,000 × 0.40 = $10,000

3.   *Consolidated Balance Sheet*

Cash	$1,400,000
Accounts receivable (net)	2,500,000
Inventories	3,000,000
Long-term investments (net) and property, plant, & equipment (net)	1,200,000*
Goodwill	300,000†
Total assets	$8,400,000
Accounts payable	$3,000,000
Bonds payable	400,000
Common stock ($10 par)	4,000,000
Retained earnings	1,000,000
Total liabilities	$8,400,000

*$4,100,000 − $3,000,000 Purchase Price + $100,000 Write-up
†$3,000,000 Price − $2,600,000 Book Value − $100,000 Write-up

4. Eighty percent of Frickle, Incorporated, was purchased at its book value: $2,600,000 × 0.80 = $2,080,000.

Cash	$1,400,000
Accounts receivable (net)	2,300,000*
Inventories	3,000,000
Long-term investments (net) and property, plant, & equipment (net)	2,020,000†
Total assets	$8,720,000

Accounts payable	$2,800,000*
Bonds payable	400,000
Common stock ($10 par)	4,000,000
Retained earnings	1,000,000
Minority interest in Frickle, Incorporated (2,600,000 × 20%)	520,000
Total liabilities	$8,720,000

*Net of intercompany transactions.
†$4,100,000 − $2,080,000 = $2,020,000

5.

Cash	$ 1,400,000
Accounts receivable	2,500,000
Inventories	3,000,000
Long-term investments (net) and property, plant, & equipment (net)	4,100,000
Total assets	$11,000,000

Accounts payable	$ 3,000,000
Bonds payable	400,000
Common stock ($10 par)	6,000,000
Retained earnings	1,600,000
Total liabilities	$11,000,000

17 STATEMENT OF CHANGES IN FINANCIAL POSITION

OBJECTIVES

After completing this chapter, you should:

1 *Understand the purpose of the statement of changes in financial position.*

2 *Be able to define funds and to identify key sources and uses of funds as well as to identify transactions which do not affect funds and are to be reported as both sources and uses to provide meaningful disclosures to financial statement users.*

3 *Know how to prepare a statement of changes in financial position, utilizing both the working capital approach and the cash approach.*

CHAPTER SUMMARY

The **statement of changes in financial position** is prepared using either *the working capital approach* or *the cash approach* in order to report how funds are obtained and used by a business. The **funds statement**, as it is frequently called, typically reports on the excess of current assets over current liabilities, with increases to working capital representing sources of funds and decreases to working capital representing uses of funds. Generally speaking, sources and uses arise from transactions that affect both current and noncurrent accounts, although generally accepted accounting practices require the listing of significant transactions affecting only noncurrent accounts as both sources and uses of funds on the statement of changes in financial position. The typical *sources* of working capital are the sale of noncurrent assets, long-term borrowing, and increases in owners' equity; the typical *uses* of working capital are the purchase of noncurrent assets, repayment of long-term debt, and decreases in owners' equity.

When preparing a statement of changes in financial position, information must be gathered from the income statement, statement of retained earnings, comparative balance sheets, and ledger accounts. After computing the increase or decrease in working capital from the current asset and current liability sections of the comparative balance sheets, the noncurrent accounts are analyzed in detail to identify the causes of the working capital increase or decrease, and the formal statement of changes in financial position is then prepared. The statement generally begins with net income, adjusted for items not affecting working capital (such as depreciation, amortization, and depletion as well as gains and losses realized in the disposal of long-term assets), and then lists other sources and uses. The final section of the statement is a schedule that summarizes the changes in each of the current asset and current liability accounts, reflecting substantive shifts across current accounts that may have little net effect on working capital but nevertheless provide information on stability and liquidity.

When the cash approach to funds is used, the change in cash is computed, then all other balance sheet accounts are analyzed in depth to compute their effect upon cash. Rather than studying each revenue and expense transaction, decreases (increases) in current assets and increases (decreases) in current liabilities can be added back to (deducted from) accrual-based net income, in addition to those adjustments to net income that are made when using the working capital approach to a funds statement, in order to derive cash provided from operations. After analyzing cash flow related to dividends, the noncurrent accounts are analyzed in a similar manner as in the working capital approach, and the formal statement of changes in financial position using the cash definition of funds is prepared.

TECHNICAL POINTS

√ *Working Capital = Current Assets − Current Liabilities*

where

> *Cash*
> + *Short-Term Investments*
> + *Accounts Receivable*
> + *Short-Term Notes Receivable*
> + *Inventories*
> _____
> *Current Assets*
>
> *Accounts Payable*
> + *Notes Payable*
> + *Accrued Payables*
> + *Short-Term Obligations*
> _____
> *Current Liabilities*
>
> *Net Income*
> + *Depreciation Expense*
> + *Amortization Expense*
> + *Depletion Expense*
> + *Losses on Long-Term Assets*
> − *Gains on Long-Term Assets*
> _____
> *Working Capital Provided from Operations*

√ Typical sources of working capital

Sale of noncurrent assets
Long-term borrowing
Increases in owners' (stockholders') equity
   Issuance of stock
   Capital contributions and donations

✓ Typical uses (applications) of working capital

Purchase of noncurrent assets
Repayment of long-term debt
Decreases in owners' (stockholders') equity
    Dividends
    Withdrawals
    Purchase of treasury stock

✓ Cash provided from operations (conversion of accrual-based net income to cash basis)

> *Working Capital from Operations*
> + *Decreases in Current Assets*
> + *Increases in Current Liabilities*
> − *Increases in Current Assets*
> − *Decreases in Current Liabilities*
>
> *Cash Provided from Operations*

Circle the letter corresponding to the best response.

MULTIPLE-CHOICE QUESTIONS

1. The conversion of convertible preferred stock into common stock
   a. would not appear on a funds flow statement
   b. would be listed as a source of funds on a funds flow statement
   c. would be listed as a use of funds on a funds flow statement
   d. would be listed as both a source and a use on a funds flow statement

2. Which of the following is not a true statement about a sources and uses of cash statement?
   a. a decrease in accounts receivable is a source of cash
   b. a decrease in inventory is a source of cash
   c. an increase in accounts payable is a source of cash
   d. an increase in marketable securities is a source of cash

3. Which of the following would be deductions from net income to convert to the cash basis?
   a. increase in merchandise inventory
   b. decrease in accounts receivable
   c. decrease in prepaid expenses
   d. increase in notes payable
   e. decrease in dividends payable

4. A company reports net income of $80,000, depreciation expense of $4,000, a gain on the sale of a building of $1,000, a loss on the sale of equipment of $11,000, and amortization of $300. The working capital provided from operations would be reported as
   a. $80,000
   b. $74,300
   c. $94,300
   d. $84,300
   e. $94,000

5. Cimaron, Inc., reported the following balance sheet amounts.

	December 31, 1983	*December 31, 1982*
Current assets	$60,000	$50,000
Current liabilities	30,000	38,000

The change in working capital in 1983 for Cimaron, Inc., was
a. an increase of $30,000
b. an increase of $18,000
c. an increase of $12,000
d. an increase of $10,000
e. an increase of $8,000

MULTIPLE-CHOICE QUESTIONS (ANSWERS)

Answer   Explanation
1. d   Nonfund exchange transactions are reported on the statement of changes as both a source and a use of funds, as a means of disclosing important changes in financial position. The conversion from preferred stock would be a source, and the conversion into common stock would be a use.
2. d   Since marketable securities represent an investment of cash, an increase in their balance is a use of cash, not a source.
3. a   An increase in inventory indicates that goods required an outlay that were not included in costs of goods sold; such an outlay results in a reduction of net income when computing current cash flow from operations. Responses (b), (c), and (d) are all additions to net income when converting to a cash basis. Response (e) involves dividends which represent distributions of earnings and would never result in an adjustment to net income to convert to cash basis.
4. c   The $94,300 of working capital derived from operations is found by taking net income of $80,000 plus $4,000 to reverse the expense reduction not requiring working capital, minus $1,000 to zero out the gain to avoid double counting of sales proceeds, plus $11,000 to zero out the loss to avoid double counting of sales proceeds and reduction for nonworking capital items, plus $300 to reverse the expense reduction not requiring working capital.
5. b   *$50,000 − $38,000 = $12,000 Working Capital 1982*
          $60,000 − $30,000 = $30,000 Working Capital 1983
          $30,000 − $12,000 = $18,000 Increase

TRUE-FALSE QUESTIONS

Indicate whether each of the following statements is true (T) or false (F).

___ 1. In the business community funds are generally defined as cash, both on hand and in the bank.

___ 2. Events and transactions that affect only current items are neither sources nor uses of funds.

___ 3. For financial statement purposes, it is not necessary to divide a source or use into the amounts placed in the common stock and paid-in capital in excess accounts; only the total need be shown.

___ 4. The sale of a piece of equipment with a book value of $30,000 that results in a recorded loss of $5,000, increases working capital by $35,000.

___ 5. If a corporation issues 40,000 shares of $5 par-value common stock at a price of $15 per share, the working capital provided is $400,000.

___ 6. A stock dividend is a use of working capital.

Answer	Explanation
1. F	While this is the common meaning to the general public, a broader definition of funds as the working capital of the enterprise is generally utilized in the business community.
2. T	Working capital increases or decreases because of transactions that affect both current and noncurrent accounts. While sources and uses of funds are disclosed for some noncurrent asset exchanges, expanding the working capital definition of funds, those transactions affecting only current items are neither sources nor uses of funds.
3. T	The detail of common stock and paid-in capital accounts has minimal information value to financial statement users.
4. F	The sales proceeds were $25,000 ($30,000 − $5,000 loss); this results in an increase to working capital regardless of the recorded gain or loss from the disposition of the equipment.
5. F	The market value is the relevant figure: 40,000 Shares × $15 = $600,000.
6. F	A stock dividend merely transfers a quantity from retained earnings to common stock and paid in capital; no current accounts are involved.

**CLASSIFI-
CATION AND
MATCHING
QUESTIONS**

Classify the following items using these symbols.

S = Source of working capital
U = Use of working capital

____   *1.* Sale of noncurrent assets
____   *2.* Purchase of treasury stock
____   *3.* Declaration of dividends
____   *4.* Long-term borrowing
____   *5.* Purchase of property
____   *6.* Withdrawals by partners
____   *7.* Issuance of preferred stock
____   *8.* Capital contributions by partners
____   *9.* Repayment of a mortgage
____   *10.* Issuance of bonds payable
____   *11.* Profitable operations (net income)
____   *12.* Incurrence of a net loss from operations

CLASSIFICATION AND MATCHING QUESTIONS (ANSWERS)

1. S   *2.* U   *3.* U   *4.* S   *5.* U   *6.* U   *7.* S   *8.* S   *9.* U   *10.* S   *11.* S   *12.* U

**QUESTIONS
CONCERNING
THE EFFECTS
OF TRANS-
ACTIONS**

Quantify the effect of the following journal entries on working capital; indicate both the direction (+) or (−) and the amount.

*Effect on
Working Capital*

1. Cash	95,000		
Discount on Bonds Payable	5,000		
Bonds Payable		100,000	_____

2. Cash   80,000
   Accumulated Depreciation: Truck   40,000
      Truck   100,000
      Gain on Sale of Truck   20,000   _____

3. Accounts Payable   40,000
      Cash   40,000   _____

4. Equipment   70,000
   Accumulated Depreciation   30,000
      Equipment   45,000
      Long-Term Notes Payable   55,000   _____

5. Cash   15,000
      Six-Month Note Payable   15,000   _____

6. Office Furniture   3,000
      Cash   1,000
      Long-Term Note Payable   2,000   _____

7. Depreciation   4,000
      Accumulated Depreciation   4,000   _____

8. Dividends Payable   18,000
      Cash   18,000   _____

QUESTIONS CONCERNING THE EFFECTS OF TRANSACTIONS (ANSWERS)

Answer   Explanation

1. +$95,000   The total funds received from issuance of debt represent the increase in working capital.

2. +$80,000   Working capital is increased by the full selling price regardless of the gain or loss effects of the transaction.

3. 0   The payment of a current liability with current assets has no net effect on working capital.

4. 0   Only noncurrent accounts are involved in this exchange of assets and issuance of a long-term note; working capital is unchanged.

5. 0   Short-term financing does not affect working capital, as both current assets and current liabilities increase by the same amount.

6. −$1,000   The acquisition reduces working capital by the cash outlay; the other two accounts are noncurrent.

7. 0   Depreciation is neither a source nor a use of working capital, as only noncurrent accounts are involved in the journal entry. The reason that depreciation is often listed under sources in a working capital statement is that net income is derived by subtracting depreciation which is not a use of funds; to reverse the effect, net income is added to depreciation to derive that portion of operating income that affects working capital.

8. 0   Dividend declaration reduces working capital not dividend payment. The payment of dividends involves only current accounts.

1. The following facts relate to Aliss, Incorporated.

	December 31, 1982, or for Year Ended December 31, 1982 (If Appropriate)	December 31, 1983, or for Year Ended December 31, 1983 (If Appropriate)
Current assets	$120,000	$220,000
Noncurrent assets	500,000	400,000
Total assets	$620,000	$620,000
Current liabilities	$150,000	$ 50,000
Noncurrent liabilities	200,000	400,000
Stockholders' equity	270,000	170,000
Total equity	$620,000	$620,000
Revenue	$300,000	$290,000
Cost of goods sold	−120,000	−130,000
Gross profit	$180,000	$160,000
Amortization expense	$ 8,000	$ 8,000
Advertising expense	24,000	24,000
Depreciation expense	40,000	40,000
Loss on sale of auto	2,000	—
Gain on disposal of typewriter	—	200
Net income	$106,000	$ 88,200
Dividends	$ 96,000	$ 80,000

a. Compute the change in working capital during 1983.

b. Compute working capital from operations for 1983.

c. With the detailed ledger information below, how did transactions involving autos influence the 1982 statement of changes in financial position? Be specific. What is the book value of autos on 12/31/82?

Autos				Accumulated Depreciation—Autos			
1/1/82	300,000	150,000	6/30/82	6/30/82	140,000	200,000	1/1/82
12/31/82	200,000						12/31/82

d. If the change in working capital during 1982 was a decline of $90,000, what was working capital on December 31, 1981?

e. Compute working capital from operations for 1982.

f. Comment on the financial condition of Aliss, Incorporated.

2. Adjust the accrual-based net income to a cash basis using the available data below. The accrual-based net income is $60,000.

Accounts Receivable		Accounts Payable		Inventory	
40,000			80,000	25,000	
200,000	130,000	180,000	150,000	140,000	150,000
110,000			50,000	15,000	

1. a.

	1983	*1982*
Current Assets	*$220,000*	*$120,000*
− Current Liabilities	*50,000*	*150,000*
Working Capital	*$170,000*	*($ 30,000)*

Increase of $200,000

b.   *$ 88,200 Net Income*
  + 8,000 Amortization
  + 40,000 Depreciation
  −   200 Gain on Disposal of Typewriter

  $ 136,000 1983 Working Capital from Operations

c. A $50,000 debit to autos is required in order to balance. This would represent purchases of noncurrent assets, typically a use of working capital.

    The $150,000 credit to autos is the original cost of autos sold during the year, while the $140,000 debit (to accumulated depreciation: autos) is the related depreciation on the assets that were sold. The book value of assets sold is $150,000 − $140,000 = $10,000, and, since the income statement in 1982 reports a loss on the sale of auto of $2,000, the sale proceeds must have been $10,000 − $2,000 = $8,000. The entire $8,000 would be a source of capital. The $2,000 loss would have to be adjusted out of net income as a nonfund item.

    The depreciation expense must be assumed to relate only to autos in order to complete the problem. Credit accumulated depreciation for the $40,000 depreciation, and the ending balance is $100,000. Hence, the book value of autos on 12/31/82 is $200,000 − $100,000 = $100,000.

    Note that the $40,000 depreciation is neither a source nor a use of working capital but is an adjustment to net income to derive working capital from operations. It is added to net income.

d.   *$(30,000) December 31, 1982, Working Capital*
  −(90,000) Decline during 1982

  $ 60,000 December 31, 1981, Working Capital

e.   *$106,000 Net Income*
  + 8,000 Amortization
  + 40,000 Depreciation
  + 2,000 Loss on Sale of Auto

  $156,000 1982 Working Capital from Operations

f. In 1982 the current ratio for Aliss was 120,000/150,000, much less than the desired rule of thumb of 2 to 1 and reflecting an inability to meet current debts. By 1983, this ratio was 220,000/50,000, a substantial change to 4.4 to 1. How did this change occur? A comparison of the working capital calculations in 1982 and 1983 indicates an increase in current assets of $100,000 and a decrease in current liabilities of $100,000. An examination of the data in the problem reflects a substantial change in noncurrent assets from $500,000 to $400,000 and an increase in noncurrent liabilities of $200,000.

    Aliss apparently has had some difficulty maintaining unsecured trade credit and has financed its 1983 operations with long-term debt. To meet current debts, noncurrent assets have been liquidated. The company's dividend policy suggests a lack of appreciation for the 1982 working capital crunch and/or a desire to distribute cash to owners rather than to retain it for distribution to creditors, should bankruptcy occur. Overall, a weak financial position exists. Earnings have fallen, as have revenues, and the excessive current ratio suggests a loss of return on assets (since long-term assets generally yield higher returns than short-term assets). The low current liabilities suggest some slowing down of day-to-day purchasing, and the large growth of noncurrent liabilities may only serve to postpone the financial and operating problems rather than to correct them.

2. $ 60,000   *Accrual-Based Net Income*
      − 70,000   *Increase in Accounts Receivable*
      − 30,000   *Decrease in Accounts Payable*
      + 10,000   *Decrease in Inventory*

      $ (30,000)   *Cash Basis Net Income*

FORSYTE CORPORATION
Comparative Balance Sheets
1984 and 1983

	December 31, 1984	December 31, 1983
ASSETS		
Current assets		
Cash	$ 600,000	$ 400,000
Marketable securities	50,000	100,000
Accounts receivable (net)	4,200,000	3,700,000
Inventory	1,100,000	900,000
Prepaid salaries	30,000	60,000
Total current assets	$5,980,000	$5,160,000
Noncurrent assets		
Land	890,000	800,000
Buildings	400,000	650,000
Accumulated depreciation: Buildings	(35,000)	(150,000)
Equipment	220,000	200,000
Accumulated depreciation: Equipment	(75,000)	(50,000)
Patents	18,000	12,000
Coal mines	82,000	390,000
Total noncurrent assets	$1,500,000	$1,852,000
Total assets	$7,480,000	$7,012,000
LIABILITIES & STOCKHOLDERS' EQUITY		
Current liabilities		
Accounts payable	$3,000,000	$2,900,000
Notes payable	200,000	800,000
Dividends payable	100,000	125,000
Taxes payable	50,000	40,000
Advances from customers	80,000	30,000
Total current liabilities	$3,430,000	$3,895,000
Long-term liabilities		
Mortgage payable	350,000	400,000
Bonds payable	300,000	100,000
Total liabilities	$4,080,000	$4,395,000
Stockholders' equity		
Common stock, par value $10	2,000,000	1,700,000
Paid-in capital in excess of par value	300,000	217,000
Retained earnings	1,100,000	700,000
Total equities	$7,480,000	$7,012,000

Income Statement
For the Year Ended December 31, 1984

Sales	$7,860,000
Cost of goods sold	5,640,000
Gross profit	$2,220,000
Expenses	
Operating and taxes	1,395,300
Building depreciation	20,000
Equipment depreciation	45,000
Amortization	1,200
Depletion	10,000
Other revenue and expense	
Gain on equipment sale	2,500
Loss on sale of building	31,000
Net income	$ 720,000

Other Information

Cash dividends declared on June 30, 1984, amounted to $320,000.

The building sold had an original cost of $250,000 and a selling price of $94,000 and included land with a book value of $10,000.

The equipment sold had an original cost of $30,000 and a book value of $10,000.

Prepare a statement of changes in financial position for Forsyte Corporation for 1984.

CHAPTER DEMONSTRATION PROBLEM (ANSWER)

Working Capital

	December 31, 1984	December 31, 1983
Current assets	$5,980,000	$5,160,000
Current liabilities	3,430,000	3,895,000
	$2,550,000	$1,265,000

Change in working capital is an increase of $1,285,000.

Analysis of Noncurrent Accounts

Land

1/1/84	800,000	10,000	Sale of Land with Building
12/31/84	890,000		

To balance, $100,000 of land must have been acquired.

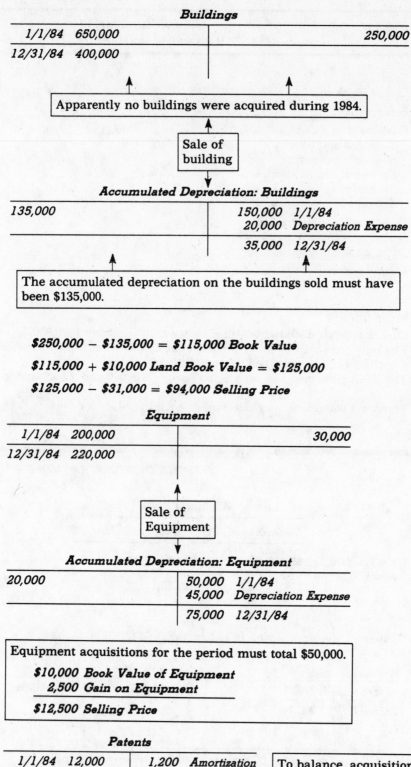

Buildings

1/1/84 650,000		250,000
12/31/84 400,000		

Apparently no buildings were acquired during 1984.

Sale of building

Accumulated Depreciation: Buildings

135,000	150,000	1/1/84
	20,000	Depreciation Expense
	35,000	12/31/84

The accumulated depreciation on the buildings sold must have been $135,000.

$250,000 − $135,000 = $115,000 Book Value

$115,000 + $10,000 Land Book Value = $125,000

$125,000 − $31,000 = $94,000 Selling Price

Equipment

1/1/84 200,000		30,000
12/31/84 220,000		

Sale of Equipment

Accumulated Depreciation: Equipment

20,000	50,000	1/1/84
	45,000	Depreciation Expense
	75,000	12/31/84

Equipment acquisitions for the period must total $50,000.

$10,000 Book Value of Equipment
  2,500 Gain on Equipment
$12,500 Selling Price

Patents

1/1/84 12,000	1,200	Amortization
12/31/84 18,000		

To balance, acquisitions of $7,200 must have been purchased for 1984.

Coal Mines

1/1/84	390,000	10,000	Depletion
12/31/84	82,000		

The $298,000 of coal mines required to balance must be those sold during the period at no gain or loss.

Mortgage Payable

	400,000	1/1/84
	350,000	12/31/84

$50,000 of the mortgage debt has been repaid.

Bonds Payable

	100,000	1/1/84
	300,000	12/31/84

$200,000 of bonds have been issued.

Common Stock, Par Value $1

	1,700,000	1/1/84
	2,000,000	12/31/84

Shares of $300,000 par value have been issued.

Paid-in Capital in Excess of Par Value

	217,000	1/1/84
	300,000	12/31/84

Additional paid-in capital on the newly issued shares total $83,000.

Retained Earnings

Cash Dividends Declared	320,000	700,000	1/1/84
		720,000	Net Income (via Closing)
		1,100,000	12/31/84

FORSYTE CORPORATION
Statement of Changes in Financial Position
For the Year Ended December 31, 1983

Sources of working capital provided from operations	
Net income	$ 720,000
Add (deduct) items not affecting working capital	
Building depreciation.	20,000
Equipment depreciation	45,000
Amortization	1,200
Depletion	10,000
Gain on sale of equipment	(2,500)
Loss on sale of building	31,000
Working capital provided from	
Operations	$ 824,700
Sale of building and land	94,000
Sale of equipment	12,500
Sale of coal mines	298,000
Issue of common stock	383,000
Issue of bonds	200,000
Total sources of working capital	$1,812,200
Uses of working capital	
Purchase of land	$ 100,000
Purchase of equipment	50,000
Declaration of dividends	320,000
Purchase of patents	7,200
Repayment of mortgage	50,000
Total uses of working capital	$ 527,200
Net increase in working capital	$1,285,000

Schedule of Changes in Working Capital Components

Increases (decreases) in current assets	
Cash	$ 200,000
Marketable securities	(50,000)
Accounts receivable (net)	500,000
Inventory	200,000
Prepaid salaries	(30,000)
	$ 820,000
Increases (decreases) in current liabilities	
Accounts payable	$ 100,000
Notes payable	(600,000)
Dividends payable	(25,000)
Taxes payable	10,000
Advances from customers	50,000
	$ (465,000)
Increase in working capital	$1,285,000

18 THE FOUNDATION OF FINANCIAL ACCOUNTING

After completing this chapter, you should:

1 *Be able to describe the objectives of financial reporting.*

2 *Understand the meaning of desirable characteristics of financial information, including relevancy, reliability, comparability, and understandability.*

3 *Know the history of generally accepted accounting principles (GAAP), including the respective roles of the Securities and Exchange Commission (SEC), American Institute of Certified Public Accountants (AICPA), the Committee on Accounting Procedure (CAP), the Accounting Principles Board (APB), and the Financial Accounting Standards Board (FASB).*

4 *Be aware of the set of assumptions and concepts which forms the basis for accounting principles: the entity assumption, the going-concern assumption, the periodicity assumption, the monetary unit assumption, the historical-cost principle, the objectivity principle, the revenue realization principle, the matching principle, the consistency principle, the disclosure principle, materiality, and conservatism.*

5 *Know how to apply the percentage of completion, cash basis, and installment methods of revenue realization and understand their advantages and disadvantages relative to point-of-sale realization.*

6 *Be able to describe what constitutes minimum acceptable disclosure.*

7 *Be aware of the potential effects of alternative reporting practices on entities' financial statements.*

CHAPTER SUMMARY

The wide variety of financial statement users requires that accounting information be general purpose with the objective of being helpful to investors, creditors, and other users in assessing cash flows, claims upon the resources of enterprises, and financial performance. To achieve this objective, the accountant strives to provide *reliable* (accurate) information without bias, which permits *comparisons* through time (primarily through *consistent* application of accounting principles), communicates to the reasonably prudent investor (i.e., is *understandable*), and is *relevant* (i.e., influences the decision maker). Such desirable information characteristics require compromise among user groups, as well as compromise among *reporting objectives.* For example, the most relevant information may not be sufficiently *objective* to become a component of financial statements.

Generally accepted accounting principles (GAAP) are the foundation for measuring and disclosing financial information and include pronouncements of the *Committee on Accounting Procedure (CAP)* of the *American Institute of Certified Public Accountants (AICPA),* the *Accounting Principles Board (APB),* and the *Financial Accounting Standards Board (FASB).* The current FASB is generally considered to have more independence, broader representation, and better resources than its predecessor, the APB. However, it has been criticized for moving too slowly and faces the risk of intervention by the *Securities and Exchange Commission (SEC),* which has the authority to set accounting principles, although in the past it has largely delegated such authority to the private sector. Accounting principles are greatly influenced by the *Internal Revenue Service (IRS), American Accounting Association (AAA),* and the *National Association of Accountants (NAA).*

In setting principles, numerous assumptions are considered, including the **entity assumption,** which requires that each entity maintain separate accounting records and prepare separate financial statements, the **going-concern assumption,** which states that the business will continue operating for long periods of time unless substantial evidence indicates otherwise, the **periodicity assumption,** which holds that an entity's life can be divided into discrete time periods for reporting purposes, and the **monetary unit assumption,** which is based on the premise that the dollar is a stable measuring unit. In addition, concepts such as the **historical-cost principle** (providing objective and definite exchange prices which are verifiable) and the **objectivity principle** are considered by the policy setters. The **revenue realization principle,** which states that revenue is earned when the earnings process is complete or virtually complete and the revenue can be objectively measured, is a primary concept which underlies GAAP and typically results in **point-of-sale recognition,** although **percentage of completion,** which recognizes revenue during the production process, is an acceptable method of realization for long-term projects, and **the installment method,** which is similar to the cash basis of accounting, is an acceptable method of realization for situations in which collectibility is uncertain. The *cash basis* of accounting, though widely used by individuals, is not in accord with GAAP.

The *matching principle* underlies the adjusting process of accounting, and coupled with the *consistency principle,* is a key component of GAAP. The **minimum disclosure principle** of GAAP requires a complete reporting of significant accounting principles, changes therein with related effects on income, impending lawsuits and contingencies, significant subsequent events, and significant business transactions.

Modifying conventions which dictate the proper handling of transactions in the accounting records based on their influence upon decision makers include *materiality* and *conservatism.* The availability of alternative accounting principles within GAAP can significantly alter the financial statements; however, such a choice among reporting techniques is essential in light of the differences in entities' operations.

TECHNICAL POINTS

√ *Desirable Information Characteristics*

Relevancy
Reliability
Comparability
Understandability

✓ Generally accepted accounting principles (GAAP) include the pronouncements of

The Committee on Accounting Procedure (CAP)
The Accounting Principles Board (APB)
The Financial Accounting Standards Board (FASB)

✓ Comparison of APB and FASB

APB	*FASB*
Eighteen to twenty-one members	Seven members supported by a staff of forty-five technical specialists
Most members were partners with national and international accounting firms	Backgrounds in public accounting, industry, government, academics, and the securities markets
Part-time, unpaid volunteers	Full-time, well-paid members

✓ Specific assumptions, principles, and concepts that underlie GAAP

Assumptions	*Principles*	*Concepts*
Entity	Historical cost	Materiality
Going concern	Objectivity	Conservatism
Periodicity	Revenue realization	
Monetary unit	Matching	
	Consistency	
	Disclosure	

✓ *Percentage of Completion Profit Allocation = (Current Period's Construction Costs ÷ Total Expected Costs over the Life of the Project*) × Estimated Profit for the Project*

where

Estimated Profit for the Project = Total Estimated Revenue − Estimated Costs

*Until final year, in which the remainder of the profit, not previously recognized but adjusted for any differences in estimated and actual costs for the project, is recorded.

✓ Installment method

Realized Profit = Cash Collected × Profit Percentage

where

$$Profit\ Percentage = \frac{Total\ Sales\ Price - Cost\ of\ Sales}{Total\ Sales\ Price}$$

MULTIPLE-CHOICE QUESTIONS

Circle the letter corresponding to the best response.

1. The concept of relevancy faces the following practical problem(s).
   a. Different users have different needs.
   b. If implemented in the strict sense, businesses would have to abandon the traditional cost basis of accounting.
   c. A given set of financial statements cannot satisfy all needs of all interested parties.
   d. All of the above.

2. The Securities and Exchange Commission (SEC)
   a. is sometimes called the watchdog of Congress
   b. has the authority to prescribe accounting principles and reporting practices for companies issuing publicly traded securities
   c. a and b
   d. none of the above

3. Members of the Financial Accounting Standards Board have backgrounds in all of the following areas except

  a. public accounting
  b. industry
  c. government
  d. academia
  e. securities market
  f. none of the above

4. If a business attempts to lessen the impact of tax law on its accounting system, the effect of such an attempt will generally be
  a. to lower taxes
  b. to lower reported income
  c. to increase reported income
  d. to provide more useful financial information

5. The AAA
  a. is a subcommittee of the AICPA
  b. issues official pronouncements
  c. is comprised primarily of accounting instructors
  d. is comprised primarily of cost and managerial accountants

6. Which of the following is commonly cited as a disadvantage of historical cost?
  a. its subjectivity
  b. its ability to be verified
  c. its distortion of income figures
  d. its objectivity

7. Revenue is said to be realized when
  a. the earnings process is complete or virtually complete
  b. the amount of revenue can be objectively measured
  c. either a or b
  d. both a and b

8. The cash basis of accounting
  a. is in accord with GAAP
  b. realizes revenue at the point of sale
  c. is widely used by individuals and small businesses
  d. is not accepted by the IRS

9. The matching principle
  a. states that all costs and expenses associated with the production of revenue should be recognized when the revenue is recognized
  b. states that all costs and expenses associated with the production of revenue should be recognized when the revenue is collected
  c. is the underlying reason behind the adjusting process
  d. a and c
  e. b and c

10. Conservatism
  a. stipulates that when alternative accounting valuations and measurements are possible, the alternative selected should be that which is least likely to overstate assets and/or net income
  b. deems the reporting of holding gains to be an acceptable practice
  c. deems write-downs below cost to be an unacceptable practice
  d. none of the above

Answer   *Explanation*

1. d   To provide all users with relevant information would require the reporting of current values, as well as historical cost, in so many different forms that some compromise would be essential to yield cost-beneficial financial statements.

2. c   Although the SEC has informally delegated its authority to prescribe GAAP, it formally holds this power.

3. f   All of the backgrounds have been represented on the board.

4. b   Generally in an attempt to minimize taxable income, reported income will decline, frequently resulting in less useful information. Taxes would not be expected to decrease due to such attempts to use one set of books.

5. c   The American Accounting Association (AAA) has no official stature in developing financial accounting standards but makes its role felt through education and persuasion. Response (*d*) refers to the NAA.

6. c   Responses (*b*) and (*d*) are advantages; response (*c*) refers to the effects of cost-based depreciation and amortization computations.

7. d   Both requirements (*a*) and (*b*) must be met.

8. c   Cash basis is not in accord with GAAP because it delays revenue realization beyond the point of sale. It is accepted by the IRS, and for this reason as well as for its simplicity it is widely used by individuals and small businesses. (Note that the IRS requires certain adjustments to be made to the cash basis to ensure that reported income is reasonable.)

9. d   Response (*b*) implies a cash basis of revenue recognition.

10. a   The idea is to offset management's tendency to be optimistic.

TRUE-FALSE QUESTIONS

Indicate whether each of the following statements is true (T) or false (F).

_____   *1.* Information is deemed relevant if it influences the actions of a decision maker.

_____   *2.* Terminology and accounting jargon aid in making financial information understandable.

_____   *3.* The establishment of GAAP means that all organizations report and measure financial activity in the same manner.

_____   *4.* The Committee on Accounting Procedure had no authority to enforce its pronouncements.

_____   *5.* Tax regulations do not directly affect financial accounting; they apply solely to the filing of income tax returns.

_____   *6.* The going-concern assumption provides some justification for the use of an accounting system based on historical cost.

_____   *7.* Most accountants recognize that cost allocations increase the usefulness of financial statements.

_____   *8.* As long as the estimates that underlie accounting numbers are reasonable, made by a competent party, and verifiable, the objectivity principle is considered to have been implemented to the greatest extent possible.

_____   *9.* Percentage of completion is permitted as an accounting method even where substantial uncertainty surrounds the estimation process.

_____   *10.* Changes in the methods of recording and reporting business transactions are allowable whenever the change results in a better or more fair presentation of an entity's economic activities.

Answer   Explanation

1. T   If not actively employed by financial statement users, information is not considered to be relevant.
2. F   Technical terminology can be troublesome to the financial statement user.
3. F   Accounting alternatives exist within GAAP, such as last-in, first-out (LIFO) and first-in, first-out (FIFO) inventory valuation techniques.
4. T   Its publications were merely "suggested" accounting practices and rules.
5. T   Despite some businesses' attempts to lessen the effects of tax law on their accounting systems by using the same accounting treatment for taxes and for financial reporting, such practices are not required.
6. T   Unless a company plans to terminate operations, the liquidation value of assets does not appear to be particularly relevant.
7. F   Since cost allocations culminate in arbitrary measures of performance, they are typically thought to diminish the usefulness of financial statements.
8. T   Personal opinion and judgment are required for such accounting measurements as depreciation, but are deemed to be objective if they meet the criteria listed.
9. F   The percentage-of-completion method can only be used when reasonable estimates of completion can be derived.
10. T   However, the reason for the change and the change's impact on net income must be disclosed in the financial statements.

CLASSIFI-CATION AND MATCHING QUESTIONS

Classify the following items using these symbols. In some cases, more than one response may be required.

APB = Refers to the Accounting Principles Board
FASB = Refers to the Financial Accounting Standards Board
CAP = Refers to the Committee on Accounting Procedure

_____ 1. Pronouncements of this rule-making body compose GAAP.
_____ 2. This body was/is independent of the AICPA.
_____ 3. Composed of between eighteen and twenty-one members.
_____ 4. Has/had no authority to enforce its pronouncements.
_____ 5. Was/is an unpaid board.
_____ 6. Ultimately issued thirty-one pronouncements.
_____ 7. Composed of seven members.
_____ 8. Members have diverse backgrounds.
_____ 9. Criticized for acting slowly.
_____ 10. Required/requires members to sever all ties with their previous employers.

CLASSIFICATION AND MATCHING QUESTIONS (ANSWERS)

1. APB, FASB, CAP 2. FASB 3. APB 4. CAP 5. APB 6. APB 7. FASB 8. FASB 9. APB, FASB 10. FASB

QUESTIONS CONCERNING THE EFFECTS OF TRANS- ACTIONS

Will the following practices tend to increase (+), decrease (−), or have no effect (0) upon reported net income for the period?

____ *1.* The use of a cash-basis realization method rather than a point-of-sale realization method

____ *2.* The application of the principle of conservatism

____ *3.* The application of the principle of materiality

____ *4.* The use of a percentage-of-completion method of revenue realization rather than completed contract

____ *5.* Compliance with the consistency principle

QUESTIONS CONCERNING THE EFFECTS OF TRANSACTIONS (ANSWERS)

Answer   Explanation

1. −   Cash basis generally delays revenue realization, tending to lower a given period's net income.

2. −   Generally, conservatism selects the alternative that is least likely to overstate net income; hence, its tendency would be to lower reported income.

3. −   Generally, materiality provides a rationale for expensing small dollar items that would otherwise be capitalized; hence, its tendency would be to lower reported income.

4. +   Percentage of completion permits an earlier recognition of income than completed contract, i.e., recognition during the production process.

5. 0   No directional effect on income is implied, as no change in reporting is implied.

EXERCISES

1. Mitchell Builders, Incorporated, has signed a $90 million contract to build a bridge over the next five years. Mitchell's accounting department has estimated total construction costs at $80 million. Compute the profit recognized in each of the next five years, assuming actual costs for each year were as follows.

Year 1 $20,000,000
Year 2 $10,000,000
Year 3 $12,000,000
Year 4 $25,000,000
Year 5 $14,500,000

2. On April 1, 1983, Turner's Furniture Company sold a dining room set to Wayne Wilson for $2,300. Wilson paid $500 down and agreed to pay the balance via 36 end-of-month installments of $50 each. If the furniture cost Turner's Furniture $1,610, prepare Turner's Furniture Company's realization schedule for this installment sale.

1.

Year	(A) Actual Costs Incurred	(B) Percentage of Work Completed (A ÷ $80,000,000)	Profit Recognized ($10,000,000 × B)
1	$20,000,000	25%	$2,500,000
2	10,000,000	12.5%	1,250,000
3	12,000,000	15%	1,500,000
4	25,000,000	31.25%	3,125,000
5	14,500,000	Remainder	125,000 Remainder
	$81,500,000		$8,500,000

2. The furniture cost $1,610, so the company has generated a $690 profit, or a 30% return, based on sales ($690 ÷ $2,300 = 30%).

Year	Cash Collected	Profit Percentage	Profit Realized
1	$ 950*	30%	$285
2	600†	30%	180
3	600†	30%	180
4	150‡	30%	45
	$2,300		$690

*$500 Down payment plus nine monthly installments of $50 each
†Twelve monthly installments of $50 each
‡Three monthly installments of $50 each

CHAPTER DEMON-STRATION PROBLEM

Filmway Pictures, Inc., is planning to make a movie and has already contracted with two leading stars. Rights to a best-selling novel have been purchased. The corporation estimates that its total revenue from box office sales will be $4 million and its total expenses for the film will be $1.5 million. The corporation estimates that if it wanted to sell the rights to the script and the two contracts with the actors, it could obtain an offer of $500,000, which would result in profit of $200,000. Filmway Pictures, Inc., is considering issuing a prospectus to attract capital for completion of the film and has requested your assistance in reporting the financial statement for this project. Tentatively, the corporation is planning to report $200,000 profit earned to date, to reflect the current market value of the planned project. It estimates that the project will not be completed for three years and is concerned as to how its financial statement will appear next year. Explain to Filmway Pictures the alternatives available to them, as well as the rationale that underlies the alternatives. Be specific and use the appropriate terminology to reflect your understanding of accounting assumptions, principles, and concepts.

CHAPTER DEMONSTRATION PROBLEM (ANSWER)

The alternatives available to Filmway Pictures, Inc., are the revenue realization techniques of completed contract or percentage of completion, both of which are acceptable under generally accepted accounting principles (GAAP). The realization principle permits the recognition of revenue when the earning process is virtually complete and the amount of revenue can be objectively determined. For a long-term project, rather than waiting until the project is completed, profit can be allocated to each period based on the percentage of the total project completed, judged by comparing the current period's project costs to the total expected costs over the life of the project. In this situation, the information implies that costs have been incurred in the amount of $300,000 ($500,000 − $200,000). Compared with the $1.5 million total expenses expected for the project, this represents $300,000/$1,500,000 or 20% of the total costs. The estimated profit on the project is $2.5 million ($4 million − $1.5 million). Hence, 20% of $2.5 million or $500,000 of earnings can be recognized in the current period. If, instead, the completed-contract method of accounting was applied, a zero earnings would be reported.

The plan to report the $200,000 profit derived from the current market value of the project is totally unacceptable according to GAAP. This can be made clear by considering the principles that underlie GAAP—specifically, the historical-cost principle and the objectivity principle. The historical-cost principle relies on the occurrence of past transactions involving independent parties which result in verifiable, objective accounting numbers. In contrast, an estimated current market value of $500,000 (a "claimed" potential offer) is subjective and related to no actual transaction. Although it is true that the realization principle discussed earlier—the percentage-of-completion technique—permits revenue recognition prior to the point of sale, the calculation of the profit that is recognized reflects actual costs incurred by the corporation, which are verifiable, and estimated revenues, the basis for which can be assessed as reasonable through a fairly objective process such as a comparison to historical and industry experience with similar projects.

Explain to Filmway Pictures, Inc., that accounting information is intended to be relevant, reliable, comparable, and understandable and will be expected to reflect such assumptions as going concern. Hence, to reflect a current market value for the project on the books, when there is neither an intention to liquidate the project, nor any means to confirm the reliability of the market value, would be irrelevant reporting of unreliable data. Furthermore, financial statements are made understandable to the reasonably prudent investor by requiring compliance with GAAP, and since historical cost rather than current market value underlies GAAP, any other approach to reporting would not be likely to communicate effectively to users. Even if the corporation had the option to report income as planned, it would more than likely choose to change its report at a later date if the current market price was not available for the project when it reached a midway point, or if the market price was less than cost. In the interest of achieving comparability, a consistent application of accounting principles is required (with some justifiable exceptions) and suggests the propriety of selecting a revenue recognition approach, which will best reflect the profit generated by the film project for its entire life. In this case, the percentage-of-completion method appears to be a reasonable approach to preparing the prospectus, as well as subsequent years' financial statements.

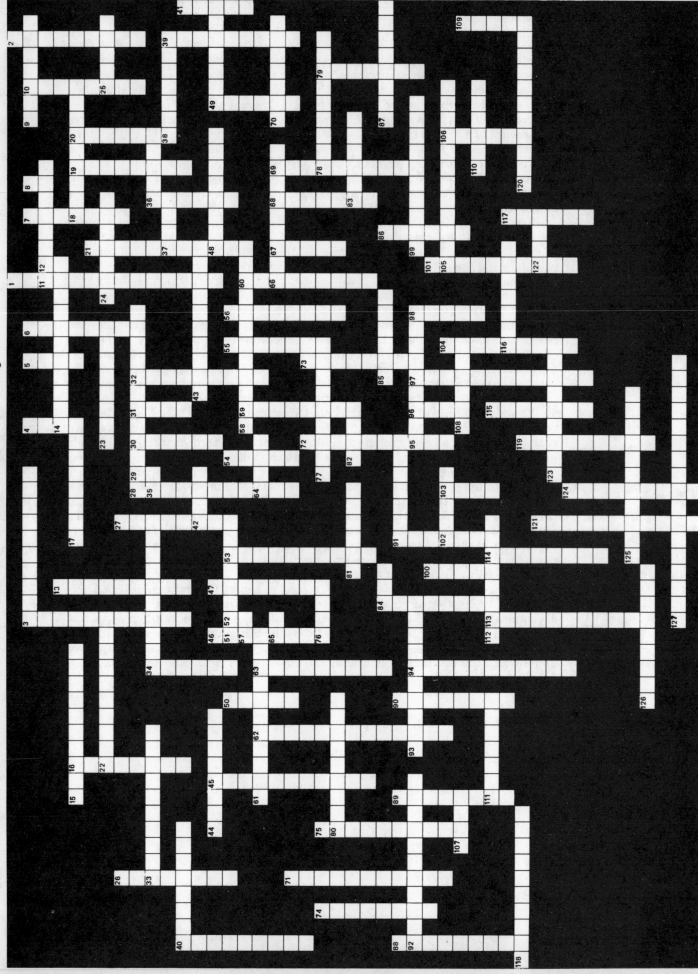

3. The _89 down_ _107 across_ _3 across_ assumes that an entity's transactions can be expressed in terms of a common measuring unit (namely, money) and that the dollar is a stable measuring unit.

9. Bonds are said to be _____ when specific assets have been pledged as security for the bondholders.

11. With _11 across_ _48 across_, interest is calculated not only on principal but on previously computed interest as well.

14. An example of an _105 across_ _14 across_ is the lending of money by a parent to its subsidiary to help to finance operations.

15. The _71 down_ _15 across_ holds that, for reporting purposes, an entity's life can be divided into discrete time periods such as quarters or years.

17. Most business combinations are accounted for by the _17 across_ _85 across_, reflecting the fact that the subsidiary's stockholders have terminated their investment by selling their shares to the parent.

18. The _39 down_ _35 across_ _20 down_ _8 down_ _18 across_ _23 across_ is a required statement that discloses the sources and uses of a business' funds.

22. The _118 across_ _65 across_ _22 across_ revenue realization method allocates profit to each accounting period on the basis of the percentage of the total project completed.

23. See 18 across.

24. When only an exchange of shares has occurred, and one could correctly conclude that the two companies have simply combined themselves to operate as a simple economic entity, the combination is deemed a _24 across_ _65 across_ _78 across_.

25. Many professionals such as lawyers and dentists use the _5 down_ _25 across_ of accounting for their practices, realizing revenue at the time that collections are received.

28. To present the operating performance and financial condition of the single economic entity, the parent company presents a _28 across_ _18 across_ _39 down_ that combines the parent's and the subsidiary's performance.

33. The _16 down_ (ies) _84 across_ _6 down_ _33 across_ is sometimes called the watchdog of Congress.

34. The foundation for measuring and disclosing the results of business transactions and events is a set of assumptions, concepts, and procedures collectively known as _119 down_ _90 down_ _53 down_ _34 across_.

35. See 18 across.

36. Many companies have begun to shy away from an outright purchase in favor of some form of _36 across_ agreement whereby they can take advantage of the tax deductibility of payments, financing without a down payment, and the assumption of the risk of obsolescence by the _108 across_.

37. A _59 down_ _37 across_ is often used to finance the purchase of real estate.

38. Transactions and events that cause working capital to increase are _38 across_ _65 across_ _54 down_.

40. Financial information must be _____; that is, the information must accurately depict the conditions it purports to represent.

42. _____ (or applications) of funds cause working capital to decrease.

43. The possession of more than 50% of the common shares outstanding for a corporation is a _120 across_ _43 across_.

44. The _44 across_ _88 down_ states that all costs and expenses associated with the production of revenue should be recognized when the revenue is recognized.

48. The _95 across_ _48 across_ _4 down_ is the actual rate and, when used in the _95 across_ _48 across_ _85 across_ _29 down_ _58 across_, results in an interest expense being recorded each period that increases in direct proportion to the total bond that is outstanding.

49. With a _____ lease, the lessee is really acquiring an asset via an installment purchase plan.

51. The interest that is printed on the bond certificate is often called the _51 across_ _73 down_ _4 down_.

57. The _100 down_ _65 across_ _122 across_ _57 across_ _110 across_ _117 down_ is used to account for long-term stock acquisitions of investors who are unable to exercise significant influence over the investee corporation.

58. _47 down_ - _82 across_ _58 across_ allocates an equal amount of discount to each interest period.

61. The _74 down_ _53 down_ _61 across_ is composed primarily of accounting instructors.

64. A _____ enables a borrower to split a large loan requirement into a number of small divisible units.

65. The _87 across_ _61 across_ _65 across_ _3 down_ is a large organization whose membership consists primarily of cost and managerial accountants.

66. A _66 across_ _64 across_ has no assets pledged as security.

70. Funds are defined as the _70 across_ _49 across_ of the enterprise, representing the excess of current assets over current liabilities.

73. Some companies prepare a _39 down_ _35 across_ _20 down_ _73 across_ _18 across_ _23 across_ using a _103 down_ _19 down_, particularly banks and insurance companies which do not classify their accounts into current and noncurrent categories.

76. The _101 down_ _76 across_ _88 down_ requires that acquisitions be recorded in the accounts at cost, with cost defined as the exchange or transaction price.

77. Under an _____ lease, the lessee signs a short-term lease agreement and treats amounts paid under the agreement as expense.

78. See 24 across.

80. The _123 across_ _53 down_ _80 across_ _67 down_ is the private sector organization currently in charge of formulating standards of financial reporting in this country.

81. The _81 across_ _75 down_ views a business as a unit that is separate and distinct from its owners and from other businesses.

82. See 58 across.

83. Affiliated companies when combined together form a single _46 down_ _83 across_.

84. See 33 across.

85. When a company acquires a substantial percentage (greater than 20%) of the voting shares of a corporation, a material economic relationship is formed between the investor and the investee and the _86 down_ _117 down_ must be used.

87. See 65 across.

91. When investors are willing to pay more than the face value of a bond, the difference between the issue price and the face value is called a _____.

92. The _111 across_ _92 across_ _104 down_ says that revenue is earned when the earnings process is complete or virtually complete and the amount of revenue can be objectively measured.

93. The _93 across_ _104 down_ requires that an entity provide a complete reporting of all facts important enough to influence the judgment of an informed user of financial information.

95. See 48 across.

99. A majority owned company is termed a _____.

102. A _102 across_ _43 across_ is initially entered in the accounts at cost (i.e., the purchase price plus any related acquisition costs such as brokers' fees and transfer taxes) and is an alternative to purchasing bonds.

105. See 14 across.

107. See 3 across.

108. The _____ is the owner of assets leased to another party.

110. See 57 across.

111. See 92 across.

112. Acquisitions of more than 50% but less than 100% of the outstanding voting stock of other corporations are common and result in the reporting of a _112 across_ _48 across_.

116. The _109 down_ _116 across_ _75 down_ states that a business will continue to operate for long periods of time unless there is substantive evidence to the contrary.

118. See 22 across.

120. See 43 across.

122. See 57 across.

123. The primary _126 across_ _29 down_ _123 across_ _124 down_ is to provide statements that are useful in satisfying different needs of different parties.

125. _____ dictates that the accountant must judge the impact and importance of each transaction (or event) to determine its proper handling in the accounting records.

126. See 123 across.

127. _____ is one of the desirable characteristics of accounting information, yet is often difficult to achieve due to troublesome terminology and jargon.

DOWN

1. Sears has a separate subsidiary that sells insurance and is an _1 down_ _99 across_ since the operations of the parent and subsidiary differ significantly.

2. Bonds may be called and replaced by an issue carrying a lower interest rate; this practice is known as _64 across_ _2 down_.

3. See 65 across.

4. See 48 across and 51 across.

5. See 25 across.

6. See 33 across.

7. A _7 down_ _26 down_ _14 across_ would be exemplified by the collection of an account receivable.

8. See 18 across.

10. A _10 down_ _64 across_ permits the issuer to pay bondholders prior to the stipulated maturity date, a feature that is often exercised should funds become available at lower interest rates.

12. A company that uses the installment basis is said to be _____ a form of the cash basis of accounting.

13. The _84 down_ _63 down_ _35 across_ _13 down_ _34 down_ _121 down_ is a national association of licensed CPAs which was responsible for forming both the CAP and APB.

16. See 33 across.

19. See 73 across.

20. See 18 across and 73 across.

21. An _21 down_ _98 down_ is required for intercompany items contained in the records of the parent and subsidiaries that do not appear in the consolidated financial statements.

26. See 7 down.

27. When bonds are sold at less than face value, the difference between the issue price and face value is commonly referred to as a _____.

28. Similar to many preferred stocks, some bonds are _____ into common shares at the option of the bondholder.

29. See 48 across and 123 across.

30. With _____ bonds, bondholders are repaid in periodic installments over a number of years.

31. Same as 82 across.

32. A _55 down_ _54 down_ _32 down_ requires issuing companies to create a special fund to repay the bond issue.

34. See 13 down.

36. The _____ is the party that uses assets leased from another party.

39. See 18 across, 28 across, and 73 across.

41. Bonds are shown at their _56 down_ _41 down_ or present value (i.e., the difference in bonds payable and any discount or the sum of bonds payable and any premium).

45. The _45 down_ _88 down_ requires that the same accounting practices be used in each reporting period with only justifiable exceptions.

46. See 83 across.

47. See 58 across.

49. A _49 down_ _64 across_ has small detachable coupons that correspond to each interest period.

50. The _53 down_ _34 across_ _50 down_ issued thirty-one pronouncements and was replaced by FASB.

52. Same as 57 across.

53. See 34 across, 61 across, 80 across, and 50 down.

54. See 38 across and 32 down.

55. See 32 down.

56. See 41 down.

59. See 37 across.

60. The provisions of a bond issue are normally stipulated in an accompanying document called a _64 across_ _60 down_.

62. _____ is a desirable information characteristic that is achieved through the use of the same accounting practices from one period to the next.

63. See 13 down.

67. See 80 across.

68. To protect the bondholders' interests, the issuing firm usually appoints a _____, a third party that monitors the issuer's adherence to the stipulated terms of the bonds.

69. Most of the bonds issued in recent years have been _____ bonds; that is, the name and address of the purchaser is entered in the issuing company's records.

71. See 15 across.

72. Bonds may be called and cancelled; this is known as _64 across_ _72 down_.

73. See 51 across.

74. See 61 across.

75. See 81 across and 116 across.

79. The _____ life of an asset when depreciated under the historical-cost principle can distort reported income relative to actual economic performance.

84. See 13 down.

86. See 85 across.

88. See 44 across, 76 across, and 45 down.

89. See 3 across.

90. See 34 across.

91. A tool known as _91 down_ _41 down_ integrates cash flows, their timing, and rates of return to quantitatively determine the amount an investor is willing to pay for a bond, or for that matter, any other investment.

94. _____ requires that accounting information be free from bias and verifiable by an independent party such as an external auditor.

96. All bonds have a _96 down_ _41 down_, that is, a set amount to be repaid on the maturity date of the bonds.

97. _____ stipulates that when alternative accounting valuations and measurements are possible, the alternative selected should be that which is least likely to overstate assets and/or net income.

98. See 21 down.

100. See 57 across.

101. See 76 across.

103. See 73 across.

104. See 92 across and 93 across.

106. The majority owner of a company is termed the _____.

109. See 116 across.

113. Sellers using the _113 down_ _117 down_, a form of cash basis, allocate a sale's profit to different accounting periods based on the amount of cash received from customers.

114. The _114 down_ _115 down_ _79 down_ administers the tax regulations that are passed by Congress.

115. See 114 down.

117. See 57 across, 85 across, and 113 down.

119. See 34 across.

121. See 13 down.

124. See 123 across.

19 FINANCIAL STATEMENTS: ANALYSIS AND THE IMPACT OF INFLATION

OBJECTIVES

After completing this chapter, you should:

1 *Be aware of the advantages to and shortcomings of various tools of financial statement analysis.*

2 *Know how to perform a horizontal analysis of comparative financial statements.*

3 *Know how to perform a vertical analysis to generate common-size statements.*

4 *Be able to describe: ratio analysis; its use in studying liquidity, activity, profitability, and coverage relationships; its adaptability in gauging almost any kind of performance; and specific ratios commonly utilized in financial analysis.*

5 *Know what is meant by trading on the equity.*

6 *Understand how to account for inflation via constant dollar accounting or a current value approach and be familiar with the related disclosure requirements of the Financial Accounting Standards Board.*

CHAPTER SUMMARY

Having prepared a set of financial statements, how can it be utilized to analyze the company's performance? Valuable tools of analysis that are frequently used to evaluate financial statements are horizontal analysis, vertical analysis, and ratio analysis. In order to be meaningful, each of these tools must be interpreted in the business and economic context to which they are applied, with particular attention to time trends and *industry norms* that are appropriately adjusted for differences in accounting practices and lines of business (e.g., through the use of segmental disclosures). The analyst should also be aware of the potential for *window dressing* (i.e., intentional manipulation of ratios by management to improve the financial picture of the company).

A **horizontal analysis** is essentially a statement of percentage changes across comparative financial statements. A **vertical analysis** is a conversion of each figure on the financial statements to a percentage of some relevant total figure on each statement (most commonly, net sales or total assets). The percentage approaches enhance the comparability of operations across time and across companies and are easier to interpret than the absolute size of financial figures.

A ratio is a mathematical expression of a relationship and can be formulated to assess any type of performance. For businesses, **ratios** are typically classified as liquidity, activity, profitability, and coverage (of obligations) ratios that assess abilities to meet current debts, management's effectiveness in using specific resources like inventory, organizations' operating success (or lack of success), and the solvency of businesses, respectively.

One means of enhancing profitability ratios is through the use of **positive leverage** (using other people's money to make money). Whenever a firm is able to trade on its equity to earn a higher return than the cost of debt and preferred stock capital, it will enhance the profits of the common stockholders.

The effect of inflation can be presented in financial statements by using the constant dollar accounting or current value accounting approach. The **constant dollar method** adjusts historical cost data by multiplying nonmonetary account balances by a general price index, such as the consumer price index, and computes the purchasing power gain (or loss) for the excess of monetary liabilities over monetary assets (or the reverse relationship) by multiplying the net balance borrowed (or loaned) by the inflation rate. The **current value method** typically uses individual assets' replacement costs to compute holding gains or holding losses (the difference in current value and historical cost). Such gains and losses are subclassified as unrealized if the assets are still owned at the end of the accounting period and as realized if the assets are sold during the period. The Financial Accounting Standards Board requires large, publicly held companies to provide supplementary information on inflationary effects upon inventories; cost of goods sold; property, plant, and equipment; and depreciation, depletion, and amortization. However, neither the constant dollar nor current value method is required to be comprehensively applied in determining income from continuing operations.

TECHNICAL POINTS

√ *Shortcomings of industry norms*

Diversified firms are unlikely to be comparable in the aggregate
Differing accounting practices may reduce comparability

√ Horizontal analysis

Percentage Change from Prior Year per Account

$$= \frac{Current\ Year\ Balance - Prior\ Year\ Balance}{Prior\ Year\ Balance}$$

√ Vertical analysis

$$Income\ Statement\ Percentage\ of\ Sales\ Analysis = \frac{Income\ Statement\ Account}{Net\ Sales}$$

$$Balance\ Sheet\ Percentage\ of\ Assets\ Analysis = \frac{Balance\ Sheet\ Account}{Total\ Assets}$$

Note: The primary advantage of vertical analysis is that it results in common-size financial statements that are comparable across time and across companies.

✓ Liquidity ratios measure the ability of a business to meet current obligations as they come due.

$$Current\ Ratio = \frac{Current\ Assets}{Current\ Liabilities}$$

Rule of thumb: 2:1

$$Quick\ Ratio = \frac{Current\ Assets\ Other\ Than\ Inventory\ and\ Prepaid\ Expenses\ (i.e.,\ Quick\ Assets)}{Current\ Liabilities}$$

Rule of thumb: 1:1

✓ Activity or turnover ratios measure management's effectiveness in using specific resources.

Accounts Receivable Turnover

$$= \frac{Net\ Sales}{\left(\frac{Beginning\ Accounts\ Receivable\ +\ Ending\ Accounts\ Receivable}{2}\right)}$$

Rule of Thumb: 365 Days/Accounts Receivable Turnover < Credit Terms + One Week for Mailing and Processing

$$Inventory\ Turnover\ Ratio = \frac{Cost\ of\ Goods\ Sold}{\left(\frac{Beginning\ Inventory\ +\ Ending\ Inventory}{2}\right)}$$

Rule of Thumb: Industry Average

✓ Profitability ratios measure an organization's operating success (or lack of success) during an accounting period.

$$Profit\ Margin\ on\ Sales = \frac{Net\ Income}{Net\ Sales}$$

Rate of Return on Assets (i.e., Return on Investment)

$$= \frac{Net\ Income\ +\ Interest\ Expense}{\left(\frac{Beginning\ Assets\ +\ Ending\ Assets}{2}\right)}$$

Return on Common Stockholders' Equity

$$= \frac{Net\ Income\ -\ Preferred\ Dividends}{\left(\frac{Beginning\ Common\ Stockholders'\ Equity\ +\ Ending\ Common\ Stockholders'\ Equity}{2}\right)}$$

$$Primary\ Earnings\ per\ Share = \frac{Net\ Income\ -\ Preferred\ Dividends}{Weighted\ Average\ Common\ Shares\ Outstanding}$$

$$Price\text{-}Earnings\ Ratio = \frac{Current\ Market\ Price\ of\ a\ Share\ of\ Common\ Stock}{Earnings\ per\ Share}$$

$$Dividend\ Payout\ Ratio = \frac{Annual\ Cash\ Dividend\ per\ Share}{Earnings\ per\ Share}$$

$$Dividend\ Yield = \frac{Annual\ Cash\ Dividend\ per\ Share}{Current\ Market\ Price\ of\ the\ Stock}$$

√ Coverage ratios measure the solvency of a business

$$\text{Debt to Total Assets} = \frac{\text{Total Debt}}{\text{Total Assets}}$$

$$\text{Total Debt to Total Stockholders' Equity} = \frac{\text{Total Debt}}{\text{Total Stockholders' Equity}}$$

$$\text{Times Interest Earned} = \frac{\text{Net Income before Income Taxes and Interest}}{\text{Interest Charges}}$$

√ Trading on the equity (using other people's money to make money): Favorable leverage results if return on investment is greater than the cost of money to make the investment.

√ Inflation is a rise in the general price level which causes a decline in the purchasing power.

√ *Constant Dollar Approach Conversion Formula = Historical Cost of Nonmonetary*

$$\text{Items} \times \frac{\text{Index Converting to}}{\text{Index Converting from}}$$

√ *Monetary Items = Contractual Claims to Receive or Pay a Fixed Amount of Cash in the Future*

√ *Purchasing Power Gain = Principal Borrowed × Inflation Rate*

Purchasing Power Loss = Principal Loaned × Inflation Rate

Note: Net gains result when monetary liabilities exceed monetary assets, and net losses result when monetary assets exceed monetary losses during a period of inflation.

√ Current value accounting: Restate assets at current value (e.g., replacement cost)

√ *Holding Gain (Loss) = Current Value − Cost*

Realized if assets are sold
Unrealized if assets are still owned at the end of the accounting period

√ Required FASB supplementary disclosures on inflation

Constant Dollar

Income from continuing operations
Purchasing power gain or loss

Current Value

Income from continuing operations
Holding gains from inventory and property, plant, & equipment (net of inflation)
Inventory and property, plant, & equipment at the end of the year

Note: Neither the constant dollar nor the current value method is required to be comprehensively applied in determining income from continuing operations. Restatements are necessary only for inventories; cost of goods sold; property, plant, & equipment; and depreciation, depletion, and amortization.

MULTIPLE-CHOICE QUESTIONS

Circle the letter corresponding to the best response.

1. If net sales in 1983 are $700,000 and in 1984 are $1,050,000, a horizontal analysis would report a percentage change of
   a. 50%
   b. 150%
   c. 66.7%
   d. 28.6%

2. The most widely used measure of liquidity is
   a. the quick ratio
   b. working capital
   c. the cash balance
   d. the current ratio

3. The general rule employed by bankers and other creditors is that the current ratio should be at least
   a. 1
   b. 1.5
   c. 2
   d. 2.5
   e. 3

4. The quick ratio, relative to the current ratio, excludes
   a. inventory from the asset base
   b. prepaid expenses from the asset base
   c. accounts receivable from the asset base
   d. inventory and prepaid expenses from the asset base
   e. inventory, prepaid expenses, and accounts receivable from the asset base

5. Inventory stockouts are more likely to occur for companies
   a. with a low inventory-turnover ratio
   b. with a high inventory-turnover ratio
   c. with either a very low or a very high inventory-turnover ratio
   d. with a high percentage of assets invested in inventory

6. Trading on the equity is favorable if
   a. a firm earns a return on long-term debt that is less than the cost of this debt
   b. a firm uses negative leverage
   c. a firm earns a return on preferred stock and long-term debt that is less than their cost
   d. a firm earns a return on preferred stock and long-term debt that is greater than their cost

7. The percentage of earnings currently being distributed to stockholders is measured by
   a. the price-earnings ratio
   b. the dividend payout ratio
   c. the dividend yield
   d. earnings per share

8. During a period of inflation, a firm had $400,000 of monetary assets and $600,000 of monetary liabilities.
   a. This firm experienced a purchasing-power gain.
   b. This firm experienced a purchasing-power loss.
   c. It cannot be determined from the information available whether the firm experienced a purchasing-power gain or loss
   d. The firm experienced neither a purchasing-power gain nor loss.

9. A price index on December 31, 1982, was 100, on December 31, 1983, was 125, and on average during 1983 was 110. If a company has sales of $800,000 that occur evenly throughout the year, the company's constant dollar income statement would report sales of
   a. $909,091
   b. $640,000
   c. $727,273
   d. $1,000,000
   e. $880,000
   f. $704,000

10. Aberack, Inc., purchased 2,000 units of inventory on April 1, 1983, at $5 per unit. By June 30, 1983, the end of the fiscal year, the replacement cost of the units had increased to $6 and 500 units remained in ending inventory. The unrealized holding gain for this inventory totals
   a. $2,000
   b. $500
   c. $1,500
   d. $250

MULTIPLE-CHOICE QUESTIONS (ANSWERS)

Answer	Explanation

1. a
$$\frac{1,050,000 - 700,000}{700,000} = 50\%$$

2. d   The current ratio assesses cash, investment receivables, inventories, and prepaid expenses in evaluating a firm's ability to meet its obligations and is the most widely used measure.

3. c   The general rule is that the current ratio should be at least 2, although the ratio is expected to vary by type of business.

4. d   These assets are not considered to be immediate sources of cash.

5. b   Too much attention on minimal inventories results in high turnovers and increases the risk of stockouts.

6. d   Positive or favorable leverage means that a firm effectively uses someone else's money to make money.

7. b
$$\frac{\textit{Annual Cash Dividends per Share}}{\textit{Earnings per Share}}$$

8. a   When monetary liabilities exceed monetary assets during a period of inflation, a purchasing power gain is realized.

9. a
$$\left(\$800,000 \times \frac{125}{110}\right) = \$909,091$$

10. b   There are 500 units unsold at year-end. 500 × ($6 − $5) = $500

TRUE-FALSE QUESTIONS

Indicate whether each of the following statements is true (T) or false (F).

____   *1.* In comparison with the current ratio, the quick ratio represents a more severe test of debt-paying ability.

____   *2.* A debt to stockholders' equity ratio of 1 signifies that the creditors and owners are providing equal amounts of funds for business operations.

____   *3.* The current ratio weights cash and near-cash items heavier than inventories and prepaids.

____   *4.* Normally, high current asset levels indicate that a company is foregoing considerable profits, as long-term investments typically generate higher returns than short-term investments.

____   *5.* The current ratio's popularity as a liquidity measure is largely due to its inability to be manipulated.

____   *6.* If a firm devoted more resources to its collection activities, it would expect its accounts receivable turnover ratio to decrease.

____   *7.* The use of net interest expense in the numerator of the return on investment ratio recognizes the tax deductibility of interest.

____ 8. Lenders encourage trading on the equity.

____ 9. The lower the debt to asset ratio, the greater the chance that owners will share in any remaining proceeds from asset liquidation.

____ 10. Neither the constant dollar nor current value method is required by the Financial Accounting Standards Board to be comprehensively applied in determining income from continuing operations.

TRUE-FALSE QUESTIONS (ANSWERS)

Answer	Explanation
1. T	Since the quick ratio excludes inventory and prepaid expenses from the numerator, it better reflects the availability of ready or "near ready" sources of cash.
2. T	This ratio is computed by dividing total debt by total stockholders' equity; it can only be 1 when the numerator and denominator are equal.
3. F	The current ratio treats all current assets equally, disregarding their individual liquidities.
4. T	Labor-saving equipment and research investments typically generate higher returns than current assets, which should be at levels that are no greater than is necessary to support operations.
5. F	A business can manipulate the current ratio upward by retiring its short-term obligations and replacing them with long-term debt.
6. F	The firm would expect its accounts receivable turnover ratio to increase, as the average collection period of receivables should be shortened by the increased collection efforts.
7. T	Interest as a tax deductible expense can be thought of as a tax savings that should be recognized as a partial offset to the cost of financing.
8. F	Generally, lenders and preferred stockholders view trading on the equity as a source of increased risk, with greater likelihood that interest and dividend requirements will not be met.
9. T	Since creditors have priority claims in the event of insolvency, the less debt outstanding, the fewer the outstanding priority claims and the more likely owners are to receive some proceeds from liquidation.
10. T	Restatements are necessary only for inventories; cost of goods sold; property, plant, & equipment; and depreciation, depletion, and amortization.

CLASSIFICATION AND MATCHING QUESTIONS

Classify the following items using these symbols.

L = Liquidity ratio
A = Activity ratio
P = Profitability ratio
C = Coverage ratio

____ 1. Accounts receivable turnover ratio
____ 2. Price-earnings ratio
____ 3. Times interest earned
____ 4. Dividend yield
____ 5. Quick ratio
____ 6. Return on common stockholders' equity
____ 7. Inventory turnover ratio
____ 8. Debt to total assets
____ 9. Profit margin on sales
____ 10. Current ratio

CLASSIFICATION AND MATCHING QUESTIONS (ANSWERS)

1. A *2.* P *3.* C *4.* P *5.* L *6.* P *7.* A *8.* C *9.* P *10.* L

QUESTIONS CONCERNING THE EFFECTS OF TRANS-ACTIONS

Does each of the following transactions increase (I), decrease (D), or have no effect on (N) the ratio indicated for a company in its first year of operations?

	Effect	
Accounts receivable turnover of twenty times	____	*1.* Made sales on account
Profit margin on sales	____	*2.* Declared dividends
Debt to total assets	____	*3.* Issued debt
Times interest earned	____	*4.* Sold for $80 inventory costing $60
Quick ratio of 0.8:1	____	*5.* Purchased inventory on account
Current ratio of 1.8:1	____	*6.* Collection of a customer's account
Return on common stockholders' equity	____	*7.* Issued preferred stock at the beginning of the year; dividends were declared during the year
Inventory turnover of fifteen times	____	*8.* A sale for $90, with related cost of goods sold of $50, was made by a salesperson
Inventory turnover of fifteen times	____	*9.* Purchased $400 of inventory
Rate of return on assets	____	*10.* Borrowed $5,000 at the beginning of the year, with a 15% interest rate

QUESTIONS CONCERNING THE EFFECTS OF TRANSACTIONS (ANSWERS)

Answer   *Explanation*

1. D   Numerator increases by same amount as denominator; since ratio is greater than one, the ratio decreases [e.g., $(20 + 1)/(1 + 1) = (21/2) = 10.5$].

2. N   Dividends affect neither net income nor sales.

3. I   Numerator and denominator increase by same amount; since the ratio can be assumed to be smaller than one, the ratio increases [e.g., $(0.5 + 1)/(1 + 1) = (1.5/2) = 0.75$].

4. I   Net income increases, thereby increasing the numerator; there is no effect on the denominator.

5. D   The numerator is unaffected and the denominator increases.

6. N   One current asset exchanged for another has no net effect on the numerator, and there is no change in the denominator.

7. D   The numerator would be reduced by related preferred dividends and there would be no change in the other components of the ratio (without some heroic assumption as to the firm's trading on the equity). Hence, the numerator decreases the ratio.

8. I   The numerator increases and the denominator decreases, resulting in an increase in the turnover ratio.

9. D   The denominator increases with no effect on the numerator.

10. D   The numerator increases by $5,000 × 15% or $750, while the denominator increases by the $5,000 principal. Without any information on the firm's ability to trade on the equity, no effect upon net income can be assumed.

EXERCISES

1. Akronic, Inc., reports the following comparative income statements.

	For the Year Ended December 31, 1984	For the Year Ended December 31, 1983
Net sales	$200,000	$150,000
Cost of goods sold	120,000	100,000
Gross profit	$ 80,000	$ 50,000
Operating expenses		
Selling	$ 2,400	$ 2,000
Administrative	1,000	1,500
Total operating expenses	$ 3,400	$ 3,500
Operating income	$ 76,600	$ 46,500
Interest expense	800	1,200
Income before income taxes	$ 75,800	$ 45,300
Income taxes at 35%	26,530	15,855
Net income	$ 49,270	$ 29,445

a. Prepare a vertical analysis for the comparative statements of Akronic, Inc.
b. Prepare a horizontal analysis for the comparative statements of Akronic, Inc.

EXERCISES (ANSWERS)

a. The first two columns in the table below compose the vertical analysis.
b. The last two columns in the table below compose the horizontal analysis.

	For the Year Ended December 31, 1984	For the Year Ended December 31, 1983	Increase (Decrease) from 1983 to 1984	Percentage Change from 1983
Net sales	100.0%	100.00%	$50,000	33.3%
Cost of goods sold	60.0	66.67	20,000	20.0
Gross profit	40.0	33.33	$30,000	60.0
Operating expenses				
Selling	1.2	1.33	$ 400	20.0
Administrative	.5	1.00	(500)	(33.3)
Total operating expenses	1.7	2.33	$ (100)	(2.9)
Operating income	38.3	31.00	$30,100	64.7
Interest expense	.4	.80	(400)	(33.3)
Income before income taxes	37.9	30.20	$30,500	67.3
Income taxes at 35%	13.3	10.57	10,675	67.3
Net income	24.6%	19.63%	$19,825	67.3

REDI-FINANCE EQUIPMENT, INC.
Comparative Income Statements
For the Years Ended December 31, 1983 and 1982

	1983	1982
Sales	$906,000,000	$803,000,000
Sales returns & allowances	6,000,000	3,000,000
Net sales	$900,000,000	$800,000,000
Cost of goods sold	630,000,000	480,000,000
Gross profit	$270,000,000	$320,000,000
Selling & administrative expenses	9,000,000	7,500,000
Interest expense	25,000,000	12,000,000
Income before taxes	$236,000,000	$300,500,000
Income taxes at 45%	106,200,000	135,225,000
Net income	$129,800,000	$165,275,000
Preferred stock dividends	$ 1,500,000	$ 1,300,000
Common stock dividends	$ 70,000,000	$ 50,000,000

REDI-FINANCE EQUIPMENT, INC.
Comparative Balance Sheets
December 31, 1983 and 1982

	1983	1982
ASSETS		
Cash	$ 20,000,000	$ 18,000,000
Marketable securities	10,000,000	10,000,000
Accounts receivable (net)	90,000,000	60,000,000
Inventory	170,000,000	100,000,000
Prepaid insurance	1,500,000	2,000,000
Land	70,000,000	70,000,000
Buildings	450,000,000	350,000,000
Accumulated depreciation: Buildings	(80,000,000)	(50,000,000)
Equipment	258,300,000	108,000,000
Accumulated depreciation: Equipment	(49,000,000)	(30,000,000)
Patent	175,000,000	54,000,000
Total assets	$1,115,800,000	$ 692,000,000
LIABILITIES		
Accounts payable	$ 90,000,000	$ 80,000,000
Notes payable	20,000,000	5,000,000
Dividends payable	20,000,000	10,000,000
Mortgages payable	60,000,000	60,000,000
Bonds payable	170,000,000	70,000,000
Total liabilities	$ 360,000,000	$ 225,000,000
STOCKHOLDERS' EQUITY		
Preferred stock	$ 12,000,000	$ 11,000,000
Paid-in capital in excess of par: Preferred	500,000	300,000
Common stock ($1 par)	35,000,000	20,000,000
Paid-in capital in excess of par: Common	500,000,000	285,700,000
Retained earnings	208,300,000	150,000,000
Total stockholders' equity	$ 755,800,000	$ 467,000,000
Total liabilities and stockholders' equity	$1,115,800,000	$ 692,000,000

A. Compute the following figures for 1983.

  1. Current ratio
  2. Quick ratio
  3. Accounts receivable turnover
  4. Inventory turnover
  5. Profit margin on sales
  6. Rate of return on assets
  7. Return on common stockholders' equity
  8. Primary earnings per share (assuming the 1983 stock issue was made June 30, 1983)
  9. Price-earnings ratio (assuming a current market price of $40)
  10. Debt to total assets
  11. Total debt to total stockholders' equity
  12. Times interest earned

B. *Briefly* comment on the results of the financial statement analysis performed in part (*A*) and suggest what your next step would be in evaluating Redi-Finance Equipment, Inc.

C. Assume the price index was as shown in the table below.

	Price Index
December 31, 1981	110
December 31, 1982	100
December 31, 1983	125
1981 Average index	105
1982 Average index	95
1983 Average index	115

If the land, building, and equipment recorded in 1982 were purchased in 1981, and the 1981 patent was purchased in 1975 when the price index was 75, what would be the constant dollar asset section of the balance sheet for Redi-Finance Equipment on December 31, 1983, and what would be its purchasing-power gain or loss?

D. Assume the following current values

	1983	*1982*
Inventory	$200,000,000	$130,000,000
Cost of goods sold	650,000,000	590,000,000
Equipment (gross)	200,000,000	130,000,000

What are the holding gains and losses for these items? Are they realized or unrealized? Are any other accounts affected by inflation's influence on the above items? Be specific in your response.

CHAPTER DEMONSTRATION PROBLEM (ANSWER)

A. 1. $\dfrac{\$291,500,000}{\$130,000,000} = 2.24$

2. $\dfrac{\$120,000,000}{\$130,000,000} = 0.92$

3. $\dfrac{\$900,000,000}{\$75,000,000} = 12$

4. $\dfrac{\$630,000,000}{\$135,000,000} = 4.7$

5. $\dfrac{\$129,800,000}{\$900,000,000} = 0.14$

6. $\dfrac{\$154,800,000}{\$903,900,000} = 0.17$

7. $\dfrac{\$128,300,000}{\left(\dfrac{\$743,300,000 + \$455,700,000}{2}\right)} = 0.21$

8. $\dfrac{\$128,300,000}{20,000,000 + \left(\dfrac{6}{12} \times 15,000,000\right)} = \$4.67$

9. $\dfrac{\$40}{\text{Answer (8)}} = \$8.57$

10. $\dfrac{\$360,000,000}{\$1,115,800,000} = 0.32$

11. $\dfrac{\$360{,}000{,}000}{\$755{,}800{,}000} = 0.48$

12. $\dfrac{\$261{,}000{,}000}{\$\ 25{,}000{,}000} = 10.44$

B. The current ratio is slightly above the general rule of thumb of 2, and the quick ratio is slightly below the general rule of thumb of 1. The accounts receivable turnover implies a collection period of 30.42 days, which corresponds well to the typical 30-day credit terms in many industries. The inventory turnover appears rather low, suggesting some risks and expenses associated with carrying costs (i.e., obsolescence, loss from mishandling or natural disasters, insurance, and storage costs). The profitability ratios cannot be interpreted without some additional trend analysis and information as to industry norms. The debt ratio suggests some possibility for increasing the extent to which the company is trading on its equity. Typically, 40 to 50% debt is deemed to be an acceptable level of risk, yet this company has a debt ratio of 32%. Clearly, common stockholders are the primary source of capital for the firm, as the debt to stockholders' equity ratio is substantially below 1, it is 0.48. The times interest earned ratio can only be evaluated with the provision of additional information as to industry norms.

The next step in evaluating Redi-Finance Equipment, Inc., would be to compute ratios for the past three to five years prior to 1983 for a time trend comparison of the company's performance in 1983 to the company's financial history. Then industry norms would be identified, with a focus on key competitors in an attempt to decipher management's strengths and weaknesses as reflected in the ratios. To facilitate comparisons with firms of varied size, a horizontal analysis should be prepared for Redi-Finance Equipment, Inc.

C. Monetary Assets = Cash + Marketable Securities + Accounts Receivable
= $120,000,000

Monetary Liabilities = Accounts Payable + Notes Payable + Dividends Payable + Mortgages Payable + Bonds Payable = $360,000,000

Monetary liabilities exceed monetary assets by $240,000,000 and the rate of inflation for 1983 is, as of year-end, 25% (the change from a 100 price index to 125). Hence, the *purchasing-power gain* is $240,000 × 25% = $60,000.

REDI-FINANCE EQUIPMENT, INC.
Constant Dollar Asset Section of the Balance Sheet
December 31, 1983

		Explanatory Details
ASSETS		
Cash	$ 20,000,000	Monetary asset
Marketable securities	10,000,000	Monetary asset
Accounts receivable (net)	90,000,000	Monetary asset
Inventory	212,500,000	Nonmonetary asset:
		$170,000,000 \times 125/100$
Prepaid insurance	1,875,000	$1,500,000 \times 125/100$
Land	79,545,455	$70,000,000 \times 125/110$
Buildings	522,727,273	$(350,000,000 \times 125/110)$
		$+ (100,000,000 \times 125/100)$
Accumulated depreciation: Buildings	(94,318,182)	$(50,000,000 \times 125/110)$
		$+ (30,000,000 \times 125/100)$
Equipment	310,602,273	$(108,000,000 \times 125/110)$
		$+ (150,300,000 \times 125/100)$
Accumulated depreciation: Equipment	(57,840,910)	$(30,000,000 \times 125/110)$
		$+ (19,000,000 \times 125/100)$
Patent	241,250,000	$(54,000,000 + 125/75)$
		$+ (121,000,000 \times 125/100)$
Total assets	$1,336,340,909	

D.

Inventory

	1983	1982
	$200,000,000	$130,000,000
	170,000,000	100,000,000
Holding gain	$ 30,000,000	$ 30,000,000

Cost of Goods Sold

	1983	1982
	$650,000,000	$590,000,000
	630,000,000	480,000,000
Holding gain	$ 20,000,000	$110,000,000

Equipment

	1983	1982
	$200,000,000	$130,000,000
	258,300,000	108,000,000
Holding gain (loss)	$ (58,300,000)	$ 22,000,000

For all assets held the gains are unrealized, whereas for all assets sold the gains are realized. It would appear that all of the above are unrealized in their respective years with the exception of cost of goods sold.

The depreciation expense and accumulated depreciation account: equipment are also affected by inflation, based on the above analysis.

20 INCOME TAXES AND BUSINESS DECISIONS

After completing this chapter, you should:

1 *Be familiar with the history of the federal income tax system, with the sources and uses of revenue to local, state, and federal governments, and with the objectives of the federal income tax system.*

2 *Know the four classes of taxpayers—individuals, corporations, estates, and trusts—and the general formula for taxable income and the tax rate for both individuals and corporations.*

3 *Be able to distinguish between progressive, proportional, and regressive taxes, as well as between marginal and average tax rates.*

4 *Understand the effect of inflation upon marginal tax rates and the rationale for the pay-as-you-earn basis for federal income taxation.*

5 *Know how to treat capital gains and losses for individuals and for corporations.*

6 *Be able to describe partnerships as "conduits" through which the tax effects of their transactions flow to the partners.*

7 *Understand interperiod tax allocation and the treatment of deferred income taxes.*

8 *Be aware of common areas for income tax planning and tax shelters to avoid (as distinct from evade) income taxes.*

9 *Know that the means of financing operations and the form of business organization can have tax consequences.*

10 *Understand the approach of the Internal Revenue Service in setting and achieving compliance requirements.*

The common saying that people are required to do two things—die and pay taxes —bears out the integral part played by taxes in everyone's economic life. Specifically, *local property taxes, states' sales taxes and excise taxes,* and *federal income taxes* provide the revenue for governmental services. Income taxation, aside from providing financial support, is used to stabilize the economy, promote economic growth and development, promote energy conservation, and meet *social objectives* including the *redistribution of wealth.*

The four classes of taxpayers are individuals, corporations, estates, and trusts. Proprietorships and partnerships act as "conduits" with respect to the distribution of taxable earnings to the owners and are not themselves taxed per se. Corporations are said to be **double-taxed,** since they pay taxes on total income and stockholders pay taxes on any dividends that are received. The tax rates are **progressive** for income taxes (i.e., the tax rate rises as taxable income rises), rather than **regressive** (i.e., the tax rate decreases as taxable income increases and vice versa) or **proportional** (i.e., the tax rate remains the same regardless of the base, as is the case for sales taxes). The **marginal rate of tax** is that rate applied to the last dollar of taxable income, which can rise rapidly as a function of inflation, and the **average rate of tax** is simply the income tax paid divided by total taxable income.

Individuals commonly use the cash basis of accounting, report all income, and exclude only that income explicitly permitted excludable by the Internal Revenue Service (IRS) to arrive at **gross income**, and then subtract business deductions and similar items to yield **adjusted gross income**. This,in turn, is reduced by *itemized deductions,* such as medical and interest expenses, to the extent that they exceed the *zero-bracket amount,* and *personal and dependent exemptions,* to yield **taxable income**. The applicable tax rates depend on marital status and head-of-household status and actually penalize married couples relative to two single working individuals. Once *prepayments* (required under the pay-as-you-earn approach to federal income taxes, intended to assure collection) and *tax credits* are deducted, the balance of tax due is remitted to the IRS or is refunded, as appropriate. Individuals receive favorable tax treatment of *capital gains and losses* and of erratic income flows through *income averaging.*

Corporations report total income and are subject to fewer *exclusions* than individuals in arriving at *gross income.* A major difference in the exclusions that are available to corporations and individuals relates to dividends; corporations can deduct 85% of any dividends received from taxable domestic corporations. Corporate deductions for business expenses and charitable contributions (up to 5% of taxable income) are subtracted to yield taxable income, to which progressive tax rates are applied. Though different in amount, tax breaks related to *capital assets* are also available to corporations. Commonly the taxes per financial accounting and per tax return will differ due to both permanent and timing differences in accounting treatment. The timing differences are subject to *interperiod tax allocation* by setting up a *deferred income tax* account.

Income tax planning can result in effective **tax avoidance** and is a recommended practice. This simply means that needless taxes are avoided, not that taxes for which one is legally liable are evaded. The latter is illegal and results in substantial penalties. Areas of tax planning include the selection of the cash versus accrual basis of accounting, the control over the timing of transactions, the choice of accounting methods for tax purposes, the structuring of transactions to minimize taxes, the choice of financing, the selection of the form of organization, and the use of *tax shelters.*

Taxes are to be paid within two and one-half months of the tax year-end by corporations and within three and one-half months by individuals. Tax compliance is monitored by the IRS through review and audits, and untimely and fraudulent returns are subject to both monetary and criminal penalties.

√ *Objectives of Federal Income Tax*

To provide financial support for the federal government
To stabilize the economy
To promote economic growth and development
To promote energy conservation
To achieve social objectives such as the redistribution of wealth

√ Classes of taxpayers: Individuals, corporations, estates, and trusts

√ *Double-taxation: The taxing of corporate earnings and the subsequent taxing of dividends to recipients*

√ *Tax Rates*

Progressive: Tax rate increases as the tax base increases
Regressive: Tax rate decreases as the tax base increases and vice versa
Proportional: Tax rate remains a constant percentage of the tax base
Marginal: Rate applied to the last dollar of taxable income
Average: Income tax paid divided by total taxable income

√ For single taxpayers the tax rate starts at 11% on income in excess of $2,300 but less than $3,400, and increases progressively to a rate of 50% on income in excess of $81,800 plus a base tax of $28,835.

√ General federal income tax formula for individuals

Total Income
— Exclusions*
Gross Income
— Deductions for Adjusted Gross Income†
Adjusted Gross Income
— Deductions from Adjusted Gross Income‡
— Personal and Dependent Exemptions§
Taxable Income
× *Applicable Tax Rates*
Gross Tax
— Prepayments and Tax Credits
Net Tax Payable

*Such as sick pay and interest on tax-free bonds.

†Trade and business expenses, trade and business expenses of employees, expenses to produce rent and royalties, alimony payments, losses from sale or exchange of property, and contributions to a retirement plan.

‡The greater of the zero-bracket amount or itemized deductions for medical and/or dental expenses, taxes, interest, charitable deductions, casualty losses, and production of income expenses. (Note that the Economic Recovery Act of 1981 also permits a charitable contribution deduction to nonitemizing taxpayers.)

§The IRS permits $1,000 per exemption—yourself, your spouse, your dependents, and an additional exemption for taxpayer's and/or spouse's blindness or age if 65 or older.

√ *Capital Gains and Losses*

Long-term capital gain or loss: Results from the sale or exchange of a capital asset held for over one year.
Short-term capital gain or loss: Results from the sale or exchange of a capital asset held for a period of one year or less.

Capital Gains and Losses for Individuals

Net short-term capital gain: Short-term capital gains minus short-term or long-term capital losses and are taxed at ordinary rates.

Net long-term capital gain: Long-term gains minus short-term losses and result in a 60% deduction from gross income.

Net short-term capital loss: Net short-term losses minus net long-term gains and reduces gross income up to a limit of $3,000.

Net long-term capital loss: Net long-term losses minus net short-term gains and one-half can be deducted from gross income up to a limit of $3,000.

Note: Any balances not currently used can be carried forward and applied to future years' incomes.

Capital Gains and Losses for Corporations

If net long-term capital gains exceed net short-term capital losses, the net capital gain is eligible for a 28% special (alternative) tax. (A corporation with less than $50,000 of taxable income can use its regular tax rate, frequently resulting in 15% to 18% special tax.)

There is no long-term capital gain deduction for corporations.

A net capital loss may be offset against net capital gains of the three preceding years and a refund applied for (this is a **carryback**), and any amount that remains can be used to offset future net capital gains in the following five years (this is called a **carryforward**).

√ General federal income tax formula for corporations

$$
\begin{array}{l}
\text{\textit{Total Income}} \\
- \text{\textit{Exclusions*}} \\
\hline
\text{\textit{Gross Income}} \\
- \text{\textit{Deductions†}} \\
\hline
\text{\textit{Taxable Income}} \\
\times \text{\textit{Applicable Tax Rates‡}} \\
\hline
\text{\textit{Gross Tax}} \\
- \text{\textit{Prepayments and Credits}} \\
\hline
\text{\textit{Net Tax Payable}} \\
\hline
\end{array}
$$

For example, 85% of any dividends received from taxable domestic corporations.

†The deduction for charitable contributions is limited to 5% of taxable income; any excess contributions can be carried forward for five years.

‡Currently, corporate tax rates are as follows:

Taxable Income	Amount Plus	Rate	Amount Over
$0 to $25,000	$ 0	15%	$ 0
$25,000 to $50,000	$ 3,750	18%	$ 25,000
$50,000 to $75,000	$ 8,250	30%	$ 50,000
$75,000 to $100,000	$15,750	40%	$ 75,000
$100,000 and over	$25,750	46%	$100,000

√ Interperiod tax allocation

Deferred Income Tax = Income Tax Expense − Income Tax Paid

If a credit balance, tax has been postponed and account is classified as a current or long-term liability

If a debit balance, tax has been prepaid and account is classified as a current or long-term asset

MULTIPLE-CHOICE QUESTIONS

Circle the letter corresponding to the best response.

1. The primary objective of income taxation is
   a. to stabilize the economy
   b. to promote economic growth and development

   c. to promote energy conservation

   d. to produce financial support for the federal government

2. Which of the following is not one of the four classes of taxpayers according to income tax law?

   a. individuals

   b. partnerships

   c. corporations

   d. estates

3. The federal income tax is a

   a. progressive tax

   b. regressive tax

   c. proportional tax

   d. none of the above

4. The deduction for two-earner married couples is a maximum of $3,000 and is computed as

   a. 10% on total income

   b. 10% of the higher-earning spouse's earned income

   c. 10% of the lower-earning spouse's earned income

   d. 10% of the difference in the higher-earning spouse's earned income and that of the lower-earning spouse's earned income

5. Which of the following is neither a deduction for adjusted gross income nor a deduction from adjusted gross income?

   a. trade and business expenses

   b. alimony payments

   c. contributions to a retirement plan

   d. sick pay

   e. taxes

6. Exclusions exist for dividends in the amount of

   a. $100 for a joint return

   b. $200 for a joint return

   c. $1,000 for a joint return

   d. $2,000 for a joint return

7. Taxpayers would choose to itemize their deductions when

   a. deductions exceed their allowed zero-bracket amount

   b. joint returns are filed

   c. medical and/or dental expenses exceed 5% of adjusted gross income

   d. deductions are less than their allowed zero-bracket amount

8. Which of the following taxes are nondeductible from adjusted gross income?

   a. real estate taxes

   b. state income taxes

   c. gift taxes

   d. general sales taxes

9. An example of an allowable deduction from adjusted gross income as a production of income expense includes

   a. commuting cost to and from work

   b. work clothes and uniforms

   c. fines and penalties

   d. funeral expenses

   e. loss from the sale of your automobile

10. John and Jean have three children, one of whom is blind and all of whom are still dependents under tax law. John is 66 years old. Jean's mother, who is 82 years old, is also a dependent under tax law. The total number of personal and dependent exemptions is

a. 7
b. 9
c. 8
d. 6

MULTIPLE-CHOICE QUESTIONS (ANSWERS)

Answer   *Explanation*

1. d   Although *(a)*, *(b)*, and *(c)* also represent objectives of income taxation, the support of federal government is the primary objective.
2. b   Income from partnerships is reported on individuals' tax returns.
3. a   The tax rate for an individual who is not married starts at 11% and ends at 50%, rising as taxable income rises.
4. c   It is limited to 10% of the lower-earning spouse's earned income up to $30,000 (i.e., a maximum deduction of $3,000).
5. d   Sick pay is an exclusion from gross income.
6. b   According to tax law, the first $100 of dividends received are excluded from taxable income; hence, for a joint return, a $200 exclusion is permitted.
7. a   The election of itemized deductions would reduce the tax liability in this situation, whereas *(b)* and *(c)* do not automatically imply that the itemization of deductions is preferable to the zero-bracket amount. Despite high medical expenses, total itemized deductions could still be less than the zero-bracket amount. Furthermore, response *(d)* implies the preferability of the zero-bracket amount.
8. c   Gift, inheritance, estate, cigarette, and alcoholic beverage taxes are not deductible from adjusted gross income.
9. b   Work clothes and uniforms, dues to professional societies and unions, and subscriptions to professional journals are all examples of allowable deductions from adjusted gross income, representing production of income expenses.
10. a   Dependents are not eligible for age or blind exemptions. However, John qualifies for an age exemption. Hence, three children, plus the mother, yield four exemptions, combined with the one exemption for Jean and the two exemptions for John.

TRUE-FALSE QUESTIONS

Indicate whether each of the following statements is true (T) or false (F).

_____ 1. Property taxes provide the primary source of governmental funds for cities and counties.

_____ 2. In 1939, over 70% of all adults paid federal income tax.

_____ 3. Double-taxation is an attribute most commonly associated with partnerships.

_____ 4. With the cash basis of accounting, revenues are recognized when cash is collected or constructively received.

_____ 5. Married taxpayers must file joint tax returns.

_____ 6. The tax law in the late seventies penalized working couples for marrying.

_____ 7. Inflation increases the proportion of taxable income flowing to the federal government, without raising the tax rates.

_____ 8. The average tax rate is that rate applied to the last dollar of taxable income.

_____ 9. Losses on property held for personal use, such as on a personal automobile, are not deductible for adjusted gross income.

_____ 10. The federal government essentially provides a subsidy to the state and local governments when it permits taxes to be deducted from adjusted gross income.

_____ 11. Contributions of money, property, and services made by individual taxpayers to or for the use of qualified charitable organizations are deductible from adjusted gross income.

_____ 12. Tax credits yield the same tax advantages as deductions from adjusted gross income.

TRUE-FALSE QUESTIONS (ANSWERS)

Answer   *Explanation*

1. T   At the state level, sales taxes and excise taxes provide the bulk of governmental funds, and at the federal level, income tax provides the primary source of funds.

2. F   In 1939, less than 6% of all persons paid federal income tax, although by 1945, 70% paid.

3. F   Double-taxation refers to the taxing of corporate earnings and subsequent taxing of dividends to recipients; hence, it relates to corporations, not to partnerships.

4. T   Constructive receipt means that the receipt is available to the taxpayer but not yet as cash (e.g., an uncashed check).

5. F   Married taxpayers are permitted to file separate returns.

6. T   In the late seventies, two persons with earnings would pay lower total taxes if they remained single than they would incur if they were married; assuming earnings of $15,000 each, the penalty was over $1,000.

7. T   This is due to inflation's effect on earnings and the marginal tax rate. (This is referred to as **bracket creep.**)

8. F   The marginal tax rate is described; the average rate is simply the total tax paid divided by the total taxable income.

9. T   Only losses from the sale or exchange of investment property are deductible for adjusted gross income.

10. T   Since the deduction lowers the net cost of the tax to those taxpayers who itemize their deductions, it can be appropriately termed a subsidy by the federal government.

11. F   Services are not deductible; only charitable contributions of money or property are deductible.

12. F   Tax credits are direct dollar-for-dollar reductions in the gross tax due, which makes them more valuable than deductions from adjusted gross income, which essentially reduce taxes only by the applicable tax rate.

CLASSIFI- CATION AND MATCHING QUESTIONS

Classify the following items using these symbols.

E = Exclusion from gross income of individuals
D = Deductions for adjusted gross income of individuals
A = Deductions from adjusted gross income of individuals

_____ 1. Trade and business expenses of employees
_____ 2. Taxes
_____ 3. Expenses to produce rent and royalties
_____ 4. Interest

_____ 5. Production of income expense
_____ 6. Social security benefits
_____ 7. Trade and business expenses
_____ 8. Combat pay
_____ 9. Medical and/or dental expenses
_____ 10. Casualty losses
_____ 11. Loss from sale or exchange of property
_____ 12. Life insurance proceeds
_____ 13. Scholarships
_____ 14. Alimony payments
_____ 15. Contribution to retirement plan
_____ 16. Charitable contributions

CLASSIFICATION AND MATCHING QUESTIONS (ANSWERS)

1. D *2.* A *3.* D *4.* A *5.* A *6.* E *7.* D *8.* E *9.* A *10.* A *11.* D *12.* E *13.* E
14. D *15.* D *16.* A

QUESTIONS CONCERNING THE EFFECTS OF TRANS-ACTIONS

Indicate whether each of the following will increase (+), decrease (−), or have no effect upon taxes payable (0).

_____ 1. The use of sum-of-the-years'-digits depreciation for tax purposes, rather than double-declining balance in the year an asset is acquired

_____ 2. The use of an installment method of revenue realization, rather than the accrual method

_____ 3. The use of FIFO rather than LIFO for book purposes during a period of inflation

_____ 4. The use of preferred stock instead of debt financing

_____ 5. The use of the corporate form of business for an individual in a 50% personal income tax bracket

QUESTIONS CONCERNING THE EFFECTS OF TRANSACTIONS (ANSWERS)

Answer   *Explanation*

1. +   Since sum-of-the-years'-digits results in a smaller depreciation expense, taxable income would be higher.

2. −   An installment basis of revenue realization will effectively defer revenue to later periods, thus decreasing the current period's taxes relative to an accrual basis.

3. +   Since LIFO must be used for book purposes if it is to be used for tax purposes, and since LIFO reduces taxes in an inflationary period, the taxes will be higher if FIFO is used for financial reporting in this situation.

4. +   While interest expense is tax deductible, preferred dividends are not.

5. −   Since the maximum tax rate for a corporation is 46%, the tax bill will be lower.

1. **Capital Asset**

Investment	Cost	Date Acquired	Date Sold	Market Value
a	$ 5,000	1/2/80	2/15/83	$ 9,000
b	$10,000	6/30/83	12/31/83	$15,000
c	$40,000	1/2/83	12/31/83	$30,000
d	$20,000	1/2/78	5/15/83	$18,000

Calculate the type of capital gain or loss per investment and describe the overall tax effect in 1983 for the individual who sold investments *(a)*, *(b)*, *(c)*, and *(d)*. If instead of an individual, a corporation held investments *(a)*, *(b)*, *(c)*, and *(d)*, what would be the overall tax effect in 1983?

2. Zee's Equipment, Inc., purchased $100,000 of equipment with an estimated residual value of $6,250 and a four-year service life on 1/2/83. The corporation uses straight-line depreciation for financial reporting purposes.

The tax law provides for cost recovery (as distinct from depreciation) for assets that are placed in service after December 31, 1980. The Accelerated Cost Recovery System (ACRS) introduced by the Economic Recovery Tax Act of 1981 strives to promote capital retention by permitting rapid recovery of capital costs. Both useful life and salvage-value concepts are eliminated from cost recovery calculations. Five different classes of capital assets are provided, each with an assigned life and a set cost recovery schedule. Assume Zee's Equipment is in the five-year class of Investment. In this case, for property placed in service after December 31, 1980, and before January 1, 1985, the cost recovery allowance for tax purposes is 15% in year 1, 22% in year 2, and 21% for years 3, 4, and 5.

Net income before depreciation and taxes is $200,000 each year, and the applicable tax rate is 30%. Record the interperiod tax allocation for 1983 through 1986.

1. a. Long-term capital gain of $4,000
  b. Short-term capital gain of $5,000
  c. Short-term capital loss of $10,000
  d. Long-term capital loss of $2,000

> $ 5,000 ($10,000 − $5,000)
> − 2,000 ($4,000 − $2,000)
> _____
> $ 3,000 *Net Short-Term Capital Losses*

Gross income would be reduced by $3,000, the limit on net short-term capital loss deductions.

If a corporation was the investor, the net short-term capital loss could be carried back three years and forward for five years. However, in 1983, the $5,000 short-term capital loss only serves to offset the $2,000 long-term capital gain, thereby eliminating any taxes on that gain; the $3,000 difference must be applied to other years in order to further reduce taxes.

2. Income tax return

	Year 1	Year 2	Year 3	Year 4	Total
Net income before depreciation and tax	$200,000	$200,000	$200,000	$200,000	$800,000
Cost recovery	15,000	22,000	21,000	21,000	79,000
Net income before tax	$185,000	$178,000	$179,000	$179,000	$721,000
Income tax expense (30%)	55,500	53,400	53,700	53,700	211,875
Net income	$129,500	$124,600	$125,300	$125,300	$504,700

Income statement

	Year 1	Year 2	Year 3	Year 4	Total
Net income before depreciation and tax	$200,000	$200,000	$200,000	$200,000	$800,000
Depreciation	23,438	23,438	23,437	23,437	93,750
Net income before tax	$176,562	$176,562	$176,563	$176,563	$706,250
Income tax (30%)	52,969	52,969	52,969	52,969	211,876
Net income	$123,593	$123,593	$123,594	$123,594	$494,374

Year 1: 1983

Income Tax Expense	52,969	
Deferred Income Tax	2,531	
Income Tax Payable		55,500
Income Tax Payable	55,500	
Cash		55,500

Year 2: 1984

Income Tax Expense	52,969	
Deferred Income Tax	431	
Income Tax Payable		53,400
Income Tax Payable	53,400	
Cash		53,400

Year 3: 1985

Income Tax Expense	52,969	
Deferred Income Tax	731	
Income Tax Payable		53,700
Income Tax Payable	53,700	
Cash		53,700

Year 4: 1986

Income Tax Expense	52,969	
Deferred Income Tax	731	
Income Tax Payable		53,700
Income Tax Payable	53,700	
Cash		53,700

Anderson's Antiques has provided you with the following data concerning the past year's operations.

Sales	$900,000
Interest on Municipal Securities	2,000
Dividends from Subsidiary	10,000
Long-Term Capital Gain	50,000
Business Expenses	600,000
Charitable Contributions	25,000
Related Federal Income Tax Payments	80,000

Anderson, the 65-year-old owner of the business, has also reported the following information concerning his personal tax situation.

Interest Income	2,000
Dividend Income	1,000
Moving Costs	4,000
Credit for Individual Retirement Account (IRA) Deposit	2,000
Itemized Deductions in Excess of Zero-Bracket Amount (not Including the Charitable Contributions Listed Above)	6,200

From a tax perspective, is Anderson better off organizing the antique business, which represents investment income (as distinct from earned income), as a sole proprietorship or as a corporation? Support your answer by computing Anderson's individual tax if the operation is a sole proprietorship relative to the tax for Anderson's Antiques, Inc.

Current tax rate schedule for single taxpayers is as follows.

Taxable Income		Tax		
Over	But Not Over	Amount Plus	Rate	Amount Over
$34,100	$41,500	$ 7,507	38%	$34,100
41,500	55,300	10,319	42%	41,500
55,300	81,800	16,115	48%	55,300
81,800		28,835	50%	81,800

Current corporate tax rates are as follows.

Taxable Income	Amount Plus	Rate	Amount Over
$0 to $25,000	$ 0	15%	$ 0
$25,000 to $50,000	3,750	18	25,000
$50,000 to $75,000	8,250	30	50,000
$75,000 to $100,000	15,750	40	75,000
$100,000 and over	25,750	46	100,000

CHAPTER DEMONSTRATION PROBLEM (ANSWER)

The following calculations are for Anderson's individual tax.

Gross income
Sales	$900,000	
Municipal interest: Excluded	0	
Dividends ($11,000 − $100)	10,900	
Net long-term capital gain	50,000	
Interest income	2,000	$962,900

Deductions for adjusted gross income
Business expenses	$600,000	
Net long-term capital gain deduction (60% × $50,000)	30,000	
Moving costs	4,000	634,000

Adjusted gross income	$328,900

Deductions from adjusted gross income
Itemized deductions in excess of zero-bracket amount	$ 6,200	
Charitable deductions	25,000	
Personal exemptions (2 × $1,000 — since 65 years old)	2,000	33,200

Taxable income	$295,700

Tax on $295,700 single ($28,835 plus 50% of amount over $81,800		$135,785
Less: Tax payments	$ 80,000	
Less: Credit for IRA deposit	2,000	82,000

Tax owed to IRS	$ 53,785

The following calculations are for Anderson's Antiques, Inc., tax.

Gross income
Sales	$900,000	
Interest on municipal securities: Excluded	0	
Dividends received (85% excluded)	1,500	
Long-term capital gain	50,000	$951,500

Deductions
Ordinary expenses	600,000
Charitable contributions*	16,738

Taxable Income	$334,762

Taxes on ordinary income
First $100,000	$ 25,750	
Remainder $184,762 @ 46%	84,991	$110,741

Taxes on capital gains ($50,000 @ 28% alternative tax)	14,000

Gross tax	$124,741
Less: Prepayments	80,000

Net tax payable	$ 44,741

*Limited to 5% of taxable income; solve the equation [($951,500 − $600,000) − 0.05 x] = x to derive the $334,762 value, 5% of which is $16,738. The remainder of charitable contributions can be carried forward to the next five years.

It is evident from these tax computations that Anderson would be better off organizing the antique business as a corporation.

21 INTRODUCTION TO MANAGERIAL AND COST ACCOUNTING

OBJECTIVES

After completing this chapter, you should:

1 *Understand the distinction between financial and managerial accounting.*

2 *Be able to describe planning, control, and decision-making applications of managerial accounting.*

3 *Know the meaning of the term cost accounting, its integration with financial and managerial accounting, its expanding application to merchandising and service organizations, including nonprofit organizations, and its interface with the other functional areas of a firm such as marketing and research.*

4 *Be able to classify cost elements as direct material, direct labor, or factory overhead and to classify cost behavior as variable or fixed.*

5 *Understand the treatment of product and period costs (particularly their influence on the computation of cost of goods manufactured, their effect upon raw material, work in process, and finished goods inventory balances) and their reflection in the financial statements.*

CHAPTER SUMMARY

While **financial accounting** is directed at *complying* with external reporting regulations at minimal cost, managerial accounting is directed at fulfilling managers' information needs in a manner that is *cost-beneficial.* In particular, **managerial accounting** has a primary role in management's *planning, control,* and *decision-making* functions. Definite objectives are frequently quantified in *budgets,* control is achieved through *feedback* on performance reports with *variance analysis* of operations, and decision making is supported by formulating performance measures that reflect both financial and qualitative factors, as well as internal information tailored to the decision context of each manager.

How much something costs is a fundamental component of pricing and operating decisions and is calculated via a **cost accounting** system which interfaces with both managerial and financial accounting, as well as other operating units such as marketing. Although cost accounting is typically viewed as being for manufacturers' use, it is adaptable and extremely useful to merchandising, service, and nonprofit organizations.

In its more traditional role, cost accounting is utilized to gather information as to the three primary cost elements of any manufacturer: *direct materials, direct labor,* and *factory overhead.* Factory overhead includes *indirect material* and *indirect labor,* as well as any other cost that does not form an integral part of the finished product or that cannot be easily traced to the finished product. The sum of direct materials and direct labor is commonly referred to as the *prime cost of manufacturing,* while the sum of direct labor and factory overhead is commonly referred to as the *conversion cost.*

A key determinant of the composition of cost accounting records is the handling of product and period costs. **Product costs** are assigned to each unit, inventoried until sold, and consist of direct materials, direct labor, and factory overhead. **Period costs** are not inventoried but are expensed, as no future benefits are expected to result from the costs; for example, paying sales commissions may greatly enhance sales this period but is unlikely to motivate the sales staff's efforts in the subsequent period unless that period's commissions are also paid.

The primary effect of manufacturers' cost accounting on the reported financial statements is the expansion of the merchandisers' inventory accounts on the balance sheet to the three types of inventory commonly held by manufacturers—raw materials, work in process, and finished goods—and the substitution of cost of goods manufactured for purchases on the income statement. A key determinant of total cost figures is *cost behavior.* Specifically, the cost accountant expects total costs to increase as production increases due to the effects of *variable costs,* but not in direct proportion due to the presence of some *fixed cost* elements which are expected to remain the same in total when changes in the *activity base* (e.g., production) occur.

TECHNICAL POINTS

√ *Primary Functions of Management*

Planning
Control
Decision making

√ *Variance = Budget − Actual*

Variance is *favorable* if actual is greater than budget for revenues or actual is less than budget for expenses
Variance is unfavorable if actual is less than budget for revenues or actual is greater than budget for expenses

√ Three primary cost elements in manufacturing

Prime costs $\left[\begin{array}{l}\text{Direct materials} \\ \text{Direct labor} \\ \text{Factory overhead}\end{array}\right.$ Conversion costs

√ *Product Costs (Costs That Are Inventoried) = Direct Materials + Direct Labor + Factory Overhead*

√ *Period Costs (Costs That Are Not Inventoried) = Costs for Which No Future Benefits Are Expected*

✓ **Manufacturer's Inventory Accounts**

Raw materials
Work in process
Finished goods

✓   **Beginning Direct Materials Inventory**
     + Net Purchases

     Direct Materials Available
     − Ending Direct Materials Inventory

     Direct Materials Used
     + Direct Labor
     + Factory Overhead

     Total Manufacturing Costs
     + Beginning Work in Process Inventory
     − Ending Work in Process Inventory

     Cost of Goods Manufactured

✓   **Beginning Finished Goods Inventory**
     + Cost of Goods Manufactured

     Goods Available for Sale
     − Ending Finished Goods Inventory

     Cost of Goods Sold

✓ **Total Variable Cost = Variable Cost per Unit × Activity Base**

where the variable cost per unit is constant

✓ **Fixed Cost per Unit** $= \dfrac{\textbf{Total Fixed Cost}}{\textbf{Activity Base}}$

where the total fixed cost is constant

MULTIPLE-CHOICE QUESTIONS

Circle the letter corresponding to the best response.

1. The cost minimization objective is appropriate for the production of
   a. external information
   b. internal information
   c. external and internal information
   d. neither external nor internal information

2. If budgeted gross profit was $352,000 and actual gross profit was $358,000, the variance
   a. is a favorable $6,000
   b. is an unfavorable $6,000
   c. cannot be computed, as a variance is only applicable to expenses
   d. cannot be computed without additional information

3. Management's functions include: (1) taking corrective action, (2) implementing plans, (3) evaluating actual performance, and (4) planning; what is the common chronological ordering of the above functions?
   a. 4, 3, 2, 1
   b. 4, 2, 1, 3
   c. 4, 2, 3, 1
   d. 4, 3, 1, 2

4. Prime costs consist of
   a. direct materials, direct labor, and factory overhead
   b. direct materials and direct labor
   c. direct materials and factory overhead
   d. direct labor and factory overhead

5. Which of the following is not a period cost?
   a. factory overhead
   b. interest
   c. sales commissions
   d. bad debts expense

6. The raw materials account
   a. includes direct materials
   b. includes indirect materials
   c. includes direct and indirect materials
   d. frequently appears on merchandisers' balance sheets

7. If cost of goods manufactured totals $300,000, beginning work in process inventory totals $15,000, and total manufacturing costs are $357,000, ending work in process inventory must be
   a. $57,000
   b. $72,000
   c. $42,000
   d. cannot be determined from the information provided

8. Fixed costs per unit
   a. remain the same as the level of activity decreases
   b. decrease as the level of activity decreases
   c. increase as the level of activity decreases
   d. behave in a similar manner to variable costs per unit

MULTIPLE-CHOICE QUESTIONS (ANSWERS)

Answer	Explanation
1. a	External reporting requirements should be satisfied at the lowest possible dollar outlay; however, cost minimization is not the appropriate objective for internal information production, as it would imply the production of no discretionary information. The manager should employ cost-benefit analysis when deciding what internal information should be produced. (Note that the cost-benefit analysis is applicable to external reporting, but it is assumed that the regulations maximize the benefits, leaving cost minimization as the responsibility of the managers.)
2. a	If actual revenue is greater than budgeted, that is "good," implying a favorable variance. Since a variance is defined as deviations from the budget, the simple difference of $6,000 can be computed ($358,000 − $352,000).
3. c	Although feedback is involved throughout such management processes, plans typically are first set, then implemented, then evaluated, and finally subjected to control measures.
4. b	Prime costs are those that are easily traced to the finished product (i.e., direct costs). Response (d) represents conversion costs.
5. a	Factory overhead is a product cost.
6. c	Both types of materials are housed in this account; a manufacturer, not a merchandiser, has this account reported on its balance sheet.
7. b	$357,000 + $15,000 − x = $300,000$; $x = $72,000
8. c	Since total costs remain the same, while activity decreases, the per unit cost increases.

Indicate whether each of the following statements is true (T) or false (F).

___ *1.* Financial accounting is characterized by an "anything goes" philosophy.

___ *2.* Frequently, the objectives of a business are in conflict with one another.

___ *3.* Internal information should be produced if the benefits derived by its use equal the costs of producing the information.

___ *4.* Recently, the emphasis on managerial accounting in companies has been declining relative to the emphasis on financial accounting.

___ *5.* The use of cost accounting by merchandising and service organizations has been expanding in recent years.

___ *6.* The distinction between product and period costs is not always clear.

___ *7.* Since nonprofit organizations are not evaluated on the "bottom line," cost accounting is not a useful tool for these organizations.

___ *8.* As the activity base increases, variable costs per unit increase.

TRUE-FALSE QUESTIONS (ANSWERS)

Answer *Explanation*

1. F   Financial accounting must comply with standards for external reporting; it is managerial accounting which can be characterized by an "anything goes" philosophy, as its purpose is to aid management in its planning, controlling, and decision making.

2. T   For example, attempts to increase market share or enhance the corporation's image regarding social accountability may well require a firm to forego short-term profit maximization. Typically, companies try to achieve consistency in their objectives as one means of reducing conflicts.

3. F   The benefits should exceed the costs to warrant the production of internal information.

4. F   Due to rampant inflation and the dynamic operating environment, the emphasis on managerial accounting within companies has been growing.

5. T   Since operating efficiency is the goal of all entities and not just of manufacturers, cost accounting has been appropriately recognized as a useful managerial tool by merchandisers and service organizations.

6. T   Costs require in-depth analysis to determine the percentage that can be appropriately inventoried and the percentage that should be expensed. Whatever classification is selected, it should be applied consistently by the company.

7. F   Since nonprofit organizations must plan, control, and make decisions to allocate their resources wisely, cost accounting can be a useful tool, despite the lack of a profit motive.

8. F   Variable costs increase in total, but the per-unit variable cost remains the same.

Classify the following items using these symbols.

DM = Direct materials
DL = Direct labor
IM = Indirect materials
IL = Indirect labor
FO = Factory overhead
SA = Selling and administrative expense

CHAPTER 21

——— *1.* Nails
——— *2.* Wages of assembly-line workers
——— *3.* Equipment depreciation
——— *4.* Seat of a chair
——— *5.* Insurance on the corporate offices
——— *6.* Machine operators
——— *7.* Repairs and maintenance
——— *8.* Plant guards
——— *9.* Sheet metal in an automobile
——— *10.* Insurance on sales staff's automobiles
——— *11.* Fabric for a clothing manufacturer
——— *12.* Glue
——— *13.* Utilities
——— *14.* Maintenance workers
——— *15.* Depreciation on office furniture

CLASSIFICATION AND MATCHING QUESTIONS (ANSWERS)

1. IM   *2.* DL   *3.* FO   *4.* DM   *5.* SA   *6.* DL   *7.* FO   *8.* IL   *9.* DM   *10.* SA   *11.* DM
12. IM   *13.* FO   *14.* IL   *15.* SA

QUESTIONS CONCERNING THE EFFECTS OF TRANSACTIONS

Indicate whether the following costs are variable and would be expected to increase in total as activity increases (+) or are fixed and would be expected to remain the same as activity increases (0).

——— *1.* Sales commissions

——— *2.* Management salaries

——— *3.* Advertising

——— *4.* Insurance

——— *5.* Direct labor

——— *6.* Straight-line depreciation

——— *7.* Supplies

——— *8.* Fuel

——— *9.* Property taxes

——— *10.* Direct material

QUESTIONS CONCERNING THE EFFECTS OF TRANSACTIONS (ANSWERS)

1. +   *2.* 0   *3.* 0*   *4.* 0   *5.* +   *6.* 0   *7.* +   *8.* +   *9.* 0   *10.* +

*This is a discretionary fixed cost and is determined by management policy.

EXERCISES

1. The following information pertains to the operations of Aben, Inc.

1983 Management salaries: $400,000 (20% relates to the factory production; 80% relates to sales and administrative activities)
1983 Production: 1 million units
Related sales in 1983: 300,000 units
Related sales in 1984: 600,000 units

Compute the effect of management salaries on the

    a. 1983 income statement
    b. 1983 balance sheet
    c. 1984 income statement
    d. 1984 balance sheet

EXERCISES (ANSWERS)

1. a.   **$400,000 × 80% = $320,000 Selling and Administrative Expenses**

Such expenses are period costs, implying a $320,000 operating expense on the 1983 income statement.

$400,000 × 20% = $80,000 Factory Overhead

Such an expense is a product cost, implying that the overhead is inventoried until its sale. Since 300,000 units of production out of a total of 1 million units are sold in 1983, 30% of this $80,000, or $24,000 will be charged to cost of goods sold on the 1983 income statement.

b.   **$80,000 × 70% = $56,000 Inventoried Factory Overhead**

Either work in process or finished goods will increase by $56,000 on the 1983 balance sheet.

c.   **$80,000 × 60% = $48,000 Product Costs Related to Goods Sold**

The cost of goods sold will increase by $48,000 on the 1984 income statement to reflect those management salaries related to factory production in 1983 which were inventoried, until sale of the related goods.

d.   **$80,000 × 10% = $8,000 Inventoried Factory Overhead**

The 100,000 units of 1983 production remaining in inventory will increase finished goods reported on the 1984 balance sheet by $8,000.

CHAPTER DEMONSTRATION PROBLEM

Performance report for department A

	Budgeted	Actual	Variance
Production	60,000 Units	70,000 Units	10,000 Units over
Direct labor	$480,000	$520,000	$40,000 Unfavorable
Direct material	$300,000	$350,000	$50,000 Unfavorable
Factory overhead	$0.20 Per dollar of direct labor	$0.19 Per dollar of direct labor	$0.01 Favorable
President's salary	$4,000	$4,200	$200 Unfavorable
Selling commissions	2% Of sales	2% Of sales	0

Assume that you are the manager for department A and have been asked to respond to the above performance report. Structure your response by line item.

Management has also requested that you provide information on the cost of goods manufactured for your department and your ideas as to the appropriate selling price for the good that you manufacture.

You have collected the following data.

Advertising Expense Allocated to Department A	$ 2,000
Direct Materials 1/1/83	40,000
Direct Materials 12/31/83	100,000
Purchases of Materials during 1983	410,000
Direct Labor	520,000
Allocation of Depreciation on Administrative Office Building	7,000
Factory Overhead	
Indirect Materials	4,000
Indirect Labor	4,000
Depreciation: Factory	1,880
Work in Process 1/1/83	95,000
Work in Process 12/31/83	110,000
Finished Goods 1/1/83	100,000
Finished Goods 12/31/83	65,000

Utilize this information to report to management, and summarize your ideas as to the appropriate selling price for the good that you manufacture. Clarify the concept of product versus period costs in your discussion of pricing policies.

CHAPTER DEMONSTRATION PROBLEM (ANSWER)

To: Management
From: Manager for department A
Re: Performance report

The first line of the performance report correctly reflects the increase in production achieved for the period by department A. Obviously, the 10,000 additional units will involve higher costs than budgeted, and unfavorable variances will automatically be reported by a static comparison of budgeted to actual.

Yet, direct labor is known to be a variable cost that will tend to vary in direct proportion to the number of units produced. Hence, the $480,000 budgeted amount implies a budgeted variable rate of $480,000 ÷ 60,000 units or $8 per unit. If the budget were adjusted to 70,000 units, it would total $560,000 (70,000 × $8) and the report would indicate a favorable variance of $40,000 rather than the currently reported unfavorable variance of $40,000.

Similarly, direct material is a variable cost, and the $300,000 budget would translate to $5 per unit. Adjusted to 70,000 units, the $350,000 total would be identical to actual costs, implying no variance whatsoever.

The factory overhead items are likely to be primarily fixed in their behavior, implying that total dollars rather than unit costs, should be the focal point. Specifically, the budgeted amount would be $0.20 × $480,000, or $96,000, and this budgeted amount should remain rather stable, even at a 70,000-unit level of production. Hence, $96,000 ÷ $520,000 = $0.184 per actual direct labor dollar. Instead of a favorable $0.01 variance, an unfavorable $0.006 variance per dollar of direct labor has been incurred.

The president's salary is an uncontrollable indirect cost that is likely to be more of an administrative cost item than a manufacturing item. The $200 unfavorable variance should not be considered department A's responsibility.

The selling commissions are selling expenses, not production costs; these commissions do not belong on department A's performance report.

DEPARTMENT A
Schedule of Cost of Goods Manufactured

Direct materials used	
Beginning direct materials inventory	*$ 40,000*
Net purchases	*410,000*
Direct materials available	*$450,000*
Less: Ending direct materials inventory	*100,000*
Direct materials used	*$350,000*
Direct labor	*520,000*
Factory overhead	
Indirect materials	*4,000*
Indirect labor	*4,000*
Depreciation: Factory	*1,880*
Total manufacturing costs	*$879,880*
Add: Beginning work in process inventory	*95,000*
	$974,880
Less: Ending work in process inventory	*110,000*
Cost of goods manufactured	*$864,880*

Cost of goods sold calculation

> **$ 100,000 Beginning Finished Goods Inventory**
> **+ 864,880 Cost of Goods Manufactured**
>
> **$ 964,880 Goods Available for Sale**
> **−   65,000 Ending Finished Goods Inventory**
>
> **$ 899,880 Cost of Goods Sold**

Since actual production was 70,000 units, the cost of goods manufactured per unit is $864,880 ÷ 70,000 Units = $12.36.

Other expenses include

> *Advertising Allocation* $2,000
> *Depreciation Allocation: Administrative*   7,000

Since these are allocated costs, they are probably going to be incurred regardless of whether department A continues to operate or not.

As department manager you should report the total manufacturing cost of $12.36 and suggest that these product costs should be covered by the selling price. You should clarify that product costs encompass direct material, direct labor, and factory overhead. They are inventoried, which could mean that some of the costs of prior periods' production remain to be covered and these may be at a higher unit cost than $12.36; this warrants consideration when setting prices. Beginning finished goods inventory is $100,000; by dividing by the units of product, a unit cost can be derived. Also, stress to top management that period costs (i.e., selling and administrative costs required to distribute the goods that are available for sale) should be considered. Such period costs are necessary to sustain ongoing operations, although they are frequently not as traceable to each unit of product. Since they are not expected to generate future benefits, they are charged each period to income and should be covered by revenue in the current period.

1. _111 down_ _1 across_ _132 across_ _69 across_ _142 down_ are primarily nonbusiness, personal expenses that are deductible by law to promote the "general welfare."

4. _4 across_ _81 across_ include cash, accounts receivable, and notes receivable and are compared with _4 across_ _75 across_ to compute companies' _98 across_ _98 down_ _125 down_ _127 across_ _135 across_.

6. _81 down_ _6 across_ _54 down_ is computed by dividing net sales by the average accounts receivable during the year.

8. A _44 across_ - _8 across_ _102 across_ should be employed to determine whether or not to generate discretionary information.

10. The ratio of net income to net sales is called the _10 across_ _70 down_ _58 across_ _50 across_.

11. _36 across_ _11 across_ is the information that is provided for managers within a company and is used for planning, control, and decision making.

12. Any differences between the income tax actually paid and the amount of income tax expense shown in the financial statements are recorded as _118 across_ _12 across_ if they represent timing differences.

13. The _13 across_ _38 across_ represents a more severe test of debt-paying ability than the current ratio by excluding merchandise inventory and prepaid expenses from the asset base.

14. _14 across_ _5 down_ are used to measure management's effectiveness in using specific resources.

17. _17 across_ _58 across_ _90 down_ _80 down_ describes the process of securing funds at fixed interest and preferred dividend rates and of investing the funds to earn a return greater than their cost.

18. _25 across_ _18 across_ represents the gross wages of the personnel who worked directly on the goods being produced.

21. _21 across_ _95 across_ contains the cost of completed production that is owned by a firm.

23. Managerial accounting plays an important role in _23 across_ _26 across_, an integral part of planning and controlling.

24. The _60 across_ - _24 across_ _38 across_ is the current market price of a share of common stock divided by earnings per share.

25. _25 across_ _2 down_ includes all materials that form an integral part of the finished product and are easily traceable to the finished product.

26. See 23 across.

30. _30 across_ _88 down_ _32 down_ _96 across_ _35 down_ are computed on the basis of assets that have been sold and are the difference between acquisition cost and replacement cost.

34. The _87 across_ _58 across_ _86 down_ _34 across_ _80 down_ measures the profits generated on the funds provided by common stockholders.

36. See 11 across.

38. The most widely used measure of liquidity is the _56 across_ _38 across_.

40. _106 across_ _29 down_ _40 across_ is a widely used measure of profitability.

41. _____ is a rise in the general price level which causes a decline in the purchasing power of the dollar.

44. _71 down_ _44 across_ is the current cost of replacing an asset with a similar asset in similar condition.

46. _56 across_ _46 across_ _39 down_ recognizes price changes in the individual assets owned by an enterprise and restates the assets in terms of their current value.

47. _47 across_ _28 down_ is oriented toward reporting the results of operations to managers and other interested parties within the firm.

50. See 10 across.

51. Owners' equity is an example of a _92 across_ _51 across_ on the balance sheet which must be adjusted to correct to a common dollar basis.

52. The _52 across_ _54 down_ _38 across_ shows the number of times the funds invested in inventory were turned into sales, thereby providing some insight regarding the effectiveness of a firm's inventory policies.

56. See 46 across.

58. The _55 down_ _66 down_ _87 across_ _58 across_ _137 across_ measures profitability from a given level of asset investment.

60. See 24 across.

62. The _82 across_ _31 down_ _62 across_ _20 down_ _89 across_ shows the percentage of total capital provided by the creditors of a business.

64. _64 across_ _39 down_ is concerned primarily with external reporting.

65. A _115 across_ _65 across_ is an enterprise created without a profit motive to meet the needs of society.

67. _74 down_ _67 across_, sometimes known as manufacturing expense or burden, consists of all factory-related costs other than direct materials and direct labor.

69. Gross income less deductions for adjusted gross income yields _132 across_ _69 across_ _142 down_.

73. _73 across_ _5 down_ are computed on the basis of sales or investment and can be used to assess an organization's operating success (or lack of) during an accounting period.

75. See 4 across.

77. A _____ acquires raw materials and uses its plant, equipment, and employees to produce a finished product.

81. _110 down_ _81 across_ are all business properties held by the taxpayer except those specifically excluded by the tax rules, such as inventory, and certain depreciable and real property used in a trade or business which are provided with favorable tax treatment when sold at a gain or a loss.

82. See 62 across.

85. With the _85 across_ _104 down_ _66 down_ _39 down_, revenues are recognized when cash is collected or constructively received.

87. Married taxpayers can file a _133 across_ _87 across_ or a separate _87 across_.

89. _89 across_ _102 across_ is a method of financial statement evaluation that can be used to study liquidity, activity, profitability, coverage of obligations, and other financial relationships.

91. The _117 down_ _126 across_ _91 across_ _63 down_ is simply the income tax paid divided by total taxable income.

92. See 51 across.

93. _93 across_ _99 across_ _79 down_ is computed by dividing net income before taxes and interest by the interest charges themselves.

94. _94 across_ _44 across_ consists of costs easily traced to the finished product; that is, direct labor plus direct materials.

95. _44 across_ _91 across_ _95 across_ _108 across_ is derived by summing the three cost elements of a manufactured product: direct materials, direct labor, and factory overhead.

96. Holding gains and losses that are _72 down_ _125 down_ _96 across_ _135 across_ relate to assets still owned at the end of the accounting period.

97. _97 across_ _16 down_ is the annual cash dividend per share divided by the current market price of the stock.

98. See 4 across.

99. See 93 across.

100. The _3 down_ _43 down_ _100 across_ is calculated by dividing the annual cash dividend per share by earnings per share.

102. See 89 across.

105. _113 across_ _105 across_ is used to determine whether a business has complied with the laws and regulations to which it is subject.

106. See 40 across.

108. See 95 across.

112. _112 across_ _22 down_ _10 down_ represents the cost of goods started but not completed.

113. See 105 across.

115. See 65 across.

116. All income not excluded is subject to federal taxation and constitutes _69 across_ _116 across_.

118. See 12 across.

119. A _148 across_ _96 across_ _96 down_ _119 across_ _151 across_ are allowed for a taxpayer and his dependent child in addition to their itemized deductions.

122. _122 across_ _114 down_ _111 down_ are those allowable nonbusiness, personal expenses that exceed the zero-bracket amount.

123. The procedure of reporting income tax expense which would have resulted if the accounting methods used for book purposes were used for income tax purposes, rather than actual income tax expense paid, is known as _128 across_ _59 down_ _123 across_.

124. When _124 across_ _111 down_ expenses such as dental and medical costs, interest, and casualty losses are reported.

126. The _141 across_ _126 across_ is that rate applied to the last dollar of taxable income.

127. _110 down_ _125 down_ _127 across_ _135 across_ result from selling

or exchanging a capital asset at an amount different from the basis of the property.

128. See 123 across.

132. See 69 across.

133. See 87 across.

134. If a taxpayer has _134 across_ _145 across_ _120 down_ _110 down_ _125 down_, 60% of these gains are permitted to be deducted from gross income when determining adjusted gross income.

135. See 127 across.

137. See 58 across.

139. Examples of _139 across_ _149 across_ between taxes implied per books and taxes per the tax return include interest on municipal bonds and expenses for key-man life insurance.

140. All taxpayer income tax returns are filed with the _124 down_ _121 down_ _140 across_.

141. See 126 across.

143. The _146 across_ _147 across_ _130 down_ (abbreviated _143 across_) was formerly called the standard deduction.

144. The use of double-declining balance for tax purposes and straight-line for book purposes creates a _____ difference which is recorded in the deferred tax account.

145. See 134 across.

146. See 143 across.

147. See 143 across.

148. See 119 across.

149. See 139 across.

150. _63 down_ _150 across_ is a smart, profitable process of minimizing current income tax liabilities by not needlessly paying income taxes, through the process of income tax planning.

151. See 119 across.

DOWN

2. See 25 across.

3. See 100 across.

5. See 14 across and 73 across.

7. Under _7 down_ _49 down_ _28 down_, historical cost data are adjusted for changes in the value (purchasing power) of the dollar by using a general price level index.

9. _9 down_ _2 down_, such as the cost of glue used in manufacturing wooden furniture, is included as a part of factory overhead.

10. See 112 across.

15. _15 down_ _44 across_ is the cost to convert raw material into finished product.

16. See 97 across.

19. A _____ is a plan expressed quantitatively in a formal report.

20. See 62 across.

22. See 112 across.

27. _27 down_ _116 across_ other than excluded income is part of taxable gross income.

28. See 47 across.

29. See 40 across.

31. See 62 across.

32. See 30 across.

33. _33 down_ _102 across_ relates each figure on a financial statement to a relevant total, stating it as a percentage of that total.

35. See 30 across.

37. A _37 down_ _131 down_ is an investment that is designed to incur business losses for investors in the short run, with the intention of achieving profits in the long run.

39. See 46 across, 64 across, and 85 across.

42. The calculation of dollar and percentage changes for corresponding items in comparative financial statements is termed _42 down_ _102 across_.

43. See 100 across.

45. Same as 58 across.

48. _48 down_ _5 down_ measure the ability of a business to meet current obligations as they come due.

49. See 7 down.

53. A _53 down_ _44 across_ varies in direct proportion to a change in an activity base.

54. See 6 across and 52 across.

55. See 58 across.

57. A _57 down_ _44 across_ remains the same in total when changes in the activity base occur.

59. See 123 across.

61. _61 down_ _5 down_ are computed to judge the solvency of a business.

63. See 91 across and 150 across.

66. See 58 across and 85 across.

68. The _____ function is an outgrowth of planning and helps to bring an organization back on target in terms of achieving the original plan.

70. See 10 across.

71. See 44 across.

72. See 96 across.

73. The cost that goes into inventory is termed a _73 down_ _44 across_.

74. See 67 across.

76. Same as 35 down.

78. A _____ is a deviation from the budget.

79. See 93 across.

80. See 17 across and 34 across.

81. See 6 across.

83. Vertical analysis results in _86 down_ - _103 down_ _64 across_ _83 down_.

84. A _84 down_ _44 across_ is a cost that is not inventoried because it does not relate to the acquisition or manufacture of inventory.

86. See 34 across and 83 down.

88. See 30 across.

90. See 17 across.

94. A _____ is the means by which an organization achieves its objectives; it involves the formulation of methods and strategies that implement a company's objectives in definite terms.

96. See 119 across.

98. See 4 across.

101. Double-taxation refers to the fact that corporate earnings are taxed _____ when distributed as dividends to stockholders.

103. See 83 down.

104. See 85 across.

105. _105 down_ _2 down_ includes the items to be processed into salable goods.

107. To analyze a company's performance, the evaluator can _107 down_ _5 down_.

109. Installment basis accounting will decrease taxes relative to the use of an _109 down_ _104 down_ method of accounting.

110. See 81 across, 127 across, and 134 across.

111. See 1 across, 122 across, and 124 across.

114. See 122 across.

117. See 91 across.

120. See 134 across.

121. See 140 across.

124. See 140 across.

125. See 4 across, 96 across, 127 across, and 134 across.

129. Same as 87 across.

130. See 143 across.

131. See 37 down.

136. Same as 149 across.

138. _63 down_ _138 down_ represents an illegal deliberate attempt to understate taxable income.

140. A holding period of a capital asset for one year or less dictates a _140 down_ - _120 down_ gain or loss.

142. See 1 across and 69 across.

22 COST ACCUMULATION SYSTEMS

OBJECTIVES

After completing this chapter, you should:

1 *Know what joint costs are.*

2 *Be aware of the sources of imprecision in the costing process.*

3 *Understand job order systems for accumulating costs.*

4 *Be able to adjust under- and overapplied overhead balances in a job costing system.*

5 *Understand process costing systems for accumulating cost.*

6 *Be able to compute equivalent units for use in assigning costs.*

7 *Know how to select the appropriate cost accounting system for a given entity and to recognize potential problem areas in assigning costs.*

CHAPTER SUMMARY

The cost accounting system utilized by producers of heterogeneous goods that are manufactured according to customer specifications or in separate batches, easily distinguishable as separate jobs, is known as a **job order system**. *Job cost sheets* accumulate direct materials and direct labor per job and factory overhead, which is applied to each job by an overhead application rate multiplied by the selected activity measure per job. To control operations, *materials requisitions* are required to transfer materials from the storeroom for use in production, and *labor time tickets* (subsequently accumulated in *labor summaries*) are required from each factory employee, reporting the job(s) and hours per job worked. These documents are the source data for the job cost sheets, which in essence can be thought of as the subsidiary ledger for work in process and finished goods.

The job order system accounts for product costs by utilizing a factory overhead account to accumulate actual costs, such as equipment depreciation, insurance, taxes, and utilities, that would typically be expenses for a merchandising operation. Actual costs are applied to jobs throughout the period and at year-end if the actual costs exceed (are less than) applied costs, overhead is considered to have been **underapplied** (**overapplied**) and a debit (credit) to cost of goods sold is recorded. Alternatively, the under- or overapplied overhead can be allocated in a theoretically preferred manner to work in process, finished goods, and cost of goods sold on some equitable basis; however, this approach can be burdensome and is only required if the more popular approach of debiting cost of goods sold results in misleading financial statements. Essentially, job costing traces costs from raw material, direct labor, and factory overhead accounts to work in process, finished goods, and, upon sale, to cost of goods sold.

The cost accounting system utilized by producers of homogeneous or similar goods that are processed on an assembly line without subdivisions for accumulating jobs is the **process costing system**. Costs are accumulated by department for direct materials, direct labor, and applied factory overhead. The physical flow of goods is accounted for and then transformed into *equivalent units* (i.e., 100 physical units 70% complete represent 70 equivalent units). Total production costs are divided by equivalent units (frequently subclassified into materials and conversion costs) to derive a *cost per equivalent unit* for use in cost assignment. A *cost of production report* is frequently prepared to summarize the flow of costs.

Both job order and process costing can be applied to service industries as well as to manufacturers, and both systems can become complicated by joint costs, a large number of products, and the requirement of estimates for such system inputs as an overhead application rate and, for process costing, equivalent units of production.

TECHNICAL POINTS

√ **Joint costs** are those costs incurred in the simultaneous production of two or more goods or services

√ *Key Documents and Reports*

Job cost sheet: Accumulates cost per job
Materials requisition: Required for issuance of materials from storeroom
Time ticket: Reports employees' hours per job
Labor summaries: Summarizes time tickets
Cost of production report: Summarizes physical unit flow, equivalent units, cost per equivalent unit, and cost assignments in a process costing system

√ *Journal Entries for a Job Costing System*

Raw Materials   XX
   Accounts Payable   XX
To record purchase of materials (both direct and indirect)

Work in Process   XX
   Raw Materials   XX
To record issue of materials for a job

Factory Overhead   XX
   Raw Materials   XX
To record issue of indirect materials

Work in Process   XX
   Wages Payable   XX
To record direct labor on a job

Factory Overhead   XX
   Wages Payable   XX
To record indirect labor

```
Factory Overhead                    XX
    Accounts Payable                    XX
    Taxes Payable                       XX
    Prepaid Insurance                   XX
    Accumulated Depreciation            XX
To record actual overhead costs

Work in Process                 XX
    Factory Overhead                XX
To record applied overhead

Finished Goods          XX
    Work in Process         XX
To record completion of a job

Cost of Goods Sold   XX
    Finished Goods          XX
To record cost of goods sold
```

✓ $\text{Overhead Application Rate} = \dfrac{\text{Estimated Factory Overhead}}{\text{Estimated Application Base}}$

✓ **Applied Overhead = Overhead Application Rate × Actual Activity**

where   Overhead is underapplied if actual factory overhead exceeds applied factory overhead. Adjusting entry is then

```
Cost of Goods Sold   XX
    Factory Overhead        XX
```

and   Overhead is overapplied if actual factory overhead is less than applied factory overhead. Adjusting entry is then

```
Factory Overhead        XX
    Cost of Goods Sold          XX
```

✓ **Equivalent Unit = Physical Units × Percentage of Completion**

✓ $\text{Cost per Equivalent Unit} = \dfrac{\text{Production Costs}}{\text{Equivalent Units Produced This Period}}$

✓ **Cost Assignment = Cost per Equivalent Unit × Equivalent Units per Inventory Class**

MULTIPLE-CHOICE QUESTIONS

Circle the letter corresponding to the best response.

1. Imprecision is not introduced into the costing process by
   a. joint costs
   b. the use of LIFO
   c. the use of specific identification
   d. the charging of overhead to inventory

2. Job order systems are not appropriate when goods are made
   a. upon the receipt of a customer order
   b. continuously on an assembly line
   c. according to customer specifications
   d. in separate batches

3. Indirect materials
   a. are charged to specific job cost sheets according to their use on particular jobs
   b. are treated as part of factory overhead
   c. include sandpaper, lubricants, and nails
   d. a and c
   e. b and c

4. The factory overhead account is debited
   a. to record estimated overhead charges
   b. actual overhead charges
   c. to record the application of factory overhead charges
   d. to transfer costs to work in process

5. Time tickets accumulate
   a. direct labor costs
   b. indirect labor costs
   c. direct and indirect labor costs
   d. information that is directly posted to job cost sheets in a job order costing system

6. Which of the following is not commonly cited as a benefit of using estimated overhead charges? The benefit of
   a. being practical
   b. permitting the figuring of total job cost at the time of job completion
   c. recording fluctuating costs that reflect lower per unit costs during peak seasonal operations
   d. tending to smooth out product costs over a period of time.

7. Which of the following application bases is most likely to be used for applying overhead in a heavily automated situation?
   a. direct labor hours
   b. machine hours
   c. direct labor cost
   d. number of employees working per day

8. Which of the following is not a criterion typically used in selecting an application base?
   a. It is one of the following bases: direct labor hours, direct labor dollars, number of employees working per day, or machine hours.
   b. It is inexpensive to compute.
   c. It is easily traced to the job or product.
   d. It has a strong cause-and-effect relationship with overhead.

9. In a job order costing system, $5,000 of depreciation on equipment used for manufacturing should be recorded as follows:
   a. Depreciation Expense   5,000
        Accumulated Depreciation: Equipment   5,000
   b. Factory Overhead   5,000
        Accumulated Depreciation: Equipment   5,000
   c. Work in Process   5,000
        Accumulated Depreciation: Equipment   5,000
   d. Cost of Goods Sold   5,000
        Accumulated Depreciation: Equipment   5,000

10. Total manufacturing costs are $200,000 for materials and $500,000 for conversion costs, or $700,000; 200,000 units have been placed into production and completed this period. Beginning work in process included 30,000 units valued at $50,000 that were 50% complete, with all materials having been added at the beginning of the process. There was no ending work in process inventory.
    a. The average production cost is $700,000/230,000 units.
    b. The equivalent units of product for further processing of work in process beginning inventory are 30,000 for materials and 15,000 for conversion costs.
    c. The equivalent units of product for the period are 200,000 + 15,000, or 215,000.
    d. The equivalent unit cost for materials was $200,000/215,000.
    e. The equivalent units of product for further processing of work in process beginning inventory are zero for materials and 15,000 for conversion costs.

Answer   *Explanation*

1. c   Specific identification attaches the cost of the units acquired to the units themselves, while each of the other responses are estimation techniques or costs that require estimation techniques to apply costs.

2. b   When production is continuous and is not subdivided into discrete jobs, process costing is appropriate, rather than job order costing.

3. e   Since indirect materials are not easily traced to jobs, they are added to factory overhead which is, in turn, applied to production.

4. b   The actual overhead charges are accumulated as debits and are applied to work in process as credits to the factory overhead account.

5. c   Both direct and indirect costs are accumulated and summarized in the form of a labor summary; it is the summary that is the source document for posting to the job cost sheets.

6. c   The benefit of overhead estimation is the avoidance of fluctuating overhead costs within the fiscal period; inventory is costed at the same rate every month.

7. b   In a heavily automated situation, much of the overhead is likely to be caused by the operation of machines.

8. a   Any application base that meets criteria *(b)*, *(c)*, and *(d)* can be applied, it does not have to be one of those mentioned in response *(a)* (for example, miles driven might be used by a bus company).

9. b   No expense is involved, as this type of depreciation is a product cost and should be charged to the factory overhead account to facilitate its application to work in process during the production period.

10. e   Since all materials are added at the beginning of the process, the $50,000 includes 100% of material costs and further processing will involve zero equivalent units for materials and 30,000 units × 50%, or 15,000 units, for conversion costs.

TRUE-FALSE QUESTIONS

Indicate whether each of the following statements is true (T) or false (F).

_____   *1.* Only an arbitrary cost allocation scheme can be employed to allocate joint costs.

_____   *2.* The determination of a job's actual overhead cost is impractical if not impossible.

_____   *3.* A credit balance in factory overhead before year-end adjusting entries represents the amount by which overhead has been underapplied.

_____   *4.* The factory overhead account is used to accumulate both actual and applied overhead.

_____   *5.* At the end of the fiscal period, overhead applied will equal total overhead incurred due to the use of the overhead application rate.

_____   *6.* The work in process/job cost sheet relationship is an example of a control account/subsidiary ledger arrangement.

_____   *7.* Continuous processing industries usually produce heterogeneous units of output.

_____   *8.* Total physical units are utilized for unit cost computation in a process costing system.

_____   *9.* Often a process and department are synonymous.

_____   *10.* Product costing and cost flow are performed in the same manner for a process costing system as for a job order system.

Answer   *Explanation*

1. T   In the early stages of production, joint costs are incurred in the simultaneous production of two or more goods and services and the products themselves are indistinguishable, implying no feasible means of applying costs in other than an arbitrary manner.

2. T   To record the costs of glue and nails would be excessively costly in terms of bookkeeping expenses regardless of how traceable such indirect materials are; some expenses such as insurance costs on plant and equipment would be almost impossible to match with anything other than a weak relationship between inputs and outputs.

3. F   A credit balance represents overapplied overhead.

4. T   Actual expenses are debits, while applications of overhead are credits to the account.

5. F   It is a rare event that these two will be equal, as estimations are required to calculate the application rate and unexpected events such as price changes from suppliers will cause actual experience to differ from that which was anticipated. Hence, an adjusting entry is typically required to close out the factory overhead account.

6. T   The job cost sheet should support the balance in the work in process control account.

7. F   Continuous processing industries usually produce homogeneous or similar units of output.

8. F   Equivalent units, rather than total physical units, are used for unit cost computations.

9. T   For example the assembly process takes place in the assembly department, the finishing in the finishing department, the packaging in the packaging department, and so forth.

10. T   Direct materials and direct labor are recorded in work in process and factory overhead is applied in an identical manner for both job order and process costing systems.

CLASSIFI-CATION AND MATCHING QUESTIONS

Classify the following items using these symbols.

J = A job order costing system is preferred for this type of operation.
P = A process costing system is preferred for this type of operation.

_____   1. Custom home builders
_____   2. Steel producer
_____   3. Claims handling by an insurance company
_____   4. Accounting and management consulting practices
_____   5. Print shops
_____   6. Petroleum producer
_____   7. Medical care
_____   8. Textile manufacturer
_____   9. Bicycle manufacturer
_____   10. Repair work

1. J   2. P   3. P   4. J   5. J   6. P   7. J   8. P   9. P   10. J

QUESTIONS CONCERNING THE EFFECTS OF TRANS-ACTIONS

Which of the following are likely to increase (+) the cost of production for the current period, which are likely to decrease (−) the cost of production for the current period, and which are unlikely to have any effect (0)?

_____ 1. The presence of a 40% completed work in process beginning inventory rather than a 50% completed work in process beginning inventory.

_____ 2. The purchase of $4,000 of nails.

_____ 3. The presence of ending work in process that is 20% completed rather than 25% completed.

_____ 4. The adjustment for underapplied overhead.

_____ 5. Sixty thousand dollars of sales commissions are incurred rather than $50,000.

QUESTIONS CONCERNING THE EFFECTS OF TRANSACTIONS (ANSWERS)

Answer	Explanation
1. +	The 40% implies 60% of the work remains to be done, while 50% implies only 50% of the work remains; 60% of the work would be expected to cost more than 50%.
2. 0	Mere purchasing does not translate into use; therefore, it cannot be implied that the cost of indirect materials used in production has increased.
3. −	The 20% completed means that costs for only 20% of production were incurred, while 25% would mean that an additional 5% of production with its related costs had been completed.
4. 0	It is the recording of actual costs that increases the costs of production, not mere adjustment of the accounts to properly charge the over- and underapplication of overhead.
5. 0	These are period costs not product costs; hence, these costs cannot have an effect on the cost of production.

EXERCISES

1. Lendin, Inc., has estimated this fiscal year's factory overhead to be $900,000 and has decided to use an application base of direct labor hours, for which a fiscal year estimate has been formulated of 30,000 hours. Actual overhead for the period has been $1 million and actual labor hours have totaled 25,000 hours.
   a. Compute the overhead application rate.
   b. What is the total overhead applied to individual jobs? Record the appropriate journal entry.
   c. Record any adjusting journal entries that would be required and explain in detail why the entries must be recorded.

2. Managramin, Inc., has 70,000 units in beginning work in process, 20% complete with respect to materials, and 10% complete with respect to conversion costs. It places an additional 150,000 units into production and has 20,000 units in ending work in process which are 45% complete with respect to materials and 30% complete with respect to conversion costs. If the beginning work in process costs $214,000 and current production costs include $500,000 of materials, $400,000 of labor, and $200,000 of overhead, what would be the cost per equivalent unit for the period?

1. a. $\dfrac{\$900,000}{30,000\ Hours} = \underline{\underline{\$30}}$

   b. $\$30 \times 25,000 = \underline{\underline{\$750,000}}$

   Work in Process   750,000
       Factory Overhead   750,000
   To record applied overhead

   c. Actual overhead totals $1 million, yet only $750,000 has been applied, resulting in underapplied overhead of $250,000. The factory overhead debit balance must be closed out to properly assign the period's total product costs to the units produced this period.

   Cost of Goods Sold   250,000
       Factory Overhead   250,000
   To adjust cost of goods sold for underapplied overhead

   Note: It is theoretically preferred to allocate such a large adjustment to work in process, finished goods, and cost of goods sold, but insufficient information is provided to do so. However, if most of the inventory produced this period has been sold, it would be acceptable to make the above entry, because the resulting financial statements would not be misleading.

2.

	Physical Units
Beginning work in process	70,000
Units started	150,000
Units to account for	220,000

	Physical Units	Equivalent Units	
		Materials	Conversion
Completed			
Beginning work in process	70,000	56,000	63,000
Units started & completed	130,000	130,000	130,000
Ending work in process	20,000	9,000	6,000
Units accounted for	220,000	195,000	199,000

	Physical Units	Costs	
		Materials	Conversion
Beginning work in process	$ 214,000	—	—
Current	1,100,000	$500,000	$600,000
To account for	$1,314,000	$500,000	$600,000
Equivalent units		195,000	199,000
Cost per equivalent unit		$2.56	$3.02

CHAPTER DEMONSTRATION PROBLEM

A. Given that the job described below is the only job worked on during the fiscal year and that factory overhead currently has a credit balance of $32, record all entries implied by the job cost sheet for Job No. 222.

JOB COST SHEET

Manufactured for:

Stock _____

Customer X _____

Job No. _____ 222 _____

Date:

Needed: _____ 8/19/83 _____

Started: _____ 11/15/82 _____

Completed: _____ 8/15/83 _____

Number of Units 2,000

Direct Materials			Direct Labor				Factory Overhead	
Date	Requisition No.	Amount	Date	Ticket No.	Hours	Amount	Date	Amount
11/15/82	777	$15,000	11/15/82	27	40	$ 400	11/15/82	$?
			12/15/82	28	43	460	12/15/82	?
			1/15/83	29	51	580	1/15/83	?
			2/15/83	30	50	572	2/15/83	?
			3/15/83	31	48	448	3/15/83	?
			8/15/83	32	52	480	8/15/83	?
					284	$2,940		$?

The overhead rate is $9 per direct labor hour.

Item	Cost Summary
Direct materials	$15,000
Direct labor	2,940
Factory overhead	?
Total cost	?

B. All costs are incurred uniformly throughout manufacturing at Effex Manufacturers. Using the following data, prepare a cost of production report in good form for Effex Manufacturers.

	Manufacturing Costs		Production
Direct materials used	$200,000	Work in process beginning of period (two-fifths completed)	30,000
Direct labor	400,000		
Applied factory overhead	100,000	Total units completed	120,000
		Ending work in process (one-fifth completed)	50,000
		Number of units started in production	140,000
Cost of beginning work in process	72,000		

CHAPTER DEMONSTRATION PROBLEM (ANSWER)

A. Work in Process   15,000
    Raw Materials   15,000

Work in Process   2,940
    Wages Payable   2,940

Note: Six different entries were made totaling the above amount.

Work in Process   2,556
    Factory Overhead   2,556

Note: Six different entries were made totaling the above amount—360, 387, 459, 450, 432, and 468—each computed as $9 \times$ Direct Labor Hours.

Finished Goods   20,496
    Work in Process   20,496

Factory Overhead   32
    Cost of Goods Sold   32
To charge off the overapplied factory overhead

B.

EFFEX MANUFACTURERS
Cost of Production Report

	Physical Units	Equivalent Units
Beginning work in process	30,000	
Units started	140,000	
Units to account for	170,000	
Completed		
Beginning work in process	30,000	18,000
Units started & completed	90,000	90,000
Ending work in process	50,000	10,000
Units accounted for	170,000	118,000
Total costs		
Beginning work in process	$ 72,000	
Current	700,000	
To account for	$772,000	

$700,000 \div 118,000 =$ __$5.93 Cost per Equivalent Unit__

EFFEX MANUFACTURERS
Cost Assignment for Completed Work

Beginning work in process		
Prior period cost	$ 72,000	
Production cost (18,000 $\times$ $5.93)	106,740	$178,740
Units started & completed (90,000 $\times$ $5.93)		533,700
Total cost of completed goods		$712,440
Ending work in process (10,000 $\times$ $5.93)		59,300
Total cost accounted for		$771,740*

*The difference from $772,000 is due to rounding.

Note: No distinction is needed between materials and conversion costs, as each type of cost is assumed in the problem to be incurred uniformly throughout manufacturing.

23 *BUDGETING*

OBJECTIVES

After completing this chapter, you should:

1 *Understand the advantages of budgeting, both short-range and long-range, and the limitations of budgeting.*

2 *Be aware of behavioral effects of budgets and the advantages of a participative budgeting approach.*

3 *Be able to describe the budget process, including the use of budget committees, cost-benefit analysis, zero-based budgeting, and continuous budgets.*

4 *Know how to prepare a master budget including expected financial statements, a sales budget, a production budget, a cash budget, and supporting schedules.*

CHAPTER SUMMARY

A formal planning process is quantified via *budgets*; **short-range budgets** reflect plans for the next year, while **long-range budgets** go beyond a year (typically three to five years, with a capital budgeting plan for a ten-year horizon). A **budget** is both a motivational and a control device and is potentially useful to both profit and not-for-profit entities; it can be particularly useful when maintained on a *continuous* basis so that twelve months of detailed budgets are always available. The establishment of specific goals for future operations and the periodic comparison of the actual operating results with these budgeted goals are important planning and control procedures. However, the advantages of budgets can disappear if a budget is utilized inappropriately, creating undue pressure on employees, destroying morale, and even encouraging employees to sabotage the entire budget process. A useful means of alleviating such ill effects is to use a participative budgeting approach in which employees are involved in setting the budget for which they are responsible.

Budgets depend upon *sales forecasts* as the building blocks of expected operations, and based on such data a budget package is developed, detailing *sales, production, and cash budgets, budgeted financial statements,* and related schedules. The package is analyzed by a *budget committee,* which is headed by a *budget director,* by means of such techniques as *cost-benefit analysis* and *zero-based budgeting* and is evaluated and often adjusted on an ongoing basis through the use of *performance reports* and the management information system.

Operating budgets detail company activities of sales, production, and *administration,* while *financial budgets* show sources and uses of money to sustain operations. Well-known accounting and business interrelationships are used to formulate budgets: the fact that one month's ending inventory is the next month's beginning inventory, collection practices, payment policies, and financing alternatives are some of the fundamentals used in budget formulation. The entire budget package is termed a **master budget** and will only be as good as the underlying estimates and efforts expended in its preparation. To be effective, day-to-day management must accompany the budgeting process.

TECHNICAL POINTS

√ *Steps in the Budget Process*

1 Estimate sales
2 Estimate production
3 Estimate revenues and costs
4 Communicate budget
5 Compare actual to budget and investigate significant deviations

√ *Total Sales Budgeted = Expected Sales in Units × Expected Selling Price per Unit*

√   *Anticipated Sales*
     + Desired Ending Inventory
     − Beginning Inventory
     _____

     Units of Production

√   *Raw Material Usage*
     + Desired Ending Raw Material Inventory Balance
     − Beginning Inventory Balance
     _____

     Raw Material Purchases

√ *Direct Labor Requirements = Number of Direct Labor Hours Required to Produce a Finished Unit × Number of Units to be Produced*

√ *Budgeted Overhead Cost = Expected Units of Production × Estimated Unit Overhead Rate*

√   *Material Cost per Unit of Finished Goods*
     + Direct Labor Cost per Unit of Finished Goods
     + Overhead Cost per Unit of Finished Goods
     _____

     Product Cost per Unit of Finished Good

✓ Cash budget

> *Beginning Cash Balance*
> + *Receipts*
> _____
> *Total Cash Available*
> − *Disbursements*
> _____
> *Cash Surplus (Deficit)*
> _____
> *Minimum Cash Balance*
> _____
> *Total Cash Needed**
> ===================
> *Financing†*

*Equals total disbursements plus minimum cash balance.
†Dollar amount depends on the available financing arrangements, although this is generally based upon the difference in the cash surplus and the total cash needed.

MULTIPLE-CHOICE QUESTIONS

Circle the letter corresponding to the best response.

1. Active participation in the budget process is not expected
   a. to be conducive to employee morale
   b. to encourage greater initiative by workers
   c. to increase budgeting pressure
   d. to increase the job satisfaction of employees

2. Indicate the chronological order of the following steps: (a) estimate revenues and costs, (b) compare actual results to the budget, (c) obtain sales estimates, (d) communicate the budget to the managers responsible for achieving the desired result, (e) estimate the level of production.
   a. c, e, a, d, b
   b. e, c, a, d, b
   c. c, e, d, a, b
   d. c, a, e, d, b

3. Which of the following methods to evaluate budget requests reviews budget proposals independently of one another?
   a. zero-based budgeting
   b. cost-benefit analysis
   c. both zero-based budgeting and cost-benefit analysis
   d. neither zero-based budgeting nor cost-benefit analysis

4. Which of the following are not cited as typical problems of zero-based budgeting?
   a. Different managers may not assign the same priority ranking to similar types of projects.
   b. Some activities cannot be eliminated.
   c. The benefits of activities such as charitable contributions are hard to determine.
   d. There is an implicit assumption that funding levels will remain the same in the future.

5. If the inventory balance is too small, a company might experience
   a. stockouts
   b. increased interest expenses
   c. increased obsolescence
   d. increased insurance costs

6. If direct laborers are paid $12 an hour and each unit of product takes 45 minutes, the cost per unit of finished product for direct labor is

  a. $12
  b. $9
  c. $540
  d. $5.40

7. Place the following steps in preparing a cash budget into chronological order: (a) ration scarce resources, (b) estimate cash payments, (c) estimate cash receipts, (d) identify projected cash shortages
  a. b, c, d, a
  b. d, c, b, a
  c. c, b, d, a
  d. d, b, c, a

8. Which of the following is not commonly cited as a means of improving cash flows?
  a. reduce dividends
  b. reduce inventory levels
  c. borrow money
  d. revise the master budget

MULTIPLE-CHOICE QUESTIONS (ANSWERS)

Answer   Explanation

1. c   Participative budgeting is considered one of the best ways to alleviate budgeting pressure and is expected to accrue the benefits described in responses (a), (b), and (d).

2. a   Sales estimates are the foundation of any budget and imply production levels, which in turn lead to revenue and expense estimates that are communicated to managers and compared to actual results.

3. b   The zero-based budgeting approach reviews proposals on a relative basis, whereas cost-benefit analysis generally reviews the benefits and expenditures in the budget proposal from each of the individual operating units independently of all others.

4. d   In fact, the most frequently cited advantage of zero-based budgeting is that such an assumption is not made; program elimination is a part of the budgetary process, with each unit starting from zero dollars in requesting funds.

5. a   The other responses all represent carrying costs, associated with maintaining an excessive inventory balance.

6. b $12 \times ¾$ Hour $= 9

7. c   Similar to operating budgets' emphasis on sales, financial budgets begin with cash receipts. The comparison of cash receipts with cash disbursements then highlights the need for additional financing.

8. c   Borrowing money does not necessarily improve cash flow; if the firm is, for example, exercising negative leverage, its cash flow is likely only to get worse as a result of borrowing.

Indicate whether each of the following statements is true (T) or false (F).

TRUE-FALSE QUESTIONS

____ 1. Monthly or quarterly adjustments to annual budgets are too time-consuming to be useful.

____ 2. Careful follow-up on budget variances is an essential element of effective budget control.

____ 3. It is desirable to have employees look on budgets as devices used by management to control worker behavior.

___ 4. The budget will typically follow the organization chart.

___ 5. Budgeting cannot replace effective day-to-day management.

___ 6. Quarterly budgets are the most effective method of controlling revenues and expenses.

___ 7. The advantage to a company of continuous budgets is that a budget for an entire year is always available.

___ 8. Preparation of the production budget is the most important element in the budgetary process.

___ 9. The ending inventory balance in one month is the beginning balance for the next month.

___ 10. Budgeting will be most effective when the budget director administers the program but delegates the budget authority and responsibility to the unit managers.

TRUE-FALSE QUESTIONS (ANSWERS)

Answer   *Explanation*

1. F   Though time-consuming, periodic adjustments result in more meaningful variance analysis than is possible from a static budget.

2. T   Such follow-up is essential, as is top-management emphasis on such review procedures.

3. F   This is an undesirable perception by employees that should only result when a budget process is used incorrectly.

4. T   A budget is typically prepared for each unit identified on the organization chart.

5. T   The budget is merely one tool to be used in managing operations and is not an end in itself.

6. F   Monthly budgets are preferable because of the shorter period involved.

7. T   Each time a month passes it is dropped from the budget and a new month is added.

8. F   The sales budget is most important, as it is the foundation for all other aspects of the budget process.

9. T   This is essentially a definition of ending inventory, that is, those goods that will be available for sale at the beginning of the next period (e.g., the next month).

10. T   This is the means by which the budget will become an effective management tool.

CLASSIFICATION AND MATCHING QUESTIONS

Classify the following budgets using these symbols.

O = Operating budget
F = Financial budget

___ 1. Sales budget
___ 2. Administrative expense budget
___ 3. Selling expense budget
___ 4. Budgeted balance sheet
___ 5. Budgeted income statement
___ 6. Production budget
___ 7. Cash budget

CLASSIFICATION AND MATCHING QUESTIONS (ANSWERS)

1. O   *2.* O   *3.* O   *4.* F   *5.* F   *6.* O   *7.* F

Indicate whether the following events will increase (+), decrease (−), or have no effect (0) upon the quantity described.

Effect Upon		*Event*
Cash collections in month of sale	____	*1.* Change of a 10-60-30 collection experience to a 15-60-25.
Cash collections	____	*2.* Depreciation of $8,000 was recorded.
Cash surplus	____	*3.* An additional $40,000 of dividends was declared and paid.
Product cost per unit of finished goods	____	*4.* An increase in the number of hours of direct labor required to produce a unit of finished goods.
Cost of raw material purchases	____	*5.* A higher level of desired ending inventory.

QUESTIONS CONCERNING THE EFFECTS OF TRANSACTIONS (ANSWERS)

Answer   *Explanation*

1. +   An additional 5% of sales on account will be collected in the month of sale.

2. 0   Depreciation has no effect on cash collections; it is a bookkeeping adjustment.

3. −   Since cash surplus is the excess of cash receipts over cash disbursements, an increased level of disbursements will reduce any excess.

4. +   More time means more cost, as one component of product cost per unit of finished good is direct labor hours required per unit of product multiplied by the direct labor hourly rate.

5. +   A higher level of desired ending inventory implies a greater quantity of purchases, which in the aggregate can be expected to cost more.

Aberac Merchandisers purchase a product for $6 per unit and sell it for $10 per unit. The finished goods inventory at the end of any given month is projected at 150% of the projected sales for the upcoming month. Collections from customers are as follows: zero in the month of sale; 60% in the month following the sale, and the remainder in the next month. Payments to vendors are made 50% in the month of purchase with the remainder paid in the next month.

Inventory at January 1, 1983, is 2,000 units. December sales were 1,500 units. Projected sales for January are 1,200 units; February, 1,800 units; and March, 1,600 units. Accounts receivable at January 1, 1983, are $23,000. Accounts·payable (for merchandise only) at January 1, 1983, are $3,200.

a. Compute December sales in dollars.
b. Compute November sales in units.
c. Compute cash collections projected for January 1983 from November sales.
d. Compute cash collections projected for January 1983 from December sales.

e. Compute December purchases.
f. Compute projected accounts receivable on January 31, 1983.
g. Compute the units of inventory projected at January 31, 1983.
h. Compute January projected purchases in units.
i. Compute February projected purchases in units.
j. Compute projected cash payments to vendors for January.
k. Compute the projected balance in accounts payable at January 31, 1983.

EXERCISES (ANSWERS)

a. *1,500 Units* $\times$ *$10 Selling Price* = $\underline{\$15,000}$

b.
$$\begin{array}{l} \$\ \ 23,000\ \textit{January 1, 1983 Accounts Receivable} \\ -\ 15,000\ \textit{December Sales} \\ \hline \$\ \ \ \ 8,000\ \textit{Sales from November Not Yet Collected} \end{array}$$

$8,000 = 40\% \cdot x$

$x = \$20,000$

$20,000 \div \$10 Selling Price = $\underline{\textit{2,000 Units}}$

c. In January, all of the receivables related to November sales will be collected, or $\underline{\$8,000}$.

d. In January, 60% of the receivables from December sales will be collected, or $15,000 \times 60\% = \underline{\$9,000}$.

e. January 1, 1983, Accounts Payable = $3,200, which represents 50% of purchases in December; hence, December purchases total $\underline{\$6,400}$.

f. On January 31, 1983, 40% of December sales will still be receivable, or $15,000 $\times$ 40\% = $6,000$, and 100% of January sales, or $10 $\times$ 1,200 = $12,000$. The total receivable would be $\underline{\$18,000}$.

g. On January 31, 1983, projected inventory is 150% of the upcoming month's projected sales, or $150\% \times 1,800$ Units = $\underline{\textit{2,700 Units}}$.

h. January projected purchases in number of units

$$\begin{array}{l} -2,000\ \textit{Beginning Inventory} \\ +1,200\ \textit{Sales for January} \\ +2,700\ \textit{Desired Ending Inventory} \\ \hline 1,900\ \textit{Purchases Required} \end{array}$$

i. February projected purchases in number of units

$$\begin{array}{l} -2,700\ \textit{Beginning Inventory} \\ +1,800\ \textit{Sales for February} \\ +2,400\ \textit{Desired Ending Inventory (1,600} \times \textit{150\%)} \\ \hline 1,500\ \textit{Purchases Required} \end{array}$$

j. In January, the entire accounts payable balance must be paid ($3,200) as well as 50% of January's purchases (1,900 Units $\times$ 50% = 950 $\times$ $6 Cost = $5,700). Hence, total projected cash payments are $\underline{\$8,900}$.

k. Accounts payable at January 31, 1983, will be 50% of January purchases or 1,900 $\times$ 50% = 950 $\times$ $6 Cost = $\underline{\$5,700}$.

BEVING CORPORATION
Balance Sheet
June 30, 1983

ASSETS

Cash	$ 50,000
Accounts receivable	459,000
Raw materials	40,000
Finished goods ($2 cost per unit)	80,000
Plant & Equipment (net)	900,000
	$1,529,000

LIABILITIES & STOCKHOLDERS' EQUITY

Accounts payable	$ 350,000
Dividends payable	50,000
Notes payable	100,000
Common stock ($1 par)	500,000
Paid in capital in excess of par	400,000
Retained earnings	129,000
	$1,529,000

Sales were $300,000 in June. Beving Corporation estimates sales (at a $2-per-unit sales price) for the next quarter as follows: July, $500,000; August, $700,000; and September, $300,000. Ten percent of each month's sales are cash sales; the remaining sales on account are collected 30% in the month of sale, 50% in the following month, and 20% in the next month. Bad debts expense is insignificant and is not considered in the budgeting process. Purchases were $200,000 in June. Beving wishes to maintain a finished goods inventory equal to 20% of the next month's sales. Beving wishes to maintain a raw materials inventory equal to 50% of the desired level of production for the next month; 4 units of material costing $0.10 per unit are required per unit of finished good. Purchases are paid for 40% in the month following purchase and 60% in the next month. June's total purchases were $200,000; accounts payable relate only to raw material purchases.

Each unit requires 6 minutes of direct labor; each hour of direct labor costs $8.00. The overhead rate for Beving Corporation is $0.60 per direct labor hour.

Estimated selling and administrative costs are $90,000 for July, $100,000 for August, and $65,000 for September.

Beving intends to declare dividends of $0.20 per share in September, 50% of which will be paid in that same month. Prior years' dividends will be paid off in July.

The note payable is due December 31, 1983, and no interim payments are to be made other than monthly interest at an annual rate of 15%. Beving Corporation has a policy of maintaining a minimum cash balance of $40,000. It has a line of credit that permits it to borrow in increments of $10,000 at 20%. Such borrowing is obtained at the beginning of the month and repaid at the end of the month, with interest paid as the loan is repaid.

Monthly income tax payments of $25,000 are required.

Depreciation for the first quarter was $70,000.

1. Prepare the following items for Beving Corporation for the three months from July 1 through September 30, 1983.
   a. Sales budget
   b. Schedule of expected cash collections
   c. Production budget (Assume October sales in units are expected to be 200,000.)
   d. Purchasing budget (Assume October production in units is expected to be 180,000.)

e. Direct labor budget

f. Overhead budget

g. Per-unit cost of finished product

h. Schedule of expected cash disbursements for purchases of raw materials

i. Cash budget

2. Prepare the budgeted income statement for Beving Corporation for the first quarter of 1983.

3. Prepare the budgeted balance sheet as of September 30, 1983.

4. What were total sales in May, 1983?

5. What were total purchases in May, 1983?

CHAPTER DEMONSTRATION PROBLEM (ANSWER)

1. a.

BEVING CORPORATION
Sales Budget
For Period Ending September 30, 1983

	July	August	September
Expected sales in units	250,000	350,000	150,000
Selling price per unit	× $2	× $2	× $2
	$500,000	$700,000	$300,000

Note: Divide the total sales provided in the problem by the $2 selling price to derive the expected sales in units.

b.

BEVING CORPORATION
Expected Cash Collections

	July	August	September	
May sales*	$270,000			] Accounts receivable 6/30/83
June sales*	135,000	$ 54,000		
July sales	135,000	225,000	$ 90,000	
August sales	—	189,000	315,000	
September sales	—	—	81,000	
Total collections of sales on account	$540,000	$468,000	$486,000	
Cash sales	50,000	70,000	30,000	
Total expected cash from sales	$590,000	$538,000	$516,000	

*The 30-50-20 collection pattern implies this balance contains both May and June sales. The problem states that June sales totaled $300,000; since 10% are cash sales, $270,000 are sales on account. As of the end of June, 70% of the June sales were still outstanding, or $189,000. Since total receivables are $459,000 on June 30, the difference in June-related receivables and the balance relates to May, or $270,000. The collection pattern indicates that the entire $270,000 of May-related receivables will be collected in July, while only 50% of the June receivables ($135,000) will be collected in July, with the remaining 20% ($54,000) collected in August.

c.

BEVING CORPORATION
Production Budget
For Period Ended September 30, 1983

	July	August	September
Expected sales (units)	250,000	350,000	150,000
Add: Desired ending inventory of finished goods*	70,000	30,000	40,000
Units needed	320,000	380,000	190,000
Less: Beginning inventory of finished goods	40,000†	70,000	30,000
Units to be produced	280,000	310,000	160,000

*20% of the next month's sales
†$80,000 Inventory ÷ $2 Cost

d.

BEVING CORPORATION
Purchasing Budget
For Period Ended September 30, 1983

	July	August	September
Units to be produced	280,000	310,000	160,000
Raw material per finished unit	× 4	× 4	× 4
Production needs	1,120,000	1,240,000	640,000
Desired ending inventory*	620,000	320,000	360,000
Total needs	1,740,000	1,560,000	1,000,000
Beginning inventory	400,000†	620,000	320,000
Raw materials to be purchased	1,340,000	940,000	680,000
Raw materials cost per unit	× $0.10	× $0.10	× $0.10
Cost of raw material purchases	$134,000	$94,000	$68,000

*50% of the next month's production, requiring 4 units of raw material per unit of product
†$40,000 Inventory ÷ $0.10 Selling Price = 400,000

e.

BEVING CORPORATION
Direct Labor Budget
For Period Ended September 30, 1983

	July	August	September
Units to be produced	280,000	310,000	160,000
Direct labor time per unit (6/60)	× 0.1	× 0.1	× 0.1
Total direct labor hours needed	28,000	31,000	16,000
Direct labor cost per hour	× $8	× $8	× $8
Total direct labor cost	$224,000	$248,000	$128,000

f.

BEVING CORPORATION
Overhead Budget
For Period Ended September 30, 1983

	July	August	September
Units to be produced	280,000	310,000	160,000
Direct labor time per unit (6/60)	× 0.1	× 0.1	× 0.1
	28,000	31,000	16,000
Overhead rate per direct labor hour	× $0.60	× $0.60	× $0.60
Total overhead	$16,800	$18,600	$ 9,600

g. $0.40   Materials (4 Units @ $0.10 per Unit)
       0.80   Direct Labor (1/10 Hour @ $8)
       0.06   Overhead ($0.60 × 1/10 Direct Labor Hour)

     $1.26

h.

BEVING CORPORATION
Expected Cash Disbursements
For Purchases of Raw Materials

	July	August	September	
May purchases	$150,000			⎫ Accounts
June purchases	80,000	$120,000		⎬ payable
July purchases	—	53,600	$ 80,400	⎭ 6/30/83
August purchases	—	—	37,600	
Total payments on purchases of raw materials	$230,000	$173,600	$118,000	

*The 0-40-60 payment policy implies June's payable balance includes 100% of June's purchases plus 60% of May's purchases.

Note: Accounts payable total all of September purchases of $68,000 plus $56,400 of August purchases, or $124,400 as of September 30, 1983.

i.

BEVING CORPORATION
Cash Budget
For the Period Ended September 30, 1983

	July	August	September
Cash balance, beginning 6/30/83*	$ 50,000	$ 42,950	$ 44,500
Add: Receipts, cash sales, and collections from customers	590,000	538,000	516,000
Total cash available	$640,000	$580,950*	$560,500
Less Disbursements:			
Less: Raw material purchases	230,000	173,600	118,000
Less: Direct labor	224,000	248,000	128,000
Less: Manufacturing overhead	16,800	18,600	9,600
Less: Selling & administrative	90,000	100,000	65,000
Less: Income taxes	25,000	25,000	25,000
Less: Dividends	50,000*	—	50,000†
Less: Interest on outstanding note‡	1,250	1,250	1,250
Total disbursements	$637,050	$566,450	$396,850
Cash surplus (deficit)	2,950	14,500	163,650
Minimum cash balance	$ 40,000	$ 40,000	$ 40,000
Total cash needed	$677,050	$606,450	$436,850
Financing			
Borrowing (at beginning)	$ 40,000	$ 30,000	
Repayment (at ending)			$ 70,000
Interest (20%)			3,000
	$ 42,950	$ 44,500	$ 90,650

*Dividends payable 6/30/83
†$0.20 × 500,000 Shares × 50% = 50,000
‡$100,000 × 15% = 15,000 ÷ 12 = 1,250

2.

BEVING CORPORATION
Budgeted Income Statement
For the First Quarter

Sales (750,000 × $2)	$1,500,000
Less: Cost of goods sold [(710,000 × $1.26) + (40,000 × $2.00)]	974,600
Gross profit	$ 525,400
Less: Selling & administrative expense	255,000
Less: Interest expense	6,750
Less: Depreciation expense	70,000
Net income before taxes	$ 193,650
Less: Income taxes	75,000
Net income	$ 118,650

3.

BEVING CORPORATION
Budgeted Balance Sheet
As of September 30, 1983

ASSETS

Cash	$ 90,650
Accounts receivable*	315,000
Raw materials (360,000 × $0.10)	36,000
Finished goods (40,000 × $1.26)	50,400
Plant & equipment (net)†	830,000
Total assets	$1,322,050

LIABILITIES & STOCKHOLDERS' EQUITY

Current liabilities	
Accounts payable	$ 124,400
Dividends payable	50,000
Note payable	100,000
Common stock ($1 par)	500,000
Paid in capital in excess of par	400,000
Retained earnings‡	147,650
	$1,322,050

*The 30-50-20 collection pattern implies that 70% of September credit sales ($189,000) and 20% of August credit sales ($126,000) are outstanding.
†$900,000 per 6/30/83 Balance Sheet − $70,000 Depreciation
‡$129,000 Beginning Retained Earnings + $118,650 Budgeted Net Income − $100,000 Budgeted Dividends.

4. Accounts receivable are $459,000 on June 30, 1983. As derived in part 1 (b), this balance includes $189,000 of June sales on account and $270,000 of May sales on account. The 30-50-20 collection pattern suggests that this May sales balance is 20% of May's sales. Therefore

$$\$270{,}000 = \frac{20}{100} \cdot x$$

$$x = \$1{,}350{,}000 \text{ Credit Sales}$$

$$\$1{,}350{,}000 = \frac{90}{100} \cdot y$$

$$y = \underline{\$1{,}500{,}000} \text{ Total May Sales (Cash Sales and Sales on Account)}$$

5. Accounts payable on 6/30/83 total $350,000, and as derived in part 1(h), $150,000 is associated with May purchases. The 0-40-60 payment policy implies that this balance is 60% of total May purchases. Therefore

$$\$150{,}000 = \frac{60}{100} \cdot x$$

$$x = \underline{\$250{,}000} \text{ Total May Purchases}$$

24 COST-VOLUME-PROFIT ANALYSIS

After completing this chapter, you should:

1 *Be able to define variable and step variable, committed and discretionary fixed, and mixed (semivariable) costs.*

2 *Understand the logic that underlies the accountant's use of linear cost lines, particularly the focus upon a relevant range.*

3 *Know how to utilize scattergraph and high-low techniques for studying cost behavior and be aware of the availability of more sophisticated techniques such as the method of least squares.*

4 *Be able to perform a cost-volume-profit analysis to assess the break-even point of operations as well as the effect of operating changes such as changes in fixed costs, contribution margin, revenues, sales price, and sales volume.*

5 *Be familiar with a break-even chart.*

6 *Be able to apply cost-volume-profit analysis to multiproduct firms.*

7 *Know the limiting assumptions upon which cost-volume-profit analysis is based.*

CHAPTER SUMMARY

A useful management tool for determining how changes in revenue, volume, and costs affect profits is known as **cost-volume-profit (CVP) analysis**. The tool rests upon the ability to define costs as either **variable costs** (fluctuating in direct proportion to changes in activity) or **fixed costs** (remaining constant regardless of the level of activity). The economists' law of economies of scale (more efficiencies are expected as production increases) and law of diminishing returns (eventually, more production leads to higher costs) are well accepted, as is the existence of such varied cost behavior as **step costs** (costs that vary only when substantial increases or decreases occur in the activity base) and **mixed or semivariable costs** (costs that contain both variable and fixed cost elements). Nevertheless, CVP analysis *assumes linear cost behavior* and the ability to classify all costs as being either fixed or variable; this is considered to be an acceptable approach as long as the CVP analysis is performed over the *relevant range* (i.e., that range with the greatest likelihood of occurrence). Within a defined range of operations fixed costs generally remain constant, linear cost behavior is common, and step costs will generally behave in either a variable or fixed manner depending on the breadth of the relevant range.

Essentially, CVP analysis graphs the variable and fixed costs of an entity and its revenue to determine the break-even point, that point at which total revenues equal total costs. The graph enables one to interpret the profit or loss of an entity at differing activity levels and can be adjusted for changes in sales price, costs, and volume to plan and analyze any proposed changes in operations. Fixed costs can be subclassified as discretionary and committed costs; **discretionary costs** are subject to management control, while **committed costs** typically cannot be changed in the short-run. CVP provides a planning device to assess the effects of such costs and related management policies.

The difficult aspect of using CVP analysis is determining the cost behavior within an entity of its expense items. Possible techniques for such a determination include scattergraphs of the observed relationships between costs and various levels of activity, the method of least squares, whereby a mathematical formula identifies the cost line with the best possible fit to the scattergraph, and the high-low method, which generalizes cost behavior by comparing the highest and lowest data points. The validity of these approaches will depend on the extent to which the data points selected for analysis are representative.

Break-even analysis can be performed using the *contribution margin* (sales minus variable costs) approach; the break-even point in units is derived by dividing fixed costs by the unit contribution margin. When a manager wishes to compute the number of sales units necessary to reach a *target net income,* the income goal can be added to the fixed costs in the numerator; and the result of the division by contribution margin will be the number of sales units required to cover both the fixed cost and the "fixed" selected net income. CVP can be diagrammed in a break-even chart to clarify interrelationships. CVP can be applied to *multiproduct firms* by computing a *weighted-average contribution percentage,* which is weighted in proportion to the predicted sales mix, and using the result in the same manner as the unit contribution margin is used in break-even analysis. The implicit assumption of such an analysis is that sales mix remains as predicted.

Other assumptions that underlie CVP are that the technology, efficiency, costs, and selling prices for the firm remain as predicted and that inventory levels remain fairly stable. By being cognizant of such assumptions, managers can identify those situations to which CVP can be applied without expecting serious deficiencies caused by the basic assumptions of the planning tool.

**TECHNICAL
POINTS**

√ Variable cost

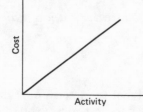

√ Step cost

√ Fixed cost

√ Mixed cost

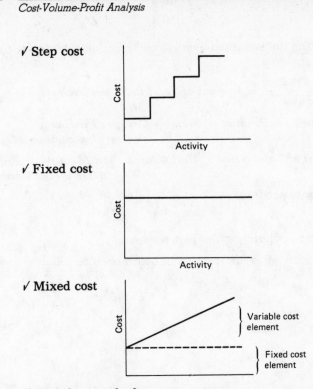

√ High-low method

> *Per Unit of Activity Variable Cost Component = (Highest Cost — Lowest Cost) ÷ (Activity Level for Highest Cost — Activity Level for Lowest Cost)*

> *Fixed Cost = Total Cost at Highest (or Lowest) Activity Level — [Per Unit of Activity Variable Cost Component × Activity Level at Highest (or Lowest) Point]*

√ Break-even point

Equation approach

> *Sales — Variable Cost — Fixed Cost = 0*

Contribution margin approach

$$\frac{\textit{Fixed Costs}}{\textit{Selling Price per Unit — Variable Cost per Unit}} = \textit{Break-even Point in Units}$$

√ Sales required to generate target net income

Equation approach

> *Sales = Variable Cost + Fixed Cost + Net Income*

Contribution margin approach

$$\frac{\textit{Fixed Costs + Net Income}}{\textit{Selling Price per Unit — Variable Cost per Unit}} = \textit{Required Sales in Units}$$

√ Break-even chart

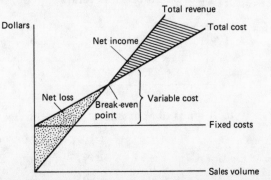

√ Steps in computing the weighted-average contribution margin for multiproduct firms

(1) $\dfrac{Sales\ per\ Product}{Total\ Sales}$ = *Percent of Total Sales per Product*

(2) *Selling Price per Product — Variable Cost per Product*
$$= Unit\ Contribution\ Margin\ per\ Product$$

(3) $\sum\limits_{1}^{n}$ *(Percent of Total Sales × Unit Contribution Margin per Product)*
$$= Weighted\text{-}Average\ Contribution\ Margin$$

where n = number of products

MULTIPLE-CHOICE QUESTIONS

Circle the letter corresponding to the best response.

1. The economic view of variable cost can be graphed as follows.

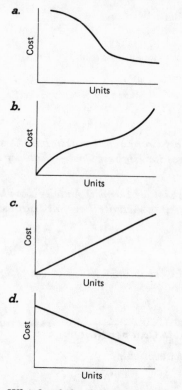

2. Which of the following statements is not true about a step cost function?
   a. Operating efficiency is maximized by being at the right-most portion of a step in a step cost function.
   b. It tends to approximate a fixed cost if extremely large activity changes are needed to force an increase in the cost function.
   c. It can be graphed as follows.

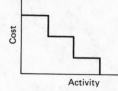

   d. It tends to approximate the behavior of a "true" variable cost.

3. Committed costs
   a. are short-term in orientation
   b. are more prone to cost elimination than discretionary costs
   c. are geared heavily to the future
   d. originate from top management's yearly appropriation decisions

4. The high-low method
   a. is based on past operating data concerning costs incurred at several various levels of activity
   b. is based on the analysis of only two data points
   c. is superior to the least-squares method of analyzing cost behavior
   d. will generally obtain the same results as those obtained by using the scattergraph technique

5. If sales are $700,000, variable costs are 40% of sales, and the average return on sales for a company is 10%, what are total fixed costs at the break-even point?
   a. $280,000
   b. $70,000
   c. $420,000
   d. $350,000

6. Indicate which of the following is an improper label for the break-even chart presented below.

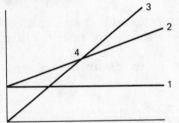

   a. 1 represents fixed costs
   b. 2 represents variable costs
   c. 3 represents total revenue
   d. 4 represents the break-even point

7. At what price must units be sold to achieve a $300 target net income if the variable costs are $2 per unit and fixed costs total $500 for 100 units of sales?
   a. $10
   b. $4
   c. $6
   d. $8

8. If forecasted sales of product A are 60,000 units at a selling price of $10 and a variable cost of $7, and forecasted sales of product B are 20,000 units at a selling price of $8 and a variable cost of $6, the "unit contribution margin for the firm" is expected to be
   a. $2.20
   b. $6.75
   c. $5.40
   d. $2.75

Answer   *Explanation*

1. b   This curve reflects both the decline in costs per unit due to efficiencies from increased production and the eventual increase in costs per unit from difficulties associated with large increases in production.

2. c   The graph for a step cost function is as follows.

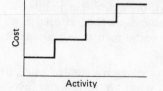

3. c   Discretionary costs are short-term, are more prone to cost elimination, and originate from annual appropriations by management.

4. b   Typically, the results of analyzing two data points will differ from the results of any technique that uses data on numerous observed cost-activity relationships. The precision of least squares and its use of a more complete data base contribute to its general superiority as a tool for analyzing cost behavior.

5. c $700,000 Sales − $280,000 Variable Costs = $420,000 Fixed Costs. The 10% average return on sales is irrelevant since the break-even point is defined to be zero net income.

6. b   This represents total costs; the distance from 1 to 2 represents the variable costs.

7. a
$$\frac{\$500 + \$300}{Selling\ Price - \$2} = 100$$

$$\frac{\$800}{Selling\ Price - \$2} = 100$$

$$\$800 = 100 \times Selling\ Price - \$200$$

$$\$1000 = 100 \times Selling\ Price$$

$$\$10 = Selling\ Price$$

8. d

Total Unit Sales	Percent of Sales		Contribution Margin		
60,000	75	×	$3	=	$2.25
20,000	25	×	$2	=	0.50
					$2.75

Weighted-average contribution margin for 80,000 units is $2.75.

TRUE-FALSE QUESTIONS

Indicate whether each of the following statements is true (T) or false (F).

____   *1.* If an activity base triples, a true variable cost should triple; if the base is halved, a variable cost should be reduced by fifty percent.

____   *2.* The accountants' variable cost per unit is constant.

____   *3.* Normally, cost-volume-profit analysis studies cost relationships that have been observed in the long-run.

____ 4. Most committed costs are not easily changed by daily business activities and decisions, and if they are cut back a firm is normally prevented from achieving long-term goals.

____ 5. The same costs can behave differently in different environments.

____ 6. The method of least squares is less accurate than the scattergraph approach to analyzing cost behavior.

____ 7. If the highest and lowest activity points span two ranges with different levels of fixed costs, the high-low method cannot be used.

____ 8. When considering a proposal such as whether to invest in an advertising campaign that is expected to increase sales, the CVP analysis must consider both the present sales volume and the additional costs and sales volume that are expected to result from the proposal.

____ 9. If the sales mix varies, the unit contribution margin for a multiproduct firm will differ.

____ 10. CVP analysis makes no assumption regarding inventory levels.

TRUE-FALSE QUESTIONS (ANSWERS)

Answer   **Explanation**

1. T   A variable cost varies in direct proportion to a change in an activity base.

2. T   It must be constant in order to maintain a directly proportional relationship to fluctuations in an activity base.

3. F   Over the long-run, most costs will change to match increases and decreases in activity; hence, CVP studies cost relationships that have been observed in the short-run.

4. T   Committed fixed costs arise from a firm's commitment to operations and are typically long-term and essential to successful operations.

5. T   It is for this reason that costs should be analyzed individually by a business incurring them rather than applying some general classification scheme.

6. F   The least-squares method is more precise, because it mathematically derives the cost line with the best possible fit to the scattergraph.

7. T   A relevant range must apply with the highest and lowest data points being representative of operations.

8. F   The analysis should evaluate only those items that change as a result of the decision; the present volume can be ignored without affecting the analysis.

9. T   For example, if more units of high contribution margin products are sold, the unit contribution margin will increase.

10. F   One of the basic assumptions of CVP analysis is that inventory levels remain fairly stable.

**CLASSIFI-
CATION AND
MATCHING
QUESTIONS**

Provide the most common classification of the following costs, using these symbols.

V = Variable cost
CF = Committed fixed cost
DF = Discretionary fixed cost
S = Step cost
M = Mixed cost

_____ *1.* Advertising
_____ *2.* Direct materials
_____ *3.* Depreciation
_____ *4.* Lease agreement requiring set rate plus percentage of sales
_____ *5.* Direct labor
_____ *6.* Insurance
_____ *7.* Property taxes
_____ *8.* Supplies
_____ *9.* Research and development
_____ *10.* Clerical staff processing customer orders
_____ *11.* Executive salaries
_____ *12.* Sales commissions
_____ *13.* Utility bills with fixed monthly charges plus charges per kilowatt hour
_____ *14.* Fuel
_____ *15.* Employee training
_____ *16.* Car rental at daily-plus-mileage rate
_____ *17.* Contributions
_____ *18.* Crew unloading goods on the receiving platform

CLASSIFICATION AND MATCHING QUESTIONS (ANSWERS)

1. DF *2.* V *3.* CF *4.* M *5.* V *6.* CF *7.* CF *8.* V *9.* DF *10.* S *11.* CF *12.* V
13. M *14.* V *15.* DF *16.* M *17.* DF *18.* S

QUESTIONS CONCERNING THE EFFECTS OF TRANS-ACTIONS

Indicate whether the following changes increase (+), decrease (−), or have no effect (0) upon the break-even point in units.

_____ *1.* An increase in the selling price

_____ *2.* An increase in contribution margin

_____ *3.* An increase in total net income

_____ *4.* An increase in fixed costs

_____ *5.* An increase in variable cost per unit

_____ *6.* An increase in target net income

_____ *7.* An increase in dollar sales

_____ *8.* An increase in total production

QUESTIONS CONCERNING THE EFFECTS OF TRANSACTIONS (ANSWERS)

Answer   *Explanation*

1. −   This increases the contribution margin per unit.

2. −   The greater the contribution margin, the fewer the units of sales required to cover total fixed costs.

3. 0   Once operations go beyond the break-even point, income will rise; however, the break-even point remains the same.

4. +   This means more fixed costs must be covered in order to reach the break-even point.

5. +   This decreases the contribution margin per unit.

6. 0   What a firm desires in income has no necessary relation to the break-even point.

7. 0   This should yield higher income but has no implications for the break-even point.

8. 0   There is no necessary change in per-unit contribution margin or total fixed costs.

EXERCISES

1. A company is operating at a $340,000 net income, incurring total fixed costs of $120,000. If its unit sales are 17,000 units, what is its contribution margin? If fixed costs increased by $130,000 what would be its net income?

2. A company sells two products in a 40/60 proportion and has a unit margin of $8.00. If the product representing 40% of sales has a contribution margin of $5, what is the contribution margin of the other product? If the sales proportions shifted to 30/70, what would be the unit contribution margin?

EXERCISES (ANSWERS)

1. $$\frac{\$120,000 + \$340,000}{x} = 17,000 \text{ Units}$$

   $$\$460,000 = 17,000x$$

   $$\underline{\$27.06} = x$$

   If fixed costs increased by $130,000, there would be a decline of total net income of $130,000, therefore net income would be $210,000.

2. $40\% \cdot \$5 = \$2$ $60\% \cdot x = \$ 6$
     $60\% \cdot x\ = \$6$ $\underline{\underline{x = \$10}}$ *Contribution Margin*
     $\qquad\qquad \overline{\$8}$

   $30\% \cdot \$5\ = \$1.50$
   $70\% \cdot \$10 = \$7.00$
   $\qquad\qquad \overline{\underline{\$8.50}}$

   Note: Since a greater proportion of the sales are items with a higher contribution margin, the unit contribution margin increases.

CHAPTER DEMON-STRATION PROBLEM

Smithdateran Corporation estimates the following operations for 1983.

Sales (184,000 units)	$920,000
Less: Variable costs of production	644,000
Less: Fixed costs of production	130,000
Less: Sales commissions (3%)	27,600
Less: Fixed selling & administrative expenses	30,000
Net income	$ 88,400

a. What is the break-even point for Smithdateran Corporation in dollars and in units?

b. If Smithdateran Corporation wishes to earn $95,000 of income, how many units of product must be sold?

c. Smithdateran Corporation is considering investing $20,000 in an advertising campaign that would be expected to increase sales by 15,000 units. Should the corporation make the investment? Quantify your answer.

d. Smithdateran is considering adding a new product line that would have sales of 46,000 units at a selling price of $20 per unit and related variable costs of $12. Fixed costs associated with the new product line would be investments in equipment leases totaling $370,000. Should the new product line be added? Quantify your answer.

 Assume Smithdateran does add the new product line, what will be the corporation's unit contribution margin?

e. One of the cost items involved in the expanded product line discussed in part (*d*) is estimated to be $70,000 at 20,000 units of production and $190,000 at 60,000 units of production. Describe the cost behavior of this cost component in a mathematical expression.

CHAPTER DEMONSTRATION PROBLEM (ANSWER)

a. Total fixed costs are $130,000 + $30,000
 Total variable costs are $644,000 + $27,600
 Per-unit variable cost is $671,600/184,000 = $3.65
 Per-unit selling price is $920,000/184,000 = $5.00
 Per-unit contribution margin is $5 − $3.65 = $1.35

$$\frac{\$160,000}{\$1.35} = \underline{\underline{118,519}} \; Units$$

$$118,519 \times \$5 = \underline{\underline{\$592,595}}$$

b.
$$\frac{\$160,000 + \$95,000}{\$1.35} = \underline{\underline{188,889}} \; Units$$

c.
$$15,000 \times \$1.35 = \$20,250$$
$$Incremental \; Fixed \; Costs = \underline{20,000}$$
$$Incremental \; Contribution \; Margin = \underline{\$250}$$

Yes, the investment should be made, because the corporation's net income will improve by $250.

d.
$$46,000 \times (\$20 - \$12) = \$368,000$$
$$Less \; Incremental \; Fixed \; Costs = \underline{370,000}$$
$$Incremental \; Contribution \; Margin = \underline{(\$2,000)}$$

No, the new product line should not be added, because the net income for the firm would decline by $2,000.

 If, however, the product were added, the corporation's unit contribution margin would be computed as follows.

	Units of Sale	Proportion of Sales	Contribution Margin per Unit		
Current product	184,000	80%	× $1.35	= $1.08	
New product	46,000	20%	× $8.00	= 1.60	
	230,000			$2.68	Weighted-Average Contribution Margin

e.

$$\frac{\$190,000 - \$70,000}{60,000 - 20,000} = \$3 \text{ per Unit Variable Cost Rate}$$

$60,000 \times \$3 = \$180,000$

$\$180,000 - \$190,000 = \$10,000$ *Fixed Cost*

or

$20,000 \times \$3 = \$60,000$

$\$60,000 - \$70,000 = \$10,000$ *Fixed Cost*

The cost takes a mixed cost form, which can be expressed as the variable cost rate times the number of units of product X plus the fixed cost, or

$\$3x + \$10,000 =$ *Total Cost at x Units of Product*

25 EXTENSION OF COST-VOLUME-PROFIT ANALYSIS FOR PERFORMANCE EVALUATION

OBJECTIVES

After completing this chapter, you should:

1 *Understand the purpose and structure of a responsibility accounting system.*

2 *Be able to distinguish between cost centers, profit centers, and investment centers.*

3 *Know how to prepare a performance report.*

4 *Understand the importance of the controllability concept and the timeliness of reporting with a responsibility accounting system.*

5 *Be able to distinguish between direct and indirect costs, as well as between controllable and uncontrollable costs.*

6 *Understand the deficiencies in cost allocations.*

7 *Know how to prepare a contribution income statement.*

8 *Understand the differences between direct and absorption costing, their respective advantages and disadvantages, and the reason that direct or variable costing is generally preferred for performance evaluation.*

9 *Be aware of the advantages of assessing performance by the use of more than one evaluative criterion and of weighting the multiple performance measures selected in terms of their relative importance in order to minimize the potential conflict, disincentives, and bias that can arise in the performance evaluation process.*

Responsibility accounting systems prepare and distribute *performance reports* that are tailored to an entity's organization chart and clearly report the costs and other facets of operations that are *controllable* by each manager and therefore the costs for which each manager is held responsible or accountable. Such a report can be directed at a **cost center** or responsibility unit in which the manager is held accountable for cost incurrence, a **profit center** or responsibility unit in which a manager is held accountable for profit, or an **investment center** or responsibility center in which the manager is held responsible for capital asset investment in addition to revenues and expenses. A timely performance report comparing budgeted figures to actual figures is issued for lower levels of the firm in detail, and in summarized form upward through the organization chart; the investment center reports will typically have information as to the center's *return on assets*. If more than one center in the firm influences a particular cost, revenue, or investment, responsibility will be assigned to that person or center with the greatest influence to whom the revenues and costs can be traced (i.e., to those responsible for their incurrence). Costs that are easily traceable are termed **direct costs**, whereas those not easily traceable are termed **indirect costs**. Since *cost allocations* tend to be arbitrary assignments of uncontrollable costs, they are typically not reported or are clearly segregated on the face of the contribution income statement.

The format of such a statement is to itemize the responsibility unit's sales less variable costs (generally assumed to be controllable) to derive the **contribution margin** and to subtract controllable fixed costs (typically, discretionary costs) to arrive at the **controllable contribution margin**. Finally, uncontrollable fixed costs (typically, committed costs) are subtracted to yield the **segment margin**. Although this is the extent of the detail for a product line and a division, the total company would also be interested in nontraceable costs being identified, as well as income taxes, to assess the total entity's net income.

The contribution margin approach requires a separation of fixed overhead expenses from cost of goods sold, as the focus is upon variable costs rather than such uncontrollable fixed costs as depreciation and insurance. The means of achieving such a separation is to apply *direct* or *variable costing*, which treats fixed manufacturing overhead expenses as a period cost, rather than a product cost, instead of the *absorption* or *full costing* method traditionally used for external reporting. In addition to facilitating performance reports geared to controllable costs, the variable costing approach interfaces well with cost-volume-profit analysis and assures that sales, not production, is the motivating force behind a given level of profit. However, drawbacks of the approach include poorer matching of expenses and revenues and the unacceptability of direct costing for external reporting.

The means of performance evaluation can dissuade employees from dysfunctional activities by using a *set of evaluative criteria* for performance measurement, rather than one sole criterion, as well as by communicating a relative *weighting scheme* for the quantitative and qualitative measures that clarify the priorities of management. Top management should take into account conflicts between objectives, how such conflicts were resolved, and sources of possible *bias* in performance evaluation when reviewing responsibility units.

√ *Responsibility Units*

Cost center: Accountable for cost incurrence
Profit center: Accountable for profit
Investment center: Accountable for profit and capital funds

√ Return on assets or return on investment (ROI) is a popular tool for evaluating investment centers.

√ *Variances or Deviations = Actual − Budgeted*

√ Format for contribution income statement

> *Net Sales*
> − *Variable Costs:*
>   *Cost of Goods Sold (per Direct Costing)*
>   *Variable Selling and Administrative Expenses*
> ───
> *Contribution Margin*
> − *Controllable Fixed Costs*
> ───
> *Controllable Contribution Margin*
> − *Uncontrollable Fixed Costs*
> ───
> *Segment Margin*

In addition, disclosures are commonly made as to total nontraceable costs.

√ Inventory valuation or product cost

Absorption Costing	Direct Costing
Direct Labor	Direct Labor
Direct Material	Direct Material
Variable Factory Overhead	Variable Factory Overhead
Fixed Factory Overhead	

√ *Difference in Net Income Computed under Absorption and Variable Costing Techniques = Fixed Overhead Cost per Unit × Number of Units Retained in Inventory from the Current Year's Production or the Number of Units Taken from Prior Years' Inventory and Sold*

√ Under absorption costing, income fluctuates with inventory levels instead of sales.

MULTIPLE-CHOICE QUESTIONS

Circle the letter corresponding to the best response.

1. A profit center is distinguishable from an investment center by the following characteristic.
   a. Profit centers are only responsible for revenues.
   b. Profit centers are only responsible for costs.
   c. Profit centers are only responsible for revenues and costs.
   d. Profit centers are only responsible for capital assets, revenues, and costs.

2. Cost allocations
   a. are extremely arbitrary
   b. tend to be controllable costs
   c. are typically included in performance evaluation
   d. b and d

3. Controllable fixed costs would not include
   a. supervisory salaries
   b. local sales promotion costs
   c. salary of the center's manager
   d. equipment rental charges if management is responsible for procuring equipment to be used in segment activities

4. Which of the following is recommended for use in figuring bonuses?
   a. segment margin
   b. contribution margin
   c. net income
   d. controllable contribution margin

5. Which of the following measures concentrates on a segment from an investment point of view?

a. controllable contribution margin
b. segment margin
c. net income
d. contribution margin

6. Full costing is not
   a. acceptable for external reporting purposes
   b. affected by fluctuations in inventory and production levels
   c. as good at matching expenses as direct costing
   d. superior for performance evaluation purposes

7. Product costs
   a. include variable overhead costs under direct and full costing
   b. are defined identically under direct and full costing
   c. include selling and administrative costs
   d. include fixed overhead costs under direct and full costing

8. If the number of units sold exceeds the units produced
   a. net income under absorption costing would be higher than net income under direct costing
   b. inventory will have increased over the period
   c. net income under absorption costing would be lower than net income under direct costing
   d. fixed manufacturing costs are being deferred

MULTIPLE-CHOICE QUESTIONS (ANSWERS)

Answer   *Explanation*

1. c   While profit centers are responsible for revenues and costs, they are not responsible for capital assets as are investment centers.

2. a   Several alternative bases can be used in cost allocation, with no clear rule available as to the optimum base; hence, allocations tend to be arbitrary, uncontrollable, and are typically disregarded in performance evaluation.

3. c   The salary costs would result from decisions made at higher levels in the organizational hierarchy.

4. d   This is the best indicator of a manager's performance, as it represents the responsibility center's contribution to firm profit.

5. b   This measure is employed in exploring the long-term advisability of keeping a segment as an operating center of the business, which is an investment decision.

6. d   Direct costing is superior for performance evaluation purposes.

7. a   These are product costs regardless of the costing method. Selling and administrative costs are always period costs. Product costs are not defined identically under the two costing approaches, as fixed overhead costs are considered to be a period cost under the direct costing approach.

8. c   Fixed overhead costs from prior periods are being taken off the balance sheet and charged against revenue via the cost of goods sold account.

TRUE-FALSE QUESTIONS

Indicate whether each of the following statements is true (T) or false (F).

_____   *1.* The thrust of responsibility accounting is that centers are charged *only* with those costs and/or revenues that are subject to their control.

_____   *2.* Cost centers should set a goal of cost minimization.

_____   *3.* Investment centers are the most complex of the responsibility centers.

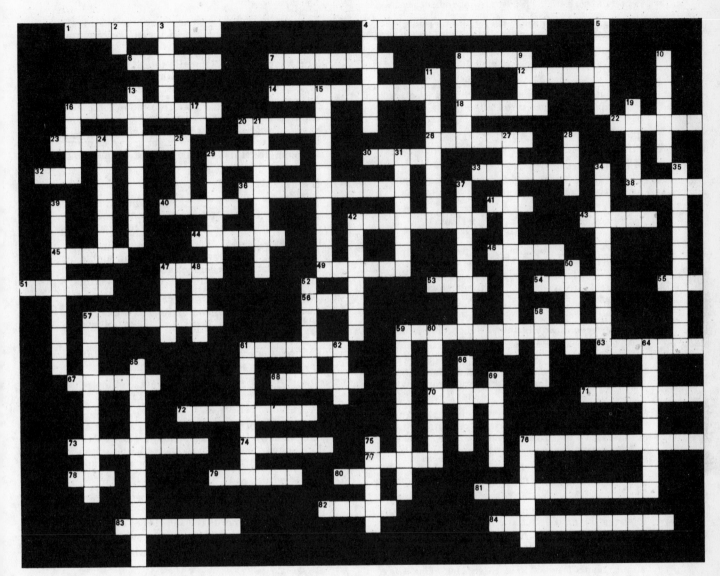

1. <u>47 across</u> <u>1 across</u> usually assigns an uncontrollable cost to segment managers in an arbitrary fashion in an attempt to have multiple responsibility centers absorb their "fair share" of indirect costs.

4. A _____ is a graphical representation of observed relationships between costs and activity levels.

6. The controllable contribution margin less uncontrollable fixed costs yields the <u>10 down</u> <u>6 across</u>.

7. <u>5 down</u> <u>7 across</u> <u>33 across</u> is consistent with contribution reporting and is frequently used for internal accounting records, although its treatment of fixed manufacturing overhead is unacceptable for external reporting purposes.

8. The costs of each job are accumulated on a separate <u>41 across</u> <u>47 across</u> <u>8 across</u>.

12. CVP analysis can be used to examine the sales necessary to generate a particular level of profit, often called the <u>3 down</u> <u>32 across</u> <u>12 across</u>.

14. Materials are issued from the storeroom or warehouse upon the receipt of a <u>60 down</u> <u>14 across</u>.

16. A <u>16 across</u> <u>75 down</u> combines the anticipated number of units to be sold with the desired ending inventory of finished goods and helps companies to protect themselves from either understocking or overstocking inventory.

18. A <u>9 down</u> <u>18 across</u> accumulates labor costs per employee each day and shows the specific job to which the employee was assigned.

20. The <u>20 across</u> <u>17 down</u> <u>43 across</u> <u>63 across</u> is a statistical technique that overcomes the imprecision of the scattergraph by using a mathematical formula to obtain the best possible fit for a cost line.

22. <u>29 across</u> <u>2 down</u> <u>22 across</u> is a very popular tool (ratio) for examining investment center performance, as it shows how effectively a center utilized its assets in generating profit.

23. <u>23 across</u> <u>61 across</u> can be classified as cash budgets, budgeted income statements, or budgeted balance sheets.

26. The <u>25 down</u> <u>26 across</u> summarizes time tickets, showing the total direct and indirect labor cost.

29. See 22 across.

30. <u>30 across</u> <u>47 down</u> are costs incurred in the simultaneous production of two or more goods or services.

32. See 12 across.

33. See 7 across.

36. <u>36 across</u> <u>42 down</u> results when a firm has applied more overhead to production than actually incurred.

38. <u>38 across</u> <u>61 across</u> generally are the result of a combination of various forecasting techniques, and are the most important element in companies' budgetary process, being the foundation for all other aspects of the budget process.

40. A <u>41 across</u> <u>40 across</u> <u>68 across</u> accumulates costs by jobs or orders which may vary in size from 1 unit to thousands of units.

41. See 40 across.

42. <u>42 across</u> <u>61 across</u> are concerned with specific company activities and include the sales budget, production budget, selling expense budget, and administrative expense budget.

43. See 20 across.

44. The <u>44 across</u> <u>75 down</u> is the comprehensive budgeting plan developed by the budget committee under the guidance of the budget director.

45. The sales budget is typically the _____ budget prepared, as it is the foundation for all other aspects of the budget process.

46. <u>57 across</u> <u>46 across</u> <u>47 down</u> arise from an organization's commitment to engage in operations and are not easily changed by daily business activities and decisions; they include the ongoing cost of plant and equipment including depreciation, insurance, and taxes.

47. See 1 across.

49. The <u>49 across</u> <u>58 down</u> <u>75 down</u> is based upon the production budget and permits management to assure it has sufficient work force for production.

51. The <u>84 across</u> <u>57 down</u> <u>51 across</u> is computed by subtracting fixed costs which are controllable by the segment's management and directly traceable to the segment from sales minus variable costs.

53. The <u>53 across</u> <u>75 down</u> plans for cash receipts and cash disbursements, and highlights the need for additional financing if cash balances fall below desired levels.

54. CVP relationships are frequently presented in a graphical format known as a <u>61 down</u> <u>54 across</u>.

55. The <u>48 down</u> <u>55 across</u> is the percentage of an individual product's sales to total sales.

56. The <u>42 down</u> <u>59 down</u> <u>56 across</u> is used to determine the estimated overhead cost of a job or product and is computed by dividing estimated factory overhead by some estimated activity base such as direct labor hours, direct labor dollars, or machine hours.

57. See 46 across.

59. <u>4 down</u> <u>80 across</u> <u>59 across</u> <u>34 down</u> <u>61 across</u> are typically estimated by individual operating units and include such items as the salaries of officers of the company, sales commissions, and advertising costs.

61. See 23 across, 38 across, and 42 across.

63. See 20 across.

67. CVP analysis stands for <u>47 across</u> - <u>74 across</u> - <u>67 across</u> <u>24 down</u>.

68. See 40 across.

70. Cost can be studied within many ranges of activity; the range with the greatest likelihood of occurrence is often termed the <u>29 down</u> <u>70 across</u>.

71. Advocates of responsibility accounting favor a <u>81 across</u> <u>71 across</u> to performance evaluation for evaluating both profit and investment centers.

72. The <u>72 across</u> <u>16 down</u> is that level of activity where revenues and costs are equal.

73. The <u>81 across</u> <u>12 across</u> <u>73 across</u> displays the segment's contribution margin, the segment's controllable contribution margin, uncontrollable fixed costs, segment margin, and income before taxes and is

considered to be a valuable responsibility accounting tool.

74. See 67 across.

76. Selling price minus the variable cost per unit is termed _76 across_ _50 down_.

77. _21 down_ _77 across_ are physical units stated in terms of finished units.

78. The _28 down_ - _78 across_ _20 across_, which focuses on extreme data points, is something of a compromise between the scattergraph and the method of least squares.

79. A _47 across_ _79 across_ is a responsibility unit in which a manager is held accountable for cost incurrence.

80. See 59 across.

81. See 71 across.

82. _82 across_ (_35 down_) _47 down_ contain both variable and fixed cost elements.

83. A _83 across_ _47 across_ varies in direct proportion to a change in an activity base.

84. See 51 across.

DOWN

2. See 22 across.

3. See 12 across.

4. See 59 across.

5. See 7 across.

8. A _52 down_ _33 across_ _8 down_ is frequently employed in steel, petroleum, chemical, and textile production where production is continuous rather than subdivided into discrete jobs.

9. See 18 across.

10. See 6 across.

11. An _11 down_ _66 down_ is the most complex of the responsibility centers; its head is concerned with both profitable operations and the effective use of capital funds.

13. The _13 down_ _75 down_ considers raw material usage, the desired ending raw material inventory balance, and the beginning inventory balance.

15. _15 down_ _42 down_ results when a firm has applied less overhead to production than actually incurred.

16. See 72 across.

17. See 20 across.

19. Same as 22 across.

21. See 77 across.

24. See 67 across.

25. See 26 across.

27. _____ accounting is a reporting system that is based on the organizational structure of a firm whereby all managers are held accountable for their department's operating results; its thrust is that centers are charged only with those costs and/or revenues that are subject to their control.

28. See 78 across.

29. See 70 across.

31. An _31 down_ _47 across_ is one which is not easily traced to a business segment.

34. See 59 across.

35. See 82 across.

37. Labor and overhead are collectively known as _37 down_ _47 across_.

39. A formal evaluation of operations usually includes a _39 down_ _69 down_, which is designed to provide the manager of a responsibility center with timely feedback of operating results.

42. See 36 across and 56 across.

47. See 30 across, 46 across, 82 across, 62 down, and 65 down.

48. See 55 across.

50. See 76 across.

52. See 8 down.

57. See 51 across.

58. See 49 across.

59. See 56 across.

60. See 14 across.

61. See 54 across.

62. Cost functions that increase only when large changes in the activity base occur are called _62 down_ _47 down_ and, when graphed, look like a staircase.

64. Under _64 down_ _76 down_ or full _76 down_, all manufacturing costs are considered product costs and are included in the valuation of inventory.

65. _65 down_ _46 across_ _47 down_ originate from top management's yearly appropriation decisions and typically include advertising, research and development, employee training, and contributions.

66. See 11 down.

69. See 39 down.

75. See 16 across, 44 across, 49 across, 53 across, and 13 down.

76. See 64 down.

26 FLEXIBLE BUDGETS AND STANDARD COSTS

OBJECTIVES

After completing this chapter, you should:

1 *Understand the procedures that are related to flexible budget construction and the benefits of using such budgets in performance evaluations.*

2 *Be able to describe what a standard cost is, how it is developed, and how it can be used to control operations.*

3 *Know how to compute material price and quantity variances, labor rate and efficiency variances, and overhead budget and volume variances.*

4 *Be aware of the common causes of each type of variance, the importance of investigating both large favorable and unfavorable variances and the role of "management by exception" as the primary tool for determining which variances are to be investigated.*

5 *Understand that a standard cost system is useful in service and not-for-profit entities as well as other nonmanufacturing operations, although its implementation frequently involves more difficult decisions regarding output and performance measurements than are required for manufacturing operations.*

6 *Know how to incorporate standards and variances into the accounting system (as explained in the Appendix).*

CHAPTER SUMMARY

Static budgets are set budgets that are not intended to reflect differences in the volume of production. In contrast, **flexible budgets** are constructed by a formula that adapts budgeted amounts to the actual volume of operations. In order for deviations from a budget to be meaningful, and not to be distorted merely by shifts in production levels, flexible budgets are generally preferable for control purposes. By multiplying the per-unit variable production costs by number of units produced and adding total fixed costs, the performance of employees can be assessed. Rather than being "blamed" for higher costs than some static budget, employees are given credit for producing more units at lower per unit costs if that, in fact, is the circumstance. Similarly, rather than "giving false praise" to employees incurring lower costs than budgeted, merely by producing fewer units, the performance of such employees will be properly evaluated in terms of the actual versus budgeted per-unit cost.

In order to determine how efficiently a company is operating, one must have a benchmark that quantifies what costs should be under reasonably efficient operating conditions (i.e., under *normal activity* conditions); **standard costs** are such a benchmark. Essentially, businesses use *historical experience* and, preferably, *engineering cost studies* to derive the standard per-unit costs of operations (direct materials, direct labor, variable overhead, and fixed overhead). The standard for each cost component has both a price and a quantity dimension and is typically reported on a *standard cost sheet*.

In this manner, the cause of any *deviation* from a budget can be isolated as being related either to the price paid or to the quantity of a cost component utilized in production (or in providing a service, for the nonmanufacturing sector). The basic form of the calculations of deviations from the materials and labor budget is a **price variance** in which Standard Price × Actual Quantity is compared with Actual Price × Actual Quantity, and a **quantity variance** in which Standard Quantity × Standard Price is compared with Actual Quantity × Standard Price. The **overhead variances**, due to their mixed cost behavior, reflect both a **budget variance**, whereby actual overhead is compared to a **flexible budget allowance** [(Standard Variable Overhead Rate × Actual Units) + Budgeted Fixed Costs], and a **volume variance**, whereby budgeted overhead is compared with applied overhead (Standard Overhead Rate × Actual Units).

By communicating cost standards, distributing monthly *performance reports,* and exercising **management by exception** (investigating significant *favorable* and *unfavorable* variances), a company can increase the cost consciousness of employees and improve overall efficiency.

The responsibility accounting system establishes a *feedback* loop that requires the identification of causes of and responsibility for variances, the recognition of interrelationships between variances, and the distinction between uncontrollable and controllable variances; feedback can be used to refine both standards and performance reports. A company utilizing a standard cost system should also set material quality and quantity specifications that permit *control* before variances occur. Furthermore, such control and efficiency techniques should be implemented in the nonmanufacturing sector, including service and not-for-profit entities. Such operations may have to spend more time establishing input and output relationships and performance standards, but the effective cost control attainable from such efforts can be expected to offset such costs.

Many companies journalize standards and variances, closing out the variance balances porportionally on the basis of ending account balances to cost of goods sold and the ending inventory of finished goods. In this manner the standard cost system becomes an integral part of the accounting system.

TECHNICAL POINTS

√ *Flexible Budget = (Variable Production Costs per Unit × Number of Units Produced) + Fixed Costs of Production*

√ Standard cost sheet format

Inputs	Standard Quantity $\times$ Standard Price $=$ Standard Cost

Direct materials
Direct labor
Variable overhead
Fixed overhead

> These are based upon normal activity (i.e., reasonably efficient operating conditions).

✓ *Material Price Variance = (Standard Price $\times$ Actual Quantity Purchased) − (Actual Price $\times$ Actual Quantity Purchased)*

✓ *Material Quantity Variance = (Standard Quantity $\times$ Standard Price) − (Actual Quantity Used in Production $\times$ Standard Price)*

✓ *Labor Rate Variance = (Standard Rate $\times$ Actual Hours) − (Actual Rate $\times$ Actual Hours)*

✓ *Labor Efficiency Variance = (Standard Hours $\times$ Standard Rate) − (Actual Hours $\times$ Standard Rate)*

✓ *Overhead Budget Variance = Actual Overhead Costs − [(Standard Variable Overhead Rate $\times$ Actual Quantity) + Budgeted Fixed Overhead Costs]*

✓ *Overhead Volume Variance = Budgeted Overhead − (Standard Overhead Rate per Unit $\times$ Actual Quantity)*

MULTIPLE-CHOICE QUESTIONS

Circle the letter corresponding to the best response.

1. Which of the following is the best description of who sets material standards?
   a. The engineering staff sets material standards.
   b. The engineering and personnel staffs set material standards.
   c. The engineering and production staffs set material standards.
   d. The production staff sets material standards.

2. Standard material prices
   a. should not include transportation charges
   b. should include transportation charges
   c. should be gross of any cash discount allowed
   d. should be net of any cash discount allowed
   e. b and d

3. Historical standards
   a. offer the advantage of simplicity
   b. are generally preferred to engineered standards
   c. avoid incorporating past inefficiencies into the standard
   d. tend to be more difficult to initially establish than are engineered standards

4. Most companies base their standards on
   a. ideal operating conditions
   b. normal activity that includes some normal loss, but does not include a provision for waste and spoilage
   c. normal activity that includes some normal loss, but does not include a provision for unscheduled repairs
   d. normal activity that includes some normal loss

5. An overhead volume variance
   a. is favorable if the actual units of production are less than the normal activity level
   b. is unfavorable if the actual units of production are less than the normal activity level
   c. is unaffected by differences in actual production and the normal activity level
   d. is favorable if actual overhead incurred is less than the flexible budget allowance, given the output produced for the period

MULTIPLE-CHOICE QUESTIONS (ANSWERS)

Answer   *Explanation*

1. c   Engineering and production staffs join efforts in setting material standards. Personnel would be involved in setting direct labor standards.

2. e   The idea is to capture the expected cost that would naturally be net of cash discounts allowed and would include transportation charges.

3. a   Engineered standards are generally preferred, because they avoid the automatic incorporation of past inefficiencies into the standard. This is true despite the greater difficulty in the initial establishment of such standards. The only advantage of historical standards is their simplicity.

4. d   Normal activity will typically include normal scrap, spoilage, and waste allowances as well as provisions for normal downtime, which will include unscheduled repairs, set-up, and rest periods for employees. Normal activity rather than some unattainable ideal standard is typically used.

5. b   This results in an underapplication of overhead and an unfavorable volume variance. Response *(d)* would result in a favorable overhead budget variance.

TRUE-FALSE QUESTIONS

Indicate whether each of the following statements is true (T) or false (F).

_____ *1.* Short-run decisions involving whether or not to accept special orders at less than normal selling prices can be made more rationally given the existence of standard costs.

_____ *2.* Variances are frequently interrelated and should not be considered in isolation.

_____ *3.* If an unfavorable quantity is attributable to substandard materials, the responsibility appropriately lies with production personnel.

_____ *4.* All variances reported on the performance report should be investigated, and corrective action should be taken.

_____ *5.* Significant favorable variances need not be subject to the same degree of scrutiny as significant unfavorable variances.

_____ *6.* The volume variance is usually uncontrollable in the short-run.

_____ *7.* Cost per Unit of Output × Actual Output will approximate total fixed overhead only if actual output is equal to normal activity.

_____ *8.* Standard cost concepts are more important in the manufacturing sector than in the nonmanufacturing sector.

TRUE-FALSE QUESTIONS (ANSWERS)

Answer   *Explanation*

1. T   Since costs must be covered in the long-run if the firm is to realize profits, information on standard costs provides a critical data base for pricing decisions.

2. T   The classic example is that purchases of substandard materials create favorable material price variances and unfavorable material quantity and/or labor efficiency variances.

3. F   In this setting, the purchasing personnel should assume most of the responsibility for the unfavorable variance.

4. F   Since investigation costs money, firms typically set limits below which variances are deemed to be insignificant; to investigate such variances would not be cost beneficial.

5. F   If such favorable variances result from loose standards, this must be detected in order to facilitate effective control by tightening standards. If the favorable results stem from improved efficiency, the entity would be foregoing the potential return it might realize from sharing the efficiency ideas with other areas of operations if it chose not to scrutinize favorable variances.

6. T   It is an indication of idle capacity.

7. T   This is essentially what the volume variance measures: whether the firm produces more or less than normal output.

8. F   Standard costing is equally important for the two sectors, as all entities require some cost control.

CLASSIFI-CATION AND MATCHING QUESTIONS

Classify the following items using the symbols provided to indicate which of the variances is more likely to result from the event or problem cited.

MP = Material price variance
MQ = Material quantity variance
LR = Labor rate variance
LE = Labor efficiency variance
OB = Overhead budget variance
OV = Overhead volume variance

____ 1. Change in mix of labor required for production
____ 2. No requirement that material requisitions be used
____ 3. Change in suppliers
____ 4. No use of competitive bidding
____ 5. Change in quality of material provided by existing supplier
____ 6. Permanent addition of a second production shift
____ 7. Price changes from existing suppliers
____ 8. Actual production volume varies from normal activity
____ 9. Excessive idle time
____ 10. Renegotiation of labor contract
____ 11. Rush orders to suppliers
____ 12. Excessive downtime

CLASSIFICATION AND MATCHING QUESTIONS (ANSWERS)

1. LR   *2.* MQ   *3.* MP   *4.* MP   *5.* MQ   *6.* OB   *7.* MP   *8.* OV   *9.* LE   *10.* LR   *11.* MP
12. LE

QUESTIONS CONCERNING THE EFFECTS OF TRANS-ACTIONS

Indicate whether the following items imply that cost of goods sold increases (+) or decreases (−) because of the transactions' effect on cost variances that are recorded in the accounts.

____ 1. The actual direct labor rate exceeds the standard labor rate.

____ 2. The adjusting entry required when actual units of output are less than the normal level of activity.

____ 3. Total direct labor hours were 7,000 to produce 3,000 units of output, which were expected to require a standard 2 direct labor hours per unit.

____ 4. The direct labor cost was $88,000 for 11,000 hours, which was expected to require a standard $9 per direct labor hour.

_____ 5. Fixed overhead costs exceed the standard fixed overhead.

_____ 6. The adjusting entry required when actual units of output are 80,000, while the company's normal activity level is 70,000 units.

QUESTIONS CONCERNING THE EFFECTS OF TRANSACTIONS (ANSWERS)

Answer   *Explanation*

1. +   An unfavorable labor rate variance would increase cost of goods sold.

2. +   Underapplied overhead results in an unfavorable volume variance. which would increase the cost of goods sold account.

3. +   An unfavorable labor efficiency variance would increase cost of goods sold.

4. −   A favorable labor rate variance—$8 versus $9 per direct labor hour—will decrease cost of goods sold.

5. +   An unfavorable overhead budget variance will increase cost of goods sold.

6. −   Overapplied overhead results in a favorable volume variance, which would decrease cost of goods sold. (Assume sales are constant as production increases.)

EXERCISES

1. Glendora Gadgets, Inc., has set a standard material usage of 3 pounds of material per unit of finished product, and this material costs $1.60 per pound. The company manufactured 50,000 units of product. A total of 170,000 pounds of material was purchased for $306,000 at the beginning of the period and 140,000 pounds of material were used in production.

Compute the material price variance and material quantity variance. Who is typically responsible for each of these variances? What is different in your approach to computing these variances from the standard formulas illustrated in Chapter 26 of *Accounting Principles*? Does this complicate any other aspects of performing a variance analysis? Be specific and quantify your response.

2. A company estimates that overhead will cost $720,000 at 80,000 direct labor hours and $810,000 at 100,000 direct labor hours. Each unit of output requires 4 direct labor hours, and normal activity in 1983 is estimated to be 20,000 units. If total overhead costs are $750,000 for actual output of 25,000 units, what are the overhead budget and volume variances for 1983?

3. Alcondale, Inc., has estimated the following variable production costs per unit.

Direct materials used	$2.00
Direct labor	8.00
Variable factory overhead	1.00

Normal production ranges from 40,000 to 60,000 units, with related fixed production costs of $148,000. Assuming actual production of 57,000 units, what would be the flexible budget for Alcondale, Inc.?

EXERCISES (ANSWERS)

1. Material price variance

   $1.60 Standard Price × *170,000 Actual Quantity Purchased = $272,000*

   $1.80 Actual Price × *170,000 Actual Quantity Purchased = $306,000*

   $272,000 − $306,000 = $34,000 Unfavorable

Material quantity variance

(3 × 50,000) Standard Quantity Used × $1.60 Standard Price = $240,000

140,000 Actual Quantity Used × $1.60 Standard Price = $224,000

$240,000 − $224,000 = $16,000 Favorable

The purchasing agent is typically responsible for the material price variance, and the production manager is typically responsible for the material quantity variance.

The key difference in the above formulas and those illustrated throughout Chapter 26 of *Accounting Principles* is that a different volume of materials was used in production than was purchased during the period. If the price variance is to capture the purchasing agent's performance, it must be based upon the total units purchased rather than the total units used in production. In contrast, the production manager's use of materials is independent of the volume of materials purchased for the period, and the material quantity variance is appropriately based upon total units used in production. In Chapter 26 the illustrations assumed that the same quantity of goods was purchased and used in production.

The difference in the total materials that are purchased and used in production complicates the ability to trace the total variance to its individual components. The typical check figure is Total Standard Cost − Total Actual Cost, or for materials

3 pounds × 50,000 × $1.60 = $240,000
Actual Costs =   306,000
$ 66,000 Unfavorable

Yet, $34,000 unfavorable plus $16,000 favorable nets to an unfavorable variance of only $18,000. The difference between $66,000 and $18,000, or $48,000, is traceable to the difference in units purchased and used [(170,000 − 140,000) × $1.60].

The analyst must be careful to reconcile any difference between units purchased and units used in production before trying to total the variance per cost component to the total difference in actual and standard costs.

2. Using the high-low method, the overhead cost formula can be derived.

$$\frac{\$810,000 - \$720,000}{100,000 - 80,000} = \frac{\$90,000}{20,000} = \$4.50 \text{ Variable Overhead Rate per Direct Labor Hour}$$

$ 810,000
− 450,000
$ 360,000 Fixed Overhead

or

$ 720,000
− 360,000
$ 360,000 Fixed Overhead

Based on normal activity of 20,000 units

Variable Overhead = $4.50 per Hour × 4 = $18.00 Standard Cost

$$\text{Fixed Overhead} = \frac{\$360,000}{20,000 \text{ Units}} = \$18 \text{ Standard Cost}$$

$750,000 Actual Overhead for 1983
  810,000 Flexible Budget Allowance*

$ 60,000 Favorable Budget Variance

*($18 × 25,000 Units) + $360,000

$810,000 Budgeted Overhead for 1983
  900,000 Applied Overhead*

$ 90,000 Favorable Volume Variance

*$36 × 25,000 Units

3. $114,000 Direct Materials (57,000 × $2)
   455,000 Direct Labor (57,000 × $8)
    57,000 Variable Factory Overhead (57,000 × $1)

$626,000 Total Variable Production Costs
  148,000 Fixed Production Costs

$774,000 Flexible Budget for 57,000 Units

CHAPTER DEMONSTRATION PROBLEM

Clandenton Corporation manufactures towels and has had engineering studies performed to assist in developing standard costs for the product at a normal activity of 400,000 units. It has set standard materials at 2 yards per unit of finished goods, costing $0.40 per yard, standard labor at 6 minutes per unit of finished goods, costing $6.00 per hour, standard variable overhead costs at $1.00 per direct labor hour, and standard fixed overhead costs at $12,000.

Actual costs for the period have been $300,000 for 820,000 yards of material purchased and used in production, $260,000 for 38,000 hours of direct labor, and $49,000 for overhead costs.

a. Prepare a standard cost sheet for Clandenton Corporation.
b. Prepare a complete variance analysis for Clandenton Corporation.
c. Record the journal entries, assuming standards and variances are incorporated in the accounting system. Allocate the variances on the basis of cost of goods sold and ending inventory with ending balances of $800,000 and $200,000, respectively.

CHAPTER DEMONSTRATION PROBLEM (ANSWER)

a.

Standard Cost Sheet
Towels

Inputs	Standard Quantity	Standard Price	Standard Cost
Direct materials	2 yards	$0.40	$0.80
Direct labor	6 minutes = 1/10 hour	$6.00	$0.60
Variable overhead	1/10 hour	$1.00	$0.10
Fixed overhead	1/10 hour	$0.30*	$0.03
			$1.53

*$12,000 ÷ 40,000 Hours = $0.30 (Based on normal activity of 40,000 hours.)

b. Abbreviations used in the complete variance analysis below include actual quantity (Aq), actual price (Ap), standard quantity (Sq), standard price (Sp), actual hours (Ah), actual rate (Ar), standard hours (Sh), and standard rate (Sr).

	$Aq \times Ap$	$Aq \times Sp$	*Variance*
Materials price	$300,000	820,000 × $0.40 = $328,000	$28,000 Favorable

	$Aq \times Sp$	$Sq \times Sp$	*Variance*
Material quantity	820,000 × $0.40 = $328,000	800,000 × $0.40 = $320,000	$8,000 Unfavorable

	$Ah \times Ar$	$Ah \times Sr$	*Variance*
Labor rate	$260,000	38,000 × $6 = $228,000	$32,000 Unfavorable

	$Ah \times Sr$	$Sh \times Sr$	*Variance*
Labor efficiency	38,000 × $6 = $228,000	40,000 × $6 = $240,000	$12,000 Favorable

Overhead budget variance

> *$49,000 Actual Overhead*
> *52,000 Budgeted Overhead ($12,000 + $0.10/Towel)*
>
> *$ 3,000 Favorable*

Overhead volume variance

> *$12,000 Budgeted Fixed Overhead*
> *12,000 Fixed Overhead Applied ($0.03 × 400,000 Towels)*
>
> *$ 0**

*This is unusual but will occur whenever actual production and normal activity are equal.

Summary of costs

> *$300,000 Direct Materials*
> *260,000 Direct Labor*
> *49,000 Overhead*
>
> *$609,000 Actual Costs*
> *612,000 Standard Costs (400,000 × $1.53)*
>
> *$ 3,000 Favorable*

Summary of variances

> *$28,000 Favorable*
> *8,000 Unfavorable*
> *32,000 Unfavorable*
> *12,000 Favorable*
> *3,000 Favorable*
> *0*
>
> *$ 3,000 Favorable*

c. Raw Materials   328,000
    Material Price Variance   28,000
    Accounts Payable   300,000

    Work in Process: Materials   320,000
    Materials Quantity Variance   8,000
      Raw Materials   328,000

    Work in Process: Labor   240,000
    Labor Rate Variance   32,000
      Labor Efficiency Variance   12,000
      Accrued Payroll   260,000

    Manufacturing Overhead Control   49,000
      Accounts Payable & Various Other Accounts   49,000

    Work in Process Overhead   52,000
      Manufacturing Overhead Applied   52,000

    Manufacturing Overhead Applied   52,000
      Overhead Budget Variance   3,000
      Manufacturing Overhead Control   49,000

    Finished Goods   612,000
      Work in Process: Materials   320,000
      Work in Process: Labor   240,000
      Work in Process: Overhead   52,000

    Material Price Variance   28,000
    Labor Efficiency Variance   12,000
    Overhead Budget Variance   3,000
      Materials Quantity Variance   8,000
      Labor Rate Variance   32,000
      Cost of Goods Sold (see table below)   2,400
      Finished Goods Inventory (see table below)   600

	Balances	Allocation
Cost of Goods Sold	$ 800,000	800/1,000,000 × $3,000
Finished Goods	200,000	200/1,000,000 × $3,000
	$1,000,000	

27 DECISION MAKING

After completing this chapter, you should:

1 **Understand the general approach to decision making by managers, particularly the focus upon relevant or differential costs and both quantitative and qualitative factors.**

2 **Be able to explain why sunk costs should be ignored in the decision process.**

3 **Know how to analyze decisions involving equipment replacement, make or buy alternatives, special order offers, the addition or deletion of products or departments, and loss leaders in both certainty and risk environments.**

4 **Understand the effects of motivational factors, opportunity costs, capacity and other limiting factors, allocation of fixed costs, utility measures, and decision constraints upon various decision contexts.**

5 **Be able to distinguish between objective and subjective probabilities, to utilize such probabilities in calculating expected values and formulating payoff matrices, and to assess the value of perfect information.**

CHAPTER SUMMARY

Day-to-day managers are faced with such decisions as whether to replace existing equipment, whether to make or buy products or product components, whether to accept special orders below normal selling price, and whether to add or to delete product lines and/or departments. Accounting information is critical to the decision process if evaluated properly. In all of these decision contexts, the focal point is upon **relevant**, or **differential**, **costs**: future costs that differ across alternatives. One cannot generalize as to the cost behavior of relevant costs, since both variable and *avoidable fixed costs* are typically included, while variable costs which do not differ across alternatives and *unavoidable fixed costs* are excluded. Once such costs are identified, either a *full project approach* can be used to reach a decision (whereby total relevant costs per alternative are computed and compared) or an *incremental approach* can be used to reach a decision (whereby only the net differences in cost across the available alternatives are analyzed). In addition to one of these quantitative approaches (preferably the full cost approach, because it is not as cumbersome when more than two alternatives are being considered and is not as likely to lead to mathematical errors), a careful consideration of *qualitative factors* is essential in reaching an optimum decision.

Sunk costs or past costs that have been incurred and can be neither retrieved nor changed by future action are irrelevant to decision making. Certain motivational factors, though one might hope they were irrelevant, can influence managers to make a decision in a manner that optimizes the manager's personal position (with respect to both short-term compensation and long-term security) but does not optimize the company's profitability over the long-term. In other words, a lack of goal congruence between managers and owners may exist, and a risk aversion by managers toward change and its related uncertainty can cause suboptimum decisions (from the perspective of stockholders).

A cost that is not recorded in the accounting records but is critical to decision making is the concept of an **opportunity cost,** which is the cost of a foregone alternative. Of similar importance in decision making is the recognition that one's goal is to maximize the contribution margin of the entire business, rather than one particular order or product, with explicit attention to factors (such as the availability of machine hours, labor, and/or floor space) that limit the generation of contribution margin. Arbitrary fixed cost allocations are common in any accounting system and should be excluded from decision making.

A final consideration in evaluating projects is the viability of using **loss leaders,** which are products that produce greater differential revenues against differential costs when sold below cost. Of course, any such strategy will require that all predicted events and outcomes are presumed to occur (i.e., **certainty**), or that the *risk* is properly captured through expected value calculations. Essentially, **expected values** are *weighted averages* of potential *payoffs.* The weighted average is the sum of the product of each possible event times its *probability,* assessed either *objectively* from past experience and/or statistical tools or *subjectively* from "gut feelings." If a decision involves numerous alternatives, a **payoff matrix** can help in structuring the decision process (the matrix is a two-dimensional table disclosing payoffs for each possible event and facilitating expected value computations). The value of *perfect information* can be computed to deduce a ceiling on the amount that should be paid for available (most likely imperfect) information; the calculation compares the diagonal of the payoff matrix to the expected value under existing conditions. Furthermore, *utility* measures can be substituted for dollars as one means of capturing qualitative factors and of capturing the effects of different decision makers upon final decisions.

Throughout the decision process, consideration should be given to *decision constraints,* for example, internal politics such as the bosses' opinions and external regulation such as the *Robinson-Patman Act.* This act forbids price discrimination and is particularly relevant to special order decision making.

TECHNICAL POINTS

√ Full project approach: Compute total relevant cost per investment alternative

√ Incremental approach: Compute net difference in relevant costs between alternatives

√ **Relevant** or **differential costs** are those future costs that differ across alternatives; they do not include sunk or past costs. They will include variable costs that differ across alternatives as well as avoidable fixed costs. In addition, opportunity costs (the costs of a foregone alternative) are relevant, although they are *not* recorded in the accounting records.

$$\checkmark \quad \textit{Expected Value} = \sum_{1}^{n} \textit{(Probability} \times \textit{Payoff or Cost)}$$

where n = the number of alternative payoffs or costs, the probabilities for which total 1.0

$\checkmark$ Payoff matrix

Events \\ Alternatives	E1	E2	E3
A1	$	$	$
A2	$	$	$
A3	$	$	$

where $ = payoffs

$\checkmark$ The blocks along the diagonal of a payoff matrix times their respective probabilities when added together, minus the expected value of existing conditions, quantify the value of perfect information.

MULTIPLE-CHOICE QUESTIONS

Circle the letter corresponding to the best response.

1. Costs are relevant if they
   a. will be incurred in the future
   b. will differ between alternatives
   c. will be incurred in the future or will differ between alternatives
   d. will be incurred in the future and will differ between alternatives

2. The incremental approach to decision analysis suffers from the serious drawbacks of
   a. being cumbersome when more than two alternatives are being considered
   b. leading to mathematical errors due to the act of netting
   c. a and b
   d. neither a nor b

3. Replacement decisions may not be made in an optimal manner due to
   a. managers' emphasis on short-term profitability
   b. the element of uncertainty
   c. the lack of congruence between performance evaluation techniques and the financial effects of decision making
   d. all of the above

4. A department or product should be eliminated
   a. if net income for the department is negative
   b. if the contribution produced is greater than the avoidable costs
   c. if the contribution produced is less than the avoidable costs
   d. if the contribution produced is less than the avoidable costs and the department is not purposefully established as a loss leader or is not being maintained due to qualitative factors

5. The objective of having a loss leader is
   a. to incur a loss to increase total profitability
   b. to decrease the markup on some units of product to increase total profitability
   c. to liquidate operations
   d. to promote complementary goods through price reduction

6. In a certainty environment
   a. objective probabilities are used to compute expected value

b. subjective probabilities are used to compute expected value
c. all predicted events and outcomes are presumed to occur
d. one knows the events that are possible and the probability of occurrence of each event

7.

Events Alternatives	0.3 10,000	0.6 15,000	0.1 30,000
10,000	$13,000	$13,000	$13,000
15,000	$11,000	$14,000	$14,000
30,000	$18,000	$20,000	$22,000

a. Perfect information is worth [0.3 ($13,000) + 0.6 ($14,000) + 0.1 ($22,000)]
b. Perfect information is worth [0.3 ($13,000) + 0.6 ($11,000) + 0.1 ($18,000)]
c. Perfect information is worth [0.3 ($13,000) + 0.6 ($14,000) + 0.1 ($22,000)] less the expected value of existing payoff conditions without the perfect information
d. Perfect information is worth [0.3 ($13,000) + 0.6 ($11,000) + 0.1 ($18,000)] less the expected value of existing payoff conditions without the perfect information

8. Utility is not
a. synonymous with money
b. a humanistic interpretation of a monetary outcome
c. quantifiable
d. likely to be a good indicator of how a decision maker will react to the results of a decision

MULTIPLE-CHOICE QUESTIONS (ANSWERS)

Answer   Explanation

1. d   Past costs and costs that are the same for alternatives are irrelevant; hence, both criteria in response *(d)* must be met in order for costs to be relevant.

2. c   These are considered to be serious drawbacks of the incremental approach and are the reason that the use of the full project approach is recommended.

3. d   Maximization of long-term income will frequently conflict with the short-term profitability emphasis of management due to performance evaluation systems that focus on the "bottom line" as well as the uncertainty involved in change.

4. d   Net income can be negative, yet if a department has a positive contribution margin the entity will be worse off if it eliminates the department, assuming such a positive contribution margin exceeds any avoidable fixed costs. Furthermore, prior to any elimination decision, qualitative factors should be considered as well as the possibility that the department is acting as a loss leader and is yielding greater differential revenues than differential costs.

5. a   One unit is actually sold below cost (not simply at a lower markup) in order to increase profitability, for example, through the promotion of complementary goods.

6. c   Responses *(a)*, *(b)*, and *(d)* relate to a risk environment.

7. c   The diagonal of a payoff matrix represents the perfect information potential but must be compared with the payoff under existing conditions to derive the value of perfect information.

8. a   Utility refers to the amount of satisfaction and dissatisfaction associated with an alternative and actually shifts away from dollars.

TRUE-FALSE QUESTIONS

Indicate whether each of the following statements is true (T) or false (F).

____ 1. Decision making is a continuous process.

____ 2. Past historical costs may serve as a basis for predicting what future costs will be and are also considered in selecting a course of action when making decisions for the future.

____ 3. Future costs that are expected to be identical for both machines being evaluated in an equipment replacement decision can be ignored; they have no bearing on the decision.

____ 4. Most business decisions are made solely on quantitative considerations.

____ 5. Book values of long-term assets are sunk costs that are important determinants of equipment replacement decisions.

____ 6. Depreciation on the new piece of equipment that is replacing old equipment is irrelevant to the decision process on whether or not to acquire such equipment.

____ 7. Fixed overhead that does not differ among the alternatives to make or to buy a product can be ignored.

____ 8. Qualitative factors that can influence make or buy decisions include the extent of dependence upon suppliers and worry about product quality, strikes against suppliers, transportation strikes and hazards, personnel changes at suppliers' offices, and product discontinuance.

____ 9. Opportunity costs are *not* recorded in the accounting records nor do they appear on financial statements.

____ 10. In order to maximize the contribution margin of an entire business, management should consider those items with the highest contribution margin per sales dollar to be the most important.

TRUE-FALSE QUESTIONS (ANSWERS)

Answer   Explanation

1. T   Since businesses are always trying to improve their operations, decision making is an ongoing process.

2. F   Old costs are just past memories and are not considered in selecting a course of action; it is the future cost that differs across alternatives that is relevant. However, historical costs can be useful in formulating predictions.

3. T   Differential costs should be the focal point in decision making and will be the sole determinants of the final decision.

4. T   Despite the importance of qualitative factors, the difficulty in evaluating such factors in dollar terms leads to decision makers commonly disregarding qualitative considerations.

5. F   Book values are sunk costs and as such are irrelevant to equipment replacement decisions. Sunk costs can be completely ignored without altering the result.

6. F   Depreciation on new equipment is relevant for the replacement decision since it represents a future cost which can be avoided by not acquiring the new equipment.

7. T   While it is not true that all fixed costs can be ignored, those that are the same across alternatives will have no effect on decision making and hence can be safely ignored.

8. T   Such quality control concerns can dictate a decision to reject the alternative of buying a product or product component.

9. T   Despite their importance to decision making, only past transactions and events are recorded in the accounting records.

10. F   Contribution margin must be analyzed in terms of factors that limit its generation, such as operating capacity, rather than stressing per-unit contribution margin. For example, a greater number of lower contribution margin units can yield a greater total dollar contribution margin than would be provided by fewer, higher-dollar contribution margin units.

CLASSIFI-CATION AND MATCHING QUESTIONS

Classify the following items using these symbols:

R = Relevant cost in this decision setting
IR = Irrelevant cost in this decision setting

____ 1. Maintenance costs on a new machine would be $500 a year compared to the $1,300 a year expected on the old machine that the company is considering replacing.

____ 2. The new car would burn 1 quart of oil every 100 miles, as does the old car being replaced.

____ 3. The book value on the machine being replaced is $40,000.

____ 4. If the company buys components rather than making them, the machine currently used in production could be leased for $1,000 a year.

____ 5. Six hundred dollars of factory overhead is charged to a department that a company plans to eliminate; this charge is related to the square feet of the plant area occupied by the department.

____ 6. Variable selling expenses of $2 per unit will not be incurred for a special order under consideration.

____ 7. Department A's display racks will be used by other departments when department A is eliminated.

____ 8. Eighty percent of the employees in department A will be fired when the department is eliminated.

CLASSIFICATION AND MATCHING QUESTIONS (ANSWERS)

Answer	Explanation
1. R	These are future costs which differ between the alternatives.
2. IR	Although a future cost is involved, it does not differ between alternatives.
3. IR	This is a sunk or past cost.
4. R	This is an opportunity cost.
5. IR	No alternative use for the space is mentioned and the cost of that portion of the plant will have to be incurred by the remaining departments.
6. R	This is a cost savings for the special order compared to standard orders.
7. IR	In other words, the cost remains whether or not the department is eliminated.
8. R	These become avoidable variable and fixed costs and differ between the alternatives of eliminating or not eliminating department A.

	Department A	Department B	Total
Sales	$20,000	$30,000	$50,000
Variable costs of manufacturing	12,000	5,000	17,000
Fixed costs			
Depreciation	2,000	3,000	5,000
Salaries	3,200	4,800	8,000
Rent	8,000	12,000	20,000
Administrative	1,600	2,400	4,000
Variable selling expenses	200	300	500
Net income	($ 7,000)	$ 2,500	($ 4,500)

QUESTIONS CONCERNING THE EFFECTS OF TRANSACTIONS

Indicate the dollar effect of the following upon total net income, give both the direction (+ or −) and the amount.

_____ 1. Department A is eliminated. Assume that all fixed costs are allocated, other than 40% of the salaries, which are paid to employees in each department and would not be incurred should department A be eliminated.

_____ 2. The company decided to use department A as a loss leader by pricing the product at $1.00 per unit instead of the present price of $2.00 per unit. It anticipates that the promotion will result in sales of 15,000 units of department A product and 30,000 units of department B (instead of the 10,000 units currently sold). Assume that the only additional costs for this loss leader approach is a cost of $1,000 for an advertising campaign.

_____ 3. Department A was eliminated (assume once again that all fixed costs are allocated other than the 40% of salaries earned by employees in department A). It was replaced by a department C, which had revenue of $40,000, variable selling and manufacturing costs of $15,000, and required fixed expenditures for equipment leases of $7,000.

_____ 4. Department B is eliminated. Assume that $2,000 of salaries and $1,000 of administrative costs will no longer be incurred, but that all other fixed costs are allocated based on sales. Furthermore, assume that $100 of the variable selling expense relates to long-term advertising and will remain after department B is closed.

QUESTIONS CONCERNING THE EFFECTS OF TRANSACTIONS (ANSWERS)

Answer   *Explanation*

1. −$6,520 $20,000 − $12,000 − $200, or $7,800, will be lost and only $3,200 × 0.4, or $1,280, of salaries will be saved, meaning a net effect on net income of $7,800 − $1,280, or $6,520, in the downward direction.

2. +$37,300   Department A will have 15,000 × $1, or $15,000, of revenue; variable costs will be $12,200/10,000 or $1.22 × 15,000, totaling $18,300. Fixed costs will remain at $14,800.

     Department B will have 30,000 × $3, or $90,000, of revenue; variable costs will be $5,300/10,000 per unit or $0.53 × 30,000, totaling $15,900. Fixed costs will remain at $22,200. Hence, department A's net income would be $15,000 − $18,300 − $14,800, or ($18,100), and department B's net income would be $90,000 − $15,900 − $22,200, or $51,900. These two figures net to $33,800 and must be reduced by the $1,000 advertising campaign to $32,800. Hence, the change in net income is from ($4,500) to $32,800, or $37,300.

3. + $11,480   From question (1), a loss of $6,520 results from eliminating department A. This is now offset by department C's contribution: $40,000 − $15,000 − $7,000, or $18,000. The net effect is an **$11,480** increase in net income.

4. − $21,800   Department B's revenue of $30,000 will be lost and expenses of $5,000 + ($300 − $100) + $2,000 + $1,000 will not be incurred. The net income effect is a decline of $30,000 − $8,200, or $21,800.

EXERCISES

1. Branda Manufacturers produce boxes for their product at the following cost.

	100,000 Boxes	Per Box
Direct materials	$12,000	$0.12
Direct labor	5,000	0.05
Variable overhead	1,000	0.01
Fixed overhead*	900	0.009
	$18,900	$0.189

*Ninety percent of this represents committed fixed overhead.

Crater's Box Company has offered to provide the 100,000 boxes at a set price of $0.18 a box. Should Branda accept the offer? Quantify your response.

2. Larry's Danish Trucks sell breakfast danish to office workers in a 10-story office building daily and is preparing a purchasing schedule. The demand fluctuates throughout the week and can be summarized as follows.

Demand for Danish	Probability
5,000 Rolls	0.1
6,000 Rolls	0.3
7,000 Rolls	0.1
8,000 Rolls	0.5

The cost of rolls is $0.20 and the selling price is $0.70. Any danish that are unsold at the end of a day must be sold at a substantial discount to a coffeeshop for $0.10. Rolls can only be purchased in lots of 5,000, of 6,000, of 7,000, or of 8,000. Prepare a payoff matrix and advise Larry's Danish as to how many rolls should be ordered. Assume that information on employee absences in the 10-story office building can be purchased to assist in planning purchases; what is the maximum amount that Larry's Danish Trucks should be willing to pay for such information?

EXERCISES (ANSWERS)

1. The costs that will be saved from not manufacturing the boxes include

$0.12	Direct Materials
0.05	Direct Labor
0.01	Variable Overhead
0.0009	Fixed Overhead (0.009 × 10%)

$0.1809

The offer by Carter's Box Company will save $0.0009 per box or $90. On a quantitative basis the offer should be accepted. However, qualitative factors such as the greater dependence on suppliers that results from buying instead of making one's own components warrant consideration.

2.

Events (demand) Alternatives (rolls purchased)	0.1 5,000	0.3 6,000	0.1 7,000	0.5 8,000
5,000	$2,500*	$2,500	$2,500	$2,500
6,000	$2,400†	$3,000‡	$3,000	$3,000
7,000	$2,300§	$2,900¶	$3,500#	$3,500
8,000	$2,200**	$2,800††	$3,400‡‡	$4,000§§

*5,000 × $0.50 Contribution Margin = $2,500.
†$2,500 − 1,000 ($0.20 − $0.10) = $2,400.
‡6,000 × $0.50 = $3,000.
§$2,500 − 2,000 ($0.10) = $2,300.
¶$3,000 − 1,000($0.10) = $2,900.
#7,000 × $0.50 = $3,500.
**$2,500 − 3,000($0.10) = $2,200.
††$3,000 − 2,000($0.10) = $2,800.
‡‡$3,500 − 1,000($0.10) = $3,400.
§§$8,000 × $0.50 = $4,000.

Expected Value Calculations

5,000: $2,500 × 1.0 = $2,500
6,000: ($2,400 × 0.1) + ($3,000 × 0.9) = $2,940
7,000: ($2,300 × 0.1) + ($2,900 × 0.3) + ($3,500 × 0.6) = $3,200
8,000: ($2,200 × 0.1) + ($2,800 × 0.3) + ($3,400 × 0.1) + ($4,000 × 0.5) = $3,400

Advise Larry's Danish Trucks to purchase 8,000 rolls; this number of rolls will yield the greatest expected value.

If the information resulted in perfect knowledge, the payoff would be

$2,500 × 0.1 = $ 250
$3,000 × 0.3 =   900
$3,500 × 0.1 =   350
$4,000 × 0.5 = 2,000
                _____
                $3,500

The difference in $3,500 and the $3,400 expected value from continually purchasing 8,000 rolls, or $100, is the value of perfect information; therefore, Larry should pay less than $100 for the information.

CHAPTER DEMON-STRATION PROBLEM

Weden Transport Company is trying to decide whether to purchase truck A or truck B. The Company can make 10 deliveries per day in truck A or 8 deliveries per day in truck B. The mileage on truck A is 15 miles per gallon, while truck B gets 20 miles per gallon. Each truck burns oil: truck A consumes 1 quart of oil every 200 miles, while truck B consumes 1 quart of oil every 300 miles. The driver for truck A is paid $16 per trip, and the driver for truck B is paid $20 per trip. The trips are each 60 miles round trip. Gas costs $1.30 per gallon and oil costs $0.80 per quart.

   a. Should Weden Transport Company purchase truck A or truck B? Support your answer with both a full project analysis and an incremental analysis. How would you proceed to make a decision?
   b. Assume that another manager questions whether truck B has mileage of 20

and proposes that mileage will depend on the particular trip, and will likely be 10 miles per gallon about 20% of the time, 15 miles per gallon about 30% of the time, and 25 miles per gallon about 50% of the time. What is the expected value of gasoline costs for truck B based on the manager's mileage estimates? Is the manager's input sufficient to alter the decision made in part *(a)*?

CHAPTER DEMONSTRATION PROBLEM (ANSWER)

a.

	Full Project Analysis		Incremental Analysis
	Truck A	*Truck B*	*Difference*
Number of deliveries	10	8	
Trip distance	60 Miles	60 Miles	
	600	480	
Mileage	÷ 15	÷ 20	
	40 Gallons	24 Gallons	
Per gallon cost	$ 1.30	$ 1.30	
	$ 52.00	$ 31.20	$20.80
Oil			
600 ÷ 200 = 3 quarts × $0.80	2.40		
480 ÷ 300 = 1.6 quarts × $0.80		1.28	1.12
Driver*			
$16 × 10 Trips	160.00		
$20 × 8 Trips		160.00	—
	$214.40	$192.48	$21.92

*This information on the cost of the driver should be deleted, as it has no effect on the decision because it does not differ across alternatives.

Based on costs, Weden Transport Company should purchase truck B, because it costs less per day to operate. However, only 8 trips can be made in truck B, while 10 trips can be made in truck A. Hence, if the revenue from 2 more trips in truck A exceeds the $21.92 difference in costs, the company should in fact buy truck A. This problem bears out two considerations: *capacity constraints* and *incremental revenues*. Both of these factors warrant consideration in this type of a purchase analysis.

Hence, information should be gathered as to the two trucks' capacities, incremental revenue per trip per truck, and the trade-offs involved in acquiring a truck that is capable of making only 8 trips rather than 10.

b.
$$480 \div 10 = 48 \times 0.2 = 9.6 \times \$1.30 = \$12.48$$
$$480 \div 15 = 32 \times 0.3 = 9.6 \times \$1.30 = 12.48$$
$$480 \div 20 = 24 \times 0.5 = 12.0 \times \$1.30 = \underline{15.60}$$
$$\underline{\underline{\$40.56}}$$

$40.56 − $31.20 = $9.36, which is less than $21.92. On a cost basis, however, the decision is not altered from part *(a)*.

28 *CAPITAL BUDGETING*

After completing this chapter, you should:

1 *Know how to compute compound interest and discounted present values for both lump sum payments and for annuities, as well as how to interpolate values from published tables when the exact interest rate desired is not reported.*

2 *Understand what is meant by the term* cost of capital.

3 *Be able to describe the capital budgeting process utilized by most companies, including the distinction between project screening and project ranking decisions.*

4 *Know how to compute the payback period, accounting rate of return, net present value, and internal rate of return for a capital investment.*

5 *Be able to describe the difference in applying capital budgeting techniques to even and to uneven cash flows.*

6 *Know how to quantify the effects of income taxes on capital budgeting.*

7 *Understand the advantages and disadvantages of the alternative methods of evaluating capital budgeting proposals as well as the benefits accrued from applying a combination of the methods when analyzing an investment proposal.*

CHAPTER SUMMARY

Capital budgeting is the term applied to long-term investment planning and analysis. It encompasses such decisions as replacement or expansion of plant and equipment and acquisitions of businesses and new product lines, including expenditures for *research and development projects*. The general approach requires management to set objectives, select measurement criteria, identify potential investments, evaluate the alternative projects using selected criteria, make a decision, assess the impact of the decision, and monitor the decision process. This approach will normally involve an initial **project screening decision** as to whether minimum preset criteria are met and a subsequent **ranking decision** as to the most attractive investment projects, given a set amount of available funds. The quantitative considerations in evaluating a capital budgeting investment can be analyzed through the **payback method,** which quantifies how long it takes to recoup the original investment, the **accounting rate of return method,** which measures the effect of an investment proposal on the return on assets percentage, the **net present value (NPV),** which incorporates the time value of money to analyze whether the project's present value of cash flow lump sums and *annuities* exceeds the present value implied by the desired rate of return (frequently the *cost of capital discount rate,* reflecting the effects of *compound interest*), and the **internal rate of return (IRR) method,** which determines the exact rate of return that equates the net present value of cash outflows to the net present value of cash inflows. Such a return is commonly compared to alternative projects' returns, as well as to the **cost of capital,** which is the cost of investment funds that are available from borrowing, issuing stock, and retaining earnings from operations.

Although the payback method is considered to be a simple *risk* measure that is useful in ranking investments, it ignores the *time value of money* as well as all cash flows beyond the payback period. Hence, it should be augmented with a *profitability measure,* such as the accounting rate of return and an approach, either NPV or IRR, that adjusts for the time value of money. The NPV method is unable to take into account large differences in original investments and useful lives; hence, each of the available analysis techniques should be augmented by the other tools, and an explicit consideration of qualitative factors, in order to capture a complete picture of risk and return.

The evaluation tools are complicated by *uneven cash flows* and *tax considerations.* However, through a systematic year-by-year analysis of cash flows and a trial-and-error approach to calculating the IRR, as well as a transformation of revenues to a net-of-tax basis and an explicit incorporation of the tax shield that is available from depreciation, the quantitative evaluation can be completed.

TECHNICAL POINTS

✓ *Payback Period for Even Cash Flows* $= \dfrac{Original\ Investment}{Even\ Yearly\ Cash\ Flow}$

✓ Payback period for uneven cash flows is determined by the number of periods' cash flows that must be added together before the sum totals the amount of the original investment; this can be represented in symbols as

$$\sum_{t=1}^{n} Uneven\ Cash\ Flows = Original\ Investment$$

where   t = periods 1 through n
         n = payback period

✓ *Accounting Rate of Return* $= \dfrac{Average\ Yearly\ Cash\ Flow - Yearly\ Depreciation}{Additional\ Investment}$

✓ Compound interest

$V = P(1.0 + i)^n$

where   V = the value at the end of the investment
         P = the original amount invested
         i = the interest rate
         n = number of years invested

✓ *Present Value* $= \dfrac{A}{(1 + i)^n}$

where   A = amount to be received in n years
       i = interest rate
       n = number of years

√ **Net Present Value = Σ Present Value of Cash Inflows − Σ Present Value of Cash Outflows**

where   the discount rate is typically the cost of capital, and cash inflows are net of taxes and reflect the tax shield that is available from depreciation.

√ **Internal Rate of Return**

For even cash flows: That percentage which corresponds to the present value of an annuity factor computed in an identical fashion as the payback period for even cash flows, i.e.,

$$\frac{Original\ Investment}{Even\ Yearly\ Cash\ Flow}$$

For uneven cash flows: That percentage which equates the net present value of cash outflows to the net present value of cash inflows, derived through trial and error

√ Interpolation from interest factor tables

$$\frac{Interest\ Rate\ with\ Higher\ Factor - Interest\ Rate\ for\ the\ Desired\ Factor}{x}$$

$$= \frac{Interest\ Rate\ with\ Higher\ Factor - Interest\ Rate\ with\ Lower\ Factor}{Higher\ Factor - Lower\ Factor}$$

where   x = amount to be subtracted from higher factor to yield desired factor

---

MULTIPLE-CHOICE QUESTIONS

Circle the letter corresponding to the best response.

1. The major concerns for capital budgeting decisions are
   a. determining the cash flows associated with the investment proposals
   b. determining the timing of the cash flows associated with the investment proposals
   c. a and b
   d. neither a nor b

2. The cost of capital
   a. is that rate which equalizes the present value of cash inflows and the present value of cash outflows
   b. is the minimum desired rate of return, determined by what it costs a company to acquire funds from investors through the sale of stocks and bonds
   c. is that rate of return earned on any project that has a positive net present value
   d. is also known as the accounting rate of return

3. A series of equal cash flows over a number of years
   a. is termed an annuity
   b. is termed a lump sum payment pattern
   c. complicates the calculation of the internal rate of return
   d. results in a payback period which is greater than the present value factor used to calculate the internal rate of return.

4. Any positive net present value
   a. indicates that the actual rate of return is less than the desired rate
   b. indicates that the actual rate of return is equal to the desired rate
   c. indicates that the actual rate of return is greater than the desired rate
   d. none of the above

5. Salvage value
   a. is a taxable cash inflow
   b. is a nontaxable cash inflow
   c. is not a cash inflow, as it was part of the original purchase price
   d. is a taxable cash outflow

6. In calculating the internal rate of return, the true interest rate
   a. falls between that rate resulting in a positive net present value and that adjacent lower rate that results in a negative net present value
   b. falls below that rate which is highest and results in a positive net present value for the investment
   c. falls above that rate which first results in a negative net present value
   d. falls between that rate resulting in a positive net present value and that adjacent higher rate that results in a negative net present value

7. Depreciation
   a. decreases the amount of taxable income
   b. is a cash expense
   c. increases the amount of taxable income
   d. has no effect on net present value calculations

8. The consideration of tax effects
   a. increases the net present value of an investment
   b. decreases the net present value of an investment
   c. has no effect on the net present value of an investment
   d. reduces the cash outflow for the purchase of an investment

MULTIPLE-CHOICE QUESTIONS (ANSWERS)

Answers	Explanation
1. c	The emphasis of capital budgeting is upon cash flows, and the time value of money dictates the importance of the timing of cash flows.
2. b	It quantifies the cost of obtaining capital. Response (a) describes the internal rate of return, and response (c) fails to realize that a net present value greater than zero implies a return in excess of the cost of capital.
3. a	It simplifies internal rate of return calculations, which in fact have a present value factor that is identical to the payback period.
4. c	Response (a) relates to a negative net present value while (b) relates to a zero net present value.
5. b	It is a cash inflow at the end of the service life which represents part of the original capital investment and hence has no tax implications.
6. d	This is the trial-and-error approach to calculating the internal rate of return.
7. a	Depreciation provides a tax shield, reducing tax payments, and thereby affecting net present value calculations.
8. b	Taxes have no effect on the original purchase price of an investment but they greatly reduce the net present value of an investment.

TRUE-FALSE QUESTIONS

Indicate whether the following statements are true (T) or false (F).

____ 1. An accountant has a major responsibility in determining the feasibility of capital budgeting projects.

____ 2. Corporate objectives are formulated by management.

_____ **3.** Qualitative measures that are relevant to capital budgeting decisions will generally relate to the overall corporate image and will generally be applied by top management.

_____ **4.** The quantitative data used to evaluate potential capital budgeting decisions emphasize cash flows and net income.

_____ **5.** A dollar received today is worth less than a dollar to be received in the future.

_____ **6.** The payback method is determined by dividing the original investment by the average yearly cash flow.

_____ **7.** A short payback period is not necessarily indicative of the desirability of an investment project.

_____ **8.** Corporations will generally not wish to accept proposals with rates of return that are less than the current rate of return.

_____ **9.** With respect to the calculation of compound interest, any combination of i (the interest rate) and n (the number of years invested) can result in only one answer that can be applied to the dollar amount invested to arrive at V (the value at the end of the investment).

_____ **10.** In essence, the present value of an annuity table is simply the sum of the present value of $1 given a specified number of years and an interest rate.

TRUE-FALSE QUESTIONS (ANSWERS)

Answer	Explanation
1. T	While not typically involved in the research activities underlying investments, the accountant is responsible for quantifying the related cash inflows and outflows and calculating the returns on investments which, in turn, implies whether or not an investment is feasible.
2. F	They are only partially formulated by management; they are also partially dictated by environmental pressures.
3. T	The focus of lower management, particularly of accountants, is the quantitative measurement of an investment's return.
4. F	Cash flows are emphasized not net income.
5. F	It is worth more, as it can be deposited in a virtually risk-free savings account and can earn interest.
6. F	This would only be true if even cash flows were earned over the life of the investment.
7. T	It is only a measure of risk; it fails to measure profitability.
8. T	This is a rule of thumb.
9. T	This is why it is possible to use prepared tables of interest factors when calculating compound interest.
10. T	This becomes obvious as one inspects prepared annuity tables and compares them to lump sum tables.

CLASSIFI-CATION AND MATCHING QUESTIONS

Indicate whether the following advantages and disadvantages are *most frequently* associated with

P = Payback method
A = Accounting-rate-of-return method
NPV = Net-present-value method
IRR = Internal-rate-of-return method

More than one response may be appropriate.

_____ 1. Ignores the time value of money
_____ 2. Fails to disclose the actual rate of return for a particular project
_____ 3. Relates directly to the financial accounting records
_____ 4. Requires a trial-and-error approach to its calculation
_____ 5. Facilitates the ranking of alternative projects by rates of return
_____ 6. Ignores the relative profitability of an investment subsequent to the period in which the original investment is recouped
_____ 7. Inadequately considers differences in expected lives and in initial outlays
_____ 8. Offers a simple measure of risk

CLASSIFICATION AND MATCHING QUESTIONS (ANSWERS)

1. P, A   *2.* NPV   *3.* A   *4.* IRR   *5.* IRR   *6.* P   *7.* NPV   *8.* P

QUESTIONS CONCERNING THE EFFECTS OF TRANS- ACTIONS

Indicate whether the following items would increase (+) the investment measures, decrease (−) the investment measures, or have no effect upon the investment measures (0) listed.

Investment Measures		Effect on Measure	
Payback period	1. ____	A project originally expected to require an outlay of $40,000 with cash inflows of $10,000 in year 1 and $30,000 in year 2 is now expected to result in cash inflows of $30,000 in year 1 and $10,000 in year 2.
Net present value	2. ____	
Accounting rate of return	3. ____	
Internal rate of return	4. ____	
Net present value	5. ____	A project which was analyzed had an estimated $40,000 salvage value at the end of 6 years; the new estimate is $30,000. The payback period was 4 years prior to this change in estimate.
Payback period	6. ____	
Accounting rate of return	7. ____	A project that was analyzed assuming $3,000 annual depreciation is now expected to result in $4,000 of depreciation expense annually; the company has a 40% effective tax rate.
Net present value	8. ____	

QUESTIONS CONCERNING THE EFFECTS OF TRANSACTIONS (ANSWERS)

Answer   *Explanation*

1. 0   The payback period is 2 years regardless of the order of the inflows.

2. +   More money available earlier in time has a higher present value, implying a higher net present value.

3. 0   The numerator of the accounting-rate-of-return calculation is average yearly cash flow, which would be ($10,000 + $30,000)/2 or $20,000, regardless of the order of the inflows.

4. +   As with NPV, IRR takes the time value of money into account.

5. **−**   The present value of a 6-year lump sum future payment of $30,000 is worth less than the present value of a 6-year lump sum future payment of $40,000.

6. **0**   The salvage value is in the sixth year, beyond the payback period of 4 years; hence, the payback period is unaffected.

7. **−**   A larger depreciation expense is subtracted from the numerator, resulting in a lower return.

8. **+**   Depreciation is not a cash outflow but does provide a tax shield, thereby reducing the cash outflow for taxes. In this setting $1,000 × 40%, or $400, of tax outflows per year will be eliminated by the increased depreciation shield.

EXERCISES

1. Andy, Alice, and Bill's Restaurant and Ice Cream Parlor is considering purchasing one of the following ice-making machines.

		Cash Flow			
	Cost	Period 1	Period 2	Period 3	Period 4
Machine 1	$40,000	$12,000	$30,000	$15,000	$15,000
Machine 2	20,000	12,000	25,000		

If the Restaurant's cost of capital is 15% and no salvage value is expected for either machine, which ice-making machine should be purchased, based on a net-present-value analysis? Comment on the investment analysis.

Periods	Present Value of $1 @ 15%
1	0.87
2	0.76
3	0.66
4	0.57

2. WW, Incorporated, invested $120,000 in a research project in 1983 from which it expected to generate cash inflows of $40,000 for 8 years. Compute the project's internal rate of return. The following tables are provided for your convenience.

Present Value of $1 Factors

Periods	8%	12%	20%	25%	30%
1	0.93	0.89	0.83	0.80	0.77
2	0.86	0.80	0.69	0.64	0.59
3	0.79	0.71	0.58	0.51	0.46
4	0.74	0.64	0.48	0.41	0.35
5	0.68	0.57	0.40	0.33	0.27
6	0.63	0.51	0.34	0.26	0.21
7	0.58	0.45	0.28	0.21	0.16
8	0.54	0.40	0.23	0.17	0.12

Present Value of Annuity of $1 for Eight Periods

8%	12%	20%	25%	30%
5.75	4.97	3.84	3.33	2.93

1. Using the net-present-value (NPV) approach

Item	Year	Cash Flows	Present Value	NPV
Machine 1	0	($40,000)	1.0	($40,000)
Cash flows	1	12,000	0.87	10,440
Cash flows	2	30,000	0.76	22,800
Cash flows	3	15,000	0.66	9,900
Cash flows	4	15,000	0.57	8,550
				$11,690
Machine 2	0	($20,000)	1.0	($20,000)
Cash flows	1	12,000	0.37	10,440
Cash flows	2	25,000	0.76	19,000
				$ 9,440

The NPV method implies that machine 1 is the better investment; however, this example bears out the shortcomings of NPV: the method does not consider the relative size of the outlays or the unequal lives. In half the time, for half the investment, machine 2 is able to generate an NPV of $9,440 relative to the $11,690 generated by machine 1 (in double the time and for twice the investment)! While the payback period per machine (1 14/15 years for machine 1 and 1 8/25 years for machine 2) is consistent with lower risk for machine 2, attention to profitability measures can bear out the substantial preferability of machine 2 as an investment. This NPV analysis demonstrates the importance of using multiple investment measures to analyze alternative investment proposals.

2. $\dfrac{\$120,000}{\$40,000} = 3.0$

Since an annuity is involved, the trial-and-error method is not required. This factor on an annuity table for 8 periods indicates that between a 25% and 30% rate of return is being earned on the project. Through the following interpolation, a more exact calculation can be obtained.

3.33 25% Value
3.00 Desired Value

0.33

3.33 25% Value
− 2.93 30% Value

0.40

$\text{Actual Rate} = 0.25 + \dfrac{0.33}{0.40}\,(0.05) = 0.25 + 0.04 = 0.29 \text{ or } \underline{\underline{29\%}}$

CHAPTER DEMON-STRATION PROBLEM

Klandike Corporation is contemplating the acquisition of a new piece of equipment that will cost $600,000 and have an estimated salvage value of $100,000 at the end of 5 years. The equipment will be depreciated by the straight-line method, and the Company's cost of capital is 10%. The following schedule of cash flows is expected:

Year	Amount
1	$ 120,000
2	130,000
3	350,000
4	300,000
5	100,000
	$1,000,000

Calculate the payback period, accounting rate of return, the net present value, and the internal rate of return for this investment. (An excerpt from present value tables is provided below for your convenience.)

Now, assume a 40% tax rate and recalculate the net present value for the investment.

Present Value of $1

Period	8%	10%	12%	15%	20%	25%
1	0.93	0.91	0.89	0.87	0.83	0.80
2	0.86	0.83	0.80	0.76	0.69	0.64
3	0.79	0.75	0.71	0.66	0.58	0.51
4	0.74	0.68	0.64	0.57	0.48	0.41
5	0.68	0.62	0.57	0.50	0.40	0.33

Period	Present Value of Annuity of $1 @ 10%
1	0.91
2	1.74
3	2.49
4	3.17
5	3.79

CHAPTER DEMONSTRATION PROBLEM (ANSWER)

Payback Period

Year	Cash Flow	Yearly Requirement	Total	Additional Needed	Payback Years
1	$120,000	$120,000	$120,000	$480,000	1
2	130,000	130,000	250,000	350,000	1
3	350,000	350,000	600,000	0	$\frac{1}{3}$

Accounting Rate of Return

$$\frac{\text{Average Yearly Cash Flow} - \text{Depreciation}}{\text{Investment}}$$

$$= \frac{\left(\dfrac{\$1,000,000}{5 \text{ Years}} - \dfrac{\$600,000 - \$100,000}{5 \text{ Years}}\right)}{\$600,000} = \frac{\$200,000 - \$100,000}{\$600,000} = \underline{16.67\%}$$

Net Present Value @ 10%

Item	Year	Cash Flows	Present Value of $1 @ 10%	Net Present Value
Machine	0	($600,000)	1.00	($600,000)
Cash flows	1	120,000	0.91	109,200
	2	130,000	0.83	107,900
	3	350,000	0.75	262,500
	4	300,000	0.68	204,000
	5	100,000	0.62	62,000
Salvage value	5	100,000	0.62	62,000
				$207,600

Internal Rate of Return

Cash Flows		Net Present Value @ 15%		Net Present Value @ 20%		Net Present Value @ 25%
($600,000)	1.00	($600,000)	1.00	($600,000)	1.00	($600,000)
120,000	0.87	104,400	0.83	99,600	0.80	96,000
130,000	0.76	98,800	0.69	89,700	0.64	83,200
350,000	0.66	231,000	0.58	203,000	0.51	178,500
300,000	0.57	171,000	0.48	144,000	0.41	123,000
100,000	0.50	50,000	0.40	40,000	0.33	33,000
100,000	0.50	50,000	0.40	40,000	0.33	33,000
		$105,200		$ 16,300		($ 53,300)

A close approximation of the expected rate can be calculated by the following interpolation of net present values.

$16,300	$16,300	Net Present Value @ 20%
0		Desired Net Present Value
	(53,300)	Net Present Value @ 25%
$16,300	$69,600	

$$\text{Rate} = 0.20 + \frac{\$16,300}{\$69,600}(0.05) = 0.20 + 0.012 = 0.212 = \underline{21.2\%}$$

After-Tax Net Present Value @ 10% (Assume 40% Tax Rate)

Item	Year	Before Tax Cash Flow	Tax	After Tax Cash Flow	Discount Factor	Net Present Value
Machine	0	($600,000)	0.0	($600,000)	1.00	($600,000)
Cash flows	1	120,000	0.6	72,000	0.91	65,520
	2	130,000	0.6	78,000	0.83	64,740
	3	350,000	0.6	210,000	0.75	157,500
	4	300,000	0.6	180,000	0.68	122,400
	5	100,000	0.6	60,000	0.62	37,200
Depreciation	1–5	100,000	0.4	40,000	3.79	151,600
Salvage value	5	100,000	0.0	100,000	0.62	62,000
						$ 60,960

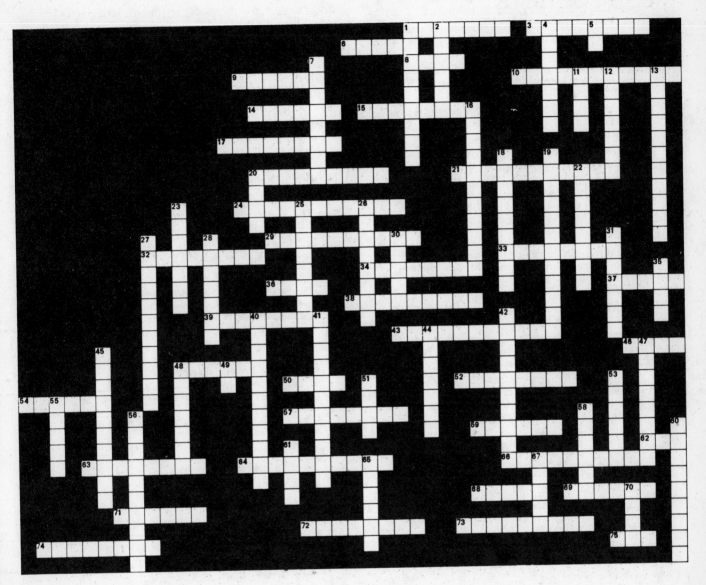

ACROSS

1. Planning for long-term investments is called <u>1 across</u> <u>73 across</u>.

3. Relevant costs can be studied in two different ways: a <u>50 across</u> <u>48 down</u> <u>3 across</u> or an <u>43 across</u> <u>3 across</u>.

6. The <u>7 down</u> <u>6 across</u> is the mathematical result of multiplying the payoff of a particular event by the event's likelihood of occurrence.

8. The difference in the actual direct labor rate and the standard rate is quantified as the <u>37 across</u> <u>8 across</u> <u>15 across</u>.

9. The <u>48 across</u> <u>9 across</u> is a two-dimensional table that discloses the payoffs for all combinations of alternatives and events.

10. An environment of <u>4 down</u> <u>10 across</u> is depicted along the diagonal of a payoff matrix.

14. A <u>35 down</u> <u>14 across</u> is a product or service offered at a price below cost; it is intended to attract customers or clients who purchase other items having a normal markup.

15. See 8 across.

17. The difference in the actual quantity of materials used in producing the period's output and the standard quantity is termed the <u>38 across</u> <u>17 across</u> <u>72 across</u>.

20. <u>45 down</u> <u>20 across</u> are essentially extrapolations of past performance.

21. A <u>29 across</u> <u>21 across</u> is a "gut feeling" about the likelihood of possible events in the future.

24. The <u>57 across</u> <u>6 across</u> <u>5 down</u> <u>4 down</u> <u>24 across</u> represents the mathematical difference between the expected value of existing conditions and the expected value of an environment where events can be predicted in advance.

29. See 21 across.

32. Many companies attempt to keep pace with changes in patterns of consumption by spending large amounts of resources on a <u>32 across</u> and <u>41 down</u> <u>48 down</u>.

33. <u>39 across</u> <u>33 across</u> extends the simple interest concept beyond one year and allows for the evaluation of decisions over extended periods of time.

34. A <u>34 across</u> <u>36 across</u> is a future cost that differs between alternatives.

36. See 34 across.

37. See 8 across.

38. See 17 across.

39. See 33 across.

43. See 3 across.

46. A <u>52 across</u> <u>46 across</u> is what a cost should be under reasonably efficient operating conditions.

48. See 9 across.

50. See 3 across.

52. The end result of developing standards is a summary <u>52 across</u> <u>61 down</u> <u>67 down</u>.

54. Most companies require a <u>40 down</u> <u>54 across</u> by responsibility area, comparing standard with actual, together with an explanation of variances.

57. See 24 across.

59. Most companies engineer a standard based on <u>59 across</u> <u>63 across</u>, or reasonably efficient operating conditions.

62. The <u>25 down</u> - <u>2 down</u> <u>62 across</u> forbids charging different prices to different customers for the same goods and services unless there are cost differences in serving the customers.

63. See 59 across.

64. The <u>64 across</u> <u>70 down</u> <u>49 down</u> <u>69 across</u> provides a measure of the effect an investment proposal will have on the return on assets percentage.

66. <u>66 across</u> <u>23 down</u> <u>68 across</u> compares the amount of current cash with a specified amount of cash to be received in the future at a specified rate of interest.

68. See 66 across.

69. See 64 across.

71. The <u>28 down</u> <u>71 across</u> measures the length of time it will take to recover the cash invested in a project.

72. A _____, in cost accounting terminology, is a deviation from standard.

73. See 1 across.

74. The difference in the actual direct labor hours used in producing the period's output and the standard direct labor hours is termed the <u>37 across</u> <u>56 down</u> <u>74 across</u>.

75. The <u>75 across</u> <u>23 down</u> <u>30 down</u> <u>71 across</u> attempts to incorporate the time value of money into the analysis of investment opportunities.

DOWN

1. In a <u>1 down</u> <u>16 down</u>, all predicted events and outcomes are presumed to occur.

2. See 62 across.

4. See 10 across and 24 across.

5. See 24 across and 26 down.

7. See 6 across.

11. A <u>11 down</u> <u>16 down</u> is one in which the possible events that can occur are known and can be weighted by their probability of occurrence.

12. A series of equal cash flows over a number of years is termed an _____.

13. The cost of a foregone alternative is termed an <u>13 down</u> <u>46 across</u>.

16. See 1 down and 11 down.

18. An <u>18 down</u> <u>27 down</u> is based on either a statistically determined outcome or past experience and is exemplified by the 0.5 probability of a head in a coin toss.

19. A cost that differs among alternatives is sometimes called a <u>19 down</u> <u>61 down</u>.

20. A past cost that has already been incurred is termed a <u>20 down</u> <u>61 down</u>.

22. Same as 33 across.

23. See 66 across and 75 across.

25. See 62 across.

26. The $\underline{\text{26 down}}$ $\underline{\text{51 down}}$ $\underline{\text{5 down}}$ $\underline{\text{69 across}}$ equates the net present value of cash outflows to net present value of cash inflows.

27. See 18 down.

28. See 71 across.

30. See 75 across.

31. _____ measures the amount of satisfaction and dissatisfaction associated with an alternative.

35. See 14 across.

40. See 54 across.

41. See 32 across.

42. $\underline{\text{42 down}}$ $\underline{\text{60 down}}$ are more difficult to initially establish than historical standards but overcome the deficiency of automatically incorporating past inefficiencies into the standards.

44. _____ is management action to assure conformity to a plan.

45. See 20 across.

47. If actual overhead incurred may have differed from the flexible budget allowance given the output produced for the building, this may be referred to as the $\underline{\text{47 down}}$ $\underline{\text{53 down}}$ $\underline{\text{72 across}}$.

48. See 3 across and 32 across.

49. See 64 across.

51. See 26 down.

53. See 47 down.

55. The difference in the actual cost of materials and the standard cost of materials is termed the $\underline{\text{38 across}}$ $\underline{\text{55 down}}$ $\underline{\text{74 across}}$.

56. See 74 across.

58. Actual production volume may have varied from normal activity, resulting in a $\underline{\text{58 down}}$ $\underline{\text{72 across}}$.

60. See 42 down.

61. See 52 across, 19 down, and 20 down.

65. Same as 59 across.

67. See 52 across.

70. See 64 across.

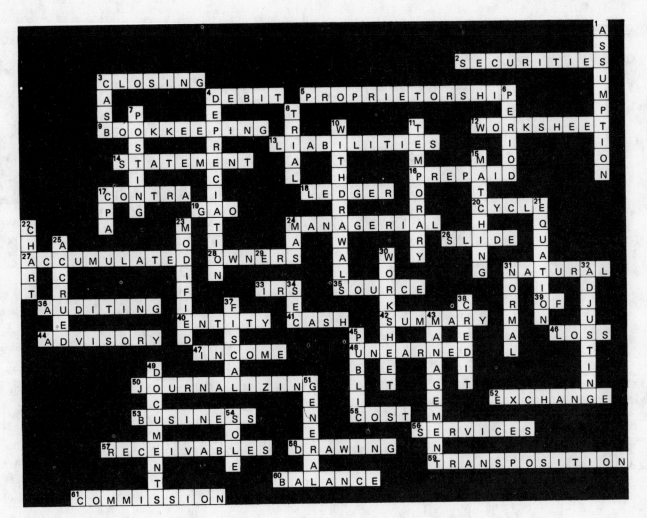

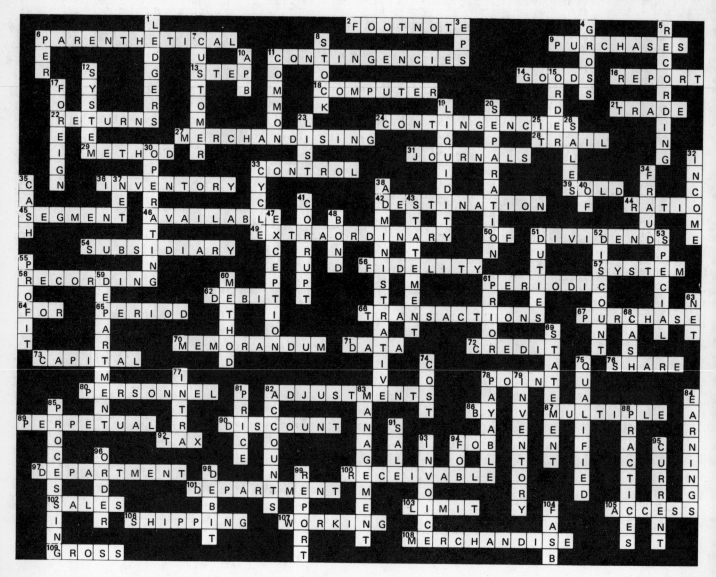

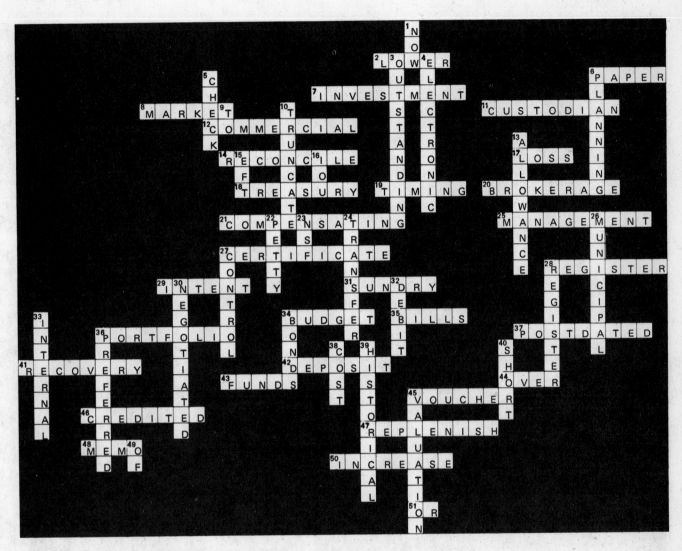

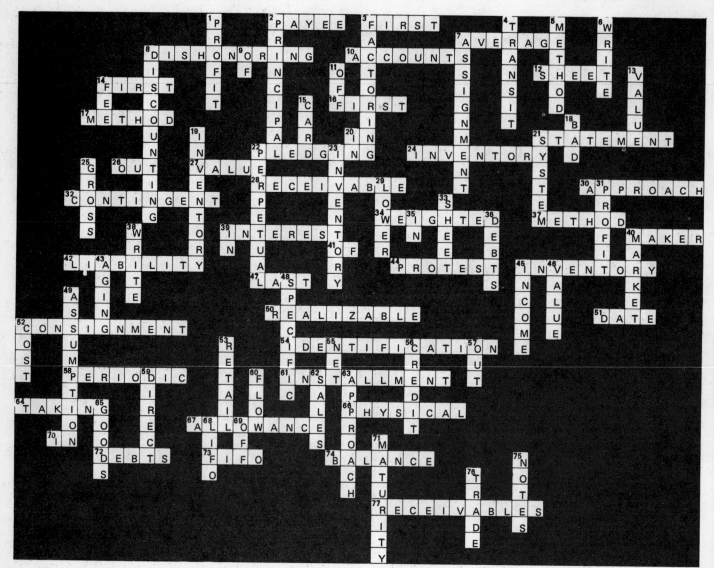

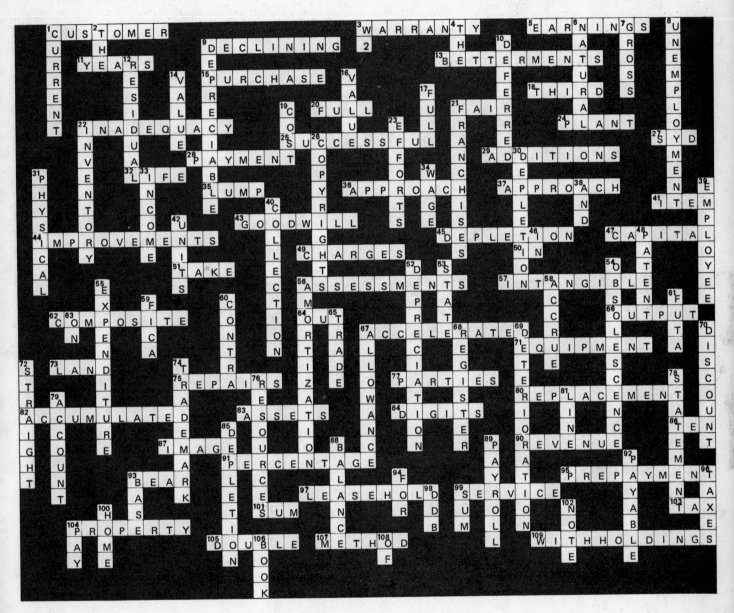

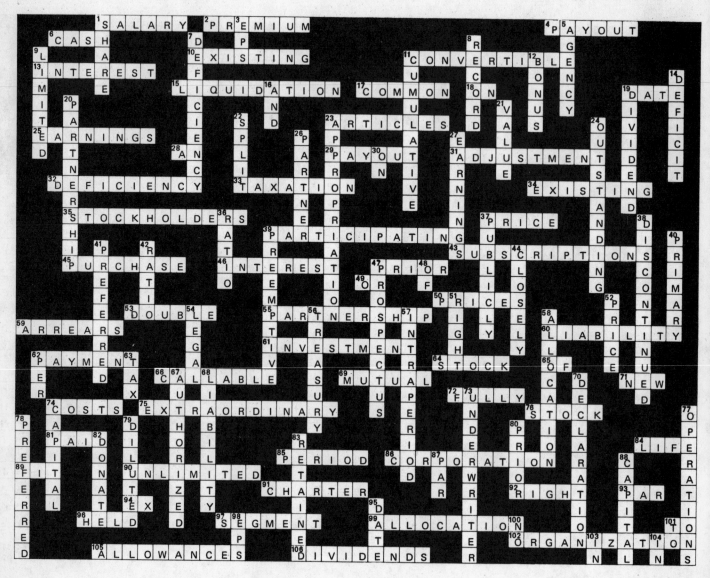

CROSSWORD PUZZLE SOLUTION for Chapters 15 through 18

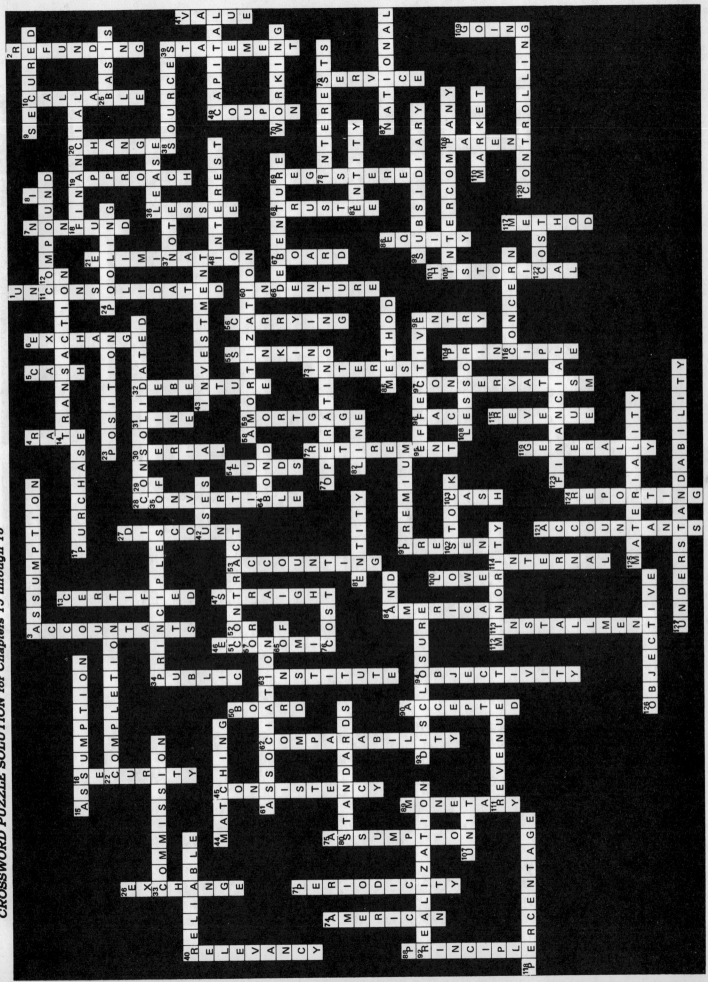

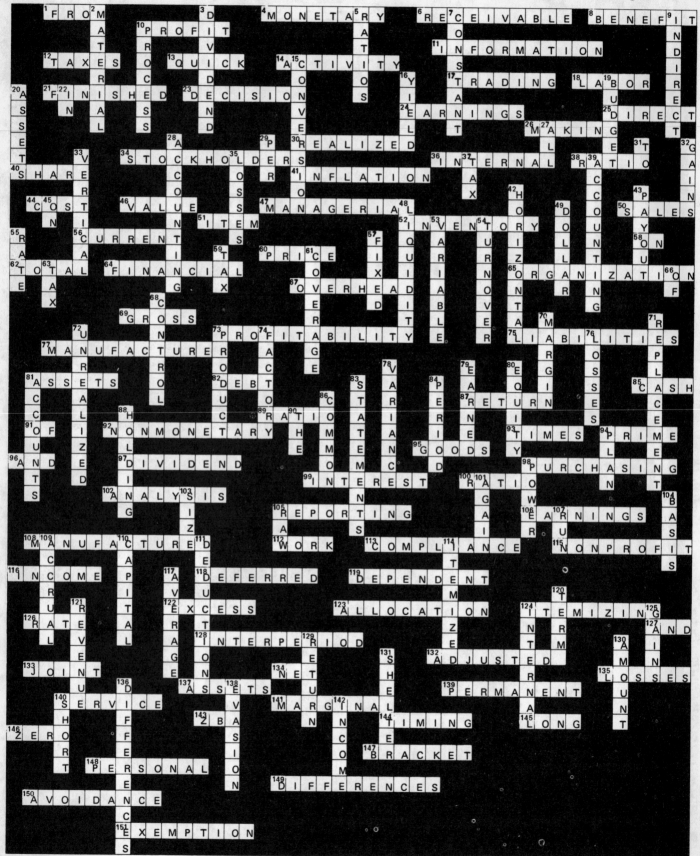

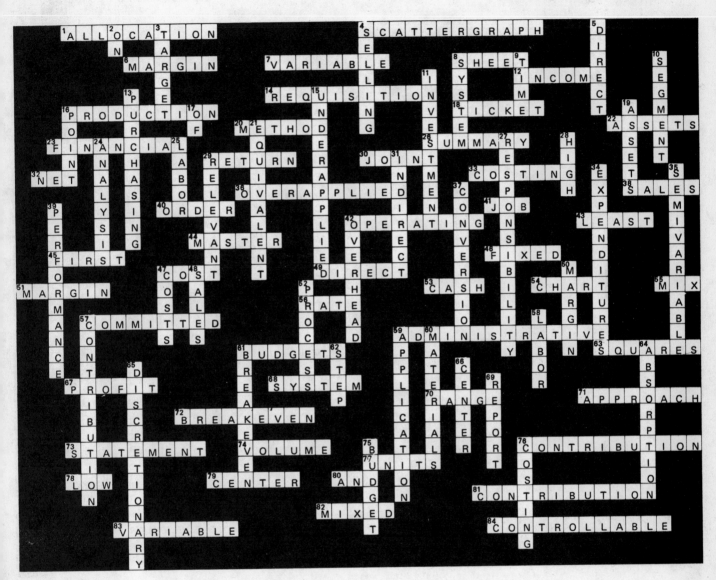

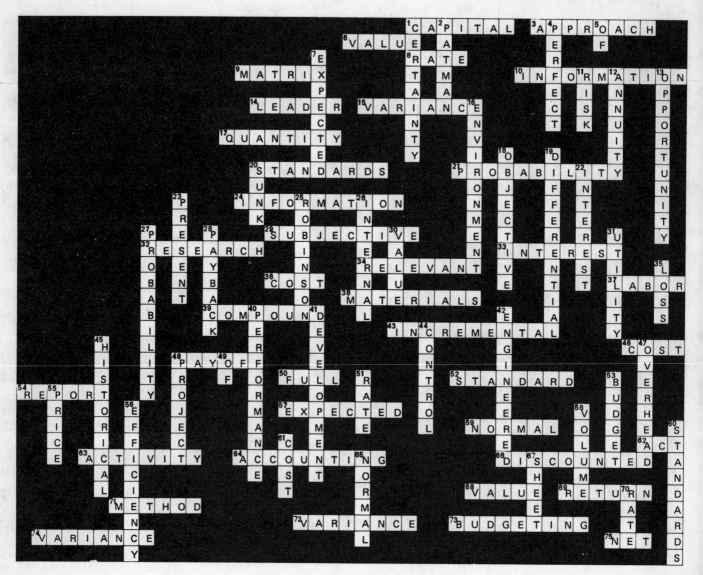

83 84 85 86   10 9 8 7 6 5 4 3 2